T0321904

Data Visualization and Statistical Literacy for Open and Big Data

Theodosia Prodromou
University of New England, Australia

A volume in the Advances in Data
Mining and Database Management
(ADMDM) Book Series

www.igi-global.com

Published in the United States of America by
    IGI Global
    Information Science Reference (an imprint of IGI Global)
    701 E. Chocolate Avenue
    Hershey PA, USA 17033
    Tel: 717-533-8845
    Fax: 717-533-8661
    E-mail: cust@igi-global.com
    Web site: http://www.igi-global.com

Library of Congress Cataloging-in-Publication Data

Names: Prodromou, Theodosia, 1974- editor.
Title: Data visualization and statistical literacy for open and big data /
    Theodosia Prodromou, editor.
Description: Hershey, PA : Information Science Reference, [2017] | Includes
    bibliographical references.
Identifiers: LCCN 2017005134| ISBN 9781522525127 (hardcover) | ISBN
    9781522525134 (ebook)
Subjects: LCSH: Information visualization. | Big data. | Statistical literacy.
Classification: LCC QA76.9.I52 D385 2017 | DDC 005.7--dc23 LC record available at https://lccn.
loc.gov/2017005134

This book is published in the IGI Global book series Advances in Data Mining and Database
Management (ADMDM) (ISSN: 2327-1981; eISSN: 2327-199X)

British Cataloguing in Publication Data
A Cataloguing in Publication record for this book is available from the British Library.

All work contributed to this book is new, previously-unpublished material.
The views expressed in this book are those of the authors, but not necessarily of the publisher.

For electronic access to this publication, please contact: eresources@igi-global.com.

Advances in Data Mining and Database Management (ADMDM) Book Series

ISSN:2327-1981
EISSN:2327-199X

Editor-in-Chief: David Taniar Monash University, Australia

MISSION

With the large amounts of information available to organizations in today's digital world, there is a need for continual research surrounding emerging methods and tools for collecting, analyzing, and storing data.

The **Advances in Data Mining & Database Management (ADMDM)** series aims to bring together research in information retrieval, data analysis, data warehousing, and related areas in order to become an ideal resource for those working and studying in these fields. IT professionals, software engineers, academicians and upper-level students will find titles within the ADMDM book series particularly useful for staying up-to-date on emerging research, theories, and applications in the fields of data mining and database management.

COVERAGE

- Cluster Analysis
- Profiling Practices
- Neural Networks
- Web-based information systems
- Enterprise Systems
- Data quality
- Customer Analytics
- Sequence Analysis
- Web Mining
- Factor Analysis

IGI Global is currently accepting manuscripts for publication within this series. To submit a proposal for a volume in this series, please contact our Acquisition Editors at Acquisitions@igi-global.com or visit: http://www.igi-global.com/publish/.

The Advances in Data Mining and Database Management (ADMDM) Book Series (ISSN 2327-1981) is published by IGI Global, 701 E. Chocolate Avenue, Hershey, PA 17033-1240, USA, www.igi-global.com. This series is composed of titles available for purchase individually; each title is edited to be contextually exclusive from any other title within the series. For pricing and ordering information please visit http://www.igi-global.com/book-series/advances-data-mining-database-management/37146. Postmaster: Send all address changes to above address. ©© 2017 IGI Global. All rights, including translation in other languages reserved by the publisher. No part of this series may be reproduced or used in any form or by any means – graphics, electronic, or mechanical, including photocopying, recording, taping, or information and retrieval systems – without written permission from the publisher, except for non commercial, educational use, including classroom teaching purposes. The views expressed in this series are those of the authors, but not necessarily of IGI Global.

Titles in this Series

For a list of additional titles in this series, please visit:
http://www.igi-global.com/book-series/advances-data-mining-database-management/37146

Web Semantics for Textual and Visual Information Retrieval
Aarti Singh (Guru Nanak Girls College, Yamuna Nagar, India) Nilanjan Dey (Techno India
College of Technology, India) Amira S. Ashour (Tanta University, Egypt & Taif University,
Saudi Arabia) and V. Santhi (VIT University,India)
Information Science Reference • ©2017 • 290pp • H/C (ISBN: 9781522524830) • US $185.00

Advancing Cloud Database Systems and Capacity Planning With Dynamic Applications
Narendra Kumar Kamila (C.V. Raman College of Engineering, India)
Information Science Reference • ©2017 • 430pp • H/C (ISBN: 9781522520139) • US $210.00

Web Data Mining and the Development of Knowledge-Based Decision Support Systems
G. Sreedhar (Rashtriya Sanskrit Vidyapeetha (Deemed University), India)
Information Science Reference • ©2017 • 409pp • H/C (ISBN: 9781522518778) • US $165.00

Intelligent Multidimensional Data Clustering and Analysis
Siddhartha Bhattacharyya (RCC Institute of Information Technology, India) Sourav De (Cooch
Behar Government Engineering College, India) Indrajit Pan (RCC Institute of Information
Technology, India) and Paramartha Dutta (Visva-Bharati University, India)
Information Science Reference • ©2017 • 450pp • H/C (ISBN: 9781522517764) • US $210.00

Emerging Trends in the Development and Application of Composite Indicators
Veljko Jeremic (University of Belgrade, Serbia) Zoran Radojicic (University of Belgrade,
Serbia) and Marina Dobrota (University of Belgrade, Serbia)
Information Science Reference • ©2017 • 402pp • H/C (ISBN: 9781522507147) • US $205.00

Web Usage Mining Techniques and Applications Across Industries
A.V. Senthil Kumar (Hindusthan College of Arts and Science, India)
Information Science Reference • ©2017 • 424pp • H/C (ISBN: 9781522506133) • US $200.00

For an enitre list of titles in this series, please visit:
http://www.igi-global.com/book-series/advances-data-mining-database-management/37146

www.igi-global.com

701 East Chocolate Avenue, Hershey, PA 17033, USA
Tel: 717-533-8845 x100 • Fax: 717-533-8661
E-Mail: cust@igi-global.com • www.igi-global.com

This book is dedicated to the memory of Professor Tim Dunne who passed away on the 18th of April 2016 in a car accident. Tim contributed a lot to statistics education both in South Africa and Internationally. He played a seminal role in the in the International Statistical Institute (ISI), International Conference on Teaching Statistics (ICOTS) and International Association for Statistical Education (IASE). He gave generously of his time and energy to build capacity in statistics, at all levels. What I valued most about him is his insight, wisdom and how well he connected with people. It was always a pleasure to talk or work with him.

Table of Contents

Section 2
Using Big Data

Section 3
Gathering and Processing Big Data

Detailed Table of Contents

Section 1
Teaching Big and Open Data

Data visualisation has blossomed into a multidisciplinary research area, and a wide range of visualisation tools has been developed at an accelerated pace. Preliminary statistical data analysis benefits from data visualisation to form the basis for decision-making. There is a greater need for people to make good inferences from visualisations. The flexible nature of current computing tools can potentially have a major impact on the learning and practice of the discipline of statistics and allow easier use of visualisations in the educational process. While this view has many merits and we support its general spirit, we argue for a valuable role for a non-visual approach at certain points. Students will employ data visualisation in an OPEN Data context. This chapter is a theoretical discussion of a framework, which emphasises explicit assumptions that help to direct inferences appropriately. In particular it addresses the common illusions of causality in student reasoning. Our discussion of points of disagreement is based on specific theoretical concerns.

This chapter focuses on statistical literacy and the practice of statistics from the perspective of middle school students and how their experiences can be enhanced by the availability of open data. The open data sets selected illustrate the types of contexts that are available and their connections to the Australian school curriculum.

The importance of visualisation is stressed and the software TinkerPlots is the tool used for students to create representations and develop the understanding necessary to analyse data and draw conclusions. Building appreciation of the practice of statistics in this way further assists students to become critical thinkers in judging the claims of others later as statistically literate adults.

Chapter 3
Elaine M. Barclay, University of New England, Australia

An understanding of crime data and analysis is central to any Criminology degree. Graduates need to know how and where to access a wide variety of secondary data sources, and understand how to read and critically evaluate crime statistics, crime maps, and quantitative research publications, and through assessment, know how to apply this learning to understanding crime rates within a community. This chapter reviews the various types of data and analysis that form a substantial part of content within a Bachelor of Criminology degree. Several types of assessment are described as examples of how to engage students in practical exercises to show them how data and analysis can provide fascinating insight into the social life of their own community.

Chapter 4
Thida Chaw Hlaing, University of New England, Australia
Julian Prior, University of New England, Australia

Statistical literacy presents many aspects about food security in the world. It highlights weaknesses, it creates awareness of threats in current situations, helps overcome challenges and creates opportunities for the future. Statistical data analysis enables existing food security interventions and programs to be reviewed and revised, and this better understanding of current situations enables more authoritative and relevant decision-making processes for the future. Statistical literacy involves skills and expertise in data description and interpretation (in words as well as in numbers) to name, explore and amend beliefs, opinions and suggestions. It helps decision-making processes about food security in a sub-nation, nation and region, as well as the world. This chapter will demonstrate the importance of open data and visualization, including its challenges and opportunities, in the food security context at national and global level to make decision-makers aware of the need to enhance their capacity for and investment in statistical literacy.

Section 2
Using Big Data

Chapter 5

Belinda A. Chiera, University of South Australia, Australia
Malgorzata W. Korolkiewicz, University of South Australia, Australia

Technological advances have led to increasingly more data becoming available, a phenomenon known as Big Data. The volume of Big Data is to the order of zettabytes, offering the promise of valuable insights with visualisation the key to unlocking these insights, however the size and variety of Big Data poses significant challenges. The fundamental principles behind tried-and-tested methods for visualising data are still as relevant as ever, although the emphasis necessarily shifts to why visualisation is being attempted. This chapter outlines the use of graph semiotics to build data visualisations for exploration and decision-making and the formulation of elementary, intermediate- and overall-level analytical questions. The public scanner database Dominick's Finer Foods, consisting of approximately 98 million observations, is used as a demonstrative case study. Common Big Data analytic tools (SAS, R and Python) are used to produce visualisations and exemplars of student work are presented, based on the outlined visualisation approach.

Chapter 6

Busayasachee Puang-Ngern, Macquarie University, Australia
Ayse A. Bilgin, Macquarie University, Australia
Timothy J. Kyng, Macquarie University, Australia

There is currently a shortage of graduates with the necessary skills for jobs in data analytics and "Big Data". Recently many new university degrees have been created to address the skills gap, but they are mostly computer science based with little coverage of statistics. In this chapter, the perceptions of graduates and academics about the types of expertise and the types of software skills required for this field are documented based on two online surveys in Australia and New Zealand. The results showed that Statistical Analysis and Statistical Software Skills were the most necessary type of expertise required. Graduates in industry identified SQL as the most necessary software skill while academics teaching in relevant disciplines identified R programming as the most necessary software skill for Big Data analysis. The authors recommend multidisciplinary degrees where the appropriate combination of skills in statistics and computing can be provided for future graduates.

Chapter 7

Spreadsheets were arguably the first information calculation and analysis tools
employed by microcomputer users, and today are arguably ubiquitously used for
information calculation and analysis. The fluctuating fortunes of PC makers coincided
with those of spreadsheet applications, although the last two decades have seen the
dominance of Microsoft Excel in the spreadsheet market. This chapter plots the
historical development of spreadsheets in general, and Excel in particular, highlighting
how new features have allowed for new forms of data analysis in the spreadsheet
environment. Microsoft has undoubtedly cast Excel as a tool for the analysis of big
data through the addition and development of features aimed at reporting on data
too large for a spreadsheet. This chapter discusses Excel's ability to handle these
data by means of an applied example. Data visualization by means of charts and
dashboards is discussed as a common strategy for dealing with large volumes of data.

Chapter 8

The teaching of statistics at the secondary level should provide statistical literacy for
students who interact with data in several everyday situations. Therefore, it is crucial
that the teacher education can provide a wider variety of situations in which teachers
can learn how to improve students' statistical literacy. The conceptualization of
sampling is crucial to understand statistical data. However, this topic is not generally
emphasized in school curriculum or in teacher education programs. This chapter
discusses a study on how primary school teachers understand issues of size and
representativeness of samples using TinkerPlots 2.0 software. The participants were
four teachers from a public school in Brazil. The research protocol followed three
phases: interviews to identify the teacher's profile and their statistical knowledge; a
familiarization session with TinkerPlots; and a session to use the software to solve
tasks involving sampling. The results showed that the teachers began to consider
aspects of data variation to determine when representative samples were presented
using TinkerPlots. The ability to select samples and analyze them seemed to contribute
to improve their understanding about sample size and representativeness. Since the
purpose of the study was to explore teacher education activities that could support
development of aspects of statistical literacy, further analysis of findings from the

study offered insights into design of tasks to help teachers teach sampling as part of statistical literacy. For example, the analysis suggested that the questions asked during the research sections should not only explore the participants´ knowledge on the sample size or the confidence level, but should also promote reflection on the meanings assigned to tasks, leading to discussion of the skills required for statistical literacy in the Big Data era.

Section 3
Gathering and Processing Big Data

Chapter 9

This chapter outlines recent ABS research in applying data visualisation to the analysis of big data for official statistics. Examples are presented from the application of a prototype analytical platform created by the ABS to two significant big data use cases. This platform – the Graphically Linked Information Discovery Environment (GLIDE) – demonstrates a new approach to representing, integrating and exploring complex information from diverse sources. This chapter discusses the role of data visualisation in meeting the analytical challenges of big data and describes the entity-relationship network model and data visualisation features implemented in GLIDE, together with examples drawn from two recent projects. It concludes and outlines future directions.

Chapter 10

Following the advent of Big Data, statistical offices have been largely exploring the use of Internet as data source for modernizing their data collection process. Particularly, prices are collected online in several statistical institutes through a technique known as web scraping. The objective of the chapter is to discuss the challenges of web scraping for setting up a continuous data collection process, exploring and classifying the more widespread techniques and presenting how they are used in practical cases. The main technical notions behind web scraping are presented and explained in order to give also to readers with no background in IT the sufficient elements to fully comprehend scraping techniques, promoting the building of mixed skills that is at the core of the spirit of modern data science. Challenges for official statistics deriving from the use of web scraping are briefly sketched. Finally, research ideas for overcoming the limitations of current techniques are presented and discussed.

Chapter 11

Kees Zeelenberg, Statistics Netherlands, The Netherlands

Barteld Braaksma, Statistics Netherlands, The Netherlands

Big data come in high volume, high velocity and high variety. Their high volume may lead to better accuracy and more details, their high velocity may lead to more frequent and more timely statistical estimates, and their high variety may give opportunities for statistics in new areas. But there are also many challenges: there are uncontrolled changes in sources that threaten continuity and comparability, and data that refer only indirectly to phenomena of statistical interest. Furthermore, big data may be highly volatile and selective: the coverage of the population to which they refer, may change from day to day, leading to inexplicable jumps in time-series. And very often, the individual observations in these big data sets lack variables that allow them to be linked to other datasets or population frames. This severely limits the possibilities for correction of selectivity and volatility. In this chapter, we describe and discuss opportunities for big data in official statistics.

Chapter 12

Franck Cotton, National Institute of Statistics and Economic Studies (INSEE), France

Daniel Gillman, U.S. Bureau of Labor Statistics (BLS), USA

Linked Open Statistical Metadata (LOSM) is Linked Open Data (LOD) applied to statistical metadata. LOD is a model for identifying, structuring, interlinking, and querying data published directly on the web. It builds on the standards of the semantic web defined by the W3C. LOD uses the Resource Description Framework (RDF), a simple data model expressing content as predicates linking resources between them or with literal properties. The simplicity of the model makes it able to represent any data, including metadata. We define statistical data as data produced through some statistical process or intended for statistical analyses, and statistical metadata as metadata describing statistical data. LOSM promotes discovery and the meaning and structure of statistical data in an automated way. Consequently, it helps with understanding and interpreting data and preventing inadequate or flawed visualizations for statistical data. This enhances statistical literacy and efforts at visualizing statistics.

Preface

CHALLENGES AND OPPORTUNITIES OF BIG DATA

Good information is invaluable for decision-making. With the explosion of computational power and digital data storage technologies, and more recently the huge increase in mobile communications devices, vast quantities of data are becoming available. But these data are unwieldy. Where data was once scarce, hard to gather, and therefore had to be subject to the very careful analytical processes familiar from mathematical statistics and probability theory, now data come in overwhelming quantity (Volume), at high speeds (velocity), and in many different forms (variety). The challenges and opportunities in Big Data arise from the attempt to use data effectively when it is available in massive Volume, at high Velocity, and in great Variety.

This book brings together a number of works that explore a range of significant issues related to Big Data. At one end of the range is concern for gathering data, as seen in the chapter on web scraping, to issues in processing data, as seen in the chapter on national statistical institutes, to concerns for using and analysing data, as seen in several chapters related to teaching with Big Data.

More and more data become available, and the future promises a greater increase, as the use of Internet-connected devices increases. It will be important to use these data effectively. How will it be gathered? How will it be used? And, perhaps most crucially, will people be able to use it effectively? This book explores both issues in how to deal with Big Data and issues in how to teach others to deal with Big Data.

This book is intended for an audience of professionals and researchers working in the field of Statistics, Statistics education, and data science. It hopes to provide insights to support educators and others concerned with open data, big data, data revolution in different types of disciplines and societies, data visualisation in statistics curriculum and statistical literacy.

This book is divided in three sections:

1. Teaching Big and Open Data;
2. Using Big Data; and
3. Gathering and Processing Big Data.

TEACHING BIG AND OPEN DATA

The section about Open Data begins with a chapter that Tim Dunne and wrote together during the ISI Congress in Brazil, 2015 prior to his untimely death. It is a theoretical discussion of a pedagogical framework, which emphasises explicit assumptions that help to make direct inferences from visualisations in OPEN Data contexts. The authors support the general spirit of a wholly visual approach to pedagogy, but they argue for a valuable role for certain non-visual verbal elements at specific points as a way of addressing common illusions of causality in student reasoning.

The second chapter by Jane Watson focuses on statistical literacy and the practice of statistics with middle school students, focusing on how their experiences can be enhanced by the availability of open data. The open data sets selected by Watson illustrate the variety of contexts that are available in teaching, especially their connections to the Australian school curriculum. The importance of visualisation is stressed and the software TinkerPlots is the tool used for students to create representations and develop the understanding necessary to analyse data and draw conclusions. Building appreciation of the practice of statistics in this way further assists students to become critical thinkers in judging the claims of others later as statistically literate adults.

Chapters 3 and 4 both focus on the use of Open Data in learning, teaching, and researching for tertiary education.

Chapter 3, by Professor Elaine Barclay, deals with the use of open data when teaching criminology. The chapter emphasises the importance of an understanding of crime data and analysis to any Criminology degree. Graduates need to know how and where to access a wide variety of secondary data sources, and understand how to read and critically evaluate crime statistics, crime maps, and quantitative research publications, and through assessment, know how to apply this learning to understanding crime rates within a community. Barclay reviews the various types of data and analysis that form a substantial part of content within a Bachelor of Criminology degree. Several types of assessment are described as examples of how to engage students in practical exercises to show them how data and analysis can provide important insight into the social fabric of their own community.

Chapter 4, by Thida Chaw Hlaing and Julian Prior, deals with the Challenges and Opportunities of Visualization of Open Data in Food Security Analysis in the world. This chapter discusses existing interventions and programs of food security that can be reviewed and revised if statistical data analyses give better understanding of current food insecurity situations for future actions, which are more authoritative and relevant in decision-making processes. They discuss how statistical literacy skills and expertise play an important role in the decision making process for food security. Thus, this book chapter will discuss the importance of open and big data in relation to food security as well as the challenges and opportunities of open data and big data in agriculture taught at tertiary education.

USING BIG DATA

Chapter 5, by Belinda Chiera and Malgorzata Korolkiewicz, focuses on the teaching of visualisation. The era of Big Data provides opportunities to adopt and adapt old approaches to address these new challenges. The authors particularly consider methods for visualising data, although the emphasis necessarily shifts to why visualisation is being attempted. This chapter outlines the use of graph semiotics to build data visualisations for exploration and decision-making and the formulation of elementary, intermediate- and overall-level analytical questions. The public scanner database Dominick's Finer Foods, consisting of approximately 98 million observations, is used as a demonstrative case study. Common Big Data analytic tools (SAS, R and Python) are used to produce visualisations, and examples of student work are presented, based on the outlined visualisation approach.

The sixth chapter, by Busayasachee Puang-Ngern, Ayse Bilgin, and Timothy Kyng, discusses the comparison of Graduates' and Academics' Perceptions of the necessary skills required for jobs in data analytics and "Big Data". In particular, in this chapter, the perceptions of graduates and academics about the types of expertise and the types of software skills required for this field are documented based on two online surveys in Australia and New Zealand. The authors recommend multidisciplinary degrees where the appropriate combination of skills in statistics and computing can be provided for future graduates.

The chapter of Jacques Raubenheimer deals with the use of Microsoft Excel for data visualization and the analysis of Big Data. This chapter plots the historical development of spreadsheets in general, and Excel in particular, highlighting how new features have allowed for new forms of data analysis in the spreadsheet environment. The chapter discusses how Microsoft has cast Excel as a tool for the analysis of big data through the addition and development of features aimed at reporting on data too large for a spreadsheet. This chapter discusses Excel's ability to handle these data by means of an applied example. Data visualization by means of charts and dashboards is discussed as a common strategy for dealing with large volumes of data.

In Chapter 8, Niedja Martins, Carlos Monteiro and Theodosia Prodromou discuss a study examining how primary school teachers understand issues of size and representativeness of samples using TinkerPlots2.0. The authors suggested that the questions of research sections should not only explore the participants´ knowledge on the sample size or the confidence level, but should also promote reflection on the meanings assigned to tasks, leading to discussion of the skills required for statistical literacy in the Big Data era.

GATHERING AND PROCESSING BIG DATA

The ninth chapter by Frederic Clarke and Chien-Hung Chien discusses recent research by the Australian Bureau of Statistics in applying data visualisation to the analysis of Big Data for official statistics. In this chapter, examples are presented from the initial use of a prototype analytical platform created by the ABS—the Graphically Linked Information Discovery Environment (GLIDE)—that aims to demonstrate new ways of representing, linking and exploring complex information from multiple diverse sources. The chapter also discusses the value of data visualisation in meeting the analytical challenges of Big Data, the entity-relationship network model and data visualisation features implemented in GLIDE, together with examples drawn from two significant use cases. It concludes and proposes future research directions.

The chapter by Antonino Virgillito and Federico Polidoro discusses the use of Internet as data source for modernizing their data collection process and the challenges of trying to set up a continuous data collection process using web scraping. They explore and classify the more widespread web scraping techniques and present how they are used in practical cases. The main technical notions behind web scraping are presented and explained in order to give readers with no background in IT the sufficient elements to fully comprehend scraping techniques, as promoting the building of mixed skills that is at the core of the spirit of modern data science. Challenges for official statistics deriving from the use of web scraping are briefly sketched. Finally, research ideas for overcoming the limitations of current techniques are presented and discussed.

In the eleventh chapter, Kees Zeelenberg and Barteld Braaksma describe and discuss opportunities for big data in official statistics and deal with the challenges of big data such as: a) uncontrolled changes in sources that threaten continuity and comparability; b) data that refer only indirectly to phenomena of statistical interest; c) big data may be highly volatile and selective: the coverage of the population to which they refer may change from day to day, leading to inexplicable jumps in time-series. And very often, the individual observations in these big data sets lack variables that allow them to be linked to other datasets or population frames.

The final chapter, by Daniel W Gillman and Franck Cotton, discusses linked Open Statistical Metadata (LOSM), a model for identifying, structuring, interlinking, and querying data published directly on the web. LOSM promotes discovery and the meaning and structure of statistical data in an automated way, helping with understanding and interpreting data and preventing inadequate or flawed visualizations for statistical data, enhancing therefore statistical literacy and efforts at visualizing statistics.

CONCLUSION

Data are proliferating at a tremendous rate. Widespread deployment of new technologies is generating ever more data, and these data can be used or misused. At present there is a need to train both people skilled to gather and process data, as well as people capable of understanding and critically examining the data and representations that they are faced with. The ability to process data well is obviously crucial, but it is perhaps more crucial that the general populace be able make effective use of the data that is presented them. In a world characterised by ever more data, the role of the informed citizen requires a degree of statistical literacy—an ability to draw effective conclusions from data without being swayed by misleading data—in order for citizens to make good decisions personally, socially, and politically. While this book does not hope answer all the important questions, it does hope to become a starting place for the discussion of such issues.

Section 1
Teaching Big and Open Data

Chapter 1
Data Visualisation and Statistics Education in the Future

Theodosia Prodromou
University of New England, Australia

Tim Dunne
University of Cape Town, South Africa

ABSTRACT

Data visualisation has blossomed into a multidisciplinary research area, and a wide range of visualisation tools has been developed at an accelerated pace. Preliminary statistical data analysis benefits from data visualisation to form the basis for decision-making. There is a greater need for people to make good inferences from visualisations. The flexible nature of current computing tools can potentially have a major impact on the learning and practice of the discipline of statistics and allow easier use of visualisations in the educational process. While this view has many merits and we support its general spirit, we argue for a valuable role for a non-visual approach at certain points. Students will employ data visualisation in an OPEN Data context. This chapter is a theoretical discussion of a framework, which emphasises explicit assumptions that help to direct inferences appropriately. In particular it addresses the common illusions of causality in student reasoning. Our discussion of points of disagreement is based on specific theoretical concerns.

DOI: 10.4018/978-1-5225-2512-7.ch001

DATA VISUALISATION

Data visualisation allows us to explore and effectively communicate relevant information about voluminous data through graphic representations. This graphic mode includes visualisation of all kinds of information, and is closely associated with research by computer scientists. From the perspective of statistical pedagogy, data visualisation can be viewed as including computer-assisted exploratory data analysis of voluminous complex data sets. In this paper we do not use the technical distinction between BIG Data and OPEN Data. We only use the term OPEN Data given our expectations of what would be used in a classroom. The new large resources of OPEN Data, such as offered by several official statistics agencies, and any of their accompanying Online analytical processing (OLAP) facilities, will be relevant to the arguments and claims of this paper. The emphasis we offer is on the coherent learning experience that can be marshalled from these resources.

Developments in computing power have greatly enhanced graphical representations in recent years. Computing advances have enabled the drawing of precise, complex displays with great ease, making rich graphics drawn for the purpose of illustrating and explaining results and relationships widely available. Moreover, computing advances have also strengthened exploratory graphical representations that in turn provided support to exploring data further. The quality and quantity of graphical representations has been improved. Many distinct displays of the same data can be drawn to shed light on hidden aspects of the information. It is important, however, to point out that the real revolution is not in the machines that calculate or provide various displays of data, but in the ways we use the data.

The advantages of graphical representations of data have been gradually appreciated and capitalised on (see, e.g., Tufte, 2001; Gal, 2002; Espinel, Bruno, & Plasencia, 2008; Batanero, Arteaga, & Ruis, 2010). These advances provide an opportunity for new avenues of education for young students of statistics. The great importance of computer software availability and associated popularity, in determining what analyses are carried out and how they are presented, is a topic of major relevance. In the world of business, the spreadsheet Excel has long been in common use for creating graphical representations of data. In the world of statistics, there are several sophisticated software packages used by statisticians, including SAS, SPSS, STATA, GENSTAT, STATISTICA, S and S-PLUS, and more recently R.

A great mass of data is being continually generated. Citizens of present and future eras will be constantly and increasingly bombarded with tables of data and graphics in media, economic forecasting, and social activities. People's decisions about their everyday lives depend increasingly on data visualisation and numerous reported figures, and these representations are not always what they seem: "There may be less in there than meets the eyes" (Huff, 1954, p. 8). Although Huff wrote this remark several decades ago about graphics used in the print media of his day, his ideas are still applicable in visual media.

It is essential to empower citizens with the skills to become informed about our world and understand the data that politicians, advertisers, and other advocates are using to promote particular causes that will impact the future of our planet. This prerequisite for citizenship embraces not just the capacity of understanding the underlying messages that the data potentially reveal; citizenship also includes critically examining statements presented in news media in terms of data and data representations, so as to recognise the varieties of misleading or distorted visualisations that miscomprehend and misrepresent data.

Misrepresentations of data may be created intentionally to obstruct the proper interpretation and to induce desired but incorrect conclusions. They may arise accidentally, for example when users are unfamiliar with using graphical software, when the data cannot be accurately conveyed, or when implicit or latent assumptions have been simply imposed on the data and inferences. Whether the deception is intentional or not, being able to recognise such distortions is a skill to be valued in citizens:

The secret language of statistics, so appealing in a fact-minded culture, is employed to sensationalise, inflate, confuse, and oversimplify. Statistical methods and statistical terms are necessary in reporting the mass data of social and economic trends, business conditions, "opinion" polls, and the census. But without writers who use the words with honesty and understanding and readers who know what they mean, the result can only be semantic nonsense. (Huff, 1954, p. 8)

These concerns remain no less pressing today, during the current revolution in our access to data and to new methods of data handling. The field of data visualisation describes ways to present information that avoid creating misleading graphs, but the problems of filtering and distilling through to any valid messages from data still exist. These two objectives of presenting and discussing suggest that visualisation tools will be very important in statistics education. To appreciate the importance that visualisation tools played in statistics, we consider some impacts of data visualisation on statistics.

In the rest of this chapter we will discuss the role and value of visualisation in statistics education, the potential and limits of a wholly visual approach, and the importance of verbalisation and the ability to shift between modes of representation.

Visualisation and Comprehension

Visualisation involves the production of a visual representation of one or more aspects of a data set. This production may include static and dynamic pictorial descriptions of multi-dimensional features. One purpose of visualisation is to allow iterations of various tools and representations, each of which constitutes engagement with the data and its possible underlying features. These representations are more familiar and friendly to sensory intuition than numerical or textual summary alone. Hence they supplement and complement other forms of sense-making from data.

While number is powerful in its domain, that domain is abstract and its nature has a restrictive impact upon its value as a sole description of features of a data set. The multiplicity of number and symbols in OPEN Data initially overwhelms or submerges the cognitive ability to search for pattern and to comprehend variation in detail. Through visualisation artefacts, the user accesses rapid cognitive processes that permit recognition of unsuspected or latent structural features of a detailed body of numbers, strings, or symbols. In consequence visualisation is part of comprehension and integrates into its communication.

While exposure to visualisation as a learning tool will incorporate a repertoire of methods and tools in current use, visualisation is itself a changing art.

Purposes of Visualisation

Wallman (1993, in Gal, 2002) termed statistical literacy as "the ability to understand and critically evaluate statistical results that permeate daily life, coupled with the ability to appreciate the contributions that statistical thinking can make in public and private, professional and personal decisions" (p. 2).

The teacher of statistical literacy has to marshal many facets of visualisation, from elicitation of pattern to salient pictorial representation of a particular specified context. Visualisation must assist with basic production of contextual meaning and interpretation through the familiar cognitive strategies:

- Describe and compare observed conditions or states in a context (at an instant).
- Describe and assess associations between categories, counts and measures (often with time aspects ignored).
- Describe and compare current changes or processes in a context (over a period, sometimes with equal inter-observation intervals).
- Describe and assess associations between changes in observed variables (over some implicit or specified time-interval lengths).

This list includes strategies for teachers to use within visualisation, which are nonetheless grounded or particularised within the visualisation contexts invoked. For the student, a visualisation of data presents a summary of some but not all features in the associated data. Fluency with visualisation implies an awareness of possible features of the data that are marginalised by any particular visualisation.

That fluency may also require an awareness of features of the data source that were never explored or observed. Necessarily, these elements are absent from the data set, and from any of its derived visualisations. These absent elements constitute an implicit framework for any sense-making and inference. For the student the task of constructing a visualisation of data will initially appear to be to represent and articulate perceptions of current phenomena as present in the data. These strategies will help the teacher to guide the students to the ability to assess, confirm or revise the assumed reliability of current belief(s) about the data.

The student must be enabled to consciously reformulate belief(s) to accommodate new perceptions. These outcomes will allow the student to extrapolate and form expectations and inferences about the future of a context, in particular the implicit or assumed context of the data set, as currently understood by the student. The beliefs, inferences and visualisations may also inform or allow retrospective insights into causation associated within the phenomena that gave rise to the data and the representation(s) as produced by the student.

In short, the purpose of visualisation is to enrich sense-making and decision-making, and a statistical literacy course will seek to gradually bring the student to conscious control of the benefits of visualisation, and awareness of its limitations.

VISUALISATION AND VERBALISATION

An explicit complement and outcome of visualisation is verbalisation. We expect that users of visualisation in social or collaborative learning contexts may blurt out initial comments and fresh insights or questions. Indeed engagement with an image that elicits such impressions in the form of language is highly desirable.

The teacher of statistical literacy has to be alert to the potential and the fragilities of these spontaneous insights and enable interchanges that allow the students to formulate and iteratively revise their impressions and reasoning in appropriate formats. These formats address assumptions, conditioning, inferences and extrapolations.

While being sensitive to age-specific development, the verbalisations precipitated by data experiences must in the end also satisfy criteria of explicitness, coherence and precision of some kind, such as descriptions of variability, and articulated assumptions necessary for extrapolation.

Around visualisation we may hope to precipitate experiences of responsible sense-making and verbalisation that become foundations of strong, confident and effective citizenship in the private and public contexts.

Assumptions Within Visualisation

One of the limitations to the wholly visual approach arises because all elicited pattern is contextual. Before the exploration for pattern begins, it may be useful to explicitly specify to students the context of interest that is embedded in the data. At a minimum, the teacher of statistical literacy has to have some knowledge of the data context and possible limitations. Such matters relate to veracity and validity, and possibly volatility, which become user-judgment responsibilities when data is analysed as evidence for inferences. This specification of context assists in understanding how processes of finding pattern may involve hidden or implicit identification and/or designation levels of aggregation or partition. Knowledge of context may give rise to a hypothesis-driven approach, but also more often to various aggregation strategies.

In an OPEN Data era, exploratory choices about which variables could be examined are not made any longer by relying exclusively on hypotheses. The data-sets are far too big and we would no longer be limited to a hypothesis-driven approach. Instead of the hypothesis-driven converging approach, we can use a data-driven approach to talk about data. We use comparisons of groups and associations between variables (correlations within cases) to gain insight into relationships between important variables in phenomena of interest. In a sense we encourage formation of multiple tentative hypotheses

Predictions based on correlations lie at the heart of big data, but with many complex relationships amongst events and variables, non-linear relationships among data variables may be operating and should be recognized or identified. Hence, the correlational relationship to be detected is more multi-faceted than in current standard elementary texts. Necessary tools to identify and compare non-linear relationships have been developed and the techniques of correlational analysis are being enhanced by novel approaches and software that can carefully tease-out non-linear relationships in data.

For education at the high school level, some of the literature (Wild, Pfannkuch, Regan, & Horton, 2011) seems to advocate completely visualised approaches of data organisation and analysis. If that goal is achievable and if it will secure entry into statistical thinking, for at least some students, there is no harm in pursuing it assiduously. An alternative view as we are arguing in this chapter, is that, worthy though the goal may be, it needs to be complemented by a committed intention to signal to students how they may explicitly and deliberately move between the modes of representation in their journeys to deeper understandings of complex and detailed constructs and methods.

The purpose of these orchestrated looser fluencies between modes is to permit and support explorations of the nature and complexity of the vast quantities of data available in the modern world in almost every type of knowledge-based decision-making. Thus the argument we examine and support in this chapter is that efforts in data visualisation, both as a constructive figural or graphical activity and as a tool of communication, will be more effective if they are linked to explicit textual and tabular representations of the same insights.

This argument admits that for many people visualisation may provide a first necessary gateway into comprehending and dealing with information complexity, but claims that their gateway(s) are widened and established by their own fluency with other representational forms of the same meanings (text and table). Likewise for those whose easy preference is for a verbal or textual form, there is a necessary complement in visualization strategies that should be their target of mastery.

One key element of the descriptive and evidential power of visualisation lies in the manner in which visualisation elicits meaningful profiles, and hence permits and supports meaningful contrasts. This outcome occurs after partitioning processes have been used to focus upon some subjectively selected salient subsets of a large data source. Students must grasp the overall abstract nature of statistical ideas by constructing comparisons within partitions of data, or comparisons between displays that present multivariate data within each partitioned group (e.g., within a group of students in a school that consist of boys and girls, and girls outperform boys on days attended and achievement scores). Since contrast and comparison are two key strategies in constructing meaning from intricate detail, the act of making visual partitions or imposing partitions before visualisation is attempted, is an explicit strategy to be invoked and taught.

Teaching of Data Types and Visualisation Repertoires

The intention to focus on data-driven processes of enquiry does not eliminate the need for statistical literacy skills when discussing the nature of manifest data. The context may warrant interpretations of either instantaneous or enduring observations or both.

The types of variables govern, to some extent, the nature and choice of most suitable graphical representation choices. While the concepts should be elicited from experience with some particular data sets, notions such as nominal, cyclical, ordinal, rank, count, and measurement data types need to be recognised and distinguished by the student. There may also be some value in distinguishing between absolute and derived measurements. For univariate descriptions there will often already be some familiarity with groups and labels, and numerical values. The connection between the frequency of specific observed labels and observed values needs to be exhibited and appreciated in bar graphs, histograms and box-whisker diagrams.

The role assigned to any variable as a response feature of direct interest, or as an explanatory variable for one or more response features of interest, is a choice of the user of visualisation. Some explicit care may be required to allow the student to comprehend the impacts and power of the assignation of explanatory status, and the conventions by which explanatory status may be signalled (e.g., partition labels, use of a horizontal axis, and so on). Lurking explanatory variables such as order in categorical groups, time in univariate time series sequences, and spatial location in geographical data sets, all permit particular choices of visualisations. For instance, sliders and curve plots for time patterns, and choropleths and isopleths for maps of spatial pattern, assist the student to simplify the visualisations to choices that find and focus upon pattern(s) that appear to matter.

The work of the naïve data explorer includes deciding on a degree of fitness for purpose(s) of a current visualisation form, or whether some other versions will give a more appealing insight. For example, a static image may be enhanced by rapid alternation between contrasted groups, or by invoking some suitable relational or dynamic re-presentation. The teacher has to be aware of these possibilities to ensure that a repertoire of options can be invoked at salient points in the exploration of a data context through visualisation.

STATISTICAL LITERACY AND UNDERSTANDING PROCESSES

The term statistical literacy carries a connotation of being able to read the products of data summary and data visualisation, and to construct meanings from those products. The noun element literacy suggests a parallel but extended skill beyond reading text and language that includes addressing verbal and numeric content.

Given some set of data from a well-specified context, we may wonder how to summarise, present or visualise the data in order to elicit and infer pattern in the data that characterises its context in some way. Often we also wish to ascertain the extent to which data appear to resonate with the current beliefs and inferences we employ or impose.

If necessary, we seek to revise our beliefs and inferences and create new understandings in the face of the data. We may make these revisions if we believe the data is inherently valid for its context, but also authoritative and appropriate for our inference-making.

Statistical literacy implies fluency with words and data manipulation sufficient to describe, explore and revise opinion and inference. This fluency will range across a continuum of notional levels of student development, covering one or more plausible sequences over grade-specific or age-specific cohorts. In an era of Open Data statistical literacy has to involve more than its original interpretation as a minimal set of statistical concepts, methods and processes from conventional statistics. It has to include exposures to and engagements with large data sets, and the exploration of plausible data summaries, which may give rise to inferences or further explorations (Wallman 1993, in Gal 2002).

Statistical literacy is a citizen imperative or democratic objective that initially involves access to and experiences of data. These experiences should permit the use of words and data manipulation in life contexts that are meaningful to the learning child and the curious adult.

IDENTIFYING AND USING SOURCES OF DATA

As groundwork for a statistical literacy course, lists of and information about BIG data sources and OPEN Data sources may be assembled. These elements can inform selection of data contexts that may be relevant or interesting. Simplified exploratory agendas can be constructed, and assumptions explicitly listed as they emerge from engaged interaction and sharing of views and impressions.

Within any source there will need to be variable exclusion and selection and role assignment (response or explanatory), identification of features, sequences of iterated visualisations, appropriate data manipulation, and verbalisation. In due course these elements merge with current prior inferences and rationales, to become revised explication of assumptions, inference and evidence.

Visualisation Within Statistical Literacy

Visualisation is seen here both as a means and as an end, supporting experiences of the production and revision of inference based upon data, as one of the goals of statistical literacy. An initial emphasis on accessible visualisation techniques, and explanation of their usefulness, should evolve into an appreciation of their limitations en route to valid use in cause–and-effect inferences.

Prerequisite ideas must include a contextualised notion of case and variable, variate values, frequency counts, relative frequencies, and numerical value summaries. There needs to be vocabulary for the student to describe both the processes invoked and their statistical outcomes. The extent of this vocabulary may still be a matter of ongoing debate.

Framework for Teaching Statistical Literacy

A new framework of statistical literacy re-visioned for the era of OPEN Data must address both foundational and dispositional considerations of student exposure. The foundation elements will have much in common with basic statistics courses of the past, in respect to rudimentary concepts of observed frequencies and number summaries, and comparison and association.

The commonalities hide at least two distinctive contrasts, firstly a focus upon experience with accessible very large data sets and visual or graphical exploration, and secondly an emphasis on engagement in data-driven practices that root statistical concepts in experience. The teacher may need to keep these contrasts explicitly in mind. Later we will propose a suitable initial framework.

Developmental Perspectives

Any student exposures to visualisation products and processes from OPEN Data sources will have to be mediated by insights into age-appropriate and/or grade-appropriate demands and skills. In an era when children are increasingly able to harness technology tricks and devices, the time horizons at which student experiences can be constructed may well be much earlier than in the past.

Within a single grade-specific statistical literacy classroom there is likely to be wide variety of access, experience, skill and comprehension associated in part with the developmental levels of the students. A major objective of the teacher is to become increasingly informed about and responsive to these differences for the choice of person-appropriate visualisation exercises.

Retrospective and Prospective Orientations

Where OPEN data sources are historic or static, the insights arising from exploration and visualisation will generally be retrospective. Students need to be aware that prospective extrapolations into extended periods are only justified by the assumption that patterns from the past will carry on unchanged in the future. In contrast, rapidly dynamic data sources may offer stronger short-term prospective inferences phased as likely predictions, but have little or no longer term relevance or utility. The teacher will need to render the contrast between using retrospective and prospective orientations as part of the conscious experience and repertoire of the students. Awareness and use of time orientation grounds the type of arguments students can explore.

Dispositional Elements

A statistical literacy course using OPEN Data sets and resources will have an objective to promote some dispositional values that enhance searches for meaning within data. Each participant begins with beliefs that, whatever their source, have been either been warranted or as yet not undermined by experience with previous related data. Students need to be made comfortable with the idea that revising an inference to take new information into account is both natural and rational.

Each student needs to address a new data context with explicit assumptions that are internally coherent, but essentially contestable. What emerges thereafter is engagement with the data and articulation of plausible inferences. Additionally, all students using OPEN Data need early exposure to the fact that all data carries ethical implications of some kind. Inferences for context carry the same ethical burdens.

Commonalities and Contrasts With Basic Statistics Courses

In the previous decade, just prior to the era of OPEN Data, several researchers in statistics education discussed the existence of new data visualisation tools. They argued that data visualisation tools created the possibility of visualising collections of actual data usable by students at the middle and high school level (Finzer, 2001; Konold & Miller, 2005), providing opportunities to include key statistical concepts not previously taught to this age of student, such as inferential reasoning (Ben-Zvi, 2006) and the process of statistical investigations (Wild & Pfannkuch, 1999).

Concepts important for statistics can be mastered with a "wholly visual approach" (Wild, Pfannkuch, Regan, & Horton, 2011, p. 252) that will, "attempt to minimise the conceptual distances between the concrete realities, including precursor practical experiences, and the dynamic imagery envisaged". This approach encourages an inferential step to be performed without having "students taking their eyes off their graphs" (p. 252) so that students can easily draw connections between question and data, and answer as quickly as possible.

This solely visual approach places working with data and making and validating visual inferences on the fly at the core of instruction, and constitutes a shift towards more holistic, process/problem-oriented approaches to learning statistics. The emphasis is on situations/data that unfold in time. However we claim that a wholly visual approach without verbalization will not necessarily connect the experience to the statistical concepts inherent in the target context.

The shift in student research from intensively focusing on mathematical tools of statistics (e.g., averages, distribution, graphs, samples, modal clumps) as embedded in the processes and contexts under investigation, to statistical processes, has raised new issues. Hancock, Kaput, and Goldsmith (1992) highlighted the challenges that students encountered when attempting to connect their statistical questions to the data required as source of evidence, and then argued for the pedagogical importance of helping students also associate their conclusions with the questions under investigation.

They argued that school statistics curricula ignored two dimensions of a statistical process: (1) connecting statistical questions to data and (2) linking conclusions from data to the questions under investigation. Focusing on the statistical *investigative cycle* (Wild & Pfannkuch, 1999) as a process of exploring the context domain of a real problem and seeking explanations in that problem context, "entails understanding the statistical investigation cycle as a process of making inferences. That is, it is not [only] the data in front of us that is of great interest, but the more general characteristics and processes that created the data. This process is indeed inferential" (Makar & Rubin, 2009, p. 84). The process seeks applicable contextual meanings in order to comprehend and perhaps replicate desirable outcomes or features latent in the data and its structure.

This process of making inferences has attracted a great deal of interest in students' informal ideas about statistical inference and people's intuitive ways of reasoning for statistical inference in diverse contexts. Researchers of statistics education over the last several years have focused on informal aspects of inferential reasoning. Makar and Rubin (2009) grappled with developing a framework for understanding the building blocks of informal statistical inference and inferential reasoning within a context of statistical investigations.

Three main principles of making informal inferences from data were identified by Makar and Rubin (2009): (1) generalising, predicting, estimating parameters, and drawing conclusions that extend beyond describing the given data; (2) using data as evidence for those generalisations; and (3) employing probabilistic language when describing the generalisation and making informal inferences that include levels of confidence or uncertainty within the conclusions drawn. A fourth principle involves (4) comparison of datasets with a model (Bakker et al., 2008).

The first principle is particularly related to the process of inference, whereas the second and third are related to statistics. When generalising beyond the data, one makes generalisations (inferences) on assumptions that the data notionally come from a sample of a specified population of which the sample is to be reasonably representative. These two assumptions are the engine of inference. Their use and control has to be properly appreciated.

The validity of any inference from a sample, which is known data, to an intended population, which is partly known and partly unknown, can be debated. The validity is predicated upon the plausibility of a usually unverifiable belief: the unobserved segment of the population, however large, is virtually identical in its data profile to the observed smaller segment in the sample. The notion of sample (at least in English) constitutes an impediment to adopting a forensic attitude to inference, because in common usage "sample" conveys a misleading assertion of precisely the representativity condition that has to be verified.

It is often difficult to distinguish descriptions of a data sample and inferences about the population from which that data was drawn (Pfannkuch, 2006), but visualisation techniques can help students when shifting their attention from describing the sample to making inferences about the population (Wild et al., 2011).

The needs of an earlier age and the constraints of technology resulted in restrictions upon the extent to which natural information-processing interactions with data emerged. Before the revolution of OPEN Data and the availability of high-performance digital technologies, the accepted convention was to make inferences about variables describing characteristics of units within populations, using observed data from samples as sets of (sometimes randomly) selected units.

This kind of thinking from samples to inferences about populations was a function of a "small data" environment. Nonetheless, at its core, OPEN Data is about making generalisations and predictions, similar to making statistical inferences. OPEN Data may be used to predict the performance of a stock market or even to predict consumers' future purchases based on their interactions at different sites on the Internet.

OPEN Data allows users see details of data we never could imagine when we were limited to smaller data sets. Visual representations of OPEN Data enable us to unravel the story of data by addressing subcategories of data that sampling cannot practically assess. By inspecting far more data than was previously possible, we are able to shift from considering error in sampling to accepting more measurement errors. With vast quantities of data, we usually need merely to have a general sense of data or to explore the data at a macro level rather than having a micro view of data. "What we lose in accuracy at the micro level we gain in insight at the macro level" (Mayer-Schönberger & Cukier, 2013, p. 14).

This shift to exploring the macro behaviour of data seems to concur with the Exploratory Data Analysis approach (EDA) that focuses explicitly on "looking at data to see what it seems to say" (Tukey, 1977, p. v), and also resonates with the important contributions of Tufte (1990, 1997) relating to the power of graphical and diagrammatic summaries of data, economies of graphical forms and representations, and his warnings about types of visualisation that distort the understanding of the data. Tufte also advocates the elimination of chart junk and redundant distracting visual elements, and offers a criterion for judging the efficacy of a (printed) diagram, the data-ink ratio. None of these insights falls away in the new environment of on-screen visualisation though the formulations may require adaptation.

DATA VISUALISATION AND LEARNING STATISTICS

The application of visualisation methods to an ever-expanding array of substantive data structures and the new developments of dynamic graphic methods that allow instantaneous and direct manipulation of graphical objects and related statistical properties bring novel applications from new technologies and permit new approaches towards teaching (e.g., modelling aspects of applications, observing valid data to adequately answer the questions), all suggesting new ways to support students' learning.

In their national curriculum, several countries encourage students to make sense of data and data representations and unravel the story that data tell (implicitly or explicitly). They promote visualisation of data as a way to meet this objective (e.g., see National Council of Teachers of Mathematics [NCTM], 2000; Australian Curriculum, Assessment and Reporting Authority [ACARA], 2016). For example, ACARA notes for students at the middle school level, interest in "data representation and interpretation," especially with identifying and investigating "issues involving continuous or large count data collected from primary and secondary sources" (p. 42) and describing and interpreting data sets in terms of location (centre) and spread. However the extent to which USA and Australian schools have successfully implemented data visualization, in which students are engaged in interpreting data, remains uncertain.

The introduction of digital technology into schools has prompted increased interest in EDA as a means of engaging students in statistical analysis, arguably reducing the need for a sophisticated understanding of theoretical statistical principles, especially those demanding an appreciation of probability theory, prior to meaningful engagement. The technology is ideally suited for supporting students as they manipulate a data set and then portray the data in a range of different representations in order to infer underlying patterns of association or perhaps trends over time.

New data visualisation tools promote a perspective on visualising collections of actual data at the middle and high school level (Finzer, 2001; Konold & Miller, 2005). They provide opportunities to include key statistical concepts not previously taught to these age cohorts, such as inferential reasoning (Ben-Zvi, 2006) and the basic process of statistical investigations (Wild & Pfannkuch, 1999). Rubin, Hammerman, and Konold (2006) argued that the use of technological tools such as TinkerPlots can rapidly enculturate their users into unlocking stories latent in data. Conceptions of statistics, and in particular statistical inference, can be mastered with a "wholly visual approach" (Wild et al., 2011, p. 252) that will, "attempt to minimise the conceptual distances between the concrete realities, including precursor practical experiences, and the dynamic imagery envisaged." This new approach exhibits the foundational difference in newer approaches to working with data as the core of instruction, towards more holistic, process/problem-oriented approaches to learning statistics.

The initial emphasis should be on making inferences based on a wholly visual approach and justifying those inferences based on characteristics of the visual graphical representations. The same basic skills used by students to perform informal inferences based on a wholly visual approach underpin strategies needed to perform informal inferences and judgments about the statistical graphs commonly available.

The skills become essential competencies to be derived from students' engagement in data visualisation and future statistics. These competencies, which underpin the essential skills for graph comprehension (Friel et al. 2001) and elements of acquisition of statistical literacy (Gal, 2002), include:

1. Data grappling skills: the ability to move data around and manipulate data using some software or programming languages;
2. An ability to create informative pictures when encountering new data;
3. Formulating and communicating a reasoned opinion about statistics (average, variation around average), confidence intervals, error bars; finding relationships between the data variables;
4. Assigning response and explanatory roles to variables in context, and reading beyond the data, including identification of relationships, in order to perform inferences or generalisations based on a wholly visual approach;
5. Forecasting and prediction, both general and specific;
6. Communication of a reasoned inference derived from data; and
7. Finding a model that in some sense best fits a data set within its context.

Some software representations help students in making inferences by exhibiting regions of the data whose patterns strongly suggest the presence of underlying models of the data.

The competencies are presented in the form of seven essential skills that might be seen as both a hierarchy of competence, and a framework for considering the ways that teachers and students could employ data visualisation when working with data in a pedagogical context.

However, the new revolutions in the era of OPEN Data visualisation and the tools for handling data have dramatically changed the practice of data exploration and comprehension. Such a slew of changes require an analogous transformation of the way the student or the citizen thinks and learns. Thus we present below some ideas about the potential use of visualisation that we specifically recommend as part of our new framework for statistical literacy education.

OPEN DATA AND STATISTICAL LITERACY

Nicholson, Ridgway, and McCusker (2013) argue that our view of what constitutes statistical literacy needs to change rapidly. Their remarks were a source of motivation to formulate a framework. Indeed, there are accessible and credible versions of data literacy that contrast with the traditional view and practice. These versions need to be embraced and explored. Furthermore, Lutsky (2013) reported that his aspiration in teaching is to strengthen quantitative reasoning. This phrase may offer a suitable theme.

Smith (2013) suggested incorporating new tools and processes if we do not want statistics to be marginalised and perceived as a redundant discipline. It is important to "not strip important information away but [to be] presenting the full complexity of the data for context and highlighting what is important" (Smith, 2013). In order to take into account the full complexity of data, we have to change the way we think about controlling and handling data. This view calls for another change to the constructs of statistical literacy (Gal, 2002) and the introduction of new constructs and principles needed for the age of OPEN Data. Although we will build upon the values, knowledge elements, and dispositional elements used to describe the constructs of statistical literacy, we recognise the urgent need for new principles and dispositions that will become the building blocks of a novel model of literacy. The OPEN Data era challenges people to become better informed about the ways in which they could harness vast bodies of data rather than small datasets, and simultaneously harness the technology that facilitates exploration of data. Some elements are listed in Table 1.

We proceed to explore these framework elements.

Seeing Plausible Inferences Within Data

Familiarity with several foundational ideas especially OPEN Data, multivariate data sets, visualisation, and data provenance and quality underlies students' ability

Table 1. Framework for teaching statistical literacy in the OPEN Data era

1. Seeing the plausible inferences within data
2. Language
3. Context, change, causality
4. Assessing data
• Evaluating the quality of evidence
• Handling new representations
• Conceiving statistics as modelling
• Action-oriented statistics

to understand the exploration and analysis of large scale multivariate data sets. The teacher needs to select some key statistical ideas that would help students to describe these data effectively. Some aspects of these key ideas can be represented by mathematical symbols or statistical terms, but their essence cannot be fully captured by technical notations. In the small-data world, both causal investigations (e.g., experimental designs) and associational analysis (e.g., categorical, ordinal and measurement relationships) have traditionally been presented as a specifiable hypothesis under test to be either falsified or adopted, and then described.

Correlations enable users to determine whether two phenomena are good proxies for each other, without shedding light on any possible causal relationships between the variables. The student will need some guidance into the arena of marshalling evidence of causal relations from associations.

Language

Some of the dissonances experienced by students with new constructs arise from the earlier multiple contextual meanings of terms adopted with fresh interpretation in a new discipline being entered by a student. In statistics such terms include possibility, probability, odds, odds ratio, normal, significant, confidence, association, regression, dependent, and cause. The familiar context or usage has to be unlearned or loosened or recontextualised, to admit entry into new understandings.

A suitable approach emerges for unlearning stable habits of constrained perceptions and thinking, namely to be able to break free of the mode by which the current understanding dominates the construction and invocation of meaning. Since that dominance is very often located in verbal modes, alternatives in forms of visual engagement, namely text, table, figure, and graph, may offer strategic advantages in the search for transformed comprehensions of obstinate words. The intrusion of such language elements into a data visualisation is not as unlikely as it may seem at face value.

Context, Change, and Cause

Initially students may tend to approach a data set as complete in itself. The practice of explicitly noting or articulating a context permits both channeling of exploration and deeper critical attention. This practice has to be acquired, and its inherent value appreciated. Experience of context being elucidated by teachers or peers, leads to appreciation of preconditions latent in the data structure and composition.

The act of articulation grounds description of relationships and associations between variables in the richness of the context. A natural tendency in the search for meaning in data is assertion of cause and effect relationships from what are merely associations. In many contexts this strategy can be demonstrated to be incomplete or unwise or false.

OPEN Data settings with an inherent time ordering of any multiple observations may lead to a focus on the derived variables of change in category or change in count or change in measure over specified sequence lengths or time intervals of interest. Contextual cues permit an appreciation of the complexity of establishing cause-and-effect relationships. The strongest levels of evidence necessarily involve association of at least one change in an explanatory variable with a change in a response variable at a suitable lag that permits the development of expected effects over time, and their eventual observation.

The application of the *investigative cycle* of Wild and Pfannkuch (1999) will necessarily lead students to contexts in which inferences and decisions involving cause and effect notions must be invoked. The complex matter of causality should not simply be left to formal higher or post-graduate levels.

Proper understanding of OPEN Data messages by students depends on their ability to distinguish the different types of data and thus reduce complex data sets into meaningful parts, and use this information to make informed decisions. Also needed is knowledge about the contexts that generate different types of data, and consideration their broad range of sources (e.g., web data, science data, graph data, user data, and transition data).

Students' familiarity with the data-generation process in social media is direct. Data such as tweets, blogs discussions, and photos/videos posted and shared by users of many Web 2.0 applications, are directly contributed by the users themselves. Most of these data are therefore unstructured, and accompanying metadata such as user names, and user identifications may be important for understanding the data and extracting necessary information to impose structure on the data.

Students must know that to understand all data, even OPEN Data, they must go through a process of data integration and cleaning, reduction, indexing, analysis, and mining. Context knowledge is the major determinant of people's familiarity with reducing large amounts of data to the meaningful parts to investigate associations within those parts. OPEN Data correlations could point towards promising areas to further explore causal relationships. If the student is not aware of the context within which data are generated, it is very difficult to identify appropriate parts and seek relationships amongst those parts.

The style of natural or naïve sense-making seeks evidence for dependable (replicable) interventions within a context, to achieve specific desired effects. It is the purposefulness of sense-making that has to be both invoked and harnessed in OPEN Data contexts.

A natural tendency in sense-making is to interpret association between variables as evidence arising from cause and effect. Thus initially students may interpret bivariate association as sufficient confirmation of causal relationship. Where this tendency occurs, the student will assign explanatory and response roles within bivariate pairs, and observe contrasts given by pairs of data cases (x_a, y_a) and (x_b, y_b).

The inherent association draws attention to observable patterns within pairs, such as $(x_a < x_b)$, far more frequently occurring with $(y_a < y_b)$ than with the converse inequality. The focus of attention is on the two original forms or contrasts of values of the variables across the cases.

Relationships across pairs of bivariate data cases must be distinguished from relationships within data cases obtained from two (or more) observations on variables of the same case as in (x_{a1}, y_{a1}) and (x_{a1}, y_{a2}). The focus is on the contrasts within the cases $(x_{a2} - x_{a1})$ and $(y_{a2} - y_{a1})$, and the patterns exhibited by the contrasts. These contrasts only become changes when we are able to invoke a time-ordering relationship within the case, with partial observations (x_{a1}, y_{a1}) always preceding (x_{a2}, y_{a2}).

A change $(x_{a2} - x_{a1})$ may be imposed upon a case a, at a specific time 1, but may require a time-lag before observation of (x_{a1}, y_{a2}) at time 2 can emerge as an associated effect $(y_{a2} - y_{a1})$.

Associations between changes over time in two variables may have a regularity of pattern within and across cases. These conditions will more strongly invite causal inferences, though they are necessary but not sufficient for that inferential purpose. The slippery notions for the student involve the data context with its latent set of assumptions, agency or imposed action, control of extraneous variables and the role of time.

One has to verify from the metadata that a suitable time-lag was allowed for in the observations. The lag has to be adequate to allow an effect to develop, but not be so large that the intrusion of other factors might become plausible explanations.

One of the prospects of data visualisation for OPEN Data is valid real world inferences, especially when evidence for causal effects for one or other set of changes is desirable or invited. The student has to be introduced at least to some appreciation of the stringency required for formal causal inferences.

If we are to encourage explorations that tap into cause and effect, we are obliged to introduce students to the conditions or assumptions necessary to warrant any causal inference. Students will have to assay the extent to which a context can supply bivariate data cases with a single candidate explanatory variable, admitting specifiable change (e.g., a dose) with a length of interaction period adequate for an associated effect to emerge and also become an observable feature of data changes in a chosen response variable.

Usually these background conditions for validity of particular causal inferences will have to be assumed to hold. Thus it is important that students exposed to OPEN Data visualisations for the elicitation of possible causal effects have sufficient awareness and appreciation for the background assumptions that are required, before available graphical evidence is deemed adequate for the purpose.

The argument here is that the all-other-things-being-equal (AOTBE) assumption, naturally made at first pass in many common-sense approaches, has to be confirmed by data analysis, in contrast to the assumption almost-all-other-things-being-equally-unknown (AAOTBEU), which is often the more accurate description. This second step re-alerts the evidential enquiry to the latent contextual assumptions driving causal inferences. Essentially the confirmation exercise provides stimulus for the elimination of redundant variables and for increasing specification of variables that may generate causal effects. Because AAOTBEU is more frequently the correct description of the data context than AOTBE. Thus any inference of causality must be carefully reasoned to ensure its validity.

Assessing Data

Ridgway, Nicholson, and McCusker (2013) discussed the idea that promotion of new statistical literacies (they argued for a variety of distinct kinds of statistical literacy) will foster appropriate dispositions and habits of minds. We see the following elements as necessary endpoints for evolving statistical literacies:

- **Evaluating the Quality of Evidence:** This element involves expecting, seeking and providing information about data sources and inserting specifications to access the metadata into displays that present multivariate data, and discussions that draw attention to the source of data generation and associated quality.
- **Conceiving Statistics as Forming Models:** The ability to use statistical models to describe a wide range of phenomena in our world and quantify an aspect of these phenomena is important. Students are usually taught statistical techniques and models and use these models focusing mainly on describing phenomena to make connections between data and chance (Bakker et al., 2008). Modelling activities are likely to increase students' understanding of how science and statistics are connected when all phenomena are modelled via mathematics (Prodromou, 2014).
- **Action-Oriented Statistics:** According to Ridgway et al. (2013), it is the purposive nature of investigation and consequent actions that will engage and enrich student learning. These circumstances then permit approaches to deeper issues:

Statistics is seen in the context of an investigative cycle, where the end point is a theoretical account and some action designed to change the current situation. A central idea is to use population data to draw conclusions and plans for action that will be applied to all subpopulations (so interaction, effect size and Simpson's paradox are exhibitable). (Ridgway et al., 2013, p. 11).

The investigative process is facilitated by visualisation tools. In order to understand students' changing experiences of how to best represent quantitative data and reason about covariation between multiple variables using the power of digital tools to represent quantities and measures in new ways, Morton et al. (2012) describe a cycle of inquiry and visual analysis:

The process starts with some task or question that about which a knowledge worker seeks to gain understanding. In the first stage, the user forages for data that may contain relevant information for their analysis task. Next, they search for a visual structure that is appropriate for the data and instantiate that structure. At this point, the user interacts with the resulting visualisation (e.g., drill down to details or roll up to summarise) to develop further insight. Once the necessary insight is obtained, the user can then make an informed decision and take action. (Morton et al., 2012, p. 807)

This cycle of visual analysis is centred around and driven by students' effective use of visualisation tools as a habit of mind. The cycle requires that the visualisation system be flexible enough to support students' feedback and allow students to investigate a variety of exploratory tasks in order to develop stronger understandings of the possible relationships between multiple variables. The cycle of visual analysis was further developed and renamed as a *cycle of inquiry and visual analysis* (Prodromou, 2014) for promoting students' inferences from data visualisations. We assert that this cycle is more than a pedagogical strategy but is intended to become a personal disposition because of its empowering effects in dealing with the dynamics of exploratory tasks when using visualization tools. All of these processes necessarily unfold in specific contexts as the settings for inference.

We need to understand how students conceptualise and experience the *cycle of inquiry and visual analysis* in order to make the cycle accessible, natural and habitual for every student.

DISCUSSION

Models that lead students into an appreciation of multivariate structure will be necessary and useful. The efficacy of the three elements for assessing data can be noted in the example of an innovative approach for multivariate categorical data offered in Wild (2013). He considered all possible combinations of responses in a multiple response item by concatenating a series of binary yes/no responses into an observed sequence of eight 1/0 characters and reporting the frequency counts of the observed strings of claimed ethnic background (Figure 1). This visualisation involves the tabular presentation of the frequencies for some of the 256 binary patterns that occur in the observations, organised from more frequent to least

Figure 1. Possible combinations of responses in a multiple response item

Combination Plot

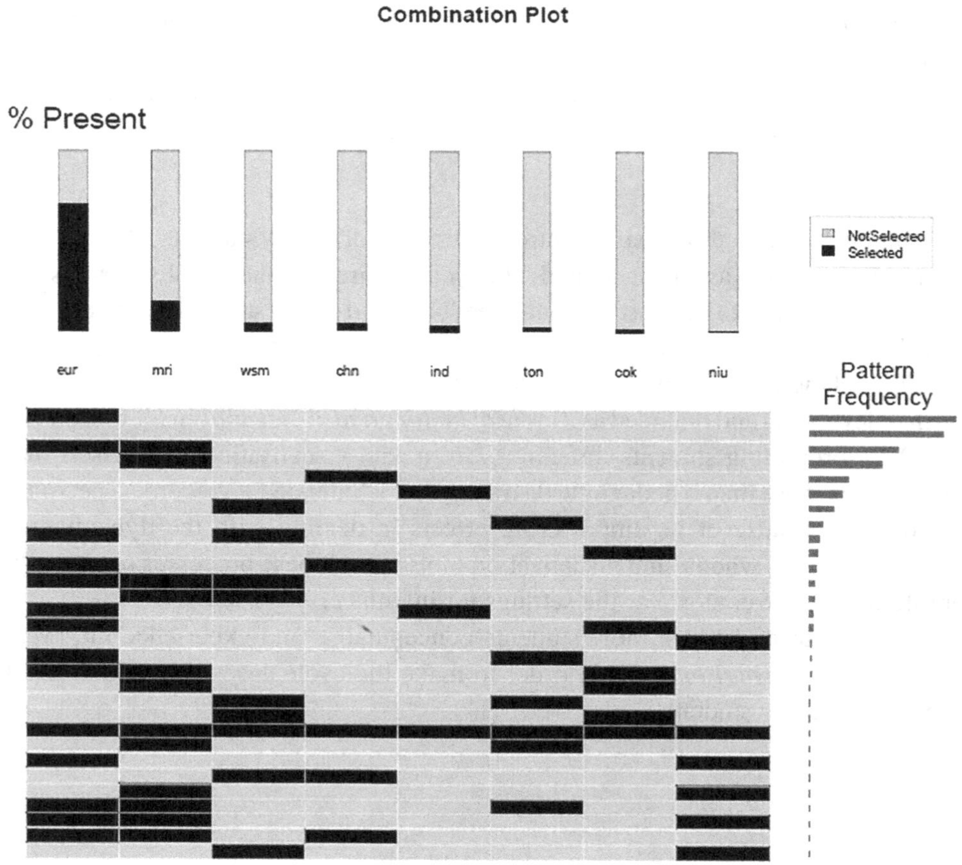

frequent 8-fold concatenations. This form of visualisation updates in 2D-space both the observations and the frequencies of correlated binary variables in a higher (8-fold) dimensional space.

There is a need to see visualisation as both product and process. As a process it has both passive and active connotations. While it is important for students to develop a smooth reading of graphical images, this objective is insufficient. They also need to begin an active attempt to pre-visualise in order engage and internalise deeper modes of interaction with visual and graphical forms.

Students have to rely on their common sense in addressing complexity. Common sense seeks threads of insights as first steps into comprehending aspects of complexity. Students start to locate elements that matter in order to begin with tentative partitions. The teacher needs to emphasise to them the iterative process of seeking relevant tentative partitions rather than any particular product fit for purpose. Initially the product is unknown, and insight into its initial state may be the first element of their learning. What is to be communicated to the student is not just the device of partitioning as a building block of process, but also the value of the final partitioning when once identified and explicitly labeled.

Partitioning leads to a focus on a part or segment of the data. When this segment is rendered relatively homogeneous with respect to some features of the complete data, its internal complexity is reduced. Thus the selected data segment's own particular internal data patterns are more likely to emerge in any data summarising activity.

Those emerging conditional patterns are the stuff of inference, whether in visual or statistical forms, and the inferences across these two forms will generally admit parallel conclusions. This fact keeps open the prospect of a formation in inference that is initially wholly visual, being later complemented with a formalised statistical approach.

CONCLUSION

We have argued the definition statistical literacy needs to be expanded to incorporate new elements and dispositions to address the OPEN Data era. In particular, technological innovations in computer architecture not only allow the storage of large volumes of data but also enable users to obtain higher-quality graphical representations that have contributed to giving a prominent role to data visualisation and more generally to data. The increase of the volume of data precipitated the need for exploratory analyses, coupled with graphical methods that very quickly demonstrate ways of productively engaging with any large data set.

Teachers of statistical literacy have to marshal many facets of visualization as a result of significant developments in information technology. All of these facets seek elicitation of pattern and salient pictorial representation of a particular specified context. The production of contextual meaning and interpretation involve familiar cognitive strategies. These strategies encompass descriptions, profiles, partitions, contrasts, comparisons and associations.

The associations may focus values for variables, contrasts of values, and changes in values. These features are discovered from and embedded in visualisations.

In fact, the key element in the success of data analysis is the strong contribution of visualisation that exploits the human capability to perceive three-dimensional space and time and invoke those elements as windows into the data. Nevertheless, in our view, a solely visual approach has to be complemented with explicit language that controls unsubstantiated attribution of cause-and-effect.

On this basis we may expect that a big change is required in teaching practice, academic programs, and teaching curricula. In consequence we have argued for an initial framework for teaching statistical literacy for an OPEN Data era. This framework seeks to orchestrate context, language, plausibility of inferences within data, attention to causality and assessing data through a critical view.

We have suggested that dispositional elements require explicit attention if statistical literacy is intended to enrich participation in the evolving world of the citizen.

As the volume of data continues to grow, making new technologies increasingly indispensable tools, there may also be a need to teach students some related computer science topics such as combinatorial optimisation, data structures, or database management.

Should this point of view be taken into consideration, a substantial change would be required in teaching practice, academic programs, and school curricula. Curricula may need to include current computer-oriented data analysis methodologies, many of which have been developed outside the field of statistics. These new methods invoke position, direction, time and movement, colour, tone, shape, and structure. The methods involve those features as tools that expose and contrast features of the data.

Data visualisation tools such as the "GapMinder World Map" graph and Tableau, for example, can display several attributes, enabling analysis of the relations between them. Visualisation tools, for example GapMinder, often have built-in access to large global datasets regarding economy, education, energy, environment, health, infrastructure, population, society, and work.

Tableau allows users to dynamically combine and visualise data from multiple heterogeneous sources by blending data. Users begin with a single data source that establishes subsequent blending operations in the visualisation. Data blending starts with the user selecting and importing fields from different data sources. Users best depict quantitative data and reason about covariation between multiple variables as represented in complex compelling visualisations within a cycle of inquiry and visual analysis (Morton, et al., 2012).

Advances in computer software and hardware have greatly simplified and enabled the production of graphical representations. These advances have also contributed to raising the expected standards. Future developments of graphic methods will indisputably include more flexible and powerful software packages that better integrate modelling and graphical representations. There will probably be developed novel and innovative graphics and some of the general design of displays will be improved.

This attention to graphical developments increases the need to understand the psychological aspects of data visualisation. These understandings will provide us with feedback about how students reason with the help of improved graphical displays, what aspects of formal inference are needed given current visualisation tools, and which methods foster students' ability to understand conventional formal conceptions and characteristics of OPEN Data sets. Ideally, there should be further progress in the formal theory of data visualisation. Nevertheless, current growth of the field already gives rise to the challenge of integrating data visualisation in statistics education for students in order that they are enabled to become competent citizens in the OPEN Data era. In consequence we infer that data visualization already constitutes a sound basis for reformulations of statistical literacy. The reformulations involve content and experiences directed by the teacher being conscious of some important endpoints in the student competences to be derived experientially from engagement with real-world data sets.

ACKNOWLEDGMENT

This chapter was written with Professor Tim Dunne before he passed away on 18 April 2016

REFERENCES

Australian Curriculum, Assessment and Reporting Authority. (2016). *Australian Curriculum, Version 8.2*. Sydney, NSW: ACARA.

Bakker, A., Kent, P., Derry, J., Noss, R., & Hoyles, C. (2008). Statistical inference at work: Statistical process control as an example. *Statistics Education Research Journal*, 7(2), 131–146. Retrieved from http://www.stat.auckland.ac.nz/~iase/serj/SERJ7%282%29_Bakker.pdf

Batanero, C., Arteaga, P., & Ruis, B. (2010). Statistical graphs produced by prospective teachers in comparing two distributions. In V. Durand-Guerrier, S. Soury-Lavergne, & F. Arzarello (Eds.), *Proceeding of the Sixth Congress of the European Society for Research in Mathematics Education,* (pp. 368-377). Lyon: ERME. Retrieved from www.inrp.fr/editions-electroniques/cerme6/

Ben-Zvi, D. (2006). Using Tinkerplots to scaffold students' informal inference and argumentation. In A. Rossman & B. Chance (Eds.), *Proceedings of the Seventh International Conference on Teaching Statistics.* Voorburg, The Netherlands: International Statistical Institute. Retrieved from http://iase-web.org/Conference_Proceedings.php?p=ICOTS_7_2006

Espinel, M. C., Bruno, A., & Plasencia, I. (2008). Statistical graphs in the training of teachers. In C. Batanero, G. Burrill, C. Reading, & A. Rossman (Eds.), *Joint ICMI/IASE Study: Teaching Statistics in School Mathematics. Challenges for Teaching and Teacher Education. Proceedings of the ICMI Study 18 and 2008 IASE Round Table Conference.* Monterrey, Mexico: International Commission on Mathematical Instruction and International Association for Statistical Education. Retrieved from: http://iase-web.org/Conference_Proceedings.php?p=ICME_11_2008.

Finzer, W. (2001). *Fathom: Dynamic Data.* Emeryville, CA: Key Curriculum. Retrieved from www.keypress.com/x5656.xml

Friel, S. N., Curcio, F. R., & Bright, G. W. (2001). Making sense of graphs: Critical factors influencing comprehension and instructional implications. *Journal for Research in Mathematics Education, 32*(2), 124–158. doi:10.2307/749671

Gal, I. (2002). Adults' statistical literacy: Meanings, components, responsibilities. *International Statistical Review, 70*(1), 1–25. doi:10.1111/j.1751-5823.2002.tb00336.x

Hancock, C., Kaput, J. J., & Goldsmith, L. T. (1992). Authentic inquiry with data: Critical barriers to classroom implementation. *Educational Psychologist, 27*(3), 337–364. doi:10.1207/s15326985ep2703_5

Huff, D. (1954). *How to Lie with Statistics.* New York, NY: W.W. Norton.

Konold, C., & Miller, C. (2005). *TinkerPlots: Dynamic data exploration.* Emeryville, CA: Key Curriculum. Retrieved from www.keypress.com/x5715.xml

Lutsky, N. (2013). *Connected Worlds: Statistical literacy in art, science, public health, and social issues.* Paper presented at the 59th WSC, Hong Kong.

Makar, K., & Rubin, A. (2009). A framework for thinking about informal statistical inference. *Statistics Education Research Journal, 8*(1), 82–105.

Mayer-Schönberger, V., & Cukier, K. (2013). *Big Data: A Revolution that will transform how we live, work, and think*. New York: Houghton Mifflin Harcourt Publishing Company.

Morton, K., Bunker, R., Mackinlay, J., Morton, R., & Stolte, C. (2012). Dynamic workload driven data integration in Tableau. In *Proceedings of the Special Interest Group on Management of Data Conference* (pp. 807-816). Retrieved from https://research.tableau.com/paper/dynamic-workload-driven-data-integration-tableau

National Council of Teachers of Mathematics. (2000). *Principles and standards for school mathematics*. Reston, VA: National Council of teachers of Mathematics.

Nicholson, J., Ridgway, J., & McCusker, S. (2013). *Statistical literacy and multivariate thinking*. Paper presented at the 59th WSC, Hong Kong.

Pfannkuch, M. (2006). Informal inferential reasoning. In A. Rossman & B. Chance (Eds.), *Working Cooperatively in Statistics Education. Proceedings of the Seventh International Research Conference on Teaching Statistics*. Voorburg, The Netherlands: International Statistical Institute.

Prodromou, T. (2014). Drawing inferences from data visualisations. *International Journal of Secondary Education, 2*(4), 66-72. Retrieved from http://article.sciencepublishinggroup.com/pdf/10.11648.j.ijsedu.20140204.12.pdf

Ridgway, J., Nicholson, J., & McCusker, S. (2013). 'Open Data' and the Semantic Web Require a Rethink on Statistics Teaching. *Technology Innovations in Statistics Education, 7*(2). Retrieved from: http://escholarship.org/uc/item/6gm8p12m

Rubin, A., Hammerman, J. K., & Konold, C. (2006). Exploring informal inference with interactive visualisation software. In A. Rossman & B. Chance (Eds.), *Working Cooperatively in Statistics Education. Proceedings of the Seventh International Research Conference on Teaching Statistics*. Voorburg, The Netherlands: International Statistical Institute.

Smith, A. (2013). *Emerging trends in data visualisation: Implications for producers of official statistics*. Paper presented at the 59th WSC, Hong Kong. Retrieved from http://www.statistics.gov.hk/wsc/IPS019-P3-S.pdf

Tufte, E. R. (1990). *Envisioning Information*. Cheshire, CT: Graphics Press.

Tufte, E. R. (1997). *Visual Explanations: Images and Quantities, Evidence and Narrative*. Cheshire, CT: Graphics Press.

Tufte, E. R. (2001). *The visual display of quantitative information. Cheshire, CT: Graphics Press.*

Tukey, J. W. (1977). *Exploratory Data Analysis.* Addison Wesley Publishing Company.

Unwin, A., Chen, C., & Hardle, W. (2008). Introduction. In C. Chen, W. Hardle, & A. Unwin (Eds.), *Handbook of Data Visualisation.* New York: Springer-Verlag. doi:10.1007/978-3-540-33037-0_1

Wallman, K. K. (1993). Enhancing statistical literacy: Enriching our society. *Journal of the American Statistical Association, 88,* 1–8.

Wild, C. J. (2013). iNZight into Time Series and Multiple-Response Data. *Proceedings of the Joint IASE/IAOS International Conference of Statistics Education for Progress Organised by the International association of Statistics Education (IASE) and the International Association for Official Statistics (IAOS).* Macau, China: IASE/IAOS. Retrieved from http://iase-web.org/documents/papers/sat2013/IASE_IAOS_2013_Paper_2.5.3_Wild_ppt.pdf

Wild, C. J., & Pfannkuch, M. (1999). Statistical thinking in empirical enquiry. *International Statistical Review, 67*(3), 223–265. doi:10.1111/j.1751-5823.1999.tb00442.x

Wild, C. J., Pfannkuch, M., Regan, M., & Horton, N. J. (2011). Conceptions of Statistical Inference. *Journal of the Royal Statistical Society. Series A, (Statistics in Society), 174*(Part 2), 247–295. doi:10.1111/j.1467-985X.2010.00678.x

Chapter 2

Open Data in Australian Schools:
Taking Statistical Literacy and the Practice of Statistics Across the Curriculum

Jane Watson
University of Tasmania, Australia

ABSTRACT

This chapter focuses on statistical literacy and the practice of statistics from the perspective of middle school students and how their experiences can be enhanced by the availability of open data. The open data sets selected illustrate the types of contexts that are available and their connections to the Australian school curriculum. The importance of visualisation is stressed and the software TinkerPlots is the tool used for students to create representations and develop the understanding necessary to analyse data and draw conclusions. Building appreciation of the practice of statistics in this way further assists students to become critical thinkers in judging the claims of others later as statistically literate adults.

INTRODUCTION

This chapter focuses on statistical literacy and the practice of statistics from the perspective of middle school students and how their experiences can be enhanced by the availability of open data. The availability of open data and big data has provided wonderful opportunities for statisticians, scientists, and social scientists to develop

DOI: 10.4018/978-1-5225-2512-7.ch002

new techniques and explore new problems (e.g., Kitchin, 2014; Mayer-Shonberger & Cukier, 2013). What has not been clear is the influence these data should have on the school curriculum, particularly the middle school where students are coming to terms with statistical literacy and the components of the practice of statistics. The suggestions made for the introduction of large, open data sets in schools (e.g., Engel, 2014; Ridgway, 2015; Ridgway, Nicholson, & McCusher, 2013; Ridgway & Smith, 2013) include two aspects relevant to this chapter, which is focussed on the middle school level. First is that open data, by their very existence, provide context for a statistical investigation, and the practice of statistics cannot take place without context (Rao, 1975). At the school level context implies cross-curriculum activities linking the mathematics curriculum meaningfully with other areas such as science, social science, and health and wellbeing. Second is the importance of visualisation and its implications for interpreting graphical presentations. In particular, the need to conceptualise multi-variate data and their representations is recognised in making sense of real world problems.

Ridgway (2015) and others base their definition of statistical literacy on the work of Gal (2002), who defined the phrase for adults as:

- *People's ability to interpret and critically evaluate statistical information, data-related arguments, or stochastic phenomena, which they may encounter in diverse contexts, and when relevant;*
- *Their ability to discuss or communicate their reactions to such statistical information, such as their understanding of the meaning of the information, their opinions about the implications of this information, or their concerns regarding the acceptability of given conclusions* (pp. 2–3).

Further, the *Guidelines for Assessment and Instruction in Statistics Education (GAISE)* for both school (Franklin et al., 2007) and college (GAISE College Report ASA Revision Committee [GAISECollegeComm], 2016) stress statistical literacy in terms of *real* data. In today's world, context with real data is likely to involve large open data sets. At the middle school level statistical literacy is seen as "the meeting point of the data and chance curriculum and the everyday world, where encounters involve unrehearsed contexts and spontaneous decision-making based on the ability to apply statistical tools, general contextual knowledge, and critical literacy" (Watson, 2006, p. 11). Reference to the curriculum places some constraints compared with what might be expected of adults. In terms of developing statistical literacy at this level Watson further suggests a three-tiered progression where students must make judgements based on

1. Understanding the statistical terminology/tools used in claims;
2. Understanding the use of the terminology/tools within the context of the claim; and
3. Possessing the ability and confidence to challenge claims made without proper statistical foundation or to support those that are legitimate.

The two aspects of open and big data sets noted above—context and visualisation—are embedded in the definition and progression for statistical literacy. Context is mentioned explicitly and visualisation provides many of the tools required for decision-making.

The implications of the descriptions of both adult and student statistical literacy do not include actually carrying out statistical investigations, only being able to judge critically claims based on the results of such investigations. The building of statistical literacy, however, is based on experiencing the practice of statistics first hand and building on appreciation of the requirements of decision-making (Franklin et al., 2007; GAISECollegeComm, 2016). As suggested by Franklin et al. there are four steps relevant as students are learning the investigative process:

- **Formulate Questions:** Anticipating variability;
- **Collect Data:** Acknowledging variability;
- **Analyze Data:** Accounting for variability;
- **Interpret Results**: Allowing for variability.

Before the phrase "open data" became part of the statistics vocabulary, precursors of relevance to the phrase at the school level included the *CensusAtSchool* initiative of the Royal Statistical Society in the United Kingdom (Connor, Davies, & Holmes, 2000; Connor & Davies, 2002; Wong, 2006). The *CensusAtSchool* project also provided software to create graphical visualisations of the data from the census. Finzer and Erickson (2005) expanded both the census and visualisation initiatives by introducing the software *Fathom* (Finzer, 2005) and using variables from US Census microdata, which have existed since 1850. *Fathom* is a powerful tool that allows students more creativity and personal decision-making about the visualisations chosen to represent the story in the data. These two types of census data are among the early examples of open data suggested for schools and the introduction of *Fathom* made accessing and handling large data sets reasonable for students at the senior school level. The obvious links to social science content began to illustrate further the importance of statistics to the school curriculum.

The implications of open data for context across the curriculum, for visualisation, and for the necessary technology tools, are kept in mind and considered in relation to the statistical skills and understanding that students are expected to possess and develop at the middle school level. They are considered in relation to the *Australian Curriculum* (Australian Curriculum, Assessment and Reporting Authority [ACARA], 2016) and research that has provided opportunities to trial activities based on open data with middle school students.

This chapter is based on expanding some of the current ideas and arguments for introducing and developing the practice of statistics in order to build statistical literacy during the middle years in association with using open data. It begins by introducing context as the foundation for interest in statistics and provides examples of open data. This is followed by evidence of the necessity to visualise data in order to find a message in them. As open data sets are usually too large to be represented by hand, a form of technology is introduced to make visualisation possible. This includes considering how middle school students should be introduced to software and how the software supports learning. Specifically, the use of open data is considered in terms of illustrating curriculum aims in relation to centres and distributions. This is followed by addressing issues related to sampling with open data populations. Combining these ingredients, open data sets are used as a basis for complete statistical investigations where students pose questions and follow the steps to reach decisions on them. Linking the components of the practice of statistics to the Big Ideas underpinning the practice is then seen to be possible through open data. Acknowledging issues associated with teachers using technology in the classroom, the chapter concludes by suggesting that the combination of the early development of statistical techniques and concepts based on open data can form a foundation for the statistical literacy required for citizenship in a world of truly big data.

Open Data: The Need for Context

At all levels of statistics education, context is the starting point for any investigation. As Rao (1975) said:

Statistics ceases to have meaning if it is not related to any practical problem. There is nothing like a purely statistical problem which statistics purports to solve. The subject in which a decision is made is not statistics. It is botany or ecology or geology and so on. (p. 152)

The context, particularly for quite young children may be local, such as suggesting improvements for the school playground (English, 2014) or collecting data on animals in the neighbourhood or scary things (Russell, Corwin, & Economopoulos, 1997). As students mature, however, and their worlds expand, there are opportunities to use open data sets as the basis for investigations. Ben-Zvi (2000) used data from the Olympic Games 100-metre sprint with Grade 7 students to explore how they would represent the winning times over the years graphically. Shaughnessy, Chance, and Kranendonk (2009) also used data from the Olympics to explore the question of whether women will ever run faster than men. They further suggested exploring eruption data from the Old Faithful Geyser and population data from the US Census.

The use of meaningful contexts implies intersecting with other curriculum areas, and although this is usually possible at the start of the middle school years, it becomes much more difficult in later years when time-tables are split strictly by the subjects taught. The *Australian Curriculum* (ACARA, 2016) is helpful in this regard by suggesting three cross-curriculum priorities: Aboriginal and Torres Strait Islander histories and cultures, Asia and Australia's engagement with Asia, and Sustainability. The curriculum also identifies seven General Capabilities to be included in each learning area. Among these is Numeracy and one of the organising elements is "Interpreting statistical information."

Watson (2012) suggested applications of interpreting statistical information for the History Curriculum (ACARA, 2016) using data sets collected for the First Fleet of convicts sent to Australia from England, early Australian explorers, and Australian prime ministers. All of these data sets were compiled for student use from open data available from Australian sources (Watson et al., 2011). Other contexts developed by Watson et al. include science (e.g., introduced animals, venomous snakes, and the weather), sport (e.g., horse racing, the Olympics, cycling, basketball, cricket, and Australian Rules football), other social science (e.g., Flying Doctors, road kill, and student time on homework and sports), and mathematics (e.g., measurement and reaction time). Given the realities of the middle school classroom and the percentage of time devoted to statistics in the curriculum, providing data sets, in some cases cleaned for student use, is an effective, practical introduction to open data from outside the classroom. Other examples, including prepared data within applications for visualisation, are provided, progressing to later levels of the curriculum, by Nicholson, Ridgway, and McCusker (2013).

Open Data: The Need for Visualisation

Open data sets are most often large data sets, which preclude the practicality of producing hand-drawn representations. Visualisation, however, is critical for teaching and learning about open data (Nicholson et al., 2013; Ridgway, 2015). Software packages, apps, or advanced spreadsheets are hence needed to provide the visualisation needed to analyse and tell the story held within the data. Although there are many statistical packages available, at the middle school level the most conducive to developing student understanding of the best ways of presenting data is *TinkerPlots: Dynamic Data Exploration* (Konold & Miller, 2011). Created from a constructivist perspective (Konold, 2007), *TinkerPlots* allows students considerable freedom in being able to produce and explore representations rather than having to make a decision on a format before choosing a ready-made graph. The importance of software such as *TinkerPlots* is that it allows students to create their own representations rather than be presented with a fait accompli graph that they are required to interpret. Many middle school students, especially in the early years, do not have the experience to make meaning from complex representations. As well as this, the curriculum is expecting students to be exploring and learning to create graphical representations that they can explain themselves. Hence presenting data via Data Cards in *TinkerPlots* as a beginning helps students identify individual variables, called Attributes by *TinkerPlots*, and use the drag-and-drop facility to explore an individual Attribute as well as relationships between two or possibly three. Although multi-variate analysis is suggested for later grades (Ridgway, 2015), at the middle school level considering even bi-variate relationships is at the fringe of the official curriculum (ACARA, 2016).

As well as producing graphs, *TinkerPlots* has a randomisation object, the Sampler, which can be used to collect random samples from a large open data set. This is an important feature given the necessity for students to experience variation in samples as the sample size increases (Ben-Zvi, Aridor, Makar, & Bakker, 2012) and as repeated samples are taken of the same size (Watson & English, 2016b). Data from open data sources can be deposited in the Sampler and then random samples collected and plotted for analysis. As Ridgway (2015) states, "The task of drawing conclusions from samples to populations is different from the task of drawing conclusions about sub-samples from populations" (p. 2). For middle school students, however, who are learning about the relationship of samples and populations, the experience of sampling from both perspectives can be valuable reinforcement. It is necessary to appreciate the variation in random samples from populations as well as considering what conclusions can be drawn from them. Although in real-world statistics single samples are typically drawn due to the cost, *TinkerPlots* and similar software packages can allow middle school students to experiment with sampling by drawing repeated samples from real-world data sets. As an example, consider a "population" of 1750 reaction times of Grade 6 students created from the Australian Bureau of Statistics (ABS) *CensusAtSchool* site (http://www.abs.gov.au/censusatschool). Figure 1 shows the layout in *TinkerPlots* with the original population—the data set downloaded from *CensusAtSchool*—and collection of a sample of size 25 (similar to a class). Once the *TinkerPlots* has the data, the Sampler allows students to create many random samples and to experiment with different samples and sampling processes, like sampling with or without replacement, and to display important values like mean and median for both sample and population.

Other affordances of *TinkerPlots* are discussed in Watson and Fitzallen (2016). *TinkerPlots* is used throughout this chapter for visualisation of open data.

Figure 1. Sampling from a population of 1750 reaction times for grade 6 students in TinkerPlots

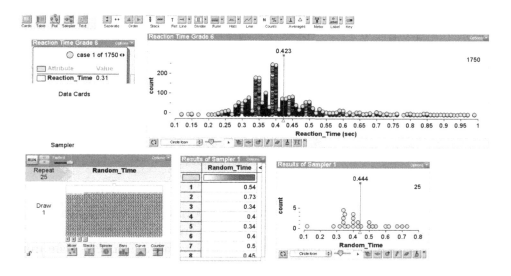

Open Data: Contexts for Specific Learning Outcomes

Ridgway (2015) and others introduce large-scale scenarios for the interpretation of open data. In the middle school classroom, however, open-data scenarios can also provide familiar contexts for considering the characteristics of data sets used in statistics, such as centres and shapes of distributions. Often data collected from the class are employed for such lessons but because they have not been perused in advance, they may not illustrate the points required. Using familiar open data sets that are known to illustrate points being made can also add motivation because students know the context well. In Australia, the popular sport of cricket provides a familiar context. Data for the batting scores of the famous player, Mark Taylor, are available online (http://www.statsci.org/data/oz/taylor.html), and can be used to teach characteristics of distributions and centres. This context relates both to the social arena of popular sport in Australian culture and to the Health and Physical Education curriculum, where sporting skills are developed over the school years. Figure 2, which shows the distribution of Mark Taylor's scores over seven years, is an excellent authentic example of a right-skewed distribution. It can be compared with other examples of left-skewed distributions, as done in Watson et al. (2011, Lesson 7.1). This is accompanied by comparison of the mean and median as measures of centre.

Figure 2. Skewed distribution of cricket scores

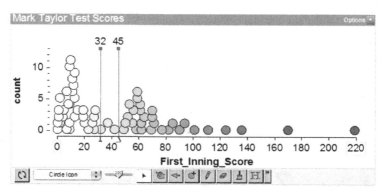

Another example of using open data for a specific learning outcome arises from a different sporting context significant in Australian culture, the Melbourne Cup, the horse race run on the first Tuesday of November each year. Data from the race are available from several sources (e.g., www.racenet.com.au/mel/default. asp, en.wikipedia.org/wiki/List_of_Melbourne_Cup_winners) and are comprised of categorical variables and numerical variables with various characteristics, including time series over the time of the race since 1861. Watson (2014) prepared a discussion for teachers focussing on measures of "typical" for the different data sets and appropriate ways of representing them visually based on activities in Watson et al. (2011, Lessons 4.1 to 4.4). Day (2013) reported using the data set and ideas with pre-service teachers.

An issue using the Melbourne Cup data is learning to use the appropriate measure of typical for different kinds of data. Figure 3 shows frequency column plots for the Attributes Sex and Age of the winners of the cup. Although similar in appearance, the plots tell different stories and although the mean is meaningful for Age (4.81 years), there are no measures of "centre" for Sex, except the mode (stallions won most often).

Introducing the Attribute Weight extends measurement to a continuous scale and in this case provides examples of mean, median, and mode, as well as discussion points for range and shape (different from Figure 2). When the box plot is introduced the symmetric Weight Attribute provides a way in *TinkerPlots* of reinforcing its meaning by displaying it with and without the associated data. Figure 4 shows the two together. The context also provides a natural way of introducing a second Attribute, for example by comparing the Weight by the Sex of the winners as is shown in Figure 5. Much discussion is possible about subsets of the data and the increasing central values for Weight.

Figure 3. Categorical and measurement data from the Melbourne Cup

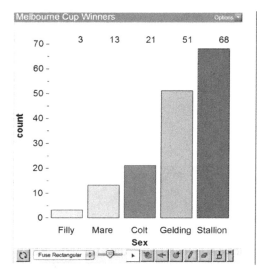 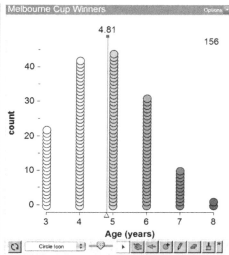

Figure 4. Plot of weight of winners of the Melbourne Cup with box plot

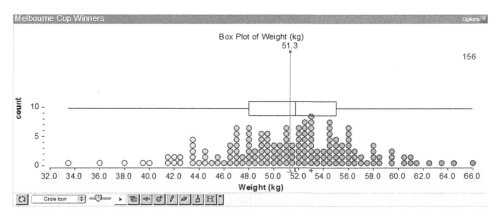

Another natural way of moving to considering two variables is by using a time series, which is common in historical contexts. This can be done with data from the running of the Melbourne Cup, but the Royal Flying Doctor Service of Australia (RFDS, 2009) provides another context of relevance to the social science or history curriculum. This service was set up in 1928 to provide access to medical services in the vast interior of Australia for cattle stations, Aboriginal communities, and outback travellers. Now more than 50 aircraft are available from 25 sites across the

Figure 5. Distribution of weight by sex for winners of the Melbourne Cup

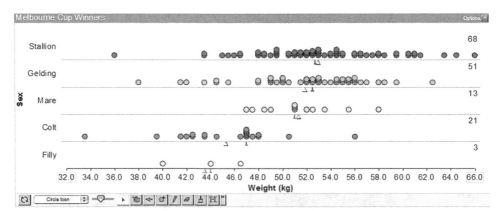

country and 250,000 people receive assistance each year. Using data from the RFDS website (http://www.flyingdoctor.net), various aspects of changes for the Service can be followed (Watson et al., 2011, Lesson 7.4). Figure 6 shows that although the number of aircraft increased over the years, so has the average number of landings per aircraft per year. These plots illustrate roughly linear growth. Non-linear change can also be introduced and shown for example by the plots in Figure 7 where the increase in the number of contacts by telephone has increased while the number of contacts by radio has decreased. These data can be the focus of a discussion concerning the change in technology for communication over the years, another aspect of the social science curriculum.

Figure 6. Increases in the RFDS over time

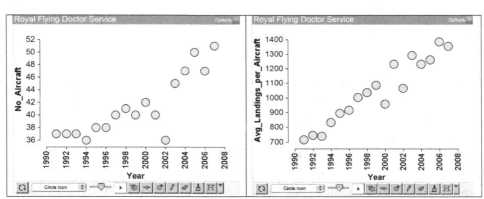

Figure 7. Differing changes in the method of contacting the RFDS over time

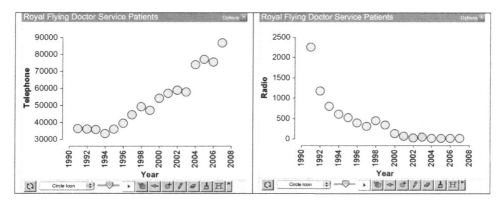

Open Data: Context for Sampling

Large open data sets provide students good opportunities to experience the properties of samples of real-world data, as mentioned earlier. Related to the History Curriculum in Australia (ACARA, 2016) is an open data set based on the First Fleet that was sent to Australia from England in 1788, carrying convicts to establish a penal colony (firstfleet.uow.edu.au/index.html). Watson et al. (2011, Lessons 6.1 and 6.2) first familiarised students with the data set by asking basic factual questions, such as about the number of males in the fleet, the percentage of females, the most common crime, and the percentages of males and females convicted of committing particular crimes. Stack and Watson (2013) described an activity based on this data set and the value of the crimes committed. The data from the variable Value_of_crime_shillings for 677 of the convicts are shown in Figure 8 with the median marked. From this population, Grade 10 students collected 100 random samples of size 10, recording the medians to compare with the median of the population. Following the process for collecting a sample shown in Figure 1, students could continue to collect 99 more samples using the History/Collect Statistics tool in *TinkerPlots*. This is shown in Figure 9, where the Median of the 100 medians is seen to be 26.75. The range of median values is 3 to 130.

This process was then repeated for 100 random samples of size 30 and Figure 10 shows the results for the 100 medians. The range for the medians of samples of size 30 is 10 to 47.5 and the Median of the 100 medians is 29.25. When the plots of the medians from the two sets of samples were compared the variation was greatly reduced for the larger sample size and the aggregate median was very much closer to the population median.

Figure 8. Population from the first fleet with data on value_of_crime_shillings

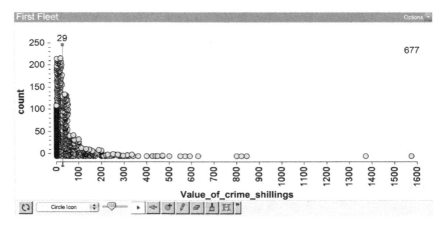

Figure 9. Collecting 100 random samples of size 10 from the first fleet and plotting the medians from the 100 samples

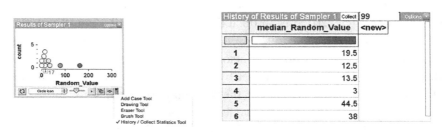

(a)

(b)

Figure 10. Plot of the medians from 100 samples of size 30 from the first fleet

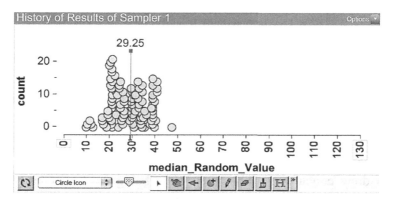

Open Data: Context for the Practice of Statistics

Recognising again the importance of experiencing the practice of statistics as the foundation for building statistical literacy, which calls for being able to interpret data but not necessarily produce formal statistical analyses (Franklin et al., 2007), the practice at the middle school level is not based on the theoretical tenets of formal statistics. Following Makar and Rubin (2009), informal inference is the basis for the practice of statistics here, where decisions about a statistical question for a population are made based on evidence (often strongly visual) presented from a sample, purposefully acknowledging uncertainty. Uncertainty is also inherent in the *p*-values of formal statistics but often it is assumed without specific mention. As noted in the Introduction, the practice of statistics involves four basic steps: posing a question (or questions) about a population, planning and collecting sample data, representing data to analyse them, and making a decision about the question/s acknowledging uncertainty due to the sample-population relationship and the method of analysis chosen (Franklin et al., 2007).

Open data can provide meaningful contexts for carrying out all steps in the practice of statistics. Using the idea of Sustainability, one of the *Australian Curriculum*'s (ACARA, 2016) cross-curriculum topics, Watson and English (2015) carried out research with a Grade 5 class that was based on questions provided by the Australian Bureau of Statistics (ABS) *CensusAtSchool* questionnaire (www.abs.gov.au/censusatschool). Students answered five yes/no questions concerning habits that were considered environmentally friendly. These are shown in Figure 11. Using the questions and class discussions as a basis, each student devised percentage criteria for Grade 5 students being environmentally friendly. Based on their class, students analysed the data, comparing the percentage of "yes" responses with their criteria.

Figure 11. Questions on being environmentally friendly

Am I environmentally friendly?	Yes	No
Our household has a water tank.		
I take shorter showers. (4 mins max)		
I turn the tap off while brushing my teeth.		
I turn off appliances (e.g., TV, computer, gaming consoles) at the power point.		
My household recycles rubbish.		

They then drew conclusions about their class being environmentally friendly. Discussion then led them to consider their class as a sample, and reach a decision about all Grade 5 students in Australia. Many points were brought out about the uncertainty of their conclusions due, for example, to the characteristics of their class compared to classes in rural schools or different parts of the country. They then used *TinkerPlots* to generate random samples the same size as their class from a "population" of 1300 Grade 5 students from around Australia prepared from the open data on the ABS website. The open data set provided an example of a population from which representative samples could be collected, as shown in Figure 1, and compared with the sample from their class. Figure 12 shows how *TinkerPlots* was used by the students in this more complex context to sample from the population for all five questions, with the percentages of "yes" and "no" appearing visually in the plots for the individual questions. This broadened the discussion to issues of

Figure 12. Collecting a random sample of 26 grade 6 students from the CensusAtSchool website to answer questions on sustainability

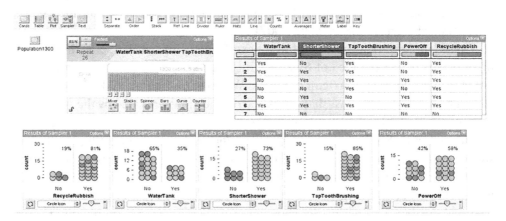

repeated sampling and increasing sample size in order to gain confidence in students' conclusions, as well as appreciation of issues related to sustainability.

Another application of open data from the ABS is related to measurement rather than categorical data. The *CensusAtSchool* site collects data on students' reaction times via students clicking a mouse on the appearance of an icon in a special box on the computer screen. This provides another opportunity to use both student data from the class as well as samples from a population the same age. In this situation, there are less likely to be cultural differences in the results for classrooms across the country than for the questions on the environment. *CensusAtSchool* also collects categorical data on the eye colour of the same students, providing an intuitive transition to comparing data across groups. Watson (2008) described a Grade 10 classroom where the teacher introduced a newspaper article based on research claiming that brown-eyed people had faster reaction times than people with eyes of other colours. The teacher challenged the students to explore this claim within their class. The class finding was that there was only a small number of students with brown eyes, but they did indeed have a faster mean reaction time on the ABS timer than the non-brown-eyed students. This led to an investigation of a random sample of size 400 from the *CensusAtSchool* site, which was used to conclude that it provided no support for the claim.

The popularity of this activity led Watson and English (2016a) to use the context with four classes of Grade 6 students who had previously explored their typical reaction time as a class using the ABS timer (Watson & English, in press). With the motivation of the question posed by the media release, the students undertook the practice of statistics, using their class as a sample to reach a conclusion for all Australian Grade 6 students. In several classes the student data favoured the brown-eyed students and the numbers for the two groups were unbalanced. Considering their samples, students appreciated the need to express uncertainty about their conclusions. Students were then given access to a data set of 1786 Grade 6 students from the ABS and generated four random samples the size of their class using the Sampler in the method shown in Figure 1, to experience the variation in samples and reconsider their decisions. Finally, the complete "population" from the ABS was used to confirm their own conclusions.

The data available from *CensusAtSchool* sites around the world (e.g., Canada [www.censusatschool.ca], Ireland [www.censusatschool.ie], Japan [census.ism. ac.jp/cas], the United Kingdom [censusatschool.com], and the United States [www. amstat.org/CensusAtSchool]) make possible some international comparisons. The importance of open data sets such as this at the school level is that they provide opportunities for teachers of the social science curriculum to explore issues that are directly related to students and where the students can collect their own personal data in the classroom.

Open Data: Context for Extending the Big Ideas of Statistics

In the classroom, activities often start from personal experience and exploring students' understanding of a context. Based on research interviews on variation and expectation (Watson & Kelly, 2005), a classroom scenario was constructed to assist teachers in building learning progressions based on authentic student responses in the context of weather (Watson, 2016). The lesson has three parts: exploring and consolidating students' understanding of the Big Ideas of Variation, Expectation, and Distribution generally; applying these ideas to explaining the weather in the Australian city of Hobart based on the average maximum daily temperature for a year of 17°C; and moving to open data for five monthly average variables for all eight Australian capital cities, including average monthly maximum temperature (www.bom.gov.au/climate/data/). In this larger hypothetical scenario the aim of the teacher is to reinforce the earlier discussion of the three Big Ideas in a much expanded context. One student picks Hobart as the coldest capital city because it is the furthest south but there is debate among class members, with another student claiming that Canberra is colder because it is inland at a higher altitude. This leads to a discussion of seasons. Figures 13 and 14 show the progression of the class discussion.

After discussing the differences in summer temperatures, winter is considered, where the mean maximum temperatures are nearly the same but the variation is different. Students are then asked to write a paragraph describing the differences for the cities for the other two seasons. The lesson concludes with a summary of the use of the Big Ideas in the discussion and reference to all of the capital cities as shown in Figures 15 and 16.

Many opportunities arise from open data based on weather statistics. The data used here came from the Australian Bureau of Meteorology (www.bom.gov/climate/data) with 54 years of monthly data for rainfall, maximum temperature, minimum temperature, average maximum temperature and average minimum temperature collected in association with Watson et al. (2011). Using filters, scatter plots, and other tools in *TinkerPlots* it is possible to pose many different questions. Some of these can be deterministic, non-statistical questions, such as "what was the highest maximum monthly temperature recorded in Australia?" The data set provides an excellent context for helping students learn to distinguish between the two types of questions (cf. Franklin et al., 2007, p. 11). For statistical questions, students then collect and analyse data to answer the questions. It is a readily accessible context related to engaging middle school students in the practice of statistics. Day (2013) reports on using this data set with pre-service teachers.

Figure 13. Applying the Big Ideas to open data about the weather

Figure 14. Applying the Big Ideas to open data about the weather (continued)

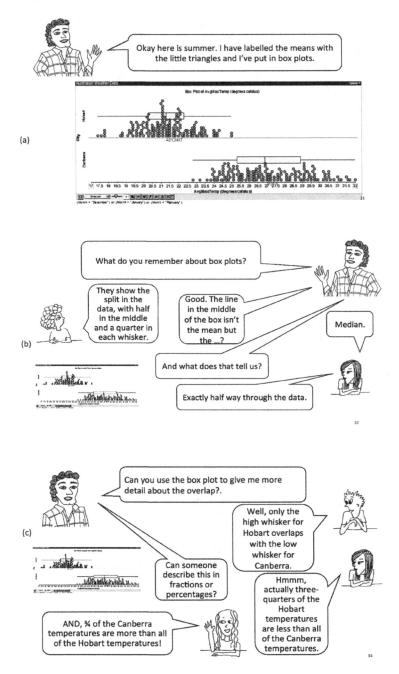

Figure 15. Review of the Big Ideas and considering the population

Figure 16. Review of the Big Ideas and considering the population (continued)

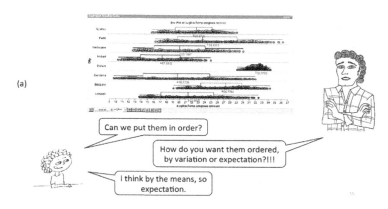

(a)

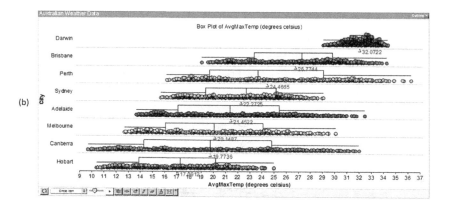

(b)

(c)

CONCLUSION

The *Australian Curriculum* (ACARA, 2016) is not explicit in referring to open data or big data but at Grades 6 and 7 of the curriculum descriptors make reference to using secondary sources of data:

- Interpret secondary data presented in digital media and elsewhere (ACMSP148), Grade 6.
- Identify and investigate issues involving numerical data collected from primary and secondary sources (ACMSP169), Grade 7.

These two aims provide motivation for activities like those described in this chapter, including collecting data from students in the class and comparing these data with open data from students the same age. Most of the activities described here are viable with students younger than Grade 7. One of the aspects of the activities that makes them accessible to younger students is the software *TinkerPlots*, which makes visualisation possible in ways that help students understand and interpret the data. Research hence suggests that it is possible and desirable to begin expanding students' world of open data in the early middle school years.

The importance of technology in the form of software like *TinkerPlots* that allows students to create their own representations must be emphasised. Pratt, Davies, and Connor (2011) discuss generally the use of technology for teaching statistics at the school level, listing some of the issues that may inhibit its use. These include teachers not prioritising technological tools, the curriculum not supporting their use, assessment not encouraging it, teachers' unwillingness to up-skill on the latest technology developments, and the use of technology reinforcing computation rather than concepts. The examples provided in this chapter show that the opportunities for using open data in the middle school are vast and can be used to motivate teachers to embrace the necessary technology and take on the challenge of developing the practice of statistics and statistical literacy, both for themselves and their students. Now that Digital Technology is being introduced into the school curriculum of many countries, including Australia (ACARA, 2016), it is hoped that the barriers noted by Pratt et al. can be overcome.

Although Ridgway et al. (2013) and others propose that understanding and working with open data should be part of the statistical literacy skills developed during the school years, open data have not been part of the general large-scale assessment of statistical literacy to this point. Currently the assessment of statistical literacy for students is based on testing that includes items based on media reports (e.g., Watson & Callingham, 2003; Callingham & Watson, 2005). These reports may be based on open data but open data sets have not been used explicitly in assessments. This is a challenge for future research into the assessment of statistical literacy given the variety of visualisations now being developed to display open data. Callingham (2011) explores the issues in relation to technology and assessment, and concludes that some of the most promising items for displaying large open data sets for analysis pose difficulties for large-scale use in terms of the time required for marking. The work of Ridgway and Nicholson (2010) with visualisations of multivariate data in classroom situations offers promise but may be difficult to use in large-scale testing.

The era of integrating open data in the middle school classroom is just beginning. The opportunities and advantages are great for cross-curriculum links to statistical investigations and statistical literacy. The challenges still remain, however, in creating awareness of the benefits, in making technology available, and in convincing teachers it is worth the investment of their time and energy. Research so far has provided much evidence that students enjoy and learn from the experience, preparing them for the adult world of big data.

REFERENCES

Australian Curriculum, Assessment and Reporting Authority. (2016). *Australian Curriculum, Version 8.2*. Sydney, NSW: ACARA.

Ben-Zvi, D. (2000). Toward understanding the role of technological tools in statistical learning. *Mathematical Thinking and Learning*, 2(1 & 2), 127–155. doi:10.1207/S15327833MTL0202_6

Ben-Zvi, D., Aridor, K., Makar, K., & Bakker, A. (2012). Students emergent articulations of uncertainty while making informal statistical inferences. *ZDM Mathematics Education*, 44(7), 913–925. doi:10.1007/s11858-012-0420-3

Callingham, R. (2011). Assessing statistical understanding in middle schools: Emerging issues in a technology-rich environment. *Technology Innovations in Statistics Education, 5*(1). Retrieved from http://escholarship.org/uc/item/3qr2p70t

Callingham, R. A., & Watson, J. M. (2005). Measuring statistical literacy. *Journal of Applied Measurement*, 6(1), 19–47. PMID:15701942

Connor, D., & Davies, N. (2002). An international resource for learning and teaching. *Teaching Statistics, 24*, 62–65. doi:10.1111/1467-9639.00087

Connor, D., Davies, N., & Holmes, P. (2000). CensusAtSchool 2000. *Teaching Statistics*, 22(3), 66–70. doi:10.1111/1467-9639.00025

Day, L. (2013). Using statistics to explore cross-curricular and social issues opportunities. *Australian Mathematics Teacher*, *69*(4), 3–7.

Engel, J. (2014). Open data, civil society and monitoring progress: Challenges for statistics education. In K. Makar, B. de Sousa, & R. Gould (Eds.), Sustainability in statistics education (Proceedings of the Ninth International Conference on Teaching Statistics, Flagstaff, USA). Voorburg, The Netherlands: International Association for Statistical Education and the International Statistical Institute. Retrieved from http://iase-web.org/icots/9/proceedings/pdfs/ICOTS9_4F4_ENGEL.pdf

English, L. D. (2014). Statistics at play. *Teaching Children Mathematics*, *21*, 37–44.

Finzer, W. (2005). *Fathom* [Computer software]. Emeryville, CA: Key Curriculum Press.

Finzer, W., & Erickson, T. (2005). Curriculum innovations based on census microdata: A meeting of statistics, mathematics and social science. In G. Burrill & M. Camden (Eds.), *Curricular development in statistics education. International Association for Statistical Education (IASE) Roundtable, Lund, Sweden, 2004* (pp. 190–203). Voorburg, The Netherlands: International Statistical Institute.

Franklin, C., Kader, G., Mewborn, D., Moreno, J., Peck, R., Perry, M., & Scheaffer, R. (2007). Guidelines for assessment and instruction in statistics education (GAISE) report: A preK-12 curriculum framework. Alexandria, VA: American Statistical Association. Retrieved from http://www.amstat.org/education/gaise/

GAISE College Report ASA Revision Committee. (2016). *Guidelines for assessment and instruction in statistics education College Report 2016*. Alexandria, VA: American Statistical Association. Retrieved from http://www.amstat.org/education/gaise/

Gal, I. (2002). Adults statistical literacy: Meanings, components, responsibilities. *International Statistical Review*, *70*(1), 1–51. doi:10.1111/j.1751-5823.2002.tb00336.x

Kitchin, R. (2014). *The data revolution: Big data, open data, data infrastructures and their consequences*. London: Sage. doi:10.4135/9781473909472

Konold, C. (2007). Designing a data analysis tool for learners. In M. C. Lovett & P. Shah (Eds.), *Thinking with data* (pp. 267–291). New York: Lawrence Erlbaum.

Konold, C., & Miller, C. D. (2011). *TinkerPlots: Dynamic data exploration* [Computer software, Version 2.2]. Emeryville, CA: Key Curriculum Press.

Makar, K., & Rubin, A. (2009). A framework for thinking about informal statistical inference. *Statistics Education Research Journal, 8*(1), 82–105. Retrieved from http://iase-web.org/documents/SERJ/SERJ8(1)_Makar_Rubin.pdf

Mayer-Schonberger, V., & Cukier, K. (2013). *Big Data: A revolution that will transform how we live, work and think*. Boston: Houghton Mifflin Harcourt.

Nicholson, J., Ridgway, J., & McCusker, S. (2013). Getting real statistics into all curriculum subject areas: Can technology make this a reality? *Technology Innovations in Statistics Education, 7*(2). Retrieved from http://escholarship.org/uc/item/7cz2w089

Pratt, D., Davies, N., & Connor, D. (2011). The role of technology in teaching and learning statistics. In C. Batanero, G. Burrill, & C. Reading (Eds.), *Teaching statistics in school mathematics – Challenges for teaching and teacher education: A joint ICMI/IASE study* (pp. 97–107). Dordrecht, The Netherlands: Springer. doi:10.1007/978-94-007-1131-0_13

Rao, C. R. (1975). Teaching of statistics at the secondary level: An interdisciplinary approach. *International Journal of Mathematical Education in Science and Technology, 6*(2), 151–162. doi:10.1080/0020739750060203

Ridgway, J. (2015). Implications of the data revolution for statistics education. *International Statistical Review*. doi:10.1111/insr.12110

Ridgway, J., & Nicholson, J. (2010). Pupils reasoning with information and misinformation. In C. Reading (Ed.), Data and context in statistics education: Towards an evidence-based society. (Proceedings of the Eighth International Conference on the Teaching of Statistics, Ljubljana, Slovenia). Voorburg, The Netherlands: International Statistical Institute. Retrieved from http://iase-web.org/documents/papers/icots8/ICOTS8_9A3_RIDGWAY.pdf

Ridgway, J., Nicholson, J., & McCusker, S. (2013). 'Open Data' and the semantic web require a rethink on statistics teaching. *Technology Innovations in Statistics Education, 7*(2). Retrieved from http://escholarship.org/uc/item/6gm8p12m

Ridgway, J., & Smith, A. (2013). Open data, official statistics and statistics education – Threats, and opportunities for collaboration. In S. Forbes & B. Phillips (Eds.), *Proceedings of the Joint IASE/IAOS Satellite Conference*. Macao, China: IASE/IAOS.

Royal Flying Doctor Service of Australia. (2009). *Look! Up in the sky. Teacher Handbook. Pilot Version*. Sydney: Author.

Russell, S. J., Corwin, R., & Economopoulos, K. (1997). *Sorting and classifying data: Does it walk, crawl, or swim?* Palo Alto, CA: Dale Seymour Publications.

Shaughnessy, J. M., Chance, B., & Kranendonk, H. (2009). *Focus on high school mathematics: Reasoning and sense making in statistics and probability.* Reston, VA: National Council of Teachers of Mathematics.

Stack, S., & Watson, J. (2013). Randomness, sample size, imagination and metacognition: Making judgments about differences in data sets. *Australian Mathematics Teacher, 69*(4), 23–30.

Watson, J. (2008). Eye colour and reaction time: An opportunity for critical statistical reasoning. *Australian Mathematics Teacher, 64*(3), 30–40.

Watson, J. (2014). What is 'typical' for different kinds of data? Examples from the Melbourne Cup. *Australian Mathematics Teacher, 70*(2), 33–40.

Watson, J. (2016). Scaffolding statistics understanding in the middle school. In W. Widjaja, E. Y-K. Loong, & L.A. Bragg (Eds.), *MATHS e^xPLOSION 2016 Mathematical Association of Victoria's Annual Conference Proceedings* (pp. 132-139). Melbourne: MAV.

Watson, J., Beswick, K., Brown, N., Callingham, R., Muir, T., & Wright, S. (2011). *Digging into Australian data with TinkerPlots.* Melbourne: Objective Learning Materials.

Watson, J., & English, L. (2015). Introducing the practice of statistics: Are we environmentally friendly? *Mathematics Education Research Journal, 27*(4), 585–613. doi:10.1007/s13394-015-0153-z

Watson, J., & English, L. (2016a). *Eye color and the practice of statistics in grade 6: Comparing two groups.* Manuscript under review.

Watson, J., & English, L. (2016b). Repeated random sampling in Year 5. *Journal of Statistics Education, 24*(1), 27–37. doi:10.1080/10691898.2016.1158026

Watson, J., & English, L. (in press). Reaction time in Grade 5: Data collection within the Practice of Statistics. *Statistics Education Research Journal.*

Watson, J., & Fitzallen, N. (2016). Statistical software and mathematics education: Affordances for learning. In L. English & D. Kirshner (Eds.), *Handbook of international research in mathematics education* (3rd ed.; pp. 563–594). New York: Taylor and Francis.

Watson, J. M. (2006). *Statistical literacy at school: Growth and goals.* Mahwah, NJ: Lawrence Erlbaum.

Watson, J. M., & Callingham, R. A. (2003). Statistical literacy: A complex hierarchical construct. *Statistics Education Research Journal, 2*(2), 3–46. Retrieved from http://iase-web.org/documents/SERJ/SERJ2(2)_Watson_Callingham.pdf

Watson, J. M., & Kelly, B. A. (2005). The winds are variable: Student intuitions about variation. *School Science and Mathematics, 105*(5), 252–269. doi:10.1111/j.1949-8594.2005.tb18165.x

Wong, I. (2006). Using CensusAtSchool data to motivate students. *Australian Mathematics Teacher, 62*(1), 38–40.

Chapter 3
Visual Criminology:
Making Sense of Crime Data and Analysis for Criminology Students

Elaine M. Barclay
University of New England, Australia

ABSTRACT

An understanding of crime data and analysis is central to any Criminology degree. Graduates need to know how and where to access a wide variety of secondary data sources, and understand how to read and critically evaluate crime statistics, crime maps, and quantitative research publications, and through assessment, know how to apply this learning to understanding crime rates within a community. This chapter reviews the various types of data and analysis that form a substantial part of content within a Bachelor of Criminology degree. Several types of assessment are described as examples of how to engage students in practical exercises to show them how data and analysis can provide fascinating insight into the social life of their own community.

INTRODUCTION

Research is a critical part of Criminology and underpins criminal justice policy and practice. It encompasses a wide and varied range of research methods to account for the diversity of social and crime issues of interest which involves the rigorous exploration and testing of disciplinary assumptions and theories through systematic empirical inquiry (Chamberlain 2013:1). Data visualization techniques are central to this endeavour to analyse, explain and present research findings (Wheeldon & Harris

DOI: 10.4018/978-1-5225-2512-7.ch003

2013). Wheeldon and Harris (2013) define this *Visual criminology* as: 'Techniques for the collection, presentation, and interrogation of data on crime and social control'.

Data visualization is increasingly important for operations for police and other agencies of the criminal justice system. It is also an important tool for teaching and explaining data analysis to students. In the sections that follow, the ways in which data visualization is employed with criminology is outlined. The nature and extent to which criminal justice agencies, especially the police, employ data visualization in developing policy and practice and evaluating 'what works' for effective crime control is also described. The value of data visualization for teaching quantitative methods to Criminology students is emphasized through a description of the design, implementation, and assessment of Criminology units that employ an experiential learning model (Kolb 1984). The chapter concludes with a call for more awareness of the need for quantitative skills that focus on data visualization, particularly spatial crime analyses as these capabilities are increasingly required by employers within the criminal justice system, and within academia.

BACKGROUND

Data Visualization Within Criminology

Criminology is a highly diverse and fragmented discipline that draws on a wide range of diverse theoretical perspectives to explain crime and other social problems (Chamberlain, 2013:1). Yet there is a common commitment among criminologists to undertaking rigorous and systematic empirical research to explore and test disciplinary assumptions and theories (Chamberlain, 2013:1, 2). Criminological research is undertaken for scholarly inquiry but also to influence government and lobby for change in social policy and within the criminal justice system. The potential to effect social change makes research in criminology a rewarding experience. However, this goal can only be achieved by conducting high-quality research (Chamberlain, 2013:2). Criminologists tend to take a positive approach to research which promotes a value-neutral and objective method of systematic observation and experiment to gather statistical evidence of 'what works' in relation to a range of criminal justice policy initiatives, interventions and crime reduction strategies (Chamberlain, 2013:2).

Data visualization plays a key role in this process through the use of graphs, plots, charts, maps, timelines, multi-level modelling and the mapping of data using GIS programs. For example, data visualization is key to the analysis and explanation of Social Network Analysis examining the ecology of crime. Social Network Data can be employed to examine the spatial distribution of crime such as the social networks among drug users (see for example Mitchell, 2000) and for drug trafficking (see Bright et al., 2012).

Similarly the graphical representations of Path Analyses provide invaluable insight into the examination of crime trajectories. For example, Jones et al. (2012) used data visualization to explain a path analysis that examined gender differences in pathways into juvenile offending.

Data Visualization is also essential for analysis of secondary data sources, such as the merging of Census Data and Official Crime Data to study socio-economic status and crime. Studies have shown that the characteristics of a neighborhood or small community can influence rates of offending (Sampson et al 1997), units of analysis such as neighborhoods, counties, or as in Australia, Local Government Areas, have geospatial properties that cannot be visualized effectively by merely using basic statistical software packages (Ferandino 2015).

Data visualization allows the data to tell its own story in the initial stages of an analysis (Maltz 2010). Visualization may identify outliers, which could be due to human error during data entry or it may mean there are some exceptional cases that require closer examination (Maltz 2010; Wheeldon & Harris 2013). Visualization can also highlight patterns or relationships in the data that can define particular groups of individuals, generate possible hypotheses, and guide subsequent analyses (Maltz 1998; Wheeldon & Harris 2013).

Maltz (2010) and Kievit et al. (2013) call for more attention to data visualization when conducting multivariate analyses. Many researchers seek to read causality into regression models that in reality are simply descriptions of the data. For example, rather than accepting regression coefficients at face value, if regression models were first investigated and validated with visualization techniques prior to analysis, it would prevent errors in the interpretation of data, and result in a deeper understanding of the subject of inquiry (Kievit et al., 2013). Results would be better explained if regression models were presented together with simple illustrative bivariate scatterplots that reveal patterns in the data and support conclusions via data visualization techniques.

Data Visualization for Testing Theories

Data visualization is also invaluable for testing criminological theory. The link between criminology and spatial analysis is well established in theories of environmental criminology, such as Brantingham and Brantingham's (1984) Crime Pattern Theory. The Brantinghams and other environmental theorists focus on the geographical distribution of crime and the daily routine activities of the people who inhabit these places. The places people go in their daily lives and the spaces they inhabit explain their risk for victimization as well as patterns of offending. People tend to move among their homes, school, work, shopping, and recreation. So do offenders. However when going about their normal legitimate activities, offenders become aware of criminal opportunities, and these places have a high risk of victimization (Brantingham & Brantingham, 1993).

The concept of place is therefore essential to crime pattern theory. Not only are places logically required (an offender must be in a place when an offence is committed), their characteristics influence the likelihood of a crime. This is because it is easier to commit crimes in the course of their daily routine than by making a special journey to do so. The Brantinghams maintain that crimes are more likely to occur the boundaries or 'edges' of areas where people live, work, shop, or play. For example, robberies or shoplifting occurs at these edges where people from different neighborhoods congregate but do not know each other well. The Brantinghams' research found that residential burglaries were more likely to occur where wealthy areas bordered poorer areas. It is environmental theory that has led to the mapping of crime incidents, identifying hot spots of crime, which has greatly improved crime problem analysis.

Another place based theory that has been frequently employed by criminologists is social disorganization theory (Jobes et al. 2004). Initially developed by the Chicago School of Sociology (Shaw & Mackay 1942), social disorganization takes an ecological approach to the study of crime by assuming that the spatial distribution of crime reflects the differing organizational structures within a neighbourhood or community (Sampson, Raudenbush & Earls, 1997). Shaw and Mackay divided the city of Chicago into zones characterised by types of population. They produced maps of the distribution of crime across five circular zones radiating out from the central business district. They found juvenile delinquency declined from the inner city areas to outer suburbs corresponding to economic factors. Income rose from the inner city slums to the wealthier and less densely populated outer suburbs. Shaw and McKay (1942) maintained that the high turnover in population which was characteristic of inner city areas, prevented the development of a stable community and resulted in 'social disorganization'.

In a study by the author and others, this theory of social disorganization was applied to rural communities of New South Wales Australia to compare and contrast variations in crime rates against census data that defined the five dimensions of social disorganization namely, (1) residential instability (i.e., high population turnover); (2) race/ethnic heterogeneity or diversity; (3) family disruption (i.e., divorce, single parent households); (4) low economic status (i.e., poverty, unemployment and other economic indicators); and (5) population (i.e., size, density and proximity to urban places) (Sampson, Raudenbush & Earls, 1997). Using cluster analysis, six community types were classified within the census data based on the demographic, social and economic dimensions of 123 rural or non-metropolitan Local Government Areas

(LGAs) across New South Wales. Comparisons of the crime rates across these six clusters revealed that clusters with higher levels of social disorganization (i.e., with population heterogeneity, residential and family instability) had the highest rates of crime. Clusters with the lowest rates of crime were more organized. Yet these groups experienced different types of crime.

When these clusters were mapped, the visualization revealed the clusters were located in approximately the same geographical areas, which suggested that people were drawn together based on similar characteristics (see Figure 1). This phenomenon would not have been identified without data visualization.

The data visualisation led to a questioning of social disorganization as the best theory to use for examining crime in rural communities. As all rural localities display different kinds of social structures, perhaps crime varies not by social disorganization, but by the differing ways communities are organized. In other words, the assumption that high crime rural communities must be more disorganized than low-crime rural communities masks reality. This led to further research to argue that forms of social organization vary not only between places, but within places as well, even those that are small and sparsely populated. Rural villages and urban neighborhoods alike do not merely display solid social structures and networks, but are in fact quite variable, both within and between, with differing forms of organization, some facilitating crime and others constraining crime, co-existing within the same place and at the same time (Donnermeyer, 2016; Barclay, et al., 2004).

Data Visualization Within the Criminal Justice System

While criminological research has a role in testing and developing theory, it also makes a significant contribution to policy and practice within the Criminal Justice System (Chamberlain, 2013, 1). However the Criminal Justice System and its associated agencies are in themselves, both producers and consumers of data and research. Police officers in Australia and in most other parts of the western world, routinely record GPS data when attending incidents and recording information. These data are then used to generate intelligence for a range of different policing models. These include Hot Spots Policing, Intelligence-Led Policing, Evidence Based Policing and Geographic Profiling.

Hotspots policing involves identifying and mapping the main crime areas in a community. Areas that receive a disproportionate number of calls to police for service are mapped and defined as hot spots of crime (Braga & Bond 2008). Police are more effective in addressing crime and disorder when they target small places that experience high crime or 'hot spots'. Places can be specific addresses, street blocks, or small clusters of addresses or neighbourhoods. Hotspot maps help determine the

Figure 1. Map of New South Wales displaying the clusters of social variables

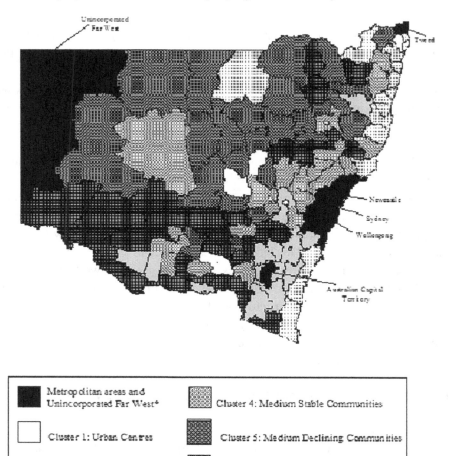

allocation of police resources and the ways in which police respond to calls and conduct patrols (Braga & Bond 2008).

Geographic profiling is another investigative approach that spatially analyzes the locations of a series of serious criminal events to determine the most likely location of an offender's residence. This technique is usually employed for serious crimes, such as serial murder or rape, arson or robbery. The mapping of criminal incidences helps police prioritize information in large-scale major crime investigations that often involve hundreds of suspects and leads. Geographic Profiling employs an environmental criminology perspective to investigate the spatial patterns of serial crimes. Probability distributions are used to generate geospatial models to be used by police for intelligence management and investigative action to identify where the offender is most likely to live (Wortley and Mazerolle 2008, p.136).

Intelligence-led policing (Ratcliff 2008) is the application of criminal intelligence analysis to facilitate crime reduction and prevention and direct effective policing strategies. Intelligence–led policing involves gathering evidence from every crime event; from informants, offender interviews, analysis of recorded crime and calls for service, surveillance of suspects, and community sources of information plus other secondary sources of intelligence, and then analysing and mapping data and developing trend analyses and response strategies (Ratcliff 2008). The data can determine objective policing tactics to support tactical, operational and strategic policing activities. The role of intelligence at a tactical level is to react to events as they happen. At an operational level, intelligence can identify areas that need to be targeted and can also be applied to more than one police district. It is used to assess patterns or trends in various types of crime over time, information gaps or flaws in investigative techniques. At the strategic level, intelligence is focused on what is driving criminal activity. For example, an increase in drug activity may be caused by changing social and economic conditions or the recent availability of certain drugs on the street, such as ice or cocaine. It identifies trends that can be addressed through relevant policy and legislative changes. Intelligence-led policing provides an objective basis for deciding priorities and resource allocation (Ratcliff, 2008).

Evidence-based policing is a relatively new approach for deciding "what works" in policing: which policies and practices are most effective for addressing crime and disorder. Police agencies have recognized the benefits of using an analysis-driven approach to decision making and work with researchers to develop, test and evaluate new theories, policies and police practices. This evidence-based approach continuously tests hypotheses through research (Sherman, 2013). Tracking police movements and practices is enabled by the use of GPS records and video recordings from body cameras/recorders worn by officers that record where they go and what occurs. Police need to attend to scientific evidence as human instincts can be wrong. Many evaluations of crime-prevention police initiatives have been found to have no effect in reducing crime or recidivism. By understanding how crime is spatially and temporally clustered, as well as identifying the environmental and situational factors that can create opportunities for crime, police can become more effective in addressing crime, disorder, and traffic problems (Sherman 2013).

These examples all show different ways that data visualisation is currently supporting efforts of Criminal Justice departments.

Community Crime Prevention

Another related use of data visualization is its benefits for community policing and community crime prevention. Visualization techniques can be used in the evaluation of the effectiveness of community crime prevention programs and for explaining crime trends within a community to the general public. In Australia, local government areas are encouraged to develop a crime prevention plan to assist their community to identify local problems and work with local police in community policing programs. Police websites in Australia provide official crime data as numbers of incidents, rates of crime per 100,000 population, and maps of crime incidents by local government or postcode area (see NSW Bureau of Crime Statistics and Research http://www.bocsar. nsw.gov.au/Pages/bocsar_crime_stats/bocsar_crime_stats.aspx). Similar services are available in most western nations (see for example, the US FBI Uniform Crime Reports http://www.ucrdatatool.gov/). These online services are continually evolving and are invaluable for criminal justice professionals, private security, community planners, the general public, as well as students and researchers.

Data Visualization is also important for evaluating crime prevention programs. The most important aspect of implementing any crime prevention program is evaluation (Eck 2005). Program evaluations investigate how a program is travelling; whether it is making a difference, and reaching the intended audience or participants. Evaluation also identifies any unintended effects of the program. It can be used to make improvements to a project as it progresses. It also shows how effectively resources have been used, which is useful because cost efficiency is usually a condition of receiving ongoing funding. A 'Good' evaluation requires a clear definition of the crime problem and a description of how it is being addressed, an overview of what was actually done and when action was taken, insight into why a program succeeded or failed in reducing crime and a collection, and a comparison of a range of 'before and after' data. Researchers may conduct surveys, security risk assessments, and systematic observations of areas (Uchida et al 2014). Data visualization can be a useful tool for presenting and explaining the findings to key stakeholders and the wider community.

Data Visualization for Teaching Criminology

Research in Criminology is an important component of the Criminology degree program at the University of New England in northern New South Wales Australia. Criminology students need to develop key qualitative and quantitative research skills, be able to read and understand research papers; know where to access available secondary data sources especially official crime data; and be able to collect, analyse, report and present empirical data that comprise a range of visualisation techniques.

As described above, such skills are increasingly important for employers within the criminal justice system.

Data visualization is a valuable teaching tool for making sense of complex data analyses for students, particularly undergraduate students who are often anxious and have limited statistical understanding (Signoretta et al., 2014). Data visualization is a way to present information and demystify statistical assumptions and analysis strategies. The concept is meaningful for students as many spend a significant amount of time engaging visually with their phones, computers, and social media (Wheeldon & Ahlberg, 2012).

As the University of New England is located in a rural region, there is a rural and agricultural focus within the courses taught and research conducted. A major part of a unit on rural criminology is the examination of official crime data between rural, regional and metropolitan areas to highlight the spatial differences in crime rates and emphasise that rural communities are not always the safe, crime-free places that they are often purported to be. For example, there are usually higher rates of violent crimes per 100,000 population in rural places than in urban areas (Barclay 2017), and this frequently surprises students.

The main assessment task for the unit requires students to conduct a crime profile of their home town. Students need to access official crime data from their state police websites and provide a profile of the main types of crime experienced in their community. Local crime rates are compared with the state crime rates to assess whether local crime is high or low relative to the state average. The sites allow students to produce their own tables, graphs and maps of crime rates for their crime profile report. Most police sites provide the opportunity to map hotspots by crime type within the community which greatly assists in this exercise. For example, Figure 2 provides an example of map of the city of Armidale and the University of New England featuring the hotspots for thefts from a motor vehicle for the years 2014 to 2016.

Students are also asked to access census data for their community to construct a social profile using factors of Social Disorganization as a guide. Data are gathered on population movements between census counts to assess residential stability; race/ethnic diversity; marital status and family structure to assess family stability; economic status including levels of income and employment, and population size, density and proximity to urban places. Lessons in small computations to assess average population growth are offered for the more advanced students. Students are encouraged to use data visualization techniques to present the data for their community.

Students then evaluate the effectiveness of Social Disorganization theory for explaining crime in their community, and if they decide it is not sufficient, to suggest a more appropriate theory. Interestingly, the majority of students choose the latter

Figure 2. Map of the hotspots of theft (steal from a motor vehicle) from July 2015 to June 2016 in Armidale, NSW, Australia
Source: BOCSAR (2016)

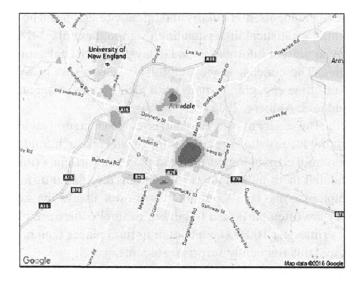

option. The exercise teaches students how and where to access various data sources, and how to analyse and interpret data. The application of the task to their home town, grounds the learning in reality.

In another unit on crime prevention, assessment requires students to conduct a security risk audit of an area in their community. This could be their home, their street, a local park, hotel, parking lot, train station, shopping centre, sports ground, farm or marine area. The process requires students to access crime data for their community including their local community crime prevention report to identify specific local crime problems and hot spots of crime. Students then generate a security risk report using data visualization such as maps, graphs, tables, photographs and diagrams of the property under risk assessment.

These assignments are structured around an experiential learning model or 'learning by doing' (Kolb 1984) which is based on the idea that experiences gained within real world activities or in a simulated learning environment facilitate student engagement and deep learning (Fry et al. 1999). When students conduct an independent inquiry into social problems and crime within their own local environment, they are frequently astonished at the nature and true extent of crime in their own community. Data visualization enables students to examine and reflect on the crime patterns and the identified 'hotspots' of crime, and critically evaluate social problems through a theoretical lens as well as their personal knowledge and life experiences.

An upper level undergraduate course on geographical information systems (GIS) is planned to meet the increasing demand for such skills within the workplace (Ferrandino 2015). However beyond the practical GIS skills, there is a need for students to learn to think critically about data analysis. Data visualization facilitates this deeper learning. Ferrandino (2015) and Althausen and Mieczkowski (2001) have argued that GIS courses for Criminology students should extend beyond the technical nature of crime mapping to incorporate theory, be interdisciplinary and integrate census data with crime mapping for a richer understanding of patterns in social and crime problems.

CONCLUSION

Data visualization is increasingly being employed within Criminology, and within the various agencies of the Criminal Justice System. There is therefore a growing need for graduates to be equipped with a high level of research skills, particularly GIS skills. For teaching purposes, visualisation techniques have the ability to reduce the barrier to understanding and appreciating quantitative research methods for some students. Students respond positively to experiential learning when assessment exercises cause them to assess crime and social data that pertain to their own community. By grounding learning in everyday reality and visually presenting crime and social data within maps of places that are familiar to students, the purpose of criminological research and the process of data analysis finally makes sense.

REFERENCES

Althausen, J. D., & Mieczkowski, T. M. (2001). The merging of criminology and geography into a course on spatial crime analysis. *Journal of Criminal Justice Education*, *12*(2), 367–383. doi:10.1080/10511250100086181

Barclay, E. M. (2017). Rural Crime. In A. Deckert & R. Sarre (Eds.), *The Australian and New Zealand Handbook of Criminology, Crime And Justice*. Palgrave MacMillan.

Barclay, E. M., Donnermeyer, J. F., & Jobes, P. C. (2004). The dark side of gemeinschaft; Criminality within rural communities. *Crime Prevention and Community Safety: An International Journal.*, *6*(3), 7–22. doi:10.1057/palgrave. cpcs.8140191

Braga, A. A., & Bond, B. J. (2008). Policing crime and disorder hot spots: A randomized controlled trial. *Criminology*, *46*(3), 577–608. doi:10.1111/j.1745-9125.2008.00124.x

Brantingham, P. J., & Brantingham, P. L. (1984). *Patterns in crime*. New York: Macmillan.

Brantingham, P. L., & Brantingham, P. J. (1993). Nodes, paths and edges: Considerations on the complexity of crime and the physical environment. *Journal of Environmental Psychology*, *13*(1), 3–28. doi:10.1016/S0272-4944(05)80212-9

Bright, D. A., Hughes, C. E., & Chalmers, J. (2012). Illuminating dark networks: A social network analysis of an Australian drug trafficking syndicate. *Crime, Law, and Social Change*, *57*(2), 151–176. doi:10.1007/s10611-011-9336-z

Bureau of Crime Statistics and Research (BOCSAR). (2016). *Crime Maps*. NSW Justice, Bureau of Crime Statistics and Research. Retrieved from http://www.bocsar.nsw.gov.au/Pages/bocsar_crime_stats/bocsar_crime_stats.aspx

Chamberlain, J. M. (2013). *Understanding Criminological Research: A Guide to Data Analysis*. London: Sage. doi:10.4135/9781473913837

Donnermeyer, J. F. (2017). Rural Criminology and Criminological Theory. In The Routledge Companion to Criminological Theory and Concepts. New York: Taylor and Francis.

Eck, J. (2005). Evaluation for lesson learning. In Handbook of Crime Prevention and Community Safety. Willan Publishing.

Eck, J. E., & Weisburd, D. (1995). Crime Places in Crime Theory. In Crime and Place. New York: Willow Tree Press.

Ferrandino, J. (2015). Using GIS to Apply Learning across the Undergraduate Criminal Justice Curriculum. *Journal of Criminal Justice Education*, *26*(1), 74–93. doi:10.1080/10511253.2014.925567

Fry, H., Kettering, S., & Marshall, S. (1999). *Teaching and Learning in Higher Education: Enhancing Academic Practice*. Kogan Page.

Jobes, P. C., Donnermeyer, J. F., Barclay, E. M., & Weinand, H. (2004). A Structural Analysis of Social Disorganisation and Crime in Rural Communities in Australia. *Australian and New Zealand Journal of Criminology*, *37*(1), 114–140. doi:10.1375/acri.37.1.114

Jones, N. J., Brown, S. L., Wanamaker, K. A., & Greiner, L. E. (2014). A quantitative exploration of gendered pathways to crime in a sample of male and female juvenile offenders. *Feminist Criminology*, *9*(2), 113–136. doi:10.1177/1557085113501850

Kievit, R. A., Frankenhuis, W. E., Waldorp, L. J., & Borsboom, D. (2013). Simpsons paradox in psychological science: A practical guide. *Frontiers in Psychology*, *4*, 513. doi:10.3389/fpsyg.2013.00513 PMID:23964259

Kolb, D. (1984). *Experiential Learning: Experience as the source of Learning and development*. Prentice-Hall.

Maltz, M. (1998). Visualizing Homicide: A Research Note. *Journal of Quantitative Criminology*, *15*(4), 397–410. doi:10.1023/A:1023081805454

Maltz, M. D. (2010). *Look before you analyze: Visualizing data in criminal justice. In Handbook of Quantitative Criminology* (pp. 25–52). Springer New York.

Michell, M. P. L. (2000). Smoke rings: Social network analysis of friendship groups, smoking and drug-taking. *Drugs Education Prevention & Policy*, *7*(1), 21–37. doi:10.1080/dep.7.1.21.37

Ratcliffe, J. (2008). *Intelligence-Led Policing*. Cullompton, UK: Willan Publishing.

Sampson, R. J., Raudenbush, S., & Earls, F. (1997). Neighborhoods and Violent Crime: A Multilevel Study of Collective Efficacy. *Science*, *277*(5328), 918–924. doi:10.1126/science.277.5328.918 PMID:9252316

Sampson, R. J., Winship, C., & Knight, C. (2013). Overview of: 'Translating Causal Claims: Principles and Strategies for Policy-Relevant Criminology. *Criminology & Public Policy*, *12*(4), 587–616. doi:10.1111/1745-9133.12027

Shaw, C. R., & McKay, H. D. (1942). *Juvenile Delinquency in Urban Areas*. Chicago: University of Chicago Press.

Sherman, L. W. (2013). The rise of evidence-based policing: Targeting, testing, and tracking. *Crime and Justice*, *42*(1), 377–451. doi:10.1086/670819

Signoretta, P., Chamberlain, J. M., & Hillier, J. (2014). A Picture Is Worth 10,000 Words: A Module to Test the Visualization Hypothesis in *Quantitative Methods Teaching. Enhancing Learning in the Social Sciences*, *6*(2), 90–104. doi:10.11120/elss.2014.00029

Uchida, C. D., Swatt, M. L., Solomon, S. E., & Varano, S. (2014). *Data-Driven Crime Prevention: New Tools for Community Involvement and Crime Control*. U.S. Department of Justice. Retrieved 28/11/16 from https://www.ncjrs.gov/pdffiles1/nij/grants/245408.pdf

Weisburd, D., Bernasco, W., & Bruinsma, G. (Eds.). (2008). *Putting crime in its place: Units of analysis in geographic criminology*. Springer Science & Business Media.

Wheeldon, J., & Harris, D. (2015). Expanding visual criminology: Definitions, data and dissemination. *Current Issues in Criminal Justice*, *27*, 141–162.

Wortley, R., & Mazerolle, L. (2008). *Environmental Criminology and Crime Analysis*. Willan Publishing.

Chapter 4
Opportunities and Challenges of Visualization and Open Data in Food Security Analysis

Thida Chaw Hlaing
University of New England, Australia

Julian Prior
University of New England, Australia

ABSTRACT

Statistical literacy presents many aspects about food security in the world. It highlights weaknesses, it creates awareness of threats in current situations, helps overcome challenges and creates opportunities for the future. Statistical data analysis enables existing food security interventions and programs to be reviewed and revised, and this better understanding of current situations enables more authoritative and relevant decision-making processes for the future. Statistical literacy involves skills and expertise in data description and interpretation (in words as well as in numbers) to name, explore and amend beliefs, opinions and suggestions. It helps decision-making processes about food security in a sub-nation, nation and region, as well as the world. This chapter will demonstrate the importance of open data and visualization, including its challenges and opportunities, in the food security context at national and global level to make decision-makers aware of the need to enhance their capacity for and investment in statistical literacy.

DOI: 10.4018/978-1-5225-2512-7.ch004

INTRODUCTION

In this era of information, communication and technological innovations, data dissemination systems and the diverse varieties of data present a number of technical challenges for various kinds of research and analysis. Private sector data and information service providers have been expanding their business by obtaining open data sets released by government and the public sector and offering them for sale. It greatly helps researchers and scientists to access open data for the analysis, modelling and visualization of their particular research topic or area. The realistic research outcomes they produce may challenge our beliefs and suggest actions for the future. The Open Knowledge Foundation describes open data as data that can be freely used, re-used and redistributed by anyone without legal, technical or social restrictions (Tammisto & Lindman, 2012, p. 298).

Accessing open dataset supports and applying them to the decision-making process could improve the lives of all people. Technological challenges have been encountered, however, due to insufficient metadata, because it is disseminated increasingly by different data organizations worldwide. For this reason, the food security situation in some developing countries goes unrecognized, mainly due to weak data analysis and visualization. A country's government or agencies and departments are always under pressure to release their big data for open access. They often cannot release the big data if they don't have permission, as is the case of isolated countries like Myanmar. In addition, profit-making data suppliers focus more on income generation from their data streams and networks than on making big data freely available.

In terms of the world's development agenda, solving the issues of food insecurity and poverty will be critical to improving rural livelihoods as well as developing very country's economy, from individual household up to the national level. However, the level of food insecurity varies from one country to another, even between regions in the same country because of different factors, causes and consequences (Joachim Von Braun, 1992). In the analysis of food security, it is hard to find major causes and provide appropriate suggestions to decision-makers, due to the limitations of data availability, accessibility and government support to re-use data.

Since data visualization has become very popular in the multisector research area, various visualization tools to process datasets have been developed and applied in the areas of agriculture and food security. In this respect, statistical analysis initially requires data visualization to give a basic understanding on which to base decisions that can reduce the stress of food insecurity. The availability and accessibility of data are therefore crucial, even though there are many reasons for insufficient data, such as weaknesses in transparency, integrity and accountability, to convey the key message that freely available open data offers great social, economic and good governance benefits to every country (Organization for Economic Cooperation and Development [OECD], 2016). Given open data availability and accessibility in the public sector, many potential research tools can give a basic understanding of food security with a model that shows multiple inter-related causes through visualized graphs, tables, charts. Open data from various sources can be applied to validate and refine these visualized food security causal models which in turn could be used to identify solutions to food insecurity.

OBJECTIVE

Without statistical literacy of data interpretation and visualization, it is not easy to explore the strength and weakness of any industry. However, when statistical literacy is applied to agriculture, which is the focus of this chapter, it can give a complete picture in order to address a situation of food insecurity, including looming risks and potential solutions. For this reason, open data and big data statistical literacy are integral both to supply of and demand for data and information.

The statistical tools used will differ, depending on data availability and accessibility as well as differences in terms of research themes and the mandate of the organizations, institutions and governments involved. Nevertheless, statistical tools will support the use of vizualisation for data interpretation, bringing more resources or skills to address the situation than just reading a text. To understand a food insecurity situation in given open data and big data, the tools the researchers apply and the way they summarise or interpret or visualize the statistical data are major challenges in order to get information and understand the data characteristics. Applying statistical concepts, methods and processes to open data and big data, that is, extending statistical literacy, will give more precise data interpretation than data reading of conventional statistics.

Statistical data presents many aspects about food security in the world. It can reveal or highlight weakness, raise awareness of threats in current situation, help overcome challenges and create opportunities for the future. Existing interventions and programs of food security can be reviewed and revised if the statistical data analysis gives better understanding of a current food insecurity situation; this better understanding in turn enables more authoritative and relevant decision-making processes for the future. Statistical literacy involves skills and expertise in data description and interpretation (in words as well as in numbers) to name, explore and amend beliefs, opinions and suggestions. It helps decision-making processes about food security in a sub-nation, nation and region, as well as the world.

This chapter will give an understanding of the importance to food security of open and big data and of the challenges of and opportunities for applying open data and big data to the agriculture sector, and by implication to food security.

THE IMPORTANCE OF VISUALIZATION AND OPEN DATA

Visualization is a better approach to understand the problems and possible solutions in multisector development issues. Having data only is not enough and we have to let the people understand what these data are and how to utilize these data. Visualization presents the available data in a form of pictures or graphs and it easily explores the concepts and trend of a particular issue to the decision-makers (Statistical Analysis System [SAS], n.d.). It helps to present the huge historical progress and future trend in trade, economic, social development, etc. at national, regional and global level. Technology-oriented-data visualization can give better interpretation of healthy and wealthy corner of the world (Rosling, 2010). Certainly, complex datasets may be applied to generate these visualized information map which is more time-effective instead of time-consuming reading text.

Liberalization of government data is very essential but the maximization of effectiveness of using open data is more crucial for the public (OECD, 2016). Ordinary citizens rarely use government datasets what researchers and business people do (OECD, 2016). The huge amounts of complex data and information in the spreadsheets and reports are not as easy to understand the given concepts as we learned from visualized graphs or charts (SAS, n.d.). Thus, the data covering the relevant information about people daily lives and habits should be available and accessible with visual presentation to allow the individual people take note and adjust their behaviour (OECD, 2016). Visualization become popular and it is internationally well accepted and applied to convey any messages and scenarios as a quick and easy tool (SAS, n.d.). Because it can point out a specific area where needs recognition or improvement with the help of researchers, practitioners, scholars in the development agenda. In the business sector, it helps to find out the influencing factors of sales and marketing, such as customer behaviour, product allocation, sales volume.

Consequently, without information and statistics, there will be no sound interpretation and visualization to explore the condition of a particular development research. Today, the availability of open data is growing through various service providers of both profit and non-profit agencies (Ubaldi, 2013). Open Knowledge Foundation (James, 2013) described the summary of full definition of open data in 2005:

Open data is data that can be freely used, shared and built-on by anyone, anywhere, for any purpose.

The more open data movement develops with the recognition of many governments and organizations, the clearer definition of open data is critical to be well-accepted. It helps to grasp the benefits of openness, and escape the risks of inconsistency between the research project and its enabling community (James, 2013). According to the OECD, the importance of open data released by the Government has been prominently recently recognized after setting the principle of this Open Government Data (OGD) in the United States in 2008 (Ubaldi, 2013).

In reality, the focus on releasing those data from public departments is not yet significant to liberalize the data as a resource to use. In addition, the potential of re-use of open data still does not meet the expected levels (Lassinantti, 2016). On the other hand, the reproduction of scientific-paper through open data should be transformed in different discipline to solve social problems out of consideration. At the same time, the researchers must be proficient to access required data in line with other discipline. Because, the transmission of scientific-research-data will not always be open and free but it must be available to access and re-use it (KAKUTA, 2016). Surprisingly, the massive quantities of data and larger datasets are gathered and delivered across the public sectors. The importance of social and economic value of the big-data creates the significant usage of data in terms of velocity and variety through socio-economic model which investigate new initiatives, sustainable growth and development.

But, such kind of dataset is not easily presentable by managing with normal tools or traditional data interpretation methods. It needs to process with the support of technological software or tools for the data organizing, searching, allocation, transporting, analysing and visualization. Then, the result of this big database analysis will be comparable with the smaller data sets of similar variety of data with the findings of disease prevalence, research quality, criminal conflicts, etc. (Ubaldi). In this connection, the importance of free big-data sets is vital to produce data visualization to determine the prevalence of food insecurity problems to help the daily lives of people.

THE IMPORTANCE OF VISUALIZATION AND OPEN DATA IN FOOD SECURITY

What Is Food Security?

A common understanding of food security, in its broadest sense is required to bridge the gap between the demand and supply of information. This requires a clear conceptual framework that embraces the full scope and all dimensions of food security as a foundation for food security information systems. Past perceptions of food security that focused on production, self-sufficiency and filling food gaps with food aid are no longer adequate given today's challenges. With growing market economies and trade liberalization, consideration of comparative advantage has helped ensure more efficient production, including of non-food commodities. With poor and traditionally food insecure communities becoming more integrated into market economies, peoples' livelihoods and opportunities for household income have become more and more important in ensuring food security. The importance of food safety and good nutritional practices has become well understood as prerequisites to ensure good health and food security (Shwe & Hlaing, 2011). The most common definition of food security was adopted by the country Leaders at the World Food Security and World Food Summit, the Rome Declaration of Food and Agriculture Organization (FAO; 1996):

Food security exists when all people, at all times, have physical and economic access to sufficient, safe and nutritious food to meet their dietary needs and food preferences for an active and healthy life. (FAO, 1996, p. 298, para. 12, 2009, para. 2)

Also, FAO has demonstrated the four dimensions of food security: Availability; Accessibility, Utilization, and Stability (Food and Agriculture Organization [FAO], 2006, p. 1). In fact, food insecurity is not stand alone (Bhutta et al., 2008; Black et al., 2008; Dangour et al., 2013; Ghattas, Barbour, Nord, Zurayk, & Sahyoun, 2013; International Food Policy Research Institute, [IFPRI], 2016; Iram & Butt, 2004; Jenkins & Scanlan, 2001; Mason, 2002; Myanmar Times, 2016; Johshin Von Braun, 1993; Wahlqvist et al., 2009). Food insecurity has other three related concepts, hunger, malnutrition and poverty as shown in Figure 1 (Food and Agriculture Organization [FAO], 2008b). If there is food deprivation in both availability and accessibility issues, it results hunger but all food insecure people will not be hungry. It may have other causes, such as inadequate micro-nutrient intake. Malnutrition occurs from food deficiencies, over-eating or imbalance of nutrient intake and it relate health care, services and environment for children. The causes of hunger and malnutrition

Figure 1. Interrelationship of food security, malnutrition, and poverty
FAO (2008b)

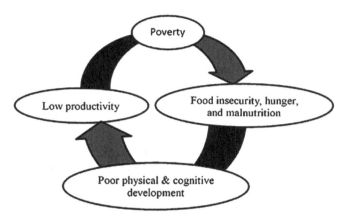

result to poverty which relates to food insecurity, health care, education, etc. This is widely accepted concept and relates to food insecurity agenda (FAO, 2008b).

Over many discussion and dialogues about food security initiatives, a number of major causes and possible solutions have been discussing to overcome the influencing factors of food insecurity, globally, regionally and nationally. For example, in relation to food availability, crop yield has been declining in many areas due to lower investment priorities in research and infrastructures. In addition, climate change as well as water scarcity and the prevalence of HIV/AIDS are also influencing factors to cause food insecurity in many regions (Rosegrant & Cline, 2003). There will be possible solutions to overcome the risks of those influencing problems, such as more investment for better yield and initiative of agriculture reform policies (Rosegrant & Cline, 2003).

It shows multiple inter-related causes of food insecurity. We need to identify major problems by providing the evidence of information and statistics. The written document of food security data and information is not very helpful to have the attention of the decision-makers immediately since it takes time to understand and judge the given information. The casual factors of food insecurity, their relationships and interconnectedness as well as the strength of their relationship may be easily recognized with the power of data analysis and visualization instead of providing the situation model in words. Data visualization is the best approach to underline the major risk factors but it could also be a technical barrier in some economic model to analysis food insecurity due to loss of statistics in some parameters.

Why Is Visualization and Open Data Important in the Analysis of Food Security in the World?

Since after the United Nations Conference of Food and Agriculture held in USA in 1943, achieving the goal of freedom from the needs of food and agriculture has taken into consideration of the world's food and agriculture problems to improve the health and nutrition of the world's population (Shaw, 2007). As a first initiative, the Conference principally agreed to establish the Food and Agriculture Organization of the United Nations (FAO) in 1943 and it was officially formed in 1945 (Shaw, 2007) emphasizing agriculture and economic policies to ensure an adequate and a suitable supply of food for all people (Shaw, 2007). FAO was intended to be a service centre of information and statistics with regards to food and agriculture as well as to provide advice to all agriculture and nutritional issues raised from all nations.

Then, FAO was initiated as a world's largest database system through Food and Agriculture Organization Statistics (FAOSTAT) (before AGROSTAT) (Food and Agriculture Organization - Economic and Social Development Department [FAO-ESDD], 2017). It became operational database system since 1986. FAOSTAT provides free datasets for 245 countries and 35 regional areas. Time series data is freely and easily accessible in most domains from the year of 1961 to most recent year (FAO, 2017). The corporate database of FAO contains a comprehensive topics of food and agriculture of production, consumption, trade, prices and resources, nutrition, etc. Besides, FAO provides the capacity development assistance for the standard methodology and national data as well as metadata collection to ensure harmonization of the collection and dissemination of reliable data for the statistical data analysis and policy making.

Also main data users of FAOSTAT are data analysts from the research institutes, International Organizations (i.e. UN, World Bank, International NGOs) as well as Universities. Data sharing from FAOSTAT depends on the indicator which the organization or agency needs and it is mostly coordinated with UN Population Division, World Bank, WHO, UNICEF, ILO, WWGI, International Road Federation, World Road Statistics and Electronic Divisions. The update of data is timely in every August of a year. Although FAOSTAT don't make user satisfaction survey (Alexa, 2017; FAOSTAT, 2017). According to the official FAOSTAT Twitter "@FAOstatistics", the number of usage to FAOSTAT reach about 100,000 visits per month. Also, from the result of preliminary assessment to study the usage of FAOSTAT, the audience are mostly from India, United States, Nigeria, Mexico and China. Based on the internet average monitoring, the visitors to FAOSTAT are the most from work followed by the school and home as shown in Figure 2 (Alexa, 2017). There is a large number of indexes of FAO Statistical database applied in the publications shown in "Google scholars". Generally, there are many number of data user access to FAO database

Figure 2. Interrelationship of food security, malnutrition, and poverty
FAO (2008b)

not only for academic research purposes but also for the reporting or assessment of International Organizations and Government agencies.

As a result, FAO database is widely accepted among the global data users but there may be many variables of missing data due to weak cooperation from the country government to release the official data. It highlighted that country governments must be aware to be stronger international incentives for a more comprehensive open data policy of food and agriculture.

For instance, Yearly FAO Hunger Map is one of the excellent visualized products released from FAO. It presents the progress of food insecurity stories of the entire world even though the written documents of "The State of Food Security in the World 2015" is available as free online published document with many reading text, data tables and visualized charts and graphs (Food and Agriculture Organization [FAO], 2016; Food and Agriculture Organization [FAO], International Fund for Agricultural Development [IFAD], & World Food Programme [WFP], 2015). But, a single colourful map briefs the overall progress of World Hunger Eradication Scheme by spotting the hunger targets driven from the Millennium Development Goals (MDGs), the update of prevalence of malnutrition of the population, and the achievement of World Food Summit target. Behind producing this map, it need big datasets to process statistical analysis and visualize the orientation of World Hunger Situation. It is comprehensive work to complete as well as the availability of all-inclusive dataset is major factor to generate visualized World Hunger Map. But it is worth to be occupied by this comprehensive work because the visualized map may draw great attention from decision-makers and policy developers which is easier to understand the problems area and the location which needs further supports for long term development.

As indicated in the FAO Hunger Map 2015 in Figure 3, the progress of every country and region can be seen through time series data process of relevant indicators from 1990-1992 to 2014-2016. At the end of MDG monitoring periods by 2015, 73 countries have achieved the target of MDG 1 to cut half of malnourished people

Figure 3. FAO hunger map 2015
FAO et al. (2015)

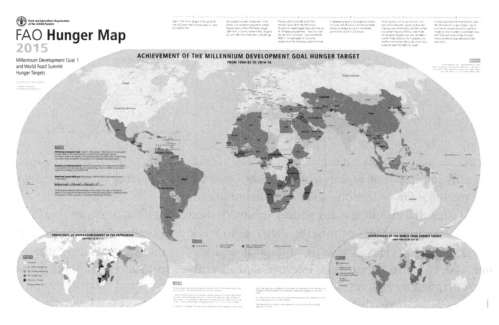

among 129 developing countries (FAO et al., 2015). Across the developing regions, the target of MDG 1 was almost achieved from 23.3 percent in 1990-1992 to 12.9 percent in 2014-2016. Among developing regions, some regions such as East, Central regions of Asia and northern and western regions of Africa shows fast progress of MDG Target 1 while other regions of Asia, African and Oceania does not give significant progress of MDG 1 target.

To address the prevalence of undernourishment, the measurement indicators are undernourishment or hunger as well as the prevalence of underweight children who are under five years old. It clearly illustrates to understand the vulnerable regions still under the high prevalence of malnourishment, such as south and central Africa as well as west and central Asia regions. Statistically, estimated 793 million of world population are still under food insufficiency situation and it may still be hard to overcome the risk of food insecurity. It present the conditions of availability and accessibility of dietary energy of individual people can be major constraints in the prevalence regions of Africa and Asia. As a result, the target of World Food Summit was not completely achieved but with noticeable progress although some other regions has lack of progress. In the populated regions, there will be many influencing factors caused to increased food insecurity and vulnerability, such as, natural and man-made disasters, political instability and domestic conflicts.

Since visualization is not just a better way to interpret the data with infographic more comprehensible, it is also a better way to achieve understanding of issues, problems, causes and solutions. Developing infographic can create descriptions which build understanding and communication to different level of audience. Another good example of world's famous infographic, namely "Hockey Stick" is one of the famous plot in statistical tools to measure climate change impact in food insecurity.

This scientific visualization as per Figure 4 shows that the world is experiencing the warmest climate in 20th Century started from 19th Century. It happened in the industrialization page of the world due to the extensive burn of coal and oil led to increase carbon dioxide in the atmosphere. It affects declination of world food production and it directly link with food availability of the households, especially in agriculture sector as well as prevalence of disease and health problems in some regions (Mann, 2013; Muller, 2004). Beside this kind of food security casual graphs, many more metaphors can produce for the better understanding of the inter-related causes to find possible solutions to improve food security.

In fact, there are some statistics and information missing which did not allow to study the situation of food insecurity and malnourishment in some regions. It was one of unfavourable technical barriers found in any statistical big-data process and analysis conducted by the scholars, researchers, practitioners and statisticians. This kind of visualized map or Hockey Stick provide the brief understanding of not only the progress of the global Food Insecurity and its related causes but also the

Figure 4. Hockey stick climate change
Mann (2013) and Muller (2004)

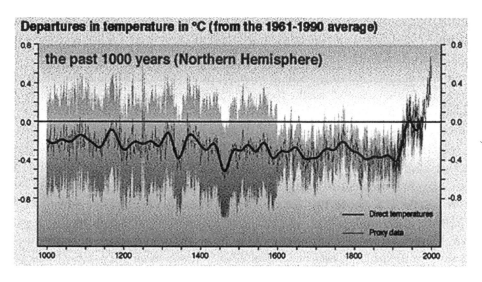

consideration of the possible problems of vulnerable conditions of food insecurity in the world. If the further information and detailed discussions are required to find out, the written documents are helpful to extend more understanding and knowledge. However, policy-makers as well as decision-makers will have more preferences on statistical visualization than the multiple reading text and data sheets.

Likewise, there are many acceptable free data sources globally available to access and it makes data users convenient to analyse for various reason of food and agriculture research (Marr, 2016). They are brilliant and internationally well-accepted in order to provide open and big data for statistical literacy. Beside world's largest online database provider of FAO in relation to the information and statistics of food and agriculture, the data sources are not really limited but the reliability and the free access of big data is a constraint for the scholars, researchers and practitioners. Among these data agencies from public sector, the United States Department of Agriculture (USDA) is one of the popular agency in terms of national and international dataset. Economic Research Service of USDA provides various data products, such as the statistics and information of food and agriculture, food safety, international markets and trade, rural economy and population, natural resources and management, etc. Apart from the statistical datasets and written documents, the Economic Research USDA has collected 70 charts and maps of the above domains and make it free available to the public as learned in Figure 5.

The statistical visualizations maps, graphs and charts together with a short summary text provided by USDA are incredibly supportive to the statistical literacy as well as it draw the attention of citizen to easily understand how agriculture contributes to National GDP, the situation of rural economy or environmental and natural resources management. Most importantly to the awareness of reducing the risks of food insecurity, the information and visualized maps, graphs, charts direct benefits firstly to the U.S citizen to understand the progress of food security at the macro and micro level.

As a brief understanding of food security in the U.S. (USDA, 2016) shown in the Figure 6, the share of food expense in total expenditure is the highest in the lowest income households in U.S in 2014; the calories intake is the highest in U.S. at 3,639 calories per day while it is only 2,206 calories in Kenya in 2013 and 2015; the income spent on total food falls from 17.5 to 9.6 percent between 1960-2014 together with declination of income share spent on food at home by showing the ignorance of recommended food balance among the citizens; the prevalence of food security in the U.S. shows that the rate of food insecure decline from 14% to 12.7% in 2014 to 2015 while 87.3% of U.S. households are recorded as food secure in 2015; For insecurity can be found more in rural and urban than in suburban areas and the significant high rate of food insecurity found at single parent, Black and

Figure 5. Open data and statistical visualization
USDA (2016)

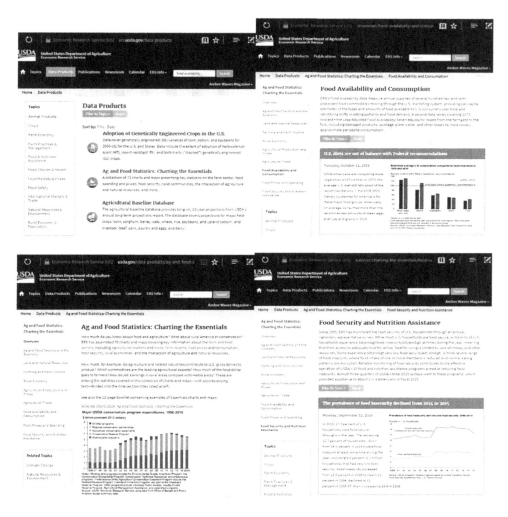

Hispanic households in the U.S.; food insecurity found more in the adults than in the children but one out of six households with children experienced food insecurity in U.S. in 2015.

These visualization about food security makes ordinary people understand straightforwardly what the situation happening in the U.S. Also, it is very accommodating to the high level decision-makers to see the actual condition of food security in both good progress and the area where the attention need to have. But, the statistics and information dissemination in terms of food security in many other government agencies are not as comprehensive and productive as the USDA do to

Figure 6. Open data and visualization
USDA (2016)

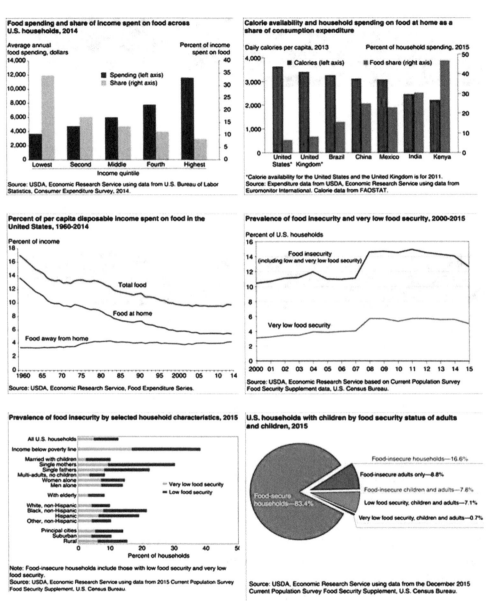

let the data users convenient in both big datasets, visualization charts and graphs. That's the reason, the scholars, researchers and practitioners have been encouraging to the public agencies and departments to aware the usefulness and importance of open data in the world today.

Visualization of Food Availability Across World Regions

In 2011, standard indicators to measure four components of food security were recommended by technical experts of the Committee on World Food Security (Committee on World Food Security (CFS)) Round Table with the consultation and judgment to analysis food security in various reasons (FAO, 2016). Based on the open database available in FAOSTAT, the status of food availability can easily be demonstrated by statistical visualization and economic modelling. Data presentation supported by visualized graphs gives better understanding of food insecurity in terms of food availability in all regions in the world. For example, it is easy to see who needs helps most and where the most vulnerable region is. Consequently, attention can be directed to further corrections or new initiatives to improve the supply of food for those people. Without this assessment enabled through visualised data, it can be hard to measure progress and to make the right decisions about food supply in vulnerable regions.

The indicators of food availability are adequacy of average dietary energy supply, average value of food production, share of dietary energy supply derived from cereals, roots and tubers, average protein supply, and average supply of animal protein (FAO, 2016).

The visualized graphs in Figure 7 present a quick snapshot of food availability in developing regions across the world. They cover Asia, Africa, Latin America and the Caribbean, Oceania, developed countries and least developed countries to illustrate the different levels of food security based on the recommended indicators. The visualized graphs demonstrated the time series datasets from 1990-1992 to 2014-2016 to compare regional trends from one period to the next. The graphs demonstrate, as an example, that the average dietary energy supply adequacy of developed countries was significantly higher than other regions, while the fastest

Figure 7. Visualization of food availability across the regions in the world
FAO (2016)

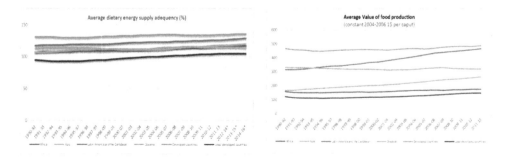

rising trend occurred in least developed countries from 2000. This indicator allows viewers to predict the sufficiency of food supply and thereby to address the causes of malnutrition in regions. In terms of average value of food production, this is steadily increasing in Latin America, the Caribbean and Asia but other regions remain the same. There is no argument that the poorer we are, the more we need a secure food supply.

Again thanks to these visualized indicators of food availability, it is easy to see that food supply is significantly high in developed countries, followed by the some other developing regions, such as Oceania, Latin America and the Caribbean. The regions where the nutritional energy supply is highly dependent on cereal, roots and tubers, such as Asia, Africa and the least developed countries, may be at high risk of food insecurity, due to such issues as political instability, climate change, and man-made and natural disasters. However, we cannot determine the prevalence of food security by food availability indicators only.

Visualization of Food Accessibility Across World Regions

Similar to food availability, the indicators of food accessibility were produced by the Committee on World Food Security (Committee on World Food Security (CFS)) Round Table in 2011. The indicators of food accessibility comprise percentage of paved roads over total roads, road density, rail line density, GDP per capita (purchasing power equivalent), domestic food price index, prevalence of undernourishment, proportion of food expenditure by the poor, and depth of food deficit. For the purposes of visualizing food accessibility in relation to food availability, the regions are the same as those mentioned above. The indicators identify mainly the socio-economic characteristics of households to find the affordability of food in the region.

Using the indicators of food accessibility, the graphs in Figure 8 are a visualization of the malnutrition experienced in poor regions, such as the least developed countries of the world, followed by developing countries in Africa, Asia, Oceania, Latin America and Caribbean. It is clear that the developed countries experience enough food accessibility. In terms of the domestic food price indicator, the least developed countries, followed by Africa and Asia, experience higher prices compared with other regions and there could be an unstable food market in these regions. Basically, it is necessary to measure the indicators of transportation resources, such as road and rail density, to establish the exact status of food accessibility. In addition, the average proportion of total household expenditure on food is an important indicator. In this respect, the statistics of some indicators of food accessibility are missing from the FAO database. This may be caused by a technical constraint or by lack of resources to identify the major poor and their needs in the regions. Such technical barriers and

Figure 8. Visualization of food accessibility indicators across the regions in the world
FAO (2016)

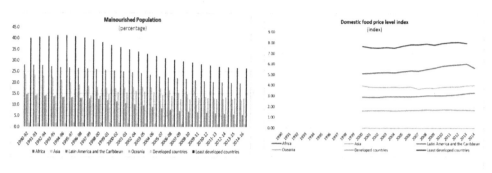

poor resources make it harder to make the best decisions about what attention and support should be added to improve food security in vulnerable regions of the world.

In summary, this section shows emphatically the importance of statistical literacy to get quick understanding of food security in all regions of the world. It is not completely possible to collect time-based food security data across the regions of the world due to a number of constraints, including the technical capacity and investment. However, there is great benefit in having open data services that allow the public to access time-based data easily and freely without having to undertake their own field surveys and data collection. This open free data is a valuable resource for research, and for the preliminary or initial assessment of food security in a particular country or region or the world as a whole. Visualized data also helps attract the interest and attention of policy makers in meeting the needs of food accessibility worldwide.

Why Is Visualization and Open Data Important in Food Security Analysis at National Level: Myanmar?

Food security is a global as well as a regional and national issue, and every nation should have a strong will and perception to reduce food insecurity for the better lives of its citizens. Consequently, policy makers must have enough understanding of social and economic strategies in relation to food security to develop evidence-based policies. In this respect, food security assessments with available information and statistics are the initial step needed to address potential problems specifically and recommend possible solutions sensibly. It is best to supply adequate and affordable food to the people of a nation before sharing surplus food with the region and the world. The right policy will not be laid down if there is no right decision. For this reason, the information stream as well as open data sources at the national level must be strong enough, with good functionality and technical capacity since it is crucial to make the right decisions and the right investment to fill gaps in food security. This section discusses these issues specifically in relation to Myanmar.

Despite open access to big datasets from the non-government sector, there are many debates and different findings in studies of poverty in Myanmar by UN agencies and other international organizations. Although they have used the same datasets, different organizations have reached different conclusions about food insecurity in Myanmar. Additional analysis using open source data, plus perhaps using other datasets not used in the original analysis, may help explain these differences and lead to greater understanding of the true situation. As food security is a complex issue, it requires big datasets from various sources to deal with the many parameters that cause food insecurity.

Many studies shows the high prevalence of poverty in all rural areas. These studies include the findings of Integrated Household Living Consumption (IHLC) surveys done by United Nations development Programme (UNDP) in collaboration with the Myanmar Ministry of National Planning and Economic Development (NPED) in 2005 and 2010 (Institute for Democracy and Electoral Assistance [IDEA] & Integrated Household Living Conditions Assistance [IHLCA], 2007; Integrated Household Living Conditions Assistance [IHLCA], 2011). These were the most comprehensive surveys and primary data collection processes ever undertaken to assess poverty levels in Myanmar. Interestingly, however, Myanmar was also recorded as reducing the prevalence of malnutrition from 62.6% in 1999-92 to 14.2% in 2014-16, an achievement that ranked it at Millennium Development Goals (MDGs) No. 1 in 2015. The number of undernourished people fell from 26.8 million in 1999-92 to 7.7 million in 2014-16 (FAO et al., 2015).

However, there was confusion over the findings of these food security assessments, due to two major constraints. The first constraint was the lack of up-to-date total population figures for 1999-92 (the last population census was done in 1974 and the updated one was done in 2014). The second constraint was the exclusion of the population in the border areas (where samples were not taken due to ongoing conflict at the time of survey) (Livelihoods and Food Security Trust Fund [LIFT], 2016). Nevertheless, the IHLCA result is the single most reliable source of knowledge and a comprehensive picture of poverty prevalence in Myanmar. In 2011, the Livelihoods and Food Security Trust Fund (LIFT) Myanmar conducted a baseline survey and a household survey to measure poverty using household consumption data. It covered 252 villages in three agro-ecological zones of the Delta/Coastal region, the Hilly region and the Central Dry Zones, as well as Rakhine State. A total of 200 samples was collected ((Livelihoods and Food Security Trust Fund [LIFT], 2012, 2016). This was one of the most popular and single food security baseline survey done in Myanmar and the outcome and baseline datasets are available to the public through the LIFT website and the Myanmar Information Management Unit (MIMU, 2014-2016).

In terms of food poverty (based on minimum food expenditure on caloric requirement for household members), 10% of the total population was affected in 2005 (IDEA & IHLCA, 2007) but this had declined to 5% by 2010 (IHLCA, 2011). Food poverty in rural areas is higher (about 5.6%) than in urban areas (2.5%). Almost 85% of total food poverty occurs in rural areas and the Ayeyarwady (18.7%), Mandalay (16%), Shan (15.4%) and Rakhine State (14.9%) are the four major contributing state/regions in national food poverty. Follow up assessment by the IHLCA (IHLCA, 2011) five after years the previous IHLCA found that 25% of the total population are below the poverty line (based on (i) minimum food expenditure on the caloric requirement of household members and (ii) reasonable non-food expenditure to meet basic needs) and this has declined from 25.6% in 2005 (IDEA & IHLCA, 2007). Poverty prevalence in rural areas is double (at 29%) that of urban areas (15%). Almost 85% of total poverty in Myanmar can be found in rural areas. The findings of UNDP show that the highest poverty occurs in mountain, coastal and delta regions, such as Chin (73%), Rakhine (44%), Tanintharyi (33%), Shan (33%) and Ayeyarwady (32%). The four major contributing states and regions to food poverty namely, Ayeyarwady (19%), followed by Mandalay (15%), Rakhine (12%) and Shan State (11%) (IHLCA, 2011) are also major contributors to national poverty rates.

It is interesting to note that the prevalence of poverty differed in the studies analysis done by the UNDP and the World Bank although they applied the same dataset and time frame of Integrated Household Living Consumption Analysis (LIFT, 2016). In 2014, the World Bank announced poverty rate for Myanmar of 37.5% in 2014, with the worst poverty in the Rakhine (78%) and Chin (71.5%) regions. (World Bank, 2014). By zone, the World Bank found that the central dry zone had the lowest poverty rate (29.5%), while the coastal area had the highest (53.1%). These are the complete opposite of previous findings from the UNDP. The World Bank applied an international method, using the cost of basic consumption expenditure (less than US$1 per household member per day), the caloric threshold of 2300 calories/day/adult and other related indicators, such as health costs, cost of durable goods, etc. to measure the poverty line across the region. Poverty occurred in landless households or those with less than 2 acres of land (World Bank, 2014).

Conversely, the result of the Household Survey (2013) undertaken by LIFT showed that 29% of the population in these zones is living in poverty. The poverty figure was completely different to a previous analysis done by the UNDP and the World Bank. It showed that the lowest poverty rate occurred in the Hilly region and the highest poverty rate was in the Central Dry Zone (LIFT, 2012, 2016). LIFT applied the extreme poverty measurement of consumption rate (less than US$1.25

per person per day). Thus, it is not possible to compare all findings of poverty rates in Myanmar since the methodologies applied by the UNDP, The World Bank and LIFT all differed (IHLCA, 2011; LIFT, 2016; World Bank, 2014). However, it cannot be denied that the highest poverty occurred in the most populated rural area in Myanmar, an area which has also suffered from prolonged food insecurity. The point here is that a single research project or assessment through statistical analysis is not always enough to examine a number of problems and recommend potential solutions, in this case to solving food insecurity.

On the other hand, however, some literature (Fujita, 2003; Kurosaki, Okamoto, Kurita, & Fujita, 2004; Okamoto, 2009) has identified two major causes of household food insecurity in relation to the agriculture sector in Myanmar. These causes are: 1) low agricultural production (and therefore low food availability) associated with less crop diversification, limited access to land, irrigation facilities, climate variability and climate change problems, and 2) weak market performance, including poor income and investment and road infrastructure in relation to food accessibility. These are the underlying causes that disrupt the food production sector on the supply side and make food access a burden, especially for the rural poor in Myanmar. Access to open data will be required in order to examine and validate these causalities and then find potential solutions to food insecurity.

A successful food security and statistic information system needs continuous monitoring as well as reliable data collection methodology to regulate the data and information. It will help to meet the demand from decision-makers for food security information and statistics, as well as from data users at different levels for different purposes, such as development partners, donor organizations, scholars, researchers, etc. In Myanmar, the public has very limited access to open data sources released by government agencies. The only source for open data released by the government in Myanmar is the Central Statistical Office (CSO; 2017 February 2), under the Ministry of Planning and Finance, where data are gathered from all ministries. Historically, the statistical data collection system of the CSO seems to have been internal data reporting from the ministries to central government and the open data is available to the public only as a published book (Shwe & Hlaing, 2011).

At present, the statistics and information of food and agriculture can access through the official Government website of CSO and Myanmar Statistical Information Service (MMSIS; 2015) (CSO, 2008; MMSIS, 2015; Planning Department, 2012, 2014). The data is divided into 17 domains at the national level and, as stated above, it is a statistical year book published by the CSO but it is not open data to access freely (CSO, 2008). The Myanmar Statistical Information Service releases the statistical database with 12 domains. Unlike the USDA database system, the CSO database service has no statistical visualization graphs or charts with short explanation text to let the citizen understand the social and economic situation with regard to food security in Myanmar. Thus, data availability and accessibility in Myanmar is a critical constraint for all users of food and agriculture sector data (Shwe & Hlaing, 2011).

In this respect, the primary data collection relating to food security was initiated by international technical agencies and development partners in Myanmar. Most of the outcomes of food security assessment or analysis are available to the international network through Myanmar Food Security Information Network (FSIN). FSIN Myanmar is a network of technical experts and information managers from 30 lead food security stakeholders joined by UN agencies, international and local NGOs and CBOs, funded by the Livelihoods and Food Security Trust Fund (LIFT) Myanmar (Food Security Information Network [FSIN], 2013a, 2013b). Thus, the information and statistical literacy of food and agriculture is stronger in the non-government organizations than in the Myanmar government agencies, although the nation-wide primary data collection is done periodically by the CSO and its related ministries. It is totally opposite to the open data services provided by the USDA, due to the statistical literacy of the database system and visualization and affordable resources. It may be that the political instability in Myanmar affects the awareness of the value of data transparency and the lack of statistical literacy in the country.

Visualization of Food Availability at National Level: Myanmar

In terms of the concept of food availability, Myanmar has been nationally food self-sufficient, with rich resources in production staple food, such as rice, pulses and fish, for decades (Byerlee, Kyaw, Thein, & Kham, 2014; Denning, Baroang, Sandar, MDRI team members, & MSU members, 2013; Food and Agriculture Organization [FAO] / World Food Programme [WFP], 2009, 2016; Haggblade & Boughton, 2013; Haggblade et al., 2014; Kyaw, 2006, 2009; Kyaw & Routray, 2006; Oo, 2012; Rammohan & Pritchard, 2014). According to the visualized graphs derived from the FAO database, the average dietary energy supply in Myanmar increased to 113% in 2014-2016 from 109% in 2012-2014 (LIFT, 2016) and 77% in 1990-1992 (FAO, 2016). Despite these indicators showing that the national food supply means self-sufficiency in terms of total calories (LIFT, 2016), there are many food-deficit households in the remotest hilly region and central dry zone area (World Food Programme. [WFP], 2012).

To food availability at the national level, food adequacy of staple grains for carbohydrate and protein in terms of total calories can be applied. Figure 9 compares the Myanmar average supply of fat, protein and animal protein per person per day (averaged over 3 years) from 1990-1992 to 2009-2011. The average protein supply increased from 42 grams per person per day in 1990-1992 to 79 grams per person per day in 2009-2011. In a similar trend, the quantity of average animal protein rose from 8 grams per person per day in 1990-1992 to 32s gram per person per day in

Figure 9. Quantity of average supply of fat, protein and animal protein in Myanmar (averaged over 3 years)
FAO (2016)

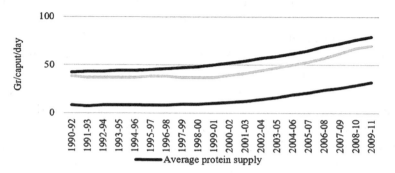

2009-2011. The average fat supply rose from 38 grams to 70 grams per person per day in the same years. According to this result, the supply of protein and fat presents no burden at the national level in Myanmar.

In comparing the average dietary energy supply adequacy of Myanmar with developed countries, developing countries, least developed countries and Asia, Myanmar's rising trend is significant in relation to the improvement of the least developing countries, as can be clearly seen in Figure 10. While Myanmar has improved its dietary energy supply sufficiently to move up and out of the least-

Figure 10. Average dietary energy supply adequacy (%) in terms of total calories in Myanmar
FAO (2016)

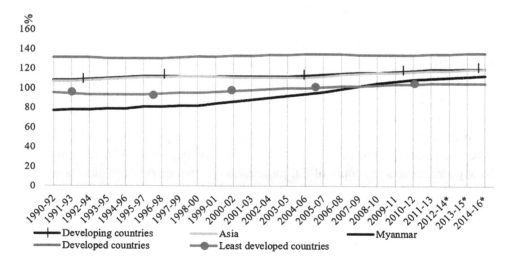

developing-country category, it still needs to improve its energy supply to reach the level of Asia and developing countries.

Interestingly, the percentage of energy derived from cereals, roots and tubers in the average dietary supply adequacy, as shown in Figure 11, has been declining slightly from 2002-2004. This may be interpreted not as a result of lower overall food production but because of increasing quantities of fat, protein and animal protein, as shown in Figure 9.

With the benefit of visualization from the FAO datasets, the state of food availability in Myanmar is quickly understandable. These data are not available from the open database of the Myanmar government sector, even though they have been reported inter-ministries and central government. As discussed earlier, this is one of the major obstacles to data availability and transparency in the country.

Visualization of Food Accessibility at National Level: Myanmar

Household food accessibility is problematic in Myanmar and it can be difficult for many families to secure their daily dietary needs. This indicator measures the quality and quantity of food that the family consume in their daily life. In addition, socio economic indicators such as the cost of food as a proportion of total expenditure, market performance and road infrastructure are important if we are to understand the problems of food accessibility (Food and Agriculture Organization [FAO], 2008a, 2008b, 2016).

Figure 11. Share of dietary energy supply derived from cereals, roots, and tubers in average dietary energy supply in Myanmar
FAO (2016)

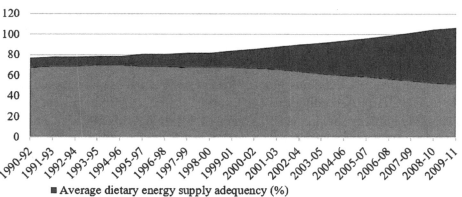

■ Average dietary energy supply adequency (%)
■ Share of dietary energy supply derived from cereals, roots and tubers (%)

Figure 12. Domestic food price level index in Myanmar
FAO (2016)

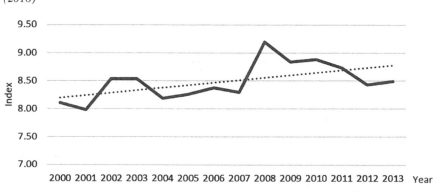

In the past, the cost of food as a proportion of total household expenditure could not be differentiated between rural and urban households in Myanmar. Thanks to big data, however, this difference can now be identified and analysed. The 2007 IHLCA survey found that national food expenditure is at a high rate of 73% of total expenditure. Food accounted for 76.3% of household expenditure in rural areas, compared to 66.3% in urban households. Poor households used 75.4% of total expenditure for food while the non-poor used a slightly smaller proportion of 72.6% (IDEA, & IHLCA. (2007). In this regard, the price of food is integral to accessing food for households. In Myanmar, the domestic food price trend is not stable, as shown in Figure 12.

The peak of domestic food costs in 2001-2003 reflect changes in market policy and the compulsory rice procurement system in Myanmar (Fujita, 2003; Kurosaki et al., 2004; Okamoto, 2009). Another spike in 2008 reflects increases in domestic food prices due to the negative impacts of the global food and oil crises on the Myanmar agriculture sector, principally higher food production costs (Hlaing et al., 2009). Thus, the fluctuation of domestic food price has associated with negative impacts to the affordable of food in rural households.

One of the most significant indicators of a household's dietary diversity (HDDS) is to measure its socioeconomic status. However, Myanmar has no national HDDS data (LIFT, 2016). According to a LIFT survey (LIFT, 2012), the lowest mean of HDD in Myanmar occurs in the Hill Region (4.80) and Rakhine State (4.74), while the Coastal Region and Dry Zone are at 5.45 and 6.28 respectively.

As discussed above, the published research and analysis of food security by researchers, practitioners, development organizations and donor agencies do help address the possible causes of and potential solutions to food insecurity in Myanmar. Although something is better than nothing, data users are still in great need of statistical analysis through modelling. Most importantly, statistical visualization is too undeveloped to give policy-makers, donors and development partners a quick overview of food insecurity and support the country's food security development program better. Interpreting Myanmar's open data and big data with visualization and relevant literature, the food security status of Myanmar can be noted as sufficient at the national level of food availability. However, it clearly shows the threats to food accessibility at household level.

The benefits of statistical literacy are well accepted and recognized worldwide as an important aspect of open and big data. In this regard, Myanmar policy makers need to consider the potential value of developing a time series visualization of food security, which does need a certain level of investment to develop a well-functioning food security open database system. Because most food security analysis begins with impact assessment, a major assumption and an economic model, these food security activities have been hindered by poor access to open data and limited data transparency on the part of the government. Such an analysis can be channelled directly to decision-makers and politicians to help them understand who are suffering the most from food shortages and where.

Poor data will continue to cause problems in many areas, from researchers and analysts all the way through to the highest-level decision makers. Poor quality data produces poor evidence and research results. Poor results lead to poor communication in terms of advice and guidance to policy makers, governments, NGOs, development agencies and donors, as well as to business leaders, and ultimately sub-optimal performance and failure to meet goals. The benefits of open data sources on infographics will give policymakers and politicians a visualized concept of the factors influencing food insecurity. Such visualized concepts will also help them to overcome the risks of food insecurity, such as resources allocation in both technical literacy and investment in food-deficit regions and the country as a whole. Visualization can become a powerful communication strategy to convey key messages about food security to decision-makers. It is a good strategic tool to educate and inform policy makers, guide food security investments, and provide a tool for monitoring and evaluating impacts.

CONCLUSION: OPPORTUNITIES AND CHALLENGES

Statistical literacy helps the decision making process to some extent, and gives development partners and donors better information with which to recognize the strengths and weakness of a current food security situation and from there to take necessary action and support the people. Food security policy objectives are positively associated with the causes of food insecurity in many households in relation to marketing policies, land policies, and cropping patterns, supported by sufficient investment in agriculture to stimulate the livelihoods of rural people in Myanmar. If insufficient investment and resources are put into the statistics and information database system, better policies and actions will never be developed in the country.

We have many opportunities in big data sites but we have many challenges as well. For example, there are three key challenges around big data currently. These are (1) possible risks from investing in data, understanding how the data will be driven and what its value is, (2) regulatory issues faced by customers in accessing and using big data, such as removing legal and technical barriers openness to accessing and using big, open data, and (3) conflicting interests between business and government over ownership and dissemination of big data via the interest. Data visualization is fundamental to understanding more about future trends of a business or industry. The application of data analysis supports the idea of key business drivers to improve weaknesses or change incorrect actions in existing programs (Samuel, n.d.). While the data itself is understandable, the data analysis adds value to the questions of what, why and how to overcome a problem and improve the business. The use of open data and big data is proliferating, governments are expanding their recognition of its many benefits, researchers and practitioners have more opportunities to use open data and the use of visualization is increasing. Thus, the opportunity to gain better understanding of food insecurity situations based on upgraded statistical data analysis tools for researchers and practitioners globally is extremely promising.

However, there are still many challenges to attaining ideal conditions of data availability and accessibility, such as transparency, integrity and accountability; these challenges continue to hinder researchers and practitioners as well as scholars and academia from finding out the root causes of, in this case, food insecurity in a particular nation or region in the world. In many research areas, the continuing problems that we face include the poor communication links between evidence gathered through research and investigation, and the influence of this evidence on policy makers, and guiding governments' and donors' investments. Visualization may become an important and powerful communication strategy to convey particularly complex concepts, such as causes of food insecurity, explaining findings, and recommending actions and investments. Thus visualization in this complex food security policy area becomes a very important strategic tool to educate and inform policy makers, guide good food security investments, and provide a tool for monitoring and evaluating impacts in a country, a region and the world as a whole.

REFERENCES

Alexa. (2017). *Site Overview: fao.org Traffic Statistics*. Alexa.

Bhutta, Z. A., Ahmed, T., Black, R. E., Cousens, S., Dewey, K., Giugliani, E., & Sachdev, H. et al. (2008). What works? Interventions for maternal and child undernutrition and survival. *Lancet, 371*(9610), 417–440. doi:10.1016/S0140-6736(07)61693-6 PMID:18206226

Black, R. E., Allen, L. H., Bhutta, Z. A., Caulfield, L. E., De Onis, M., Ezzati, M., & Rivera, J. et al. (2008). Maternal and child undernutrition: Global and regional exposures and health consequences. *Lancet, 371*(9608), 243–260. doi:10.1016/S0140-6736(07)61690-0 PMID:18207566

Byerlee, D. R., Kyaw, D., Thein, U. S., & Kham, L. S. (2014). *Agribusiness models for inclusive growth in Myanmar: Diagnosis and ways forward*. Michigan State University, Department of Agricultural, Food, and Resource Economics.

Central Statistical Organization. (2017, February 2). *Welcome to CSO Website: Provider of official statistics of Myanmar*. Retrieved from http://www.csostat.gov.mm/

Dangour, A. D., Hawkesworth, S., Shankar, B., Watson, L., Srinivasan, C. S., Morgan, E. H.,... Waage, J. (2013). Can nutrition be promoted through agriculture-led food price policies? A systematic review. *BMJ Open, 3*(6). doi: 10.1136/bmj.f370310.1136/bmjopen-2013-002937

Denning, G., Baroang, K., & Sandar, T. M. (2013). Rice Productivity Improvement in Myanmar: USAID. Michigan State University, Myanmar Development Resource Institute - Centre for Economic and Social Development (MDRI-CESD).

Food and Agriculture Organization. (1996). *Rome Declaration on World Food Security, World Food Summit*. Retrieved from http://www.fao.org/docrep/003/w3613e/w3613e00.HTM

Food and Agriculture Organization. (2006). *Food Security Policy Brief*. FAO.

Food and Agriculture Organization. (2008a). *E-Learning to meet the needs of agriculture and food security professionals*. Retrieved 28.07.2016, from Food and Agriculture Organization of the United Nations and European Unions: http://www.fao.org/elearning/#/elc/en/Course/FC

Food and Agriculture Organization. (2008b). *An Introduction to the Basic Concepts of Food Security*. EC - FAO Food Security Programme. Retrieved from www.foodsec.org/docs/concepts_guide.pdf

Food and Agriculture Organization. (2009). *Declaration of the World Summit on Food Security*. United Nations of Food and Agriculture Organization.

Food and Agriculture Organization, International Fund for Agricultural Development, & World Food Programme. (2015). The State of Food Insecurity in the World 2015. Meeting the 2015 international hunger targets: Taking stock of uneven progress. Rome: Food and Agriculture Organization of the United Nations, International Fund for Agricultural Development and World Food Programme.

Food and Agriculture Organization. (2016). *Food security indicators*. Retrieved 3.8.2016, from Food and Agriculture Organization of the United Nations, and other international organizations http://www.fao.org/economic/ess/ess-fs/ess-fadata/en/#. V6GrW6J5Lqk

Food and Agriculture Organization. (2017). *Statistics at FAO*. Retrieved from http://www.fao.org/statistics/en/

Food and Agriculture Organization / World Food Programme. (2009). *FAO/WFP Crop and Food Security Assessment Mission to Myanmar*. Rome: Food and Agriculture Organization of the United Nations and World Food Programme.

Food and Agriculture Organization / World Food Programme. (2016). *FAO/WFP Crop Food Security Assessment Mission to Myanmar*. Rome: Food and Agriculture Organization of the United Nations and World Food Programme.

Food and Agriculture Organization - Economic and Social Development Department. (2017). *Statistics*. Retrieved from http://www.fao.org/economic/ess/ess-home/ess-about/en/

Food and Agriculture Organization Statistics. (2017). *How many visit to FAOSTAT per month?* (T. C. Hlaing, Ed.). FAO.

Food Security Information Network. (2013a). Food Security Information Network. *Food Security Monitoring Bulletin*.

Food Security Information Network. (2013b). *Resilience Measurement.* Paper presented at the Technical Working Group Consultative Meeting, Rome, Italy.

Fujita, K. (2003). Policy-Initiated Expansion of Summer Rice under Constraints of Rural Credit in Myanmar in the 1990s -Perspectives from a Village Study in Ayeyarwaddy Division. The Economic Review, 54(4).

Ghattas, H., Barbour, J. M., Nord, M., Zurayk, R., & Sahyoun, N. R. (2013). Household food security is associated with agricultural livelihoods and diet quality in a marginalized community of rural Bedouins in Lebanon. *The Journal of Nutrition*, *143*(10), 1666–1671. doi:10.3945/jn.113.176388 PMID:23946340

Haggblade, S., & Boughton, D. (2013). *A Strategic Agricultural Sector and Food Security Diagnostic for Myanmar*. Michigan State University, Department of Agricultural, Food, and Resource Economics.

Haggblade, S., Boughton, D., Cho, K. M., Denning, G., Kloeppinger-Todd, R., Oo, Z., & Wilson, S. et al. (2014). Strategic Choices Shaping Agricultural Performance and Food Security in Myanmar. *Journal of International Affairs*, *67*(2), 55.

Hlaing, T. C., Kuwabara, T., Cuong, N. H., Bounnad, C., Kubo, T., & Ito, S. (2009). International Competitiveness in Rice Exports under High Oil Prices. 農業経営研究, *47*(2), 202-205.

Institute for Democracy and Electoral Assistance & Integrated Household Living Conditions Assistance. (2007). Integrated Household Living Conditions Assistance Survey in Myanmar: Poverty Profile. Yangon, Myanmar: IDEA International Institute (Canada), IHLCA Project Technical Unit, Ministry of National Planning and Economic Development (MNPED) and United Nations Development Program (UNDP).

Integrated Household Living Conditions Assistance. (2011). Integrated Household Living Conditions Assistance Survey in Myanmar (2009-2010) - Poverty Profile. Yangon, Myanmar: Ministry of National Planning and Economic Development (MNPED), Swedish International Development Cooperation Agency (SIDA), United Nations Children Emergency Fund (UNICEF) and United Nations Development Program (UNDP).

International Food Policy Research Institute. (2016). *Global Nutrition Report 2016: From Promise to Impact: Ending Malnutrition by 2030* [Press release]. Retrieved from http://ebrary.ifpri.org/utils/getfile/collection/p15738coll2/id/130354/filename/130565.pdf

Iram, U., & Butt, M. S. (2004). Determinants of household food security: An empirical analysis for Pakistan. *International Journal of Social Economics*, *31*(7/8), 753–766. doi:10.1108/03068290410546011

James, L. (2013). *Defining Open Data*. Retrieved from http://blog.okfn. org/2013/10/03/defining-open-data/

Jenkins, J. C., & Scanlan, S. J. (2001). Food security in less developed countries, 1970 to 1990. *American Sociological Review*, *66*(5), 718–744. doi:10.2307/3088955

Kakuta, S. (2016). Prospect of Open Data on Labor Division of Scientific Research. *MACRO REVIEW*, *28*(1), 39–41.

Kurosaki, T., Okamoto, I., Kurita, K., & Fujita, K. (2004). *Rich Periphery, Poor Center: Myanmar's Rural Economy under Partial Transition to a Market Economy*. Academic Press.

Kyaw, D. (2006). *Rural poverty analysis in Myanmar: a micro level study in the dry zone* (Ph. D. dissertation). School of Environment, Resources and Development, Asian Institute of Technology, Bangkok, Thailand.

Kyaw, D. (2009). Rural Households' Food Security Status and Coping Strategies to Food Insecurity in Myanmar. V.R.F. Series, Institute of Developing Economies, Japan External Trade Organization, 444, 83.

Kyaw, D., & Routray, J. K. (2006). Gender and rural poverty in Myanmar: A micro level study in the dry zone. *Journal of Agriculture and Rural Development in the Tropics and Subtropics*, *107*(2), 103–114.

Lassinantti, J. (2016). *Re-use of open data from public sector-Towards a definition*. Information Polity.

Livelihoods and Food Security Trust Fund. (2012). *Baseline survey results: July 2012*. Retrieved 16.8.2016, from Livelihoods and Food Security Trust Fund http://www.lift-fund.org/downloads/LIFT%20Baseline%20Survey%20Report%20-%20July%202012.pdf

Livelihoods and Food Security Trust Fund. (2016). Undernutrition in Myanmar, Part 1: A Secondary Analysis of LIFT 2013 Household Survey Data. In *Learn A Consortium of: Save the Children, ACF, Helen Keller International funded by Livelihoods and Food Security Trust Fund (Vol. 1): Livelihoods and Food Security Trust Fund*. Save the Children, ACF, Helen Keller International.

Mann, M. E. (2013). *The hockey stick and the climate wars: Dispatches from the front lines*. Columbia University Press. doi:10.7312/columbia/9780231152556.001.0001

Marr, B. (2016). *Big Data: 33 Brilliant And Free Data Sources For 2016*. Academic Press.

Mason, J. B. (2002). *Measuring hunger and malnutrition.* Paper presented at the International Scientific Symposium, Rome, Italy.

MIMU. (2014-2016). *Baseline Datasets-Myanmar Information Management Unit.* Retrieved 27.1.2017, from http://www.themimu.info/baseline-datasets

MMSIS. (2015). *Statistical Database: from Myanmar Statistical Information Service.* Retrieved from http://www.mmsis.gov.mm/

Muller, R. (2004). Global warming bombshell. *Technology Review, 15,* 14–15.

Myanmar Census 2014. (2015). *The 2014 Myanmar Population and Housing Census: The Union Report* (Vol. 2). Myanmar: Department of Population, Ministry of Immigration and Population.

Myanmar Times. (2016, December 9). *Myanmar is still the third-most malnourished country in Southeast Asia by ghatt WFP Myanmar.* Retrieved from http://www. mmtimes.com/index.php/national-news/18665-myanmar-is-still-the-third-most-malnourished-country-in-southeast-asia.html

Okamoto, I. (2009). Transformation of the Rice Marketing System after Market Liberalization in Myanmar. In K. Fujita, F. Mieno & I. Okamoto (Eds.), The economic transition in Myanmar after 1988: Market economy versus state control (Vol. 1, pp. 216-245). NUS Press associated by Kyoto University Press.

Oo, T. H. (2012). Devising a new agricultural strategy to enhance Myanmar's rural economy. In N. Cheesman, M. Skidmore, & T. Wilson (Eds.), *Myanmar's transition: Opening, obstacles and opportunities* (pp. 156–181). Singapore: Institute of Southeast Asian Studies.

Organization for Economic Cooperation and Development. (2016). *Open Government Data-Rebooting Public Service Delivery: How can open government data help to drive innovation? In OECD Comparative Study* (p. 26). OECD.

Planning Department. (2012). *Monthly Expenditure of Urban and Rural Households by State and Region.* Retrieved 15.09.2015, from Central Statistical Organization, Ministry of Planning and Finance: http://mmsis.gov.mm/statHtml/statHtml.do

Planning Department. (2014). *Statistical Data: Share of Gross Domestic Product (At Current Producers' Prices).* Retrieved 14.09.2015, from Central Statistical Organization, Ministry of Planning and Finance: http://mmsis.gov.mm/statHtml/statHtml.do

Rammohan, A., & Pritchard, B. (2014). The role of landholding as a determinant of food and nutrition insecurity in rural Myanmar. *World Development, 64*, 597–608. doi:10.1016/j.worlddev.2014.06.029

Rosegrant, M. W., & Cline, S. A. (2003). Global food security: Challenges and policies. *Science, 302*(5652), 1917–1919. doi:10.1126/science.1092958 PMID:14671289

Rosling, H. (2010). *Hans Rosling's 200 Countries, 200 Years, 4 Minutes*. Retrieved from https://www.youtube.com/watch?v=jbkSRLYSojo

Samuel, S. (n.d.). History of Data Visualization. *Data Visualization: What it is and why it matters*. Retrieved from http://www.sas.com/en_au/insights/big-data/data-visualization.html

Shaw, D. J. (2007). *World food security*. Academic Press.

Shwe, T. M., & Hlaing, T. C. (2011). *Scoping study on food security and nutrition information in Myanmar. National Consultant's Report of the Project: Support to the EC Programme on Linking Information and Decision-Making to Improve Food Security for Selected Greater Mekong Sub-Regional Countries*. Rome: FAO.

Statistical Analysis System. (n.d.). *Data Visualization: What it is and why it matters*. Retrieved from http://www.sas.com/en_au/insights/big-data/data-visualization.html

Tammisto, Y., & Lindman, J. (2012). *Definition of open data services in software business*. Paper presented at the International Conference of Software Business. doi:10.1007/978-3-642-30746-1_28

Ubaldi, B. (2013). Open Government Data: Towards Empirical Analysis of Open Government Data Initiatives. *OECD Working Papers on Public Governance, 22*.

US Department of Agriculture. (2016, August 22). *International Markets & Trade*. Retrieved 21 January 2017, from https://www.ers.usda.gov/topics/international-markets-trade/

US Department of Agriculture. (2017, January 25). *Data Products, Economic Research Service, United States Department of Agriculture*. Retrieved 21 January 2017, from https://www.ers.usda.gov/data-products/?topicId=0&sort=UpdateDate&sortdir=desc

Von Braun, J. (1992). *Improving food security of the poor: Concept, policy, and programs*. Intl Food Policy Res Inst.

Von Braun, J. (1993). *Urban food insecurity and malnutrition in developing countries: Trends, policies, and research implications*. Intl Food Policy Res Inst.

Wahlqvist, M. L., Keatinge, J. D. H., Butler, C. D., Friel, S., McKay, J., Easdown, W., & Li, D. et al. (2009). A Food in Health Security (FIHS) platform in the Asia-Pacific Region: The way forward. *Asia Pacific Journal of Clinical Nutrition, 18*(4), 688–702. PMID:19965367

World Bank. (2014). *Myanmar-Systematic Country Diagnostic: Ending poverty and boosting shared prosperity in a time of transition.* Washington, DC: World Bank Group.

World Food Programme. (2012). *WFP in Myanmar: Looking forward 2013-2017.* Yangon: World Food Programme, Myanmar. Retrieved from http://www.wfp.org/content/wfp-myanmar-looking-forward-2013-2017

Section 2
Using Big Data

Chapter 5

Teaching Visualisation in the Age of Big Data:
Adopting Old Approaches to Address New Challenges

Belinda A. Chiera
University of South Australia, Australia

Malgorzata W. Korolkiewicz
University of South Australia, Australia

ABSTRACT

Technological advances have led to increasingly more data becoming available, a phenomenon known as Big Data. The volume of Big Data is to the order of zettabytes, offering the promise of valuable insights with visualisation the key to unlocking these insights, however the size and variety of Big Data poses significant challenges. The fundamental principles behind tried-and-tested methods for visualising data are still as relevant as ever, although the emphasis necessarily shifts to why visualisation is being attempted. This chapter outlines the use of graph semiotics to build data visualisations for exploration and decision-making and the formulation of elementary, intermediate- and overall-level analytical questions. The public scanner database Dominick's Finer Foods, consisting of approximately 98 million observations, is used as a demonstrative case study. Common Big Data analytic tools (SAS, R and Python) are used to produce visualisations and exemplars of student work are presented, based on the outlined visualisation approach.

DOI: 10.4018/978-1-5225-2512-7.ch005

INTRODUCTION

Recent technological advances have led to data collection at a rate never seen before, from sources such as climate sensors, transaction records, social media and videos, to name a few. With the advent of *Big Data* come insights at a previously unseen depth and breadth of detail. Operational decisions are increasingly based on data rather than experience or intuition (McAfee & Brynjolfsson, 2012) and more broadly, a shift in perspective is under way on the relationship between data and knowledge generation (Ekbia et al, 2015).

Big Data is typically defined in terms of its *Variety*, *Velocity* and *Volume*. Variety refers to expanding the concept of data to include unstructured sources such as text, audio, video or click streams. Velocity is the speed at which data arrive and how frequently data change. Volume is the size of the data, which for Big Data runs to the order of petabytes (1000^5) through to zettabytes (1000^7).

Visualisation is a potentially valuable way to make sense of Big Data, to uncover features, trends or patterns to produce actionable analysis and provide deeper insight (SAS Institute Inc., 2014). There is an increased focus on visualisation over formal data analysis, partly due to the proliferation of easy-to-use web-based visualisation tools (e.g., Tableau Online), and partly due to an added emphasis on the power of well-designed visualisations and the demand for a new type of Big Data 'dataviz' analyst (McCosker, & Wilken, 2014). However, the opaque character of large data sets makes it difficult to describe in a systematic way how to effectively translate Big Data into visual or other kinds of knowledge. Furthermore, a 'black box' approach to generating data visualisations puts data analysts at risk of producing ornate and visually pleasing graphics that are otherwise useless.

The use of visualisation as a tool for data exploration and/or decision-making is not a new phenomenon. Data visualisation has long been an important component of data analysis, whether the intent is that of data exploration or as part of a model building exercise. However, the challenges underlying the visualisation of Big Data are still relatively new; often the choice to visualise is between simple graphics using a simple palette of colours to distinguish information or to present overly complicated but aesthetically pleasing graphics, which may obfuscate and distort key relationships between variables. Previous work in the literature suggests a tendency to approach Big Data by repeating analytical behaviours typically reserved for smaller, purpose-built data sets (e.g., Gelper, Wilms, & Croux 2015; Toro-Gonz´alez McCluskey, & Mittelhammer 2014; Huang, Fildes, & Soopramanien 2014). There appears, however, to be less emphasis on the exploration of Big Data itself to formulate questions that drive analysis.

In this chapter, a portable framework is proposed to arm aspiring visual analysts with tools to decide what is/is not useful when visualising Big Data. The target audience is working professionals seeking to expand or formalise their data analytics skills through postgraduate university study. Based on the authors' teaching experience in this context, introducing a framework for visualising Big Data through real-life case studies is advocated, instead of presenting students with an encyclopaedia of methods and graphical displays.

Despite the new challenges introduced by the emergence of Big Data, visualisation techniques themselves need not be new – *lessons from the past* in the form of tried-and-tested graphs can still be effective – however with a new way to perceive the data. This chapter adopts the seminal work of Bertin (1967) and extensions in Tufte (1983) in the field of *graph semiotics,* to explore and harness the scope of Big Data to formulate meaningful questions and drive analysis. To illustrate graph semiotics, the Dominick's Finer Foods (DFF) scanner database is used. Dominick's Finer Foods (DFF) is a Chicago supermarket chain and its scanner database is publicly available at https://research.chicagobooth.edu/kilts/marketing-databases/dominickscourtesy of James M. Kilts Center, University of Chicago Booth School of Business. The use of graph semiotics is further demonstrated to formulate three levels of questions from the supermarket database: elementary-, intermediate- and overall-level, before presenting conclusions.

There are many visualisation tools available; some come from established analytics software companies (e.g., Tableau, SAS or IBM), with others emerging as open source applications. For the purposes of visualisation in this chapter, SAS, R and Python form the focus, which together with Hadoop, are considered to be the key tools for Data Science (Oancea & Dragoecsu 2014).

GRAPH SEMIOTICS: A VISUALISATION METHODOLOGY FOR THE EXPLORATION OF BIG DATA

Issues, Controversies, Problems Arising From Visualising Big Data

The impetus underlying visualisation is the construction and/or answering of questions about the data. Survey results reported in Wang, Wang & Alexander (2015) indicated that improved decision making was the main motivation for visualisation (77% of respondents) as well as better ad-hoc data analysis (44% of respondents) and improved collaboration and information sharing (41% of respondents). Growing popularity plus wider recognition of the role of visualisation in decision making aside, a common problem of visualisation is the belief that all data need to be visualised or that only 'good' data should be visualised to support decision-making (Simon, 2014). Equally problematic is the myth of visualisation providing certainty in insight; visualisations can be manipulated leading to erroneous decision making processes (Simon, 2014).

Scalability and dynamics pose major obstacles to visualisation, as well as the high dimensionality of Big Data and the unstructured nature of the data itself, which are often captured in the form of graphs, tables and texts (Wang et al., 2015). Visualisation of Big Data is further challenged by visual noise in the data and the issue of large image perception, that is by actual physical perception limits – visualisation of every data point will lead to over-plotting and thus overwhelm the decision maker's perceptual and cognitive abilities (Gorodov & Gubarev, 2013), whereas over-simplification of the data can lead to information loss (Liu, Jiangz, & Heer, 2013). A solid set of principles to avoid such data distortion is required.

Bertin (1967) Approach to Visualisation and Its Extensions

It was suggested in Bertin (1967) that a question about data can be defined by its *type* and *level*, where it was claimed there are as many types of questions as components (variables) in the data. For example, in a data set containing two variables (date and stock price) there are two types of questions that can be posed: (1) *On a given date, what is the stock price?*; and (2) *For a given stock price, on what date(s) was it attained?* (Bertin, 1967).

The *level* of a question can be defined as:

1. **Elementary:** In an elementary-level question, the focus is on individual elements in the data (e.g., places, time snapshots or objects);
2. **Intermediate:** Intermediate-level questions focus on general aspects of the data over time and space, typically involving some, but not all of the data; or
3. **Overall:** Overall-level questions also focus on general aspects of the data over time and space, however all of the data are typically of interest.

It was further postulated in (Bertin, 1967) that there are at least as many types of questions as physical dimensions used to construct the graphic. Only data of a temporal nature was considered in Bertin (1967), however this work was extended to spatio-temporal data in Koussoulakou & Kraak (1995), where the distinction between question types can be independently applied to both the temporal and spatial data, thereby adding the concept of *dimension* to the graphic. Finally, MacEachren & Kraak (1997) extend the classification of questions asked of spatio-temporal data by *query,* namely *if* (existence), *when* (location in time), *how long* (duration), *how often* (temporal texture), *how fast* (rate of change), *what order* (sequence in the data) and the seventh focuses on grouping, by investigating which data points fall together.

Data visualisation embodies at least two distinct purposes: (1) to communicate information meaningfully; and (2) to 'solve a problem' (Bertin, 1967). It is suggested the latter purpose can be achieved by answering and/or postulating questions from data visualisation, as was the approach in the originating work (Bertin, 1967). In this same spirit, graph semiotics are adopted in this chapter and the visualisations contained therein. At the crux of graph semiotics are *retinal variables,* originally proposed by Bertin (1967) with extensions provided by MacKinley (1986). These variables are presented in Figure 1 by data type. The perceived accuracy of each retinal variable is also indicated, which can be used to make informed choices about data visualisation, rather than blindly rotating through a selection of visualisations. Note that not all retinal variables are applicable across all data types, however they are included for the sake of completion.

Each retinal variable can be explained as follows:

- **Position:** The position of graphing symbol relative to the axes;
- **Length:** The length of the graphing symbol;
- **Angle:** The mathematical angle of the plotted data;
- **Orientation:** The slope of the data;
- **Area:** The area of the plotting symbol;
- **Volume:** The volume of the plotting symbol;
- **Density:** The distance between plotted observations;
- **Colour Saturation:** Transparency levels of colour to highlight differences;
- **Colour Hue:** Shades of colour to highlight differences;

Figure 1. The retinal variables applied to data type for visualisation with accuracy as indicated. Starred items indicate retinal variables not relevant to the specific data type.

Perceived Accuracy	Quantitative Variables Discrete, Continuous		Qualitative Variables			
			Ordinal		Nominal	
Most Accurate	Position		Position		Position	
	Length		Density		Colour Hue	
	Angle		Colour Saturation		Texture	
	Orientation		Colour Hue		Connection	
	Area		Texture		Containment	
	Volume		Connection		Density	
	Density		Containment		Colour Saturation	
	Colour Saturation		Length		Shape	
	Colour Hue		Angle		Length	
	Texture*		Orientation		Angle	
	Connection*		Area		Orientation	
	Containment*		Volume		Area	
Least Accurate	Shape*		Shape*		Volume	

- **Texture:** Patterns used within the plotted shapes, typically used to distinguish between groups;
- **Containment:** A portion of the data that is grouped together (e.g., a pie wedge in a pie chart), which can be nested indicating a hierarchy;
- **Connection:** Connectivity between individual data points; and
- **Shape:** The graphic symbol used to represent the data.

The usefulness of the retinal variables was experimentally verified in subsequent research (Cleveland & McGill, 1984) and more recently (Wigdor, Shen, Forlines, & Balakrishnan,, 2007) with the ranking indicating the accuracy with which these variables was perceived, as shown in Figure 1. The variables Position and Size were the most accurately perceived whilst Shape was the least accurate, with the work extended to include qualitative data (Cleveland & McGill, 1984; MacKinley, 1986, Wigdor et al., 2007).

One other issue is the data set itself. While the focus of this chapter is on visualisation of data, it should be noted that data are rarely provided in a visualisation-ready format. Data management can, and often necessarily involves, cleaning and merging data from disparate sources by means of database-style merging and joining operations, as well as summarising data over merged frames or by groups of interest. However, given the volume and inconsistencies of Big Data, viewing the raw data to check validity is not possible. For this reason, pre-processing Big Data takes much forethought coupled with computer language skills.

The programming language *Python* is useful in this regard, specifically the built-in *Pandas* (PANel DAta Structures) library for data cleaning and merging. Python was chosen in the analysis that follows as it provides data structures that are amenable to large volumes of data and can be used for the fast removal of missing values, fast merging of database entries and slicing the data into smaller subsets, ready for visualisation and question formulation. Complementing this choice is the use of R and SAS for the visualisation itself.

BIG DATA: VISUALISATION FOR INSIGHT AND EXPLORATION

The concept of *dimension, type* and *level* of a question, as well as *query* type, combined with graph semiotics, is now demonstrated with the aid of the R and SAS programming languages and their respective visualisation libraries. A case study is adopted to provide an appropriate data set. The Dominick's Finer Foods (DFF) supermarket scanner database is used, courtesy of the James M. Kilts Center, University of Chicago Booth School of Business.

The DFF supermarket database contains data recorded weekly from September 1989 to May 1997, yielding approximately 98 million observations that are non-homogeneous in time with some missing records. The database is split into 60 files which are classified as either:

1. **General Files:** Capturing sales and store-level demographics; and
2. **Category-Specific:** For the different grocery items stocked, broadly defined across 29 categories. Each item category is defined across two files; the first contains product description information (name, size) for all brands contained within the item category. The second file contains information including weekly sales data such as *store, item price, units sold, total dollar sales.* In the visualisation that follows, a selection of supermarket items will be used.

A distinguishing characteristic of the DFF database is the classification of the stores according to price tier. Although product prices are set on a chain-wide basis, price variation occurs across the stores based on pricing strategies that best fit within each store's local market structure and competition level. Supermarkets in the DFF database are thus consigned to either the *low, medium* or *high* price tiers, while a fourth price tier, called the *CubFighter,* is assigned to those Dominick's Finer Foods stores located within close proximity and therefore in direct competition with a store from the alternative, competing supermarket called Cub Foods (Levy, Lee, Chen, Kauffman, & Bergen, 2011).

Adhering to the claim that questions can be asked by any combination of *dimension, type* and *level,* together with a *query,* the product of question *type* and *level* gives the minimum number of questions that can be asked to drive the data analytics along each *dimension* (temporal and/or spatial). Sample questions that can be asked of the DFF database along either *dimension* and across each *level*, are given in Table 1. The use of *query* is included naturally in these questions.

Although the approach outlined in Table 1 appears to support formulating questions of interest before visualisation of data, it is suggested that this approach can be reverse engineered so that questions can be drawn from rigorously produced visualisations, thereby guiding not just the decision-making process itself, but aiding the data analyst in understanding which questions could be asked in the first place.

As noted throughout, visualisation of elementary-level questions typically involves a single observation, providing focused insights. In Figure 2 the first of three examples of elementary level questions is depicted. Recalling there are at least as many types of questions as physical dimensions used to construct the plot (Bertin, 1967) and as the temporal dimension is fixed (week 103), this first visualisation focuses on the spatial domain. Thus sample questions could be: *What is the total volume of cheese profit in Store 5? or Which store has the maximum total dollar profit from selling*

Table 1. Sample questions based on type, level, dimension, and query, using the DFF database

Space	Elementary Level	Intermediate Level	Overall Level
Time			
Elementary Level	What is the profit from cheese sales at Store 81 in week 103?	At which stores is profit from cheese sales in excess of $5,000?	At which stores does the highest cheese profit occur in Week 103?
Intermediate Level	How does profit from cheese sales at Store 81 change between weeks 103 and 107?	At which stores does cheese sales profit exceed $5,000 between weeks 103 and 107?	At which stores does the highest cheese profit occur between weeks 103 and 107?
Overall Level	What is the trend in profit from cheese sales over the entire recorded period?	At which stores does cheese sales profit exceed $5,000 over the entire recorded period?	What is the trend in high cheese profits over the entire recorded period?

cheese? The former is a specific question requiring some level of knowledge of the database, whereas the latter is purely exploratory in spirit illustrating the reverse engineering of the process, helping the analyst to derive meaningful information from the database. In Figure 2, the answer to the generalised question, *Which store has the maximum total dollar profit from selling cheese in Week 103* is store 81, which is illustrated using the retinal variables *Position* (profit levels) and *Colour Hue* (maximum profit) over a selection of the stores. Note that the variable type plotted is quantitative only.

A second type of elementary-level question is depicted in the rainfall plot of Figure 3 using the retinal variable *Position*, while *Colour Hue* is used solely for aesthetic purposes. Adding the qualitative variable *Price Tier*, indicating the store classification, allows for elementary-level questions such as *Which Price Tier has the largest variability in cheese sales?* or *Which Price Tier sells the most cheese?* This plot type combines both quantitative and qualitative variables and focuses on the spatio-temporal dimensions of the data.

Visualising over all stores in the database, and increasing the number of components (variables) to include the quantitative variable *Zone*, capturing the Price Tier of each store is depicted in Figure 4 via a 100% stacked bar chart. The other variables of interest are cheese profit in each store over time, thus capturing two types of categorical information: *Year* and *Price Tier*. The retinal variables *Position* and *Colour* are used with the inherent temporal and spatial dimensions of the data (weekly profit over geographically disparate stores) to represent a quantitative variable (cheese profit) and two types of qualitative variables (ordinal and nominal). Thus questions can be formulated over either or both of these dimensions, e.g., *Which Price Tier had the*

Figure 2. Dot plot of cheese profit by store

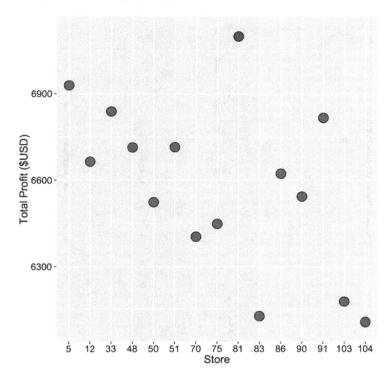

highest cheese profit? In 1992, in which Price Tier do stores attain the highest profit for cheese? In which year did stores in the "High" Price Tier see the lowest profit for cheese? As there are 3 types of components visualised (Weeks, Year, Cheese Profit) covering both temporal and spatial aspects of the data, there are a minimum of 3x2 or 6 questions that can be asked based on this single graphic.

Intermediate-level questions involve several items, thus while elementary-level questions are useful to provide quick, focused insights, intermediate-level questions can be used to reveal a larger amount of detail about the data. It is possible now to represent the interplay between specific and general information from the database. For example, possible questions to be asked include *product sales over a week* (temporal) or *the five stores with the highest weekly sales* (spatial). Figures 5 and 6 depict bubble plots which use the retinal variables *Position, Colour Hue, Shape, Density* and *Size* to represent profit and price (quantitative) by Price Tier (qualitative), where bubble size is directly proportional to product price. Questions can thus focus on quantitative variables, e.g. *Is there a relationship between cheese price and profit?* or on qualitative variables, e.g., *Is there a relationship between front-end candies prices and profits across price tiers?*

Figure 3. Rainfall plot of cheese by price tier

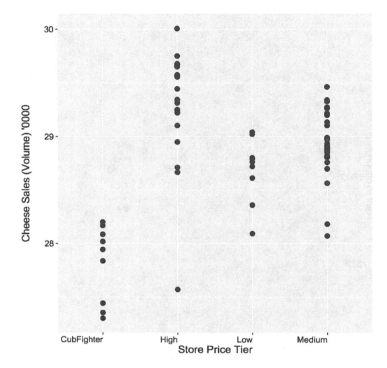

Figure 4. 100% stacked bar chart of cheese profit by price tier between 1991-1997

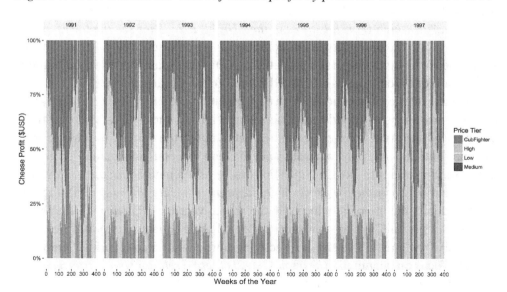

Figure 5. Bubble plot of cheese profit across the DFF supermarkets

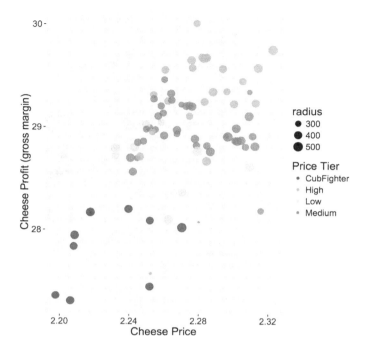

A cautionary tale echoing concerns raised in Simon (2014) demonstrates that not all plots are useful. An RDI (Raw data/Descriptive statistics/Inferential statistics) plot is presented in Figure 7 via a boxplot, capturing detailed information about Cheese and Cracker sales across Price Tiers. However much of this fine data detail is obscured by scale differences across the four price tiers, specifically the Medium price tier, thereby dwarfing this fine detail with variability in sales. Besides capturing this variability in the data, otherwise use of the boxplot in this case makes comparisons cumbersome. On the other hand, the butterfly plot of Figure 8 offers a variation on a simple bar chart by utilising an extra retinal variable — *Orientation* — and in doing so provides a more informative comparison of the average sales levels.

Overall-level questions focus on general trends across the data set as a whole (Bertin, 1967). Time series plots and other time-based plots are useful in this regard with smaller databases, however traditional time series plots often do not scale well in that they cause the issue of large image perception generated by over-plotting to overwhelm the decision maker's perceptual and cognitive abilities (Gorodov & Gubarev, 2013). Thus although it is possible to glean very general trends in this case, there is still an opportunity loss in that retinal variables are not being properly utilised to convey more subtle information.

Figure 6. Bubble plot of front-end candies profit across the DFF supermarkets

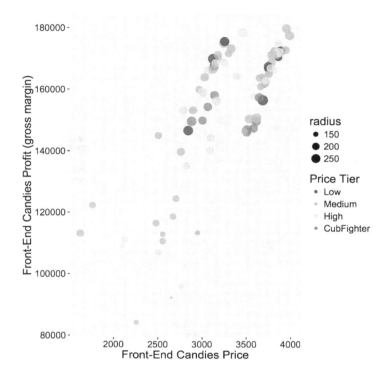

Figure 7. Box plot of cheese and cracker sales by price tier

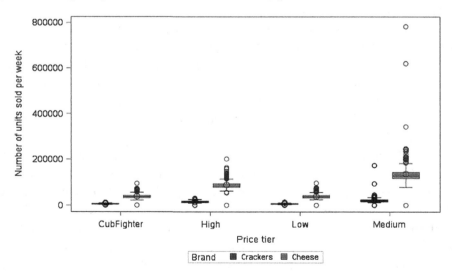

Figure 8. Butterfly plot of cheese and cracker sales by price tier (mean, in thousands)

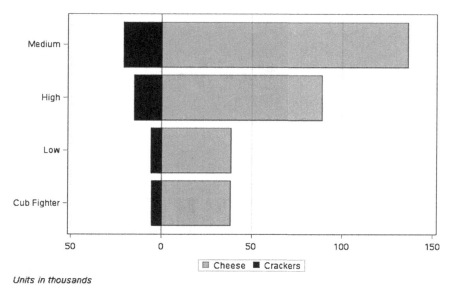

Units in thousands

An example of a plot capturing all relevant information is given in Figure 9, underscoring concerns raised in Gorodov & Gubarev (2013). However, through the addition of the retinal variables *Colour Hue* and *Containment,* the same data can be captured for informative insight (Figure 10) in a calendar heat map in which impressions of the information contained within the data can be easily and quickly gained. For example, questions such as *What is the general trend of cheese sales over time?* focusing on the temporal dimension of the data can be asked and answered.

Adding a qualitative variable extends the visualisation to a treemap (Figure 11). Treemaps are used to capture inherent hierarchy in the data and are automatically defined by four variables, two of which must be quantitative and two of which must be qualitative. With regards to retinal variables, *Size, Colour Hue, Colour Saturation* and *Containment* are required. The qualitative item of interest is used to form the containers (individual rectangles or 'tiles'), with the qualitative group to which the item belongs used to create separate areas in the map. One of the two quantitative variables is used to scale the size of each rectangle while the second quantitative variable assigns the colour hue to each container. The advantage of the treemap display is the easy intake of general patterns that would otherwise be obfuscated by data volume as in Figure 9.

In the example in Figure 11, a treemap of the front-end-candies data uses the qualitative variables Store and Price Tier and the quantitative variables Price and Profit. The identity of each rectangular container in the treemap uniquely corresponds

Figure 9. A plot of weekly cheese sales (number of units sold by store)

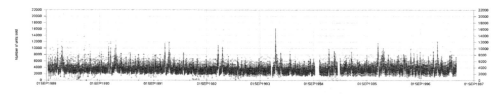

Figure 10. Calendar heat map of maximum weekly cheese profit

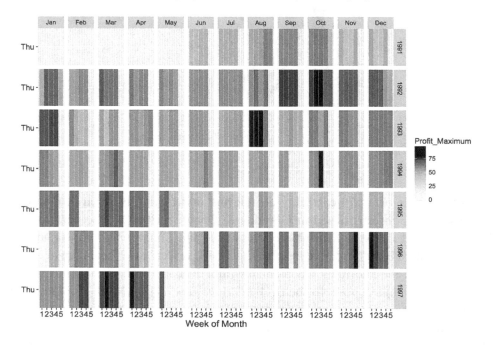

Figure 11. Treemap of front-end candies by price, movement, and price tier

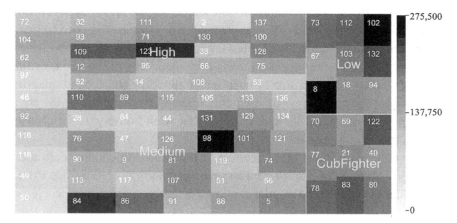

to a store while Price Tier is used to create groupings by dividing the map into four separate areas. The size of each tile corresponds to the price of front-end-candies at a given store, while the color hue represents the profit made by each store, with the minimum and maximum values indicated by the heat map legend. Thus while the price of front-end candies appears to be relatively uniform across all stores in each Price Tier, the colour variation indicates variability in buying patterns, e.g., stores in the Low and CubFighter Price Tiers. Questions postulated from a treemap include *Which stores are generating high profits? What is the relationship between front-end-candies prices and profit? Which price tiers make the largest profit selling front-end-candies? Do stores within a price tier set the price of front-end-candies consistently against one another?*

Figure 12 depicts another variation of a time series plot – the streamgraph. In Simon (2014) it was suggested that for the purpose of understanding large datasets, visualisation tools should be interactive to allow users another dimension through which to understand and extract insights from the data, as well as to provide the opportunity to iteratively improve questions asked of the data.

The streamgraph is one such example of an interactive plot, providing a variation of a time series plot by displaying changes in the data over time across different groups of interest. However, the streamgraph also has the added functionality of interactivity and in this case, the ability to depict the behaviour of multiple groups simultaneously. The size of each individual stream that makes up the streamgraph is proportional to the values in each group, with the x-axis dedicated to the time

Figure 12. Streamgraph of beer sales by store

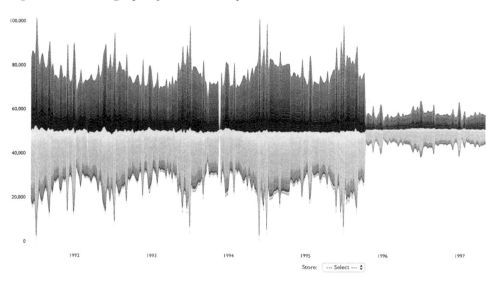

scale, as in a traditional time series plot. Streamgraphs are useful to uncover trends in Big Data as a large number of groups can be considered simultaneously, allowing the data analyst to discover peaks, troughs or shifts of interest in the data, as well as the existence of any periodic patterns.

Figure 12 shows a streamgraph of beer profit made in every store over the entire time period represented in the data set. In this case the retinal variables *Length*, *Orientation* and *Color Hue* are used to combine quantitative information (beer profit) with qualitative groups (stores). The streamgraph also adds interactivity, as indicated in Figure 12, in which a drop-down menu (labelled *Store* in Figure 12) allows for the selection of a single store. However, the drop-down menu is not the only means through which to single out data, or in this case, a store of interest. The streamgraph is also sensitive to cursor movements running over the graph, and will indicate in real time over which store the cursor is hovering. Figure 13 thus depicts the selection of Store 121 via the mouse cursor, a method which has the added benefit of providing not just the store identity, but the value of the beer profit made by Store 121 at that particular point in time. In Figure 13 this profit is $1,097 (USD) as indicated in the top left-hand corner of the graphic. Thus questions that can be asked about the data based on the streamgraph in Figure 12 include *What is the overall trend of beer prices? Does beer price behaviour change over time? Are there repetitive patterns to beer price behaviour?* Then, coupled with the retinal variable *Color Saturation* to select a store of interest, based on Figure 13, others questions include *What is the overall trend of beer prices at a particular store? Does*

Figure 13. Streamgraph of beer sales for store 121

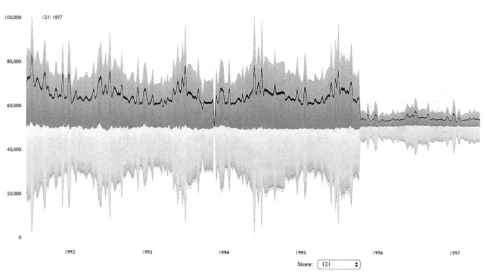

the trend of this store behave similarly to the overall pattern? and so forth, allowing for overall-level questions that compare specific item behavior (e.g., a store) with the overall trend in the data.

It is observed that the streamgraph is a prime example of a visualisation tool which while promising multiple benefits can, like the traditional time series plot, easily suffer from issues such as the large image perception problem (Gorodov & Gubarev, 2013) and over-simplification of the data (Liu et al., 2013). Specifically, categories with smaller values can be overshadowed by categories with larger values, nor is it possible to easily read the exact values visualised. However, unlike the traditional time series plot, the streamgraph provides an interactive component which overcomes, to some extent, these concerns and for this reason should be used interactively, rather than represented with a static image, to support and aid the exploration of overall trends contained within the data.

STUDENT EXEMPLARS: LESSONS FROM TEACHING PRACTICE

The principles presented within this chapter were applied in teaching practice at the postgraduate level. The postgraduate target audience was predominantly composed of working professionals with no or limited prior background in programming and/ or Statistics. Through coursework in which the students were taught Python, R, SAS and Statistics, students were encouraged to apply the principles presented in this chapter to visualise real-world Big Data collected and pre-processed by the students themselves. In this section exemplars of such student work are presented, across three different analytical tasks:

1. Mining blog posts by country, to classify the general emotions expressed by country, as part of the *We Feel Fine* project (http://wefeelfine.org/);
2. Illustrating the distribution of billionaires across the world, using the billionaire list published annually by Forbes magazine; and
3. Analysing iPhone passcodes using Benford's Law, to determine whether data are fraudulent.

The exemplar from the first task is shown in Figure 14 in which a student used the retinal variables *Size, Density* and *Colour Hue* to visualise a country's overall mood based on data mined from blog posts expressing a multitude of feelings, with brighter colours reflecting brighter moods and vice versa. To create the data set, students wrote a Python script to scrape blog posts across a selection of countries. The blog posts were then mined for words relating to feelings, which were compared to a pre-supplied list of emotions from the *We Feel Fine* project, to determine whether the mined word was to be included in the visualisation. In the exemplar shown the student produced bubble plots of the mined feelings, capturing both quantitative and qualitative information. Specifically, *Colour Hue* and *Density* were utilised to facilitate an easy comparison of the qualitative data (feelings) between countries while *Size* was used to represent the quantitative data, namely counts of each feeling expressed. The contrast between the frequency and mood of Australian blog posts versus those posted by individuals in Yemen was demonstrated, from which it was determined there were a larger variety of feelings expressed in Australian blog posts and the mood of these blog posts typically captured a happier tone with more positive emotions expressed.

In Figure 15, another student used *Size, Position and Colour* to visualise billionaire net worth and age (2014 data) across the world. While the data set used in this case would not be classified as 'Big Data' having less than 2000 records, it posed many of the challenges inherent in working with Big Data. The characteristics of the data that were most difficult to represent effectively were the large differences in the number and net worth of billionaires across different regions of the world. The student's choice to present the variables Age and NetWorth using a bubble plot with bubble sizes determined by the numbers of billionaires making the Forbes list in different regions, proved to be quite effective in highlighting regional similarities and differences.

The final exemplar presented here comes from an analysis of iPhone passcodes; a data set of actual iPhone passcodes augmented with computer-simulated passcodes and presented to students, with the challenge of determining whether the data were

Figure 14. A country's mood by blog post. In this exemplar, the student compared Australia and Yemen, producing plots using Python.

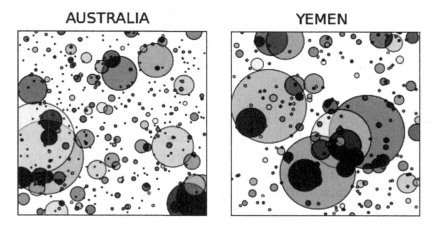

Figure 15. Male billionaires by region. Student exemplar produced using SAS.

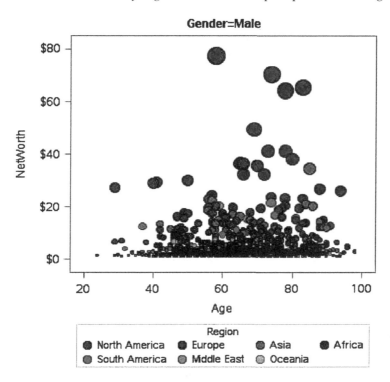

fraudulent. Students used Benford's law over the iPhone passcodes, computing the expected distribution of first numbers in the four-digit passcode and then comparing this expected distribution with the actual distribution of first numbers in the four-digit passcode. The result was presented as in Figure 16, showing the distribution of the numbers 1 to 9 in the aggregation of 204,432 four-digit iPhone passcodes. The student in this case used *Position, Size* and *Shape* to compare the computed with the actual distribution and based on the visualisation, correctly concluded the data were fraudulent. Based on the chosen visualisation the student was also able to indicate which digits were over- or under-represented in the iPhone passcode data set, providing justification for the conclusion that fraudulent activity had taken place. These exemplars illustrate the outcome of using newly developed computing skills, combined with graph semiotics, in support of deriving insights from Big Data without sacrificing too much of clarity and accuracy.

Figure 16. The distribution of the first digit of iPhone passcodes versus the expected distribution using Benford's Law. Student exemplar produced using R.

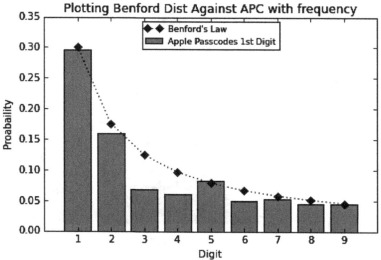

FUTURE RESEARCH DIRECTIONS

Visualisation is by no means a new area for consideration, however visualisation of Big Data is a new frontier in its own right that warrants further exploration. The principles that have guided visualisation thus far still hold for Big Data, in particular that: the chosen graphics should be appropriate for the data that is being visualised; data should not be distorted for the sake of an aesthetic image; and good visualisation supports the formulation of meaningful questions and/or insights about the data, however is not a substitute for rigorous data analysis.

However, while the tried-and-tested principles of visualisation provide a solid foundation for representing Big Data graphically, there is still a need for evolution in the current state-of-the-art. The call for interactive visualisation (Simon, 2014) marks an area for current and future exploration, which will likely become more widespread in use as visualisation software becomes more sophisticated. Irrespective of the sophistication of any graphics tool however, is the need for a systematic approach to support the art of visualising Big Data according to well-grounded statistical principles.

Another area of interest not explored in this chapter, but of value for future exploration, is the extension of the graph semiotics principles conveyed here to the visualisation of associated metadata of the variables. Visualising data about data has the power to potentially provide an information-rich representation of an even bigger amount of Big Data, increasing the power of the analyst to extract deeper, context-enriched insights from the data. However, such visualisation needs to be carefully balanced against the challenge of ensuring that the visual representation adheres to the basic principles of effective graphic display, to ensure the analyst and other users of the graphics are not overwhelmed by information.

Finally, while there is a hierarchy of effectiveness for representing variables in a visualisation (MacKinley, 1986), with the advent of Big Data and more recently, the move towards interactivity as a new component of visualisation, further formal testing of the effectiveness of the suggested ordering of the retinal variables, and the overall approach outlined here, would be beneficial. In particular, graph semiotics plays a role in the larger field of data visualisation and its associated visualisation vocabulary, which to date has been grounded in traditional (static) graphic representations of data. Given the nature and velocity at which Big Data arrives, allowing for interactive graphics that can be manipulated by the user, and/ or graphics updated in real time, suggests an opportunity to expand the visualisation vocabulary to harness this new potential in information representation.

CONCLUSION

Recent advances in the new age of Big Data have challenged the concept of data visualisation, due to its speed, size and diversity. In this chapter it was suggested that tried-and-tested techniques—*lessons from the past*—can be adopted for Big Data visualisation to drive the formulation of meaningful questions. Graphs and charts used to derive insights from data can effectively be those decision makers are accustomed to seeing—but a new way to look at the data is typically required. This chapter used graph semiotics to depict multiple characteristics of data through retinal variables, which drove the formulation of elementary-, intermediate- and overall-level questions. These techniques were applied using a case study based on Dominick's Finer Foods. Insights from Big Data were demonstrated with commonly-used visualisations, including exemplars of student work. By applying modern graphics to Big Data, with foundations still traceable to retinal variables (Bertin, 1967), lessons from the past were shown to support data visualisation in the future.

REFERENCES

Bertin, J. (1967). *Semiology of Graphics: Diagrams, Networks, Maps*. Madison, WI: The University of Wisconsin Press.

Cleveland, W. S., & McGill, R. (1984). Graphical perception: Theory, experimentation and application to the development of graphical methods. *Journal of the American Statistical Association, 79*(387), 531–554. doi:10.1080/01621459.1984.10478080

Ekbia, H., Mattioli, M., Kouper, I., Arave, G., Ghazinejad, A., Bowman, T., & Sugimoto, C. R. et al. (2015). Big data, bigger dilemmas: A critical review. *Journal of the Association for Information Science and Technology, 66*(8), 1523–1545. doi:10.1002/asi.23294

Gelper, S., Wilms, I., & Croux, C. (2015). Identifying demand effects in a large network of product categories. *Journal of Retailing, 92*(1), 25–39. doi:10.1016/j.jretai.2015.05.005

Gorodov, E. Y., & Gubarev, V. V. (2013). Analytical review of data visualization methods in application to big data. *Journal of Electrical and Computer Engineering, 2013*, 1–7. doi:10.1155/2013/969458

Huang, T., Fildes, R., & Soopramanien, D. (2014). The value of competitive information in forecasting FMCG retail product sales and the variable selection problem. *European Journal of Operational Research, 237*(2), 738–748. doi:10.1016/j.ejor.2014.02.022

Koussoulakou, A., & Kraak, M. J. (1995). Spatio-temporal maps and cartographic communication. *The Cartographic Journal, 29*(2), 101–108. doi:10.1179/caj.1992.29.2.101

Levy, D., Lee, D., Chen, H., Kauffman, R. J., & Bergen, M. (2011). Price points and price rigidity. *The Review of Economics and Statistics, 93*(4), 1417–1431. doi:10.1162/REST_a_00178

Liu, Z., Jiangz, B., & Heer, J. (2013). imMens: Real-time Visual Querying of Big Data. *Eurographics Conference on Visualization (EuroVis), 32*(3), 421-430. doi:10.1111/cgf.12129

MacEachren, A. M., & Kraak, M. J. (1997). Exploratory cartographic visualization: Advancing the agenda. *Computers & Geosciences, 23*(4), 335–343. doi:10.1016/S0098-3004(97)00018-6

Mackinlay, J. (1986). Automating the design of graphical presentations of relational information. *ACM Transactions on Graphics, 5*(2), 110–141. doi:10.1145/22949.22950

McAfee, A., & Brynjolfsson, E. (2012). Big data: The management revolution. *Harvard Business Review, 90*(10), 60–68. PMID:23074865

McCosker, A., & Wilken, R. (2014). Rethinking big data as visual knowledge: The sublime and the diagrammatic in data visualisation. *Visual Studies, 29*(2), 155–164. doi:10.1080/1472586X.2014.887268

Oancea, B., & Dragoecsu, R. M. (2014). Integrating R and Hadoop for big data analysis. *Revista Romana de Statistica, 2*(62), 83–94.

SAS Institute Inc. (2014). *Data visualization techniques: From basics to big data with SAS Visual Analytics* [White Paper]. Retrieved 14 November 2016 from http://www.sas.com/content/ dam/SAS/en_us/doc/whitepaper1/data-visualization-techniques-106006.pdf

Simon, P. (2014). *The visual organization: Data visualization, big data, and the quest for better decisions*. Wiley.

Toro-Gonz'alez, D., McCluskey, J. J., & Mittelhammer, R. C. (2014). Beer snobs do exist: Estimation of beer demand by type. *Journal of Agricultural and Resource Economics, 39*(2), 1–14.

Tufte, E. R. (1983). *The visual display of quantitative information*. Cheshire, CT: Graphics Press.

Wang, L., Wang, G., & Alexander, C. A. (2015). Big data and visualization: Methods, challenges and technology progress. *Digital Technologies, 1*(1), 33–38.

Wigdor, D., Shen, C., Forlines, C., & Balakrishnan, R. (2007). Perception of elementary graphical elements in tabletop and multi-surface environments. In *CHI '07: Proceedings of the SIGCHI conference on Human factors in computing systems*. New York, NY: ACM Publications. doi:10.1145/1240624.1240701

Chapter 6
Comparison of Graduates' and Academics' Perceptions of the Skills Required for Big Data Analysis:
Statistics Education in the Age of Big Data

Busayasachee Puang-Ngern
Macquarie University, Australia

Ayse A. Bilgin
Macquarie University, Australia

Timothy J. Kyng
Macquarie University, Australia

ABSTRACT

There is currently a shortage of graduates with the necessary skills for jobs in data analytics and "Big Data". Recently many new university degrees have been created to address the skills gap, but they are mostly computer science based with little coverage of statistics. In this chapter, the perceptions of graduates and academics about the types of expertise and the types of software skills required for this field are documented based on two online surveys in Australia and New Zealand. The results showed that Statistical Analysis and Statistical Software Skills were the most necessary type of expertise required. Graduates in industry identified SQL as the most necessary software skill while academics teaching in relevant disciplines identified R programming as the most necessary software skill for Big Data analysis. The authors recommend multidisciplinary degrees where the appropriate combination of skills in statistics and computing can be provided for future graduates.

DOI: 10.4018/978-1-5225-2512-7.ch006

INTRODUCTION

Nobody can imagine a part of the developed world where more than half of the population is illiterate. In the developing world there might still be small pockets of the population who would benefit from learning to read and write, although they would be a minority. What about numerical and statistical literacy? Unfortunately, even in the developed world, we cannot be so confident as to say that people with numerical skills and statistical literacy are the majority (OECD, 2016, p.13). The need to educate people on statistical skills and literacy has been becoming more urgent with advent of the "Big Data" era, especially where most of the educators of the "Big Data" users and analysts are from computer science departments.

Around the world, there is an explosion of "data science" and "Big Data" degrees which were initiated by computer science departments who may lack the expertise to provide statistical literacy and statistical knowledge to future data scientists. Most Australian universities offer degree programs at both undergraduate and postgraduate level in mathematics, statistics, and computer science, however there does not seem to be a good example of collaboration between these three disciplines to educate future data scientists who would be dealing with "Big Data" analysis (Kyng, Bilgin, & Puang-Ngern, 2016; Puang-Ngern, 2015). Unfortunately the need to collaborate is not obvious to either the majority of the computer science academics or to the majority of the statistics academics. The authors argue that computer science academics believe that data science is all about computing. The structure of currently available data science degrees (which have subjects mainly offered by computer science departments) is a manifestation of what they think data science is, such that these degrees do not have as much statistics as needed for data scientists. The authors also argue that the majority of the statistics academics prefer to ignore data science with the expectation that "data science" is a temporary fad and a rebadging of statistical science by IT professionals which will go away soon. The miniscule number of presentations related to data science in the international statistics education conferences since 2010 is an indication of this ignorance. There were zero in ICOTS 8 (2010) and in IASE satellite (2011 and 2013); one in IASE roundtable (Finzer, 2012); five in ICOTS 9 (Kudo et al., 2014; Ridgway et al., 2014; McNamara & Hansen, 2014; Kaplan et al., 2014; Horton et al., 2014); one in IASE satellite (Kyng et al., 2015) and three in the last IASE roundtable (Schwab-McCoy, 2016; Gould, 2016; Bergen, 2016). These conferences are well attended by the statistics education community and influence the ideas of many attendees. The limited number of presentations during these conferences on data science/Big Data is an indication of the lack of interest in data science by statistics educators.

For a recent talk (10th March 2015) to the Statistics Society of New South Wales (Australia), Professor Thomas Lumley of the University of Auckland (New Zealand) wrote "Mainstream statistics ignored computing for many years ..... Practical estimation of conditional probabilities and conditional distributions in large data sets was often left to computer science and informatics. Although statistics started behind, we are catching up: many individual statisticians and some statistics departments are taking computing seriously. More importantly, applied statistics has a long tradition of understanding how to formulate questions: large-scale empirical data can tell you a lot of things, but not what your question is. Big Data are not only Big but Complex, Messy, Badly Sampled, and Creepy. These are problems that statistics has thought about for some time, so we have the opportunity to take all the shiny computing technology that other people have developed and use it to re-establish statistics at the centre of data science". Glance (2013) also pointed out that a combination of computational, statistical and mathematical skills are required in Big Data analysis and data visualization. It is clear that expertise in one discipline is not enough.

There is anecdotal evidence and reported personal views, especially by computer scientists, regarding the required skills for the data science workforce (Song & Zhu, 2015), however there does not seem to be any research in the literature which incorporates current workforce perceptions and academic perceptions of this important emerging new industry required job – "data scientist"—and its relevance to statistics education. Admittedly, computer science departments are investing time and resources into Big Data and data science research and developing degrees (McAfee et al., 2012). In the business world, the importance of data scientists and evidence-based decision making is well recognized. It is even advertised as *"The Sexiest Job of the 21st Century"* (Davenport & Patil, 2012). However statistics educators also need to provide input to identify the skills required for data scientists and contribute to the literature in this field (ASA, 2014). The aims of this chapter are to identify the important areas of both generic expertise and specific software skills required to equip graduates for work in the data science/Big Data field, to compare the perceptions of academics and graduates in industry about these issues, and to better inform curriculum design in universities.

BACKGROUND

In the past, gathering data to analyze was costly and time consuming. Surveys had to be carefully designed; the sampling methodology had to be developed to achieve a representative sample of the population studied so that bias was eliminated, if possible. Also in the past, statistics and computing education were closely tied to mathematics education. Until relatively recently many statistical calculations were done by hand and tables of statistical distributions were used for application of statistical theory, which might still be the case for some (Bilgin et al., 2014). University statistics degree programs tended to focus on mathematical statistical theory rather than application, even for non-statisticians such as social scientists and engineers who were studying statistics to apply it in their own area. With the adoption of statistical software, statistics education slowly became more applied for both non-statistics majors and statistics majors than was the case two decades ago.

Nowadays, in the world of information technology, data collection and generation is pervasive. Data about people are recorded from many different sources including customer contact centers, customer loyalty cards, websites and social media such as Google, Facebook, and LinkedIn. Facebook is the best face recognition platform (Anthony, 2014), even better than the FBI's face recognition software (85% accuracy versus 98% accuracy) (LaChance, 2016). Many industry studies have reported significant growth in data storage, as well as in jobs related to data analytics, and Big Data analysis. Ninety percent of global data has been generated over the last two years (Bradshaw, 2013; Trondheim, 2013). Moreover, the world's data is predicted to experience forty percent growth per year (Manyika et al., 2011). There are billions to trillions of records about millions of people. The Computer Age, or Information Age in respect to technology is transforming society into the Big Data era due to the massive and rapid growth in data collection and storage (Boyd & Crawford, 2011; Brown, Chui, & Manyika, 2011; McAfee & Brynjolfsson, 2012; Zikopoulos et al., 2011). There is a flood of data being collected and available for analysis, which makes sampling a lesser issue, however the quality of the data collected is often poor and not subject to quality control. So there may now be a very large volume of data but much of it may be of low quality.

Statistics education and computer science education are also changing. The increasing capabilities and importance of statistical software facilitates the development of new statistical methods such as bootstrapping and makes other methods such as Generalized Linear Models (GLMs) practical to use whereas in the past this wasn't the case. Software has and is revolutionizing the discipline of statistics and not just in the Big Data / data science field but in traditional application of statistical methods. In particular, free open source software such as R and packages developed for it facilitates the availability and usage of both traditional and new statistical methods for both experienced statistical practitioners and recent graduates at minimal cost to employers. r

The focus on the mathematical approach to statistics education is limiting the available time to cover required software skills which might need to be reduced to make space in degree programs for students to learn more about software and software skills. There is still a need to educate students heading for a career in data science about mathematics and statistical theory in addition to computer science. A multidisciplinary approach to their education will enable them to have skills to develop new algorithms, theories and applications for statistics and computing. However theory-based work is likely to be a specialist role for statisticians and computer scientists, not for data scientists who seek employment in industry. Undoubtedly it is good for graduates to be equipped with the skills to understand the theory behind what they do as well as being able to do the statistical analysis and use the software tools required, however due to time pressures in the degree programs, it is difficult to teach everyone every skill in a multidisciplinary degree. After all only a small number of people is needed to discover/innovate new statistical methods but many people are needed to apply/use the discovery/innovation to enable larger benefits to society. The wireless network is a good example of that, a small group created it, many learnt to install it and then many more benefitted from it. Therefore educating graduates to be statistically literate regardless of which area they are going to work on has crucial importance for society. In today's workforce, professionals with skills in data analysis and computing are highly valued, and sought after because the volume of data being collected is huge, and the capacity to analyse the data is limited. The number of people with the right skills in statistical analysis and computing who could work in Big Data fields is limited relative to the demand for them.

The term 'Big Data' is believed to have originated from Silicon Graphics, a big computer graphic company, in the middle of the 1990s and was made noteworthy by John Mashey (Diebold, 2012; Lohr, 2013). There is no single agreed definition of *"statistics"*, therefore it is not surprising that there is no single universally agreed definition of *"Big Data"* either (DeMauro et al., 2016). It can be argued that "big" is a relative word. In the 19th century, statisticians had "big" data sets when the number of observations approached 100 with a handful of variables, since they analyzed the data without computers or user friendly software tools. Recently, Big Data refers to data sets that contain a huge volume of diverse and complex data. They are difficult to process and analyze using traditional statistical techniques and ordinary database tools. Big Data refers not only to the volume of data, but also to the technology (including tools and processes) required to access, store and analyze the data (Manyika et al., 2011). Hurwitz et al. (2013) proposed that Big Data is the capability to manage and analyze these data at the appropriate velocity within a suitable time frame that allows for reasonable reaction to events on a real-time basis.

An expansion of Big Data has led to an increased number of job opportunities. Gartner (2015) forecasted that the growth in Big Data will produce 4.4 million IT jobs globally. Bradshaw (2013) also stated that for each new IT job created there will be three new non-IT positions which require analytical skills to analyze and extract useful information from this massive volume of data. The McKinsey Global Institute (Manyika et al., 2011) forecasted a shortage of 1.5 million data-savvy managers with proficiency in effective decision making using Big Data analysis. The demand for graduates with the right skills and experience is growing exponentially with the increased demand for evidence based decision making in industry (ASA, 2014).

Most Australian Universities offer degree programs in statistics, computer science, mathematics, information technology, information systems, and engineering. Graduates with these university qualifications have been the essential source of entry level employees in the Big Data field in Australia. However the required combination of computational, statistical, mathematical skills and data visualization (Glance, 2013) are rarely part of a standalone degree program. Data scientists would benefit from obtaining a degree with a combination of the different disciplines, such as mathematics, statistics and computer science.

The Occupational Information Network (O*NET), which was developed under the sponsorship of the US Department of Labor/Employment and Training Administration, lists three domains for the required knowledge for statisticians (O*Net, 2016). These three domains are mathematics, including knowledge of arithmetic, algebra, geometry, calculus, statistics, and their applications; computers and electronics, including knowledge of circuit boards, processors, chips, electronic equipment, and computer hardware and software, including applications and programming; and English language, including knowledge of the structure and content of the English language, including the meaning and spelling of words, rules of composition, and grammar. There is no occupation in this network named "data scientist", however there are various occupations listed under data scientist which include computer and information research scientists; statisticians; computer systems analysts; mathematicians and software developers, systems software (Figure 1). It is clear that there are more computer science oriented positions than statistics oriented positions, however could this be related to who is teaching data scientists?

This chapter examines the existence of a (hypothesized) mismatch between the demands of industry and government for appropriately trained people to work as data scientists and the supply of such people, particularly in Australia, by universities. The authors specifically report the perceived missing required computational skills and the perceived required type of expertise (e.g., statistical analysis and statistical software skills, programming) for mathematics, statistics and computing graduates who would have better employability if their educators (universities) implement modified courses in the future.

MAIN FOCUS OF THE CHAPTER

The main focus of this chapter is to document what is missing from the university degree programs in data science and provide guidance for academic statisticians in general, and not just those who specialize in statistical education which is a subset

Figure 1. O*NET data science search results

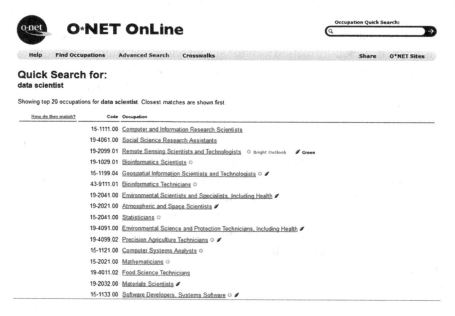

of the academic statistical community, about how the statistics discipline should respond to the new discipline of data science. The authors would like an awakening in the academic statistical community so that they are aware of the developments in Big Data field, the need to respond and to take seriously the implications of data science education being dominated by computer science departments.

Analysis of data has been central to statistics education since the establishment of the discipline but recently this has become of great interest to computer scientists, with new hardware and software being developed to automate and extend our ability to analyse and process data. There seemed to be an unspoken agreement between statisticians and computer scientists for so long in which computer scientists developed software tools to enable storage, retrieval and analysis of the data, and statisticians developed algorithms for data analysis and applied these algorithms to real data. Recently, this implicit agreement seems to have broken down, and computer scientists are claiming to be experts in data analysis ("data scientists") without proper knowledge of the work already developed by the statistical community, without statistical literacy or statistical thinking. Many statistics educators are ignorant of the fact that this is happening. They see data science as another fad or buzz word and expect that it will go away if they ignore it.

The authors would like to warn the academic statistical community and make them aware of the threat posed by complacency in the circumstances that currently apply. "Data scientists" are now being hired for many jobs that once were for statisticians. Many of our graduates are now getting jobs in "data science" and they are learning to use the various software tools and packages in the workplace, despite our graduates having no formal training as "data scientists". However many of the new data science degrees are "owned" by computer science departments and the way they teach their students may make it inaccessible for our students. We should be teaching data science skills to our statistics students in a way that makes it accessible to them, and not vacate the field to let it be taken over by our computer science colleagues and graduates.

METHODOLOGY AND DATA COLLECTION

The ethical aspects of this study were approved by the Macquarie University Human Research Ethics Committee (Reference No: 5201400282). Participation in the study was entirely voluntary and anonymous. To be able to reach many participants, online surveys were created using the Qualtrics Surveys software (https://mqedu.qualtrics. com/ControlPanel/). The authors planned to conduct a two-stage study. The first stage was an online survey, and the results of it are reported in this chapter. The second stage is semi-structured interviews and this will be reported in later publications.

Two groups of participants in Australia and New Zealand were surveyed. The first group was academics in targeted relevant departments. For the academic workforce an invitation to participate to the study was sent to all academics who can be identified in 39 Australian and 8 New Zealand universities by using their public web pages within the statistics, computer science, actuarial science, information systems, information technology, mathematics and marketing departments in 2014. The second group was graduates in the data analytics work force. The authors identified the population of the workforce as the cohort of people working in data science jobs who graduated between 2003 and 2014 in statistics, computer science, actuarial science, information technology and mathematics disciplines. There is no easy way to identify graduates working in Big Data analytics, unlike the academics where they can be easily identified via information available on the web pages of the universities. Accordingly therefore the authors used snowball sampling for the graduate survey to be able to access a larger number and wider range of graduates starting with the graduates from two Australian universities.

A sample of job advertisements for data science / data analytics jobs was analysed, as well as semi-structured discussions with recent graduates who were currently working in the industry and with academics in our professional networks. This was used to identify which skills and software tools would be relevant for inclusion in the surveys. Ten skills were identified based on these discussions and analysis and these ten skills were: Statistical Analysis and Software Skills, Statistical Learning, Mathematics, Data mining, Machine learning, Artificial Intelligence, Programming, Marketing, Business Analysis and Accounting. In addition the following seventeen software tools were identified as relevant for inclusion in the surveys: Base SAS, SAS Enterprise Miner, SPSS Analytics, SPSS Modeler, WinBUGS, Matlab, R, Java, VBA, Hadoop, MapReduce, noSQL, SQL, JaQL, Hive, Oracle, and Python.

Surveys

The questionnaires for the academics and graduates were designed separately for each group but the topics addressed in both questionnaires were quite similar to facilitate comparison between academics' and graduates' perspectives, and identify similarities and differences between their perspectives. Some questions required selecting a rating from "strongly agree" to "strongly disagree" using a five point Likert scale for various statements or options. Both surveys had two questions on generic skills, expertise required for employment in the Big Data / data science field (see Appendix, Figures 5 and 6), two questions on software tools and skills, four questions on demographics of the participants and their experience in the Big Data field. One open-ended question in both surveys was included for additional comments. Pilot surveys for both questionnaires were undertaken and this guided us to revise some of the questions.

The academic survey had sixteen questions while the graduate survey had twenty-one questions. In addition to the questions common to both surveys, the academic survey had seven questions regarding the workplace, their University, faculty, and department, as well as their working experience in the Big Data field; and five questions relating to the degree programs and subjects offered in participants' departments that are relevant to Big Data / data analytics/ data science, such as Machine Learning, Statistical Learning, Data Mining, and Statistical Analysis as well as the number of students graduating from their departments and the number of students enrolled in those relevant subjects each year. Similarly the graduate survey had extra questions related to participants' education (four questions), their workplace information (6 questions) and their opinions about the graduates employed in Big Data / data analytics roles (3 questions).

Participants

The academics' email addresses from 39 Australian and 8 New Zealand universities' websites were collected during the period April - May 2014. The target group was academics in the Statistics, Computer Science, Actuarial Science, Information Systems, Information Technology, Mathematics, and Marketing disciplines. In total, there were 127 potential university departments in Australian universities and 31 for New Zealand universities. Moreover, there were responses from 5 university departments in the United Kingdom, Austria, Canada, and the United States. From 163 university departments sampled, there were 62 university departments that responded. The response rate for the university departments was 38%.

The email list of prospective participants for the graduate survey was gathered from two Australian universities: Macquarie University and Western Sydney University. The graduates in our list included people who graduated between 2003 and 2014 with one of the following qualifications: Bachelor degree, Postgraduate Certificate, Postgraduate Diploma, and/or Master degree. Current Master's degree students were also included since majority of them are working and undertaking their studies concurrent to their day jobs. The target disciplines were: Statistics, Computer Science, Actuarial Science, Information Technology, and Mathematics. 442 invitations to graduates were sent out and these asked them to forward the invitation to people who they think would be in the target population (e.g., their work colleagues and other). 48 responses were received for the graduate survey. Although it is impossible to calculate a response rate for snowball sampling because the number of invitees are unknown, if the initial invitees are taken as if the total invited people, the response rate for the graduate survey would have been considered to be equal to 10.86% (48/442).

RESULTS

In this chapter the survey results about the required skills and software tools/skills are presented. Detailed analysis of the results about various groups of academics and graduates are also documented.

Perceptions of Skills Required for the Big Data Workforce

Academics were asked their opinion about the types of expertise that are required for graduates working in the Big Data field and whether or not students acquire such expertise in this area during their studies. Similarly graduates were asked their opinions about the type of expertise required to work with Big Data and whether or not they have this expertise. The average ratings of graduates and of academics were close to each other for all skills listed in the survey, suggesting strong consistency between academics' and graduates' views on the required types of expertise (Figure 2). Both academics (86%) and graduates (86%) consistently rated Statistical Analysis and Statistical Software Skills as the most necessary type of expertise required for working in the Big Data field (Agree and Strongly Agree combined). Almost half

Figure 2. The average ratings of expertise required for Big Data analytics

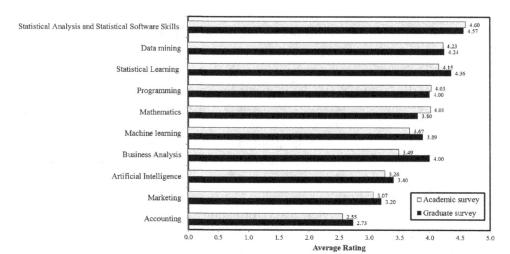

(47%) of the academic respondents stated that graduates had already been trained in these skills at university and 51% of the graduates agreed that they had these skills. Data Mining, Statistical Learning and Programming were the second, third and fourth most valued skills although the rankings were slightly different for the academics and for the graduates. Mathematics was the fifth ranking skill identified by the academics but not by the graduates, who suggested Business Analysis for the fifth place. The only category of expertise that was rated as not important for working in the Big Data workforce was Accounting which had the lowest ratings overall for both groups of participants.

Table 1 presents the results for graduate participants about the perceived importance of skills based on the disciplines they completed their studies in, while Table 2 presents the results for academic participants about the perceived importance of skills based on the disciplines they work in. The tables show the pattern of perceived importance of skills and how it varies by discipline. The importance of Statistical Analysis and Statistical Software Skills is rated highly by academics in business and statistics disciplines. Academics and graduates in the computing discipline rated the importance of the Statistical skills lower than academics and graduates from other disciplines did. Could that be because they are unable to judge the importance (unknown unknowns)?

Data mining was rated higher by academics in computing and marketing than by academics from other areas. Graduates from the statistics discipline gave a higher rating for data mining skills than did graduates from other disciplines and rated it almost as important as skills in statistical analysis / statistical software, whereas

Table 1. The average ratings of required skills for big data analytics, grouped by graduates' disciplines

Type of expertise	Graduate														
	Statistics			Computing			Business			Marketing			Other		
	AR	SE	SS	AR	SE	SS	AR	SE	SS	AR	SE	SS	AR	SE	SS
Statistical Analysis and Statistical Software Skills	4.73	0.12	15	4.20	0.25	10	4.85	0.10	13	4.00	0.58	3	4.40	0.40	5
Data mining	4.71	0.13	14	3.80	0.42	10	4.54	0.22	13	2.67	0.88	3	4.00	0.55	5
Statistical Learning	4.53	0.17	15	3.80	0.39	10	4.69	0.13	13	4.00	1.00	2	4.20	0.20	5
Programming	4.40	0.19	15	3.70	0.50	10	4.08	0.37	13	3.67	0.67	3	3.40	0.51	5
Machine learning	4.33	0.21	15	3.30	0.33	10	4.15	0.25	13	4.00	1.00	2	3.00	0.55	5
Business Analysis	4.07	0.25	15	3.70	0.37	10	4.31	0.24	13	5.00	0.00	2	3.20	0.20	5
Mathematics	4.00	0.22	15	3.33	0.41	9	4.15	0.22	13	3.67	0.67	3	3.20	0.58	5
Artificial Intelligence	3.27	0.27	15	3.40	0.40	10	3.85	0.27	13	3.00	0.00	2	2.80	0.37	5
Marketing	3.07	0.23	15	2.89	0.39	9	3.77	0.36	13	3.67	0.88	3	2.40	0.60	5
Accounting	2.40	0.35	15	2.60	0.22	10	3.50	0.36	12	2.50	1.50	2	2.20	0.73	5

*AR = Average Rating, SE = Standard Error, SS = Sample Size

Table 2. The average ratings of required skills for big data analytics, grouped by academics' disciplines

Type of expertise	Academic														
	Statistics			Computing			Business			Marketing			Other		
	AR	SE	SS	AR	SE	SS	AR	SE	SS	AR	SE	SS	AR	SE	SS
Statistical Analysis and Statistical Software Skills	4.90	0.10	20	4.34	0.16	29	5.00	0.00	10	4.50	0.31	14	4.44	0.24	9
Statistical Learning	4.50	0.17	18	3.93	0.18	28	4.44	0.24	9	4.21	0.32	14	3.78	0.32	9
Programming	4.50	0.19	18	4.21	0.13	29	3.67	0.47	9	3.36	0.36	14	3.89	0.20	9
Mathematics	4.10	0.23	20	3.97	0.16	29	4.20	0.20	10	3.86	0.21	14	4.00	0.17	9
Data mining	3.95	0.26	19	4.48	0.14	29	3.89	0.35	9	4.50	0.31	14	3.89	0.42	9
Machine learning	3.82	0.30	17	3.97	0.18	29	3.14	0.55	7	3.31	0.35	13	3.33	0.17	9
Business Analysis	3.00	0.32	17	3.32	0.19	28	4.22	0.40	9	4.31	0.26	13	3.00	0.33	9
Artificial Intelligence	2.88	0.27	17	3.72	0.17	29	2.78	0.43	9	3.00	0.26	14	3.33	0.24	9
Marketing	2.38	0.31	16	2.90	0.17	29	3.14	0.51	7	4.31	0.21	13	3.00	0.33	9
Accounting	2.06	0.30	16	2.54	0.17	28	2.56	0.41	9	3.00	0.23	14	2.78	0.28	9

*AR = Average Rating, SE = Standard Error, SS = Sample Size

graduates in the marketing discipline rated data mining skills lowest. Artificial intelligence (AI) was rated lower by academics in the business discipline than by other academics but it was rated higher by graduates in business than by graduates from other disciplines. Machine learning was rated higher by academics in the computing discipline than by graduates in the same field, who gave it the lowest rating in the survey. Interestingly, programming was rated higher by academics and graduates in the statistics discipline than by academics and graduates in the computing discipline. Could this result be considered an outcry for a collaborative degree? The average rating of marketing skills was highest for the academics in marketing and for the graduates from the business discipline. Business analysis skills were rated higher by graduates in all disciplines than by academics while the biggest gap between the graduates and academics was in the statistics discipline.

Perceptions of Software Skills Required for the Big Data Workforce

Both academics and graduates were asked about the expertise in software tools necessary for Big Data analysis, whether these software tools were used in teaching students by academics, and whether the software tools are used in graduates' workplaces, by graduates themselves, for the analysis of Big Data or not.

R programming had a higher average rating by academics than by graduates and SQL had a higher average rating by graduates than by academics (Figure 3). Not surprisingly, R programming and SQL were software tools with the highest proportions of usage according to both academics and graduates.

The graduate survey had higher average ratings than the academic survey for most of the software tools, with big differences in ratings between graduates and academics for noSQL, SQL, Hive, IBM SPSS Modeler and Base SAS (Figure 3). For R, Python and Matlab, academics' average ratings were higher than graduates' average ratings. MapReduce, SAS Enterprise Miner and SPSS Analytics had similar

Figure 3. The average ratings of software tools importance for Big Data analytics

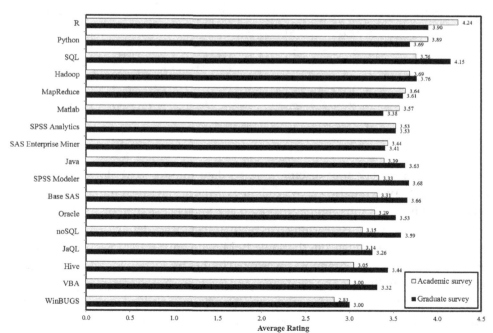

results for both groups. R programming (average rating of 4.24 out of 5) was the most important software skill according to academics, followed by Python (3.89). However, these ratings were much lower in the graduate survey with R programming rated 3.90 and Python rated 3.69. The most important software skill in graduates' opinion was SQL (4.15). WinBUGS was seen to be an unimportant software tool for Big Data analysis (it had the lowest average ratings for both groups).

The average ratings of software tools importance for Big Data analytics by graduates and by academics can be seen in Table 3. In this table, the results are presented for those participants who use the tool separately from those who don't use the tool. When the ratings were compared (see Table 3), it was found that most of them were rated more highly by graduates than by academics, except for Hive, Java and IBM SPSS Analytics. MapReduce had the highest average ratings with academics, while graduates rated SQL as the most important software tool. Hive had the biggest gap in ratings where academics who used Hive for teaching rated (4.00) higher than graduates who used it in their workplace (3.50), while SQL had the biggest gap in rating that academics (3.71) rated lower than graduates (4.72). The second most important software tools were Java and SAS Enterprise Miner for academics and graduates, respectively. R programming was the third most important

Table 3. The average ratings of software tools importance for big data analytics, grouped by academics' and graduates' use of the software

| Software tool | Academic | | | | | | Graduate | | | | | |
| | Yes | | | No | | | Yes | | | No | | |
	AR	SE	SS	AR	SE	SS	AR	SE	SS	AR	SE	SS
MapReduce	4.50	0.34	6	3.53	0.24	17	4.50	0.50	2	3.58	0.20	24
Java	4.36	0.20	11	2.76	0.29	17	4.00	0.22	15	3.37	0.27	19
R	4.33	0.18	27	3.67	0.33	9	4.50	0.18	16	3.31	0.20	16
SAS Enterprise Miner	4.14	0.26	7	3.35	0.23	20	4.60	0.24	5	3.21	0.18	24
SPSS Analytics	4.07	0.22	14	3.33	0.30	15	3.79	0.24	14	3.40	0.21	15
Matlab	4.07	0.23	15	3.31	0.25	16	4.00	0.50	8	3.09	0.19	23
noSQL	4.00	0.00	1	3.00	0.24	19	4.40	0.40	5	3.45	0.23	22
Hive	4.00	0.58	3	2.75	0.19	16	3.50	0.50	2	3.43	0.19	23
Base SAS	3.89	0.31	9	3.28	0.25	18	4.36	0.24	11	3.35	0.17	17
Hadoop	3.83	0.48	6	3.75	0.24	20	4.40	0.40	5	3.77	0.23	22
SPSS Modeler	3.80	0.36	10	3.19	0.26	16	4.11	0.20	9	3.65	0.21	20
JaQL	3.80	0.37	5	2.87	0.26	15	4.00	0.00	1	3.30	0.16	20
Python	3.73	0.21	15	3.50	0.31	14	4.29	0.29	7	3.47	0.21	19
SQL	3.71	0.24	14	3.25	0.35	12	4.72	0.11	18	3.73	0.28	15
Oracle	3.64	0.20	11	2.83	0.32	12	4.29	0.29	7	3.42	0.19	24
WinBUGS	3.20	0.66	5	2.71	0.19	17	4.00	0.41	4	2.78	0.14	23
VBA	3.00	0.00	2	2.83	0.27	18	3.64	0.23	14	3.29	0.22	17

*AR = Average Rating, SE = Standard Error, SS = Sample Size

software for both groups. The ratings of MapReduce and Matlab by the two groups were similar. WinBUGS had a relatively low rating except among graduates who use it in their workplace.

The average ratings of software tools importance for Big Data analysis according to discipline are presented in Table 4 for academics and in Table 5 for graduates. The results indicate that Java, SQL and Oracle were rated more highly by graduates than by academics in all disciplines. R programming was ranked more highly by academics than by graduates across all disciplines. In the marketing discipline, academics ranked many software tools more highly than the graduates did. SQL was ranked higher by graduates in the business discipline than by the academics, while a similar pattern is observed for noSQL in the computing discipline. Opposite patterns were observed for SAS Enterprise Miner, R, noSQL, Hadoop, and Python in the marketing discipline (i.e., academics ranked these higher than graduates).

The average ratings of software tools' importance for Big Data analytics by graduates' company operating area (Table 6) were mostly higher for graduates in data analytics than in finance. The exceptions were for SAS Enterprise Miner, IBM SPSS Modeler, Hive and R. The higher rankings of software tools by graduates in data analytics were for SQL, Base SAS, Python, Hadoop and Oracle. For Oracle

Table 4. The average ratings of software tools importance for big data analytics, grouped by academics' disciplines

| Software tool | Academic | | | | | | | | | | | | | | |
| | Statistics | | | Computing | | | Business | | | Marketing | | | Other | | |
	AR	SE	SS	AR	SE	SS	AR	SE	SS	AR	SE	SS	AR	SE	SS
R	4.32	0.23	19	4.27	0.13	22	4.00	0.38	8	4.43	0.37	7	4.00	0.31	7
Python	4.27	0.21	15	3.94	0.22	18	3.00	0.49	7	4.00	0.27	8	3.75	0.31	8
SQL	3.85	0.36	13	4.00	0.16	20	2.83	0.54	6	3.83	0.40	6	3.67	0.41	9
Hadoop	3.75	0.28	12	3.82	0.21	17	2.83	0.48	6	4.00	0.45	6	3.71	0.29	7
MapReduce	3.82	0.26	11	3.94	0.20	17	2.67	0.42	6	3.33	0.33	6	3.71	0.29	7
Matlab	3.59	0.29	17	3.47	0.18	19	3.86	0.26	7	3.43	0.37	7	3.63	0.46	8
SPSS Analytics	3.43	0.29	14	3.50	0.21	20	3.67	0.37	9	3.78	0.40	9	3.20	0.58	5
SAS Enterprise Miner	3.43	0.25	14	3.25	0.22	20	3.71	0.42	7	3.78	0.36	9	3.20	0.66	5
Java	3.31	0.28	16	3.64	0.19	22	2.57	0.37	7	4.00	0.26	6	3.00	0.55	5
SPSS Modeler	3.21	0.28	14	3.15	0.18	20	3.50	0.50	6	3.78	0.40	9	3.40	0.68	5
Base SAS	3.47	0.26	15	3.11	0.20	19	3.17	0.31	6	3.88	0.35	8	3.00	0.52	6
Oracle	3.22	0.43	9	3.45	0.21	20	2.86	0.40	7	3.86	0.26	7	2.67	0.33	6
noSQL	3.13	0.40	8	3.13	0.18	16	2.67	0.42	6	4.20	0.49	5	2.83	0.48	6
JaQL	3.40	0.37	10	3.13	0.15	16	2.67	0.42	6	3.67	0.42	6	2.60	0.40	5
Hive	3.38	0.46	8	2.94	0.14	16	2.67	0.42	6	3.67	0.42	6	2.60	0.40	5
VBA	3.36	0.31	11	2.69	0.22	16	2.83	0.48	6	3.50	0.22	6	2.80	0.49	5
WinBUGS	3.07	0.34	14	2.63	0.13	16	3.00	0.32	5	2.83	0.31	6	2.60	0.40	5

*AR = Average Rating, SE = Standard Error, SS = Sample Size

140

Table 5. The average ratings of software tools importance for big data analytics, grouped by graduates' disciplines

Software tool	Graduate														
	Statistics			Computing			Business			Marketing			Other		
	AR	SE	SS	AR	SE	SS	AR	SE	SS	AR	SE	SS	AR	SE	SS
R	4.29	0.22	14	3.89	0.35	9	3.80	0.25	10	3.00	0.00	1	3.20	0.37	5
SQL	4.25	0.28	12	4.44	0.24	9	4.00	0.33	12	4.00	1.00	2	3.80	0.37	5
Base SAS	4.17	0.24	12	3.29	0.36	7	3.70	0.26	10	3.00	0.00	1	3.00	0.32	5
Hadoop	4.00	0.30	12	3.89	0.42	9	3.29	0.29	7	3.00	0.00	1	3.80	0.49	5
SPSS Modeler	4.00	0.23	14	3.14	0.26	7	4.00	0.26	10	3.00	0.00	1	3.00	0.45	5
Python	3.82	0.30	11	4.11	0.26	9	3.30	0.26	10	3.00	0.00	1	3.50	0.50	4
SAS Enterprise Miner	3.77	0.23	13	3.00	0.22	7	3.70	0.26	10	2.00	1.00	2	3.00	0.55	5
MapReduce	3.73	0.30	11	3.78	0.36	9	3.38	0.26	8	3.00	0.00	1	3.50	0.50	4
Hive	3.73	0.30	11	3.25	0.31	8	3.25	0.16	8	3.00	0.00	1	3.50	0.50	4
Oracle	3.67	0.31	12	3.63	0.26	8	3.36	0.28	11	4.00	1.00	2	3.20	0.20	5
SPSS Analytics	3.57	0.25	14	3.14	0.26	7	4.00	0.26	10	3.00	0.00	1	3.00	0.41	4
Java	3.57	0.34	14	3.67	0.33	9	3.36	0.20	11	4.33	0.67	3	4.00	0.41	4
noSQL	3.42	0.36	12	4.11	0.31	9	3.38	0.26	8	3.00	0.00	1	3.50	0.50	4
Matlab	3.36	0.29	14	3.78	0.43	9	3.45	0.34	11	3.00	0.00	1	2.50	0.29	4
VBA	3.36	0.29	14	3.00	0.27	8	3.50	0.22	10	4.00	1.00	2	3.00	0.41	4
JaQL	3.14	0.34	7	3.38	0.18	8	3.38	0.26	8	3.00	0.00	1	3.00	0.00	3
WinBUGS	2.92	0.29	12	2.88	0.23	8	3.44	0.24	9	3.00	0.00	1	2.50	0.29	4

*AR = Average Rating, SE = Standard Error, SS = Sample Size

Table 6. The average ratings of software tools importance for big data analytics, grouped by graduates' company operating area

Software tool	Graduate								
	Data analytics			Finance			Other		
	AR	SE	SS	AR	SE	SS	AR	SE	SS
SQL	4.38	0.32	8	3.85	0.27	13	4.26	0.21	19
Base SAS	4.14	0.34	7	3.67	0.26	12	3.44	0.22	16
Python	4.00	0.33	8	3.50	0.29	12	3.67	0.21	15
Hadoop	4.00	0.38	7	3.64	0.28	11	3.75	0.30	16
Oracle	4.00	0.38	8	3.00	0.11	13	3.71	0.22	17
Java	3.91	0.39	11	3.62	0.21	13	3.47	0.24	17
R	3.89	0.31	9	3.92	0.24	13	3.88	0.24	17
SPSS Analytics	3.75	0.31	8	3.67	0.22	12	3.31	0.24	16
SPSS Modeler	3.75	0.31	8	3.83	0.24	12	3.53	0.24	17
noSQL	3.75	0.37	8	3.27	0.33	11	3.73	0.25	15
MapReduce	3.71	0.36	7	3.64	0.28	11	3.53	0.26	15
JaQL	3.67	0.42	6	3.00	0.00	9	3.25	0.18	12
VBA	3.67	0.29	9	3.15	0.22	13	3.25	0.25	16
Hive	3.57	0.30	7	3.64	0.28	11	3.21	0.21	14
Matlab	3.56	0.24	9	3.23	0.30	13	3.41	0.32	17
SAS Enterprise Miner	3.38	0.46	8	3.58	0.26	12	3.29	0.21	17
WinBUGS	3.25	0.16	8	3.10	0.23	10	2.81	0.25	16

*AR = Average Rating, SE = Standard Error, SS = Sample Size

141

and JaQL, the ratings by graduates in finance were a lot lower than for graduates in data analytics.

The research reported in this chapter included participants mainly from Australia and New Zealand, therefore the results might need to be interpreted with caution. The participants might not be a representative sample of the population. For example although all academics from relevant departments in 39 Australian and 8 New Zealand universities were invited to participate, only a small number of them responded to the survey. In the graduate survey, it is not clear whether a representative sample is achieved since it is not possible to identify the population characteristics.

CONCLUSION AND DISCUSSIONS

A new hybrid type of career, the 'data scientist' has emerged recently. Some academics and graduates in statistics regard 'data science' as applied statistics whereas academics and graduates from computer science may see it as a new set of software skills and tools belonging in the realm of computer science, not statistics. In this chapter the authors have investigated the perceptions of graduates working in the new field of Big Data analytics / data science and the perceptions of academics working in disciplines producing graduates likely to work in that field, such as statistics, mathematics and computing. The differences between academics' perceptions and graduates' perceptions (for those working in the field) about the areas of expertise and the types of software tools required for working in Big Data analytics / data science have been examined. The results presented in this chapter can help to inform university academics about the design of the curriculum for degrees in Statistics, Computing, Mathematics, and Data Science.

Our research into the Australian data science / data analytics work force and educational institutions training people for this work force has investigated the skills needed (as perceived by graduates working in the industry) and taught (as perceived by academics). The most important type of expertise required for Big Data analytics according to both academics and graduates is "Statistical Analysis and Statistical Software Skills", followed by "Data Mining" and "Statistical Learning". This is good news for statisticians and for the future of statistics as a discipline and requires action to collaborate with computer scientists to teach future data scientists. In addition, university education for statisticians will need to change to incorporate a lot more content relating to computers and software. To free up some space to accommodate these into curriculum, we might need to restructure the statistical curriculum to reduce the emphasis on theoretical mathematical statistics or make it a specialization within statistics, with applied statistics/data science as a separate specialization. Mathematical statistics might only be relevant to niche students who are more interested in theory or pursuing a PhD in statistics but not for the wider cohort of students who might want to use their statistical skills in highly competitive data science jobs.

A range of different software tools are used in industry and in academia for Big Data analysis. Some software tools may be more suited to teaching than to industry practice. This may partly explain the differences between the results for academics and for graduates in the average importance ratings and level of usage of different software tools. The R statistical software package is open source and widely used in academia. It has a higher average rating and higher level of usage according to academics than according to graduates in industry. For SQL the opposite is true. Some software tools have very low levels of usage in industry. For instance, Hive, JaQL, and MapReduce had less than 10% of the graduates saying it is used in their workplaces.

When graduates join the workplace they should be capable of learning new software tools. It is not necessary for university degrees to provide training in all of the software tools that have been identified as being used in industry, because during the last two decades universities are incorporating *"learning to learn" and "life-long learner"* emphasis and skills to their degree programs as one of the most important employee required generic skills (Delors, 1996; Commission of the European Communities, 2001; OECD, 2001). Graduates graduate as able learners. However being exposed to certain software tools that are used for certain kinds of analysis/tasks, is necessary to enable skills transfer from one software tool to another. For example, learning one kind of data mining software, IBM SPSS Modeler, along with the theory behind it would enable students to easily learn and use another data mining software, SAS Enterprise Miner, if they have to in their work, because knowledge and experience they gained with one software will be transferable and software tools are usually similar to each other for specific analysis.

The noteworthy differences between the results from the academic and graduate surveys about the importance of software tools were as follows.

- Most software tools were on average rated more highly by graduates than by academics, except R programming, Python, and Matlab where academics' average ratings were higher.
- noSQL, SQL, Hive, IBM SPSS Modeler, and Base SAS had much lower importance rating by academics than by graduates.
- Most software tools had a big gap in the proportion of usage between academics and graduates use in their work, except for IBM SPSS Modeler. This points to a mismatch in software tools used in education and in industry for Big Data analysis.

- Hive had a higher average rating by academics than by graduates working in Big Data analysis.
- Java, SQL, and Oracle had a higher average importance ratings by graduates than by academics in all disciplines.
- R programming was identified as more important by academics from all disciplines than by graduates.
- The academics in the marketing discipline rated many software tools as more important than graduates did in marketing discipline.
- SQL was seen as more important by the graduates in the business discipline than by academics in the same discipline, while a similar pattern is observed for noSQL in computing discipline. Opposite patterns were observed for SAS Enterprise Miner, R, noSQL, Hadoop, and Python in marketing discipline (i.e., academics rated higher than graduates).

It is unfortunate for statisticians that many new degrees in the Big Data field are usually owned and taught by computer science departments, which might lack the expertise to teach statistical literacy and statistical knowledge to future data scientists. The authors recommend that data science degrees should include software skills as well as statistical skills for Big Data analysis. Universities could consider giving students exposure to some of the software tools used in industrial applications of data analytics. It might also be beneficial for universities to consider including the software tools identified in this study as 'important' and 'mostly used' into their academic curricula, especially in the computing, statistics and mathematics disciplines. This recommendation is in line with the Curriculum Guidelines for Undergraduate Programs in Statistical Science written by the American Statistical Association (2014); as recommended by the President of the Statistical Society of Canada, Prof John Petkau (2014) and the Australian Government, Department of Finance and Deregulation Big Data Strategy paper (Australian Government, 2013).

The disciplines of computer science and statistics approach data analytics in quite different ways. The computer science approach involves creating software for pattern recognition and development of models for prediction. This includes machine learning, statistical learning, and genetic algorithms. It tends to produce complex models, sometimes lacking a sensible or intuitive or theoretical interpretation. The aim of the data analysis is to find patterns and possibly correlations, which might be quite descriptive, exploratory and could be misleading, especially if the correlations are interpreted as causations without proper experimental design. Learning analytics dashboards (Atif et al., 2013) and customer relationship dashboards (Cahyati & Prananto, 2015) are examples for such analysis. For many years, statisticians named this kind of analysis "data dredging", "data fishing" or "data snooping" because the process starts with analysis, not with a "question" to be answered or a "problem" to be solved.

On the other hand, statistical science aims to provide evidence to answer questions or solve problems. Therefore developing data collection methodologies, understanding data and the relationships between variables in the data are at the core of statistical analysis. Statisticians help researchers to design studies for data collection, to formulate and test hypotheses and theories. So statisticians are more inclined to obtain models which have an intelligible interpretation or which fit into some theoretical conceptual framework, not just in the statistical science domain but also in the domain where the data is obtained and where the research questions or theories arise.

A collaborative and multi-discipline approach is required to achieve the best outcomes for future graduates (Miller, 2014), because the required skills and expertise cannot be covered completely by only one discipline (Figure 4) (Conway 2016, Hoerl et al., 2014; DeVeaux et al., 2016). The steps in statistical analysis and statistical thinking would be beneficial to any data exploration to enable quality decision making.

It can be argued that the departmental or discipline based funding in Australian universities is a road block to creating such multidisciplinary degrees, when the

Figure 4. The data science Venn diagram
(Conway, 2016)

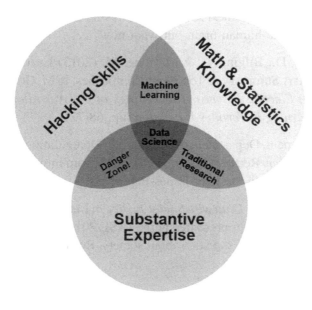

survival of the department or discipline depends on the number of students they have. When a single discipline degree is created the relevant income from the students flow to the discipline that owns the degree. Therefore executive enlightenment and support is crucial to enable collaboration and cooperation and to reduce the fear of losing students to competition in such multidisciplinary degrees.

ACKNOWLEDGMENT

The authors would like to thank Chulalongkorn University in Thailand for providing scholarship to one of the authors to study in Australia. The authors also wish to thank all of the academics and graduates who took part in this study by completing the surveys, without them the authors would not be able to undertake this research. Their opinions are valuable.

REFERENCES

American Statistical Association. (2014). *Curriculum Guidelines for Undergraduate Programs in Statistical Science*. Retrieved March 6, 2015, from http://www.amstat.org/education/pdfs/guidelines2014-11-15.pdf

Anthony, S. (2014). *Facebook's facial recognition software is now as accurate as the human brain, but what now?* ExtremeTech. Retrieved October 12, 2016, from http://www.extremetech.com/extreme/178777-facebooks-facial-recognition-software-is-now-as-accurate-as-the-human-brain-but-what-now

Atif, A., Richards, D., Bilgin, A., & Marrone, M. (2013) Learning Analytics in Higher Education: A Summary of Tools and Approaches. In M. Gosper, J. Hedberg, H. Carter (Eds.), *Electric Dreams. Proceedings of the Australasian Society for Computers in Learning in Tertiary Education* (pp. 68-72).

Australian Government, Department of Finance and Deregulation. (2013). *Big Data Strategy - Issues Paper*. Retrieved October 14, 2014 from http://www.finance.gov.au/files/2013/03/Big-Data-Strategy-Issues-Paper1.pdf

Bergen, S. (2016). *Melding Data with Social Justice in Undergraduate Statistics and Data Science Courses*. Paper presented at the IASE 2016 Roundtable Conference: Promoting understanding of statistics about society, Berlin, Germany.

Bilgin, A. A., Primi, C., Chiesi, F., Lopez, M. V., Fabrizio, M. C., Quinn, V. F.,... Graham, P. L. (2014). A Comparison of First Year Statistics Units' Content and Contexts in a Multinational Study: With a Case Study for the Validation of ASSIST in Australia. In *Topics from Australian Conferences on Teaching Statistics: OZCOTS 2008-2012* (pp. 189-210). Springer Science+Business Media.

Boyd, D., & Crawford, K. (2011). *Six provocations for big data.* Paper presented at: A Decade in Internet Time: Symposium on the Dynamics of the Internet and Society, Oxford, UK.

Bradshaw, L. (2012). Big Data and What it Means. *Business Horizon Q., 7*, 32–35.

Brown, B., Chui, M., & Manyika, J. (2011). Are you ready for the era of 'big data'. *The McKinsey Quarterly, 4*, 24–35.

Cahyadi, A., & Prananto, A. (2015). Reflecting design thinking: A case study of the process of designing dashboards. *Journal of Systems and Information Technology, 17*(3), 286–306. doi:10.1108/JSIT-03-2015-0018

Commission of the European Communities. (2001). *Making a European Area of Lifelong Learning a Reality.* Retrieved October 18, 2016 from http://aei.pitt.edu/42878/1/com2001_0678.pdf

Conway, D. (2016). *The data science Venn diagram.* Retrieved October 12, 2016, from https://s3.amazonaws.com/aws.drewconway.com/viz/venn_diagram/data_science.html

Davenport, T. H., & Patil, D. J. (2012). Data Scientist: The Sexiest Job Of the 21st Century. *Harvard Business Review, 90*(10), 70–76. PMID:23074866

De Mauro, A., Greco, M., & Grimaldi, M. (2016). A formal definition of Big Data based on its essential features. *Library Review, 65*(3), 122–135. doi:10.1108/LR-06-2015-0061

De Veaux, R.D., Hoerl, R.W. & Snee, R. D. (2016, August). Big Data and the Missing Links. *Statistical Analysis and Data Mining: The ASA Data Science Journal.* doi: 10.1002/sam.11303

Delors, J. (1996). *Learning: The treasure within Report to UNESCO of the International Commission on Education for the Twenty-first Century.* UNESCO Publishing.

Diebold, F. X. (2012). *A Personal Perspective on the Origin(s) and Development of "Big Data": The Phenomenon, the Term, and the Discipline.* Retrieved from http://www.ssc.upenn.edu/~fdiebold/papers/paper112/Diebold_Big_Data.pdf

Finzer, W. (2012). *The data science education dilemma*. Paper presented at the IASE Roundtable Conference: Technology in Statistics Education: Virtualities and Realities, Cebu, The Philippines.

Gartner Orlando (FL). (2012). *Gartner Says Big Data Creates Big Jobs: 4.4 Million IT Jobs Globally to Support Big Data By 2015*. Retrieved February 8, 2015 from http://www.gartner.com/newsroom/id/2207915

Glance, D. (2013). *Solving Big Data's big skills shortage*. Perth: The Conversation. Retrieved February 8, 2015 from http://theconversation.com/solving-big-datas-big-skills-shortage-20352

Gould, R. (2016). *Preparing secondary teachers to teach data science: lessons learned*. Paper presented at the IASE 2016 Roundtable Conference: Promoting understanding of statistics about society, Berlin, Germany.

Hoerl, R.W., Snee, R. D. & De Veaux, R.D. (2014). Applying Statistical Thinking to 'Big Data' Problems. *Wiley Interdisciplinary Reviews: Computational Statistics*, 6, 222–232. doi: 10.1002/wics.1306

Horton, N., Baumer, B., & Wickham, H. (2014). *Teaching precursors to data science in introductory and second courses in statistics*. Paper presented at the ICOTS-9: Sustainability in statistics education, Flagstaff, AZ.

Hurwitz, J., Nugent, A., Halper, F., & Kaufman, M. (2013). *Big data for dummies*. Hoboken, NJ: Wiley.

IASE Satellite. (2011). *International Association for Statistical Education: Statistics Education and Outreach*. Dublin, Ireland: Author.

IASE Satellite. (2013). *The Joint IASE/IAOS Satellite Conference on Statistics Education and Outreach: Statistics Education for Progress: Youth and Official Statistics*. Macao, China: Author.

ICOTS-8. (2010). *International Conferences on Teaching Statistics: Data and Context in Statistics Education: Towards an Evidence-Based Society*. Ljubljana, Slovenia: Author.

Kaplan, D., Overvoorde, P., & Shoop, E. (2014). *Integrating big data into the science curriculum*. Paper presented at the ICOTS-9: Sustainability in statistics education, Flagstaff, AZ.

Kudo, T., Yoshihiro Hayashi, Y., Watanabe, M., Morikawa, T., Furutani, T., & Iwasaki, M. (2014). *Challenges and issues in developing real-world curriculum for data scientists in Japan*. Paper presented at the ICOTS-9: Sustainability in statistics education, Flagstaff, AZ.

Kyng, T., Bilgin, A., & Puang-Ngern, B. (2015). *Data Science: Is it statistics or computer science? Statistics education in the age of big data*. IASE 2015 Satellite Conference on Advances in statistics education: developments, experiences, and assessments, Rio de Janeiro, Brazil.

Kyng, T. J., Bilgin, A. A., & Puang-Ngern, B. (2016). *Big Data, Data Science, Computer Science and Statistics Education*. Paper presented at the OZCOTS 2016, Canberra, Australia.

LaChance, N. (2016). *Facebook's Facial Recognition Software Is Different From The FBI's. Here's Why*. Retrieved October 12, 2016, from http://www.npr.org/sections/alltechconsidered/2016/05/18/477819617/facebooks-facial-recognition-software-is-different-from-the-fbis-heres-why

Lohr, S. (2013). The Origins of 'Big Data': An Etymological Detective Story. *The New York Times*. Retrieved from http://bits.blogs.nytimes.com/2013/02/01/the-origins-of-big-data-an-etymological-detective-story/?_r=0

Manyika, J., Chui, M., Brown, B., Bughin, J., Dobbs, R., Roxburgh, C., & Hung Byers, A. (2011). *Big Data: The next frontier for innovation, competition, and Productivity*. San Francisco, CA: McKinsey Global Institute.

McAfee, A., & Brynjolfsson, E. (2012). Big data: The management revolution. *Harvard Business Review*, *90*(10), 60–66. PMID:23074865

McNamara, A., & Hansen, M. (2014). *Teaching data science to teenagers*. Paper presented at the ICOTS-9: Sustainability in statistics education, Flagstaff, AZ.

Miller, S. (2014). Collaborative Approaches Needed to Close the Big Data Skills Gap. *Journal of Organization Design*, *3*(1), 26–30. doi:10.7146/jod.9823

O*NET Resource Centre. (2016). Retrieved October 12, 2016 from http://www.onetcenter.org/overview.html

OECD. (2001). *Lifelong Learning for All: Policy Directions*. OECD Publishing. Retrieved October 18, 2016 from http://www.oecd.org/officialdocuments/publicdisplaydocumentpdf/?cote=DEELSA/ED/CERI/CD(2000)12/PART1/REV2&docLanguage=En

OECD. (2016). *Equations and Inequalities: Making Mathematics Accessible to All, PISA*. Paris: OECD Publishing. doi:10.1787/9789264258495-en

Petkau, J. (2014). President's Message. *SSC Liason*, *28*(4), 3–7. PMID:24707580

Puang-Ngern, B. (2015). *Big data and its implications for the statistics profession and statistics education* (Unpublished Master of Research Thesis). Macquarie University, Sydney, Australia.

Ridgway, J., Nicholson, J., & Sean McCusker, S. (2014). *Exploring "white flight" via open data and big data*. Paper presented at the ICOTS-9: Sustainability in statistics education, Flagstaff, AZ.

Schwab-McCoy, A. (2016). *Developing A First-Year Seminar Course in Statistics and Data Science*. Paper presented at the IASE 2016 Roundtable Conference: Promoting understanding of statistics about society, Berlin, Germany.

Song, I.-Y., & Zhu, Y. (2015). Big data and data science: What should we teach? *Expert Systems: International Journal of Knowledge Engineering and Neural Networks*. doi:10.1111/exsy.12130

Trondheim (NO). (2013). *SINTEF. Big Data, for better or worse: 90% of world's data generated over last two years*. Retrieved February 8, 2015 Feb 8 from http://www.sintef.no/home/corporate-news/Big-Data--for-better-or-worse/

Zikopoulos, P., Eaton, C., deRoos, D., Deutsch, T., & Lapis, G. (2011). *Understanding big data: Analytics for enterprise class hadoop and streaming data*. New York: McGraw-Hill Osborne Media.

APPENDIX: ACADEMIC AND GRADUATE SURVEYS EXPERTISE QUESTIONS

Figure 5. Expertise questions from academic survey

	In your opinion, which type of expertise is required for graduate students to be employed in the big data field? Please indicate your level of agreement with the following statements:						Do students acquire expertise in this area?	
	Strongly Disagree	Disagree	Neutral	Agree	Strongly Agree	N/A	Yes	No
Statistical Analysis and Statistical Software Skills	○	○	○	○	○	○	○	○
Statistical Learning	○	○	○	○	○	○	○	○
Mathematics	○	○	○	○	○	○	○	○
Data mining	○	○	○	○	○	○	○	○
Machine learning	○	○	○	○	○	○	○	○
Artificial Intelligence	○	○	○	○	○	○	○	○
Programming	○	○	○	○	○	○	○	○
Marketing	○	○	○	○	○	○	○	○
Business Analysis	○	○	○	○	○	○	○	○
Accounting	○	○	○	○	○	○	○	○
Other, please specify	○	○	○	○	○	○	○	○

Figure 6. Expertise questions from graduate survey

	In your opinion, which type of expertise is required to work with big data? Please indicate your level of agreement with the following statements:						Do you have this expertise yourself?	
	Strongly Disagree	Disagree	Neutral	Agree	Strongly Agree	N/A	Yes	No
Statistical Analysis and Statistical Software Skills	○	○	○	○	○	○	○	○
Statistical Learning	○	○	○	○	○	○	○	○
Mathematics	○	○	○	○	○	○	○	○
Data mining	○	○	○	○	○	○	○	○
Machine learning	○	○	○	○	○	○	○	○
Artificial Intelligence	○	○	○	○	○	○	○	○
Programming	○	○	○	○	○	○	○	○
Marketing	○	○	○	○	○	○	○	○
Business Analysis	○	○	○	○	○	○	○	○
Accounting	○	○	○	○	○	○	○	○
Other, please specify	○	○	○	○	○	○	○	○

Chapter 7

Excel–lence in Data Visualization?
The Use of Microsoft Excel for Data Visualization and the Analysis of Big Data

Jacques Raubenheimer
University of the Free State, South Africa & The University of Sydney, Australia

ABSTRACT

Spreadsheets were arguably the first information calculation and analysis tools employed by microcomputer users, and today are arguably ubiquitously used for information calculation and analysis. The fluctuating fortunes of PC makers coincided with those of spreadsheet applications, although the last two decades have seen the dominance of Microsoft Excel in the spreadsheet market. This chapter plots the historical development of spreadsheets in general, and Excel in particular, highlighting how new features have allowed for new forms of data analysis in the spreadsheet environment. Microsoft has undoubtedly cast Excel as a tool for the analysis of big data through the addition and development of features aimed at reporting on data too large for a spreadsheet. This chapter discusses Excel's ability to handle these data by means of an applied example. Data visualization by means of charts and dashboards is discussed as a common strategy for dealing with large volumes of data.

DOI: 10.4018/978-1-5225-2512-7.ch007

INTRODUCTION

Since the dawn of writing, humans have endeavored to capture data. Early tools were primitive, with limited capacity (as with early clay tablets inscribed with a stylus) and limited durability (as papyrus and vellum degraded quickly over time). None can argue that both storage capacity and longevity have increased since the introduction of electronic computing and electronic storage, paralleling what has come to be known as Moore's law (cf. Moore, 1965) even though Moore himself notes that his "law" will eventually prove to be unsustainable (Courtland, 2015). Martin Hilbert (2012; cf. also Hilbert & López, 2012a, 2012b) defines the start of the digital age as that point at which the world's digital storage capacity exceeded its analog storage capacity—which he puts at the year 2002. It is exactly this growth in storage capacity that has facilitated the rise of big data. But with storage comes the desire to retrieve and then to analyze, and for this, we need tools that can handle big data.

Microsoft Excel was a relatively late entrant to the spreadsheet market, but since then it has become the de facto spreadsheet program, holding—by some estimates—up to 95% of the market share for spreadsheets. As such, Excel is, for many, the first line tool they turn to for data analysis and data visualization. For better or worse, Microsoft has placed voluminous resources behind its efforts to position Excel as a big data analysis tool (Sharma & Ellis, 2016). This chapter will plot that development and will examine what Excel offers the user who wants to make forays into working with big data.

HISTORY

The democratization of electronic information can truly be said to have started with the advent of the personal computer, and spreadsheets have played a central role in that process, to such an extent that Hesse and Scerno (2009) pointedly state:

It was VisiCalc (in approximately 1981) and the development of electronic spreadsheets that advanced PC sales beyond word processing machines and changed the definition of secretary (eliminating much of the work that secretaries had done) to administrative assistant. Wang redefined the secretary's job; however, with their word processing and spreadsheet capabilities, PCs redefined the secretary.... We contend that without the electronic spreadsheet, PCs might have remained hobby tools or game machines. (pp. 159-160)

History of Spreadsheets in General

The concept of a spreadsheet predates personal computers, with one of the earliest references (then as "spread sheet") being listed in Kohler's dictionary for accountants of 1952 (Mattessich, n.d.). Early accounting work was done by Richard Mattessich on the idea of the computerization of spreadsheets (1961, 1964). The first actual computerization of these ideas (LANPAR) was done by Rene Pardo and Remy Landau in 1969 (Pardo, 2000). However, it is commonly held that the utility of personal computers first became evident with the 1979 release of a spreadsheet program for the Apple II: VisiCalc (cf. Power, 2004), the first so-called "killer app" (Brandel, 1999; Grad, 2007; Walkenbach, 2010, p. 11). VisiCalc was developed based on Dan Bricklin and Bob Frankston's experience working with paper-based calculation problems in business school, independent of earlier computerizations (Bricklin, 2009b, 2015; Frankston, 1999; Power, 2004), so much so that Grad (2007) details how Bricklin's prior experiences with word processing proved far more pivotal in the development of VisiCalc than actual accounting experience. Not only was a spreadsheet application the first "killer app" for personal computers, but spreadsheets could arguably be called the first area for the battle of software supremacy, even predating operating system battles. Things developed very quickly after the release of VisiCalc: SuperCalc was released in 1980, and Microsoft's Multiplan in 1982. Multiplan's fleeting early popularity was quickly lost to the superior Lotus 1-2-3 released in January 1983 (Campbell-Kelly, 2007, p. 15; Kapor, 2007, p. 37).

History of Microsoft Excel

In an effort to regain market share from Lotus 1-2-3, Microsoft discontinued Multiplan—1987 saw version 3 as the last release of Multiplan (Campbell-Kelly, 2007, p. 16)—and supplanted it with Excel, which was released on 30 September 1985 for the new Apple Macintosh (Campbell-Kelly, 2007, p. 16; Weber, 2010). Excel was aimed not just at outsmarting Lotus 1-2-3, but at actively courting over Lotus 1-2-3 users, replacing the Multiplan R1C1 referencing system for signifying cell addresses (which is still optionally available—and even occasionally useful—in the Excel interface) with the A1 referencing system pioneered by VisiCalc and also used in Lotus 1-2-3, opening Lotus 1-2-3 files (allowing users to convert easily), and even going to the point of knowingly duplicating a Lotus 1-2-3 date error (Microsoft, 2015; Tan, 2009). Two factors ensured Excel's subsequent dominance in the electronic spreadsheet market: Excel, capitalizing on the graphic capabilities of the Macintosh, was the first spreadsheet software to employ a graphical user interface, which made it very popular with general users (Campbell-Kelly, 2007).

Second, Excel's next update was released concurrently with the release of Microsoft Windows—the first Windows release of Excel (numbered 2.0 in order to synchronize with the already-released second Macintosh version) included the run-time version of Windows (Campbell-Kelly, 2007, p. 16; Walkenbach, 2010, p. 16)—and Excel had no other significant competitor spreadsheet software in the Windows environment until Lotus 1-2-3 for Windows was released in August 1991 (Campbell-Kelly, 2007, p. 17). By that time, Excel had already significantly extended its market lead (Power, 2004). Excel has since seen twelve further major releases (released on a median of every two years), skipping version 6 when the version numbering of all the Microsoft Office applications was synchronized for Office 95 (Walkenbach, 2010, p. 18), and also version 13 when all the Microsoft Office applications jumped from version 12 (Office 2007) to version 14 (Office 2010), presumably in order to appease superstitious triskaidekaphobic customers. The future of Excel in terms of releases is changing, with Microsoft (2016n) pursuing a cross-platform, cross-market strategy, synchronous also with its changed strategy for Windows, in which Excel appears in different flavors (mainly, at present, Excel as part of Office 2016 and Excel as part of Office 365) and on different platforms (Windows, Mac, iOS, WebApps). The importance of this is that not all features are available in all versions/platforms, and also that the idea of a major release is fading in favor of incremental updates—see, for example, the "What's new in Excel 2016 for Windows" web page, which lists updates (including new features) for September 2015, and then every month from January to September, excepting February (Microsoft, 2016m).

Dual Ubiquity of Spreadsheets and Excel

It is sufficient to conclude that, to a large degree, the popularity of early personal computers was driven by software, with numerous reports of customers purchasing the computer for the single motive of using one particular software item, and—more often than not—that item was a spreadsheet program (Brandel, 1999; Bricklin, 2006, 2013, 2015; Campbell-Kelly, 2007; Garfinkel, n.d.; Grad, 2007; Power, 2004). It is thus no surprise that spreadsheets are near-ubiquitous. Additionally, Microsoft Excel has successfully captured the spreadsheet market: If a user, especially a business or academic user, has a computer, it can safely be assumed that the computer will have a spreadsheet program on it, and furthermore, that the program could very well be Microsoft Excel (Kwak, 2013; Lynn, 2016). Estimates of Excel's market share will always remain only estimates, but Excel's growth was such that it was able to grab about 10% of the market with its initial release on the Apple Macintosh and extend that to 70% by the early 1990s (Campbell-Kelly, 2007, p. 17), then to 80%–90% by the turn of the century (Fylstra, Lasdon, Watson, & Waren, 1998, p. 29), and up to 95% by 2007 and onwards (Campbell-Kelly, 2007, p. 18; Great Speculations, 2013; Walkenbach, n.d.). Because of its prevalence, the remainder of this chapter will discuss data analysis and data visualization in Microsoft Excel only.

Development of Data Analysis and Data Visualization Tools in Microsoft Excel

Microsoft has continually sought to include new features in successive releases of Excel that would extend its data analysis capabilities, and maintain its appeal to its user base. It is beyond the scope of this chapter to list all the new features incorporated in each release, but several features relevant to how Excel can read, analyze and display data, are listed in Table 1. With future updates to Excel, this list will become immediately dated, but it will provide a historical basis to which the reader can append post-2016 information.

Concerning data visualization, Microsoft originally released what was known as Microsoft Chart as an adjunct charting program together with Multiplan. This tool was then rebranded as Microsoft Graph with the early versions of Excel, although Excel has long had its own charting engine. Microsoft Graph is still packaged with Microsoft Office for compatibility reasons, although all Office applications have used Excel's charting engine since Office 2007, making Office 2003 the last version to natively include Microsoft Graph for charting in applications other than Excel), and Excel having its own (very similar-looking) charts much earlier than that.

EXCEL TOOLS

It is impossible to demonstrate the scope of Excel's capabilities in a single chapter, let alone a single book. The aim, rather, is to provide an overview of what Excel is capable of in terms of accessing data, analyzing data, and visualizing data.

Tools for Data Access

Microsoft designed Excel from the start to be able to access data in other formats, beginning, as previously mentioned, with its ability to woo over Lotus 1-2-3 users by reading the Lotus 1-2-3 format (Campbell-Kelly, 2007). For many years, Excel has been able to read only a relatively "standard" set of data formats, although the list was quite extensive, including variously delimited text files, html, xml, several database formats, and files of competitor spreadsheet formats. This was the status quo up until Excel 2007. However, with Excel 2010, as the big data revolution gained momentum, this changed. The standard version of Excel maintained its normal set of

Table 1. Data access, analysis, and display tools introduced in Microsoft Excel

Year	Version	Branded Version	New Features
1990	3		Solver add-in 3D charts
1992	4		Microsoft Excel 4.0 Macro language
1993	5		Microsoft Excel 4.0 Macro language replaced with Microsoft Excel Visual Basic PivotTables as a data analysis response to Lotus 1-2-3's Improv
1995	7	Excel 95	Natively 32-bit
1997	8	Excel 97	Excel Visual Basic replaced with more robust Visual Basic for Applications (along with VBA implementation in other Microsoft Office applications)
1999	9	Excel 2000	Read html data PivotCharts allow visualization of data analyzed with PivotTables
2001	10	Excel 2002/XP	No important new features
2003	11	Excel 2003	Read XML data "Lists" introduced
2007	12	Excel 2007	Lists rebranded and extended as "Tables" Data stored in new OXML file format, which allows significant data compression Microsoft Graph replaced with internal Excel graphing engine (although the same selection of charts is offered) Excel also becomes the default charting engine for all other Office applications New larger worksheet size extends worksheet from 65 536/2^{16} rows by 256/2^{8} columns (for 2^{24} cells) to 1 048 576/2^{20} rows by 16 384/2^{14} columns (for 2^{34} cells)
2010	14	Excel 2010	Sparklines Data Slicers New Solver add-in Power Pivot add-in allows data from multiple sources to be combined in single PivotTable Power Query add-in Support for high-performance computing
2013	15	Excel 2013	Chart tools significantly altered Data slicers extended to tables New Excel Data Model allows PivotTables to incorporate more than one table New data sources Online Analytical Processing (OLAP) cubes allow Multidimensional Expression (MDX) calculation in PivotTables
2016	16	Excel 2016	Several new chart types Power Query rebranded as Get And Transform Power Map rebranded and incorporated as 3D Maps

(Duggirala, 2011; Fylstra, 2016; Microsoft, 2010b, 2013b, 2016m; Walkenbach, 2010) import capabilities, but users could augment this with a new add-in from Microsoft itself: Power Query (For Excel 2010 and 2013, Power Query had to be installed as an additional add-in, but since Excel 2016/365, Power Query is included natively under the rebranded name Get & Transform), which added access to a much wider variety of additional data sources. This list of possible data sources has also been steadily expanding since its first iteration in Excel 2010. Table 2 shows the list of possible data source options provided from the Get & Transform ribbon menu, also indicating which items form part of the "standard" set of Excel data import tools. It

Table 2. Possible data sources for get and transform (power query) as at October 2016

Category	Data Sources
File	Excel workbooks CSV files* XML files* Text files* Import files from folder
Database	SQL Server database* Microsoft Access database* SQL Server Analysis Services database* Oracle database IBM DB2 database MySQL database PostgreSQL database Sybase database Teradata database
Azure	Azure SQL database Azure Marketplace* Azure HDInsight Azure Blob storage Azure Table storage
Online Services	SharePoint Online list Microsoft Exchange online Dynamics CRM online Facebook Salesforce objects Salesforce reports
Other Sources	Web pages* SharePoint lists OData feeds* Hadoop files Active Directory Microsoft Exchange ODBC* Blank queries
Data catalog search	

* Indicates items listed in "standard" Get External Data tools of Excel

should also be noted that the Data catalog search option provides further access to various data stores (e.g., accessing data from Wikipedia or Google Analytics) via the Microsoft Power BI service (for which a subscription is needed).

One further element, though, was what allowed Excel to step up to the domain of the analysis of big data: Power Query freed it from the confines of the worksheet. Even Microsoft Access, the Microsoft Office database application, has a 2 GB limit on the size of a database file that can be created (Microsoft, 2016a), which, even in the compressed.accdb format, is limiting. Excel 2016 shares this file-size limit on its 32-bit version, but not on its 64-bit version (Microsoft, 2016f), although Microsoft (2016h) has allowed 32-bit versions of Excel 2013/2016 to access more system memory as of its June 2016 update. Furthermore, since Excel 2007, the worksheet size has been increased from 2^{24} to 2^{34} cells, but that still enforced a practical limit of 1 048 575 records (assuming only one row for data headers). However, with Power Query and the accompanying Power Pivot (discussed below), Excel was transformed to the reporting front end for massive datasets. Bill Jelen (2010, pp. 1–2) vividly describes his amazement as Microsoft employee Donald Farmer demonstrated the analysis of a 100-million-row dataset in Excel at the 2009 Excel MVP summit. Nonetheless, what may be thought of as an even bigger—yet more easily overlooked—constraint that was removed was that Excel now contains a tool to create, and even infer, relationships between datasets in much the same way as classical database programs could. Before Power Query, these relationships had to be built laboriously and manually by analysts in Excel, using tools such as the VLOOKUP function.

Tools for Data Analysis

The very idea underlying the spreadsheet concept is that of analysis (Bricklin, 2009a, 2009b). From the outset, thus, Excel has incorporated tools for analysis, typified by its inclusion of PivotTables in the native version of Excel 5, while Lotus 1-2-3 users had to buy Improv at an additional cost (Jelen, 2010, p. 4). However, analysis needs vary greatly, and analysis of big data requires a specific set of tools.

Language Tools

The simplest of Excel's tools are those that perform analyses in the traditional spreadsheet environment: Functions. Every new version of Excel contains more functions, so that Excel 2016 lists 341 functions "out-of-the-box" (Microsoft, 2016f), and even more new functions are added in the incremental updates (Microsoft, 2016m). Apart from this, VBA (discussed next) allows the creation of user-defined functions (UDFs), potentially allowing an unlimited number of in-cell analysis tools. The Excel functions are grouped into various general categories (listed according to the numerical value of the VBA *MacroOptions.Category* method):

- Financial
- Date and time
- Math and trigonometry
- Statistical
- Lookup and reference
- Database
- Text
- Logical
- Information
- Engineering
- Cube
- Web

In addition to this are the categories Compatibility (where functions from older versions that have been superseded by newer functions are included for compatibility reasons), Macro Control, and DDE/External. Functions generally require what are called arguments (some of which may be optional) on which the function will then perform a certain calculation. Provided the data is in an Excel workbook, functions can perform all manner of calculations on the data, and some functions can also import data into an Excel workbook (e.g., the CUBE or WEBSERVICE functions). A good example of an analytic function is the FORECAST set of functions.

The possibility of using VBA allows all manner of analytic extensibility to Excel tools. The simplest example of this is the creation of a UDF in VBA, but tools such as these can be, and regularly are, created to open, reorder, and analyze data, even automating the creation of reports.

In the move to the analysis of big data, however, Microsoft has added additional language tools (which also bridge to the next category of tools discussed below): The first of these is the Data Analysis Expression (DAX) language introduced with Power Pivot for Excel 2010 (see https://www.microsoft.com/en/library/ee634396). These are essentially similar to Excel worksheet functions, but are only used within Power Pivot PivotTables (cf. Jelen, 2010, p. 110 ff.). DAX functions are calculated on every row of data underlying the PivotTable, and present new calculation results that can then be analyzed and/or summarized using the PivotTable. Furthermore, Microsoft (2016i) has added the Power Query Formula Language—which Allington

(2016) suggests should be called PQL (with a pronunciation similar to that used for SQL)—which allows extensive manipulation and transformation of data in the process of loading that data to Excel via Power Query (see https://www.microsoft.com/library/mt253322).

PivotTables

The general idea behind pivot tables was developed by Pito Salas, who discovered that data in spreadsheets are organized in discernible patterns, and that an understanding of these patterns could be used to analyze and summarize that data. This was implemented in Lotus 1-2-3's Improv, released in 1991 (Garfinkel, n.d.). In 1993, Microsoft responded with the introduction of PivotTables (Microsoft's trademarked name for the product). The simple idea behind an Excel PivotTable is that it can take a table of data, and all the data in a column can be used in summary, or can be compared to other fields in some form of cross tabulation.

Specialized Tools for Data Analysis

Microsoft has incorporated various additional analysis tools in Excel that allow more complex analysis. One of the first of these was the Solver tool, which was created by Dan Fylstra's company Frontline Systems. Fylstra was involved in the development of VisiCalc through his first company, Personal Software, which was later renamed VisiCorp (Bricklin, 2009b; Grad, 2007; Power, 2004), and Frontline Systems first developed the What-If Solver for Lotus 1-2-3 in 1990, and then a Solver add-in for Excel 3 in 1991 (Fylstra, 2016; Fylstra et al., 1998). This add-in was shipped with Excel, although it had to be installed additionally by the user if required. The Solver add-in was predated by Microsoft's own more primitive Goal Seek tool, but it was Solver that gave Excel users the power of analysis-modelling that they desired (Fylstra et al., 1998, p. 31).

Despite incremental improvements, the solver tool remained in essentially the same format through successive versions until Excel 2007, but in Excel 2010 the Solver was totally revamped, with a new interface, new algorithms, and improved modelling capabilities (Microsoft, 2010b).

Excel has also, from very early versions, contained tools for evaluating and predicting various scenarios, viz., the Scenario Manager (Microsoft, 2016j), Goal Seek, which allows simpler scenarios with only one input variable (Microsoft, 2016k), and, in Excel 2016, the ability to create a forecast sheet (Microsoft, 2016c).

Statistical Tools

This category actually spans the earlier language tools (Excel has numerous statistical functions built in) and also the category of specialized tools, but it deserves a separate discussion, as the analysis of big data frequently involves statistical manipulation and/or analysis of the data. For many years, Excel's statistical functions have come under fire for problems related to their accuracy (Almiron, Lopes, & Oliveira, 2010; Apigian & Gambill, 2004; Keeling & Pavur, 2004; Knüsel, 1998, 2005; McCullough, 2008; McCullough & Wilson, 1999, 2002), although even then, it has been shown that in select cases, the critics did not understand Excel's operation properly (Berger, 2007). Microsoft eventually attempted to address some of these issues in both Excel 2003 (Microsoft, 2004) and then more comprehensively in Excel 2010 (Microsoft, 2010b), introducing a large number of new functions using a new function naming format (e.g., CHIDIST was superseded by CHISQ.DIST and CHISQ.DIST.RT) to distinguish them from the older functions. The older functions were moved to a new Compatibility function category. These corrections seem to have satisfied most criticisms, although some concerns remain (Knüsel, 2011; Mélard, 2014). In short, the use of spreadsheets, and Excel in particular, for some statistical analysis has received greater acceptance (Nash, 2006).

Regardless, Excel has been used for a considerable amount of statistical analysis, motivating Brian Ripley's (2002, p. 7) oft-quoted line: "Let's not kid ourselves: the most widely used piece of software for statistics is Excel." Selected examples for illustration are using Excel for simulation (Laverty, Miket, & Kelly, 2002; Seila, 2004), meta-analysis (Neyeloff, Fuchs, & Moreira, 2012), confirmatory factor analysis (Miles, 2005), regression analysis (Graves, 1997), and even, somewhat surprisingly, for the analysis of large bodies of qualitative data (Meyer & Avery, 2008; Ose, 2016). It should be noted that, for quantitative analyses, the Solver add-in mentioned previously is often employed. Various other add-ins from third parties extend Excel's reach to even more specialized statistical analyses, although these are too numerous to be listed here.

Excel has also been "repurposed" as a data-store/interface for R (Heiberger & Neuwirth, 2009), and numerous statistical packages are available as add-ins for Excel. As one example, the statistics add-in/tutorial Real Statistics using Excel (http://www.real-statistics.com) has become increasingly popular (Zaiontz, 2015).

One final tool which has shipped with Excel for many years as a post-installable add-in (in much the same way as Solver), is the Data Analysis ToolPak—developed for Microsoft by GreyMatter International (Microsoft, 1994)—which allows certain basic statistical analyses to be calculated on data stored on a worksheet (Microsoft, 2016l). No exact documentation noting any changes to this tool could be found, and this author can also not recall any changes since at least Excel version 4 (Microsoft, 1994, 1997). The analyses provided in the ToolPak include:

- ANOVA: Single Factor
- ANOVA: Two-Factor with Replication
- ANOVA: Two-Factor without Replication
- Correlation
- Covariance
- Descriptive Statistics
- Exponential Smoothing
- F-Test Two-Sample for Variances
- Fourier Analysis
- Histogram
- Regression (least squares linear regression)
- Moving Average
- Random Number Generation
- Rank and Percentile
- Sampling
- t-Test: Paired Two-Sample for Means
- t-Test: Two-Sample Assuming Equal Variances
- t-Test: Two-Sample Assuming Unequal Variances
- z-Test: Paired Two-Sample for Means

Tools for Data Visualization

The ability to visualize a presentation of data is not merely a method to make graphics showing what we already know about the data; it should be a means by which we can come to new and deeper insights about data. Pioneered by the likes of Edward Tufte (1983, 1990, 1997, 2006; see also www.edwardtufte.com) and Howard Wainer (1997, 2005, 2009), and finding several new modern-day proponents like Stephen Few (2004, 2006, 2009, 2013; see also www.perceptualedge.com), data visualization has become a specialty of its own. Although the earliest spreadsheet programs were developed for computers that had only the most rudimentary display capabilities, the initial focus was merely on the calculation of data values, rather than on the graphical display of data. However, as the hardware improved, graphical display was soon added. Excel, as the market leader in spreadsheets, also includes several tools for data visualization.

Charts

Excel has included charts natively since very early in its life, but the offering of charts has remained the basic (and relatively inadequate) list of column, bar, pie, doughnut, scatter, line, area, surface, radar, stock, and bubble charts, through to

Excel 2013. Users who wished to create other chart types either had to rely on some very creative hacks to get the end result (e.g., Peltier, 2011a, 2011b), or rely on third-party add-ins to get the desired charts (e.g., Peltier, 2016b).

However, some changes were made through the years. First, while the other Office applications had to make do with Microsoft Graph, which had a very limited data sheet, Excel allowed charts based on much larger datasets stored in a worksheet, and that data range increased as the worksheet size increased in Excel 2007 and later versions. Furthermore, PivotCharts, introduced with Excel 2000, allowed charts based not only on raw data, but also on the analysis of that data using PivotTable methods.

Second, Microsoft has devoted considerably more resources towards improving Excel's data visualization since Excel 2007. Excel 2007 included a total revamp of the charting process, replacing the bottom-up 5-step Chart Wizard, in which every component of a chart had to be specified before the end product was created, with a much faster top-down charting process, where the chart was created in a default format, and then modified as desired. Excel 2007 still included only the same basic offering of chart types as before, but did allow for vastly expanded formatting capabilities—some would say too much so (Peltier, 2008b).

Excel 2010 did not produce much improvement in terms of charts per se, but did introduce better in-cell graphics discussed below. However, in Excel 2013 large modifications (sometimes to the chagrin of long-time users) were made to the chart creation user interface (many dialogs were replaced with panes, which are arguably slower to use). Some big improvements did, however, result from this upgrade: The previously experimental Microsoft Chart Advisor was incorporated as a standard part of the interface, allowing Excel to "examine" the user's data and recommend the best chart type for its display. Furthermore, an improved method for creating charts that combine various elements (such as a bar chart with a line chart displayed on a secondary axis) was introduced in the ability to create "combo" charts. But still no new chart types were introduced.

The biggest changes, however, were introduced with Excel 2016 (Microsoft, 2016m), where the organization of the charts was rearranged, and, while the original eleven chart types (with their variations, such as 2D and 3D versions) were retained, a further six new chart types were introduced (Table 3). One more type (funnel charts) was added in the January 2016 Office 365 update (Microsoft, 2016d, 2016m).

However, the Microsoft Excel team has shown intent for further development, canvassing user feedback on how to plan the implementation of new charting features (Peltier, 2016a). Time, and successive upgrades, will reveal what Excel will be capable of in terms of charting in the future.

Table 3. New chart types in Excel 2016

New Organizational Grouping	Chart Type
Column or Bar	Column
	Bar
Pie or Doughnut	Pie
	Doughnut
Line or Area	Line
	Area
Scatter or Bubble	Scatter
	Bubble
Surface or Radar	Surface
	Radar
Waterfall or Stock	Waterfall*
	Funnel*
	Stock
Hierarchy	Treemap*
	Sunburst*
Statistic	Histogram*
	Pareto*
	Box and whisker*

* Added in Excel 2016

In-Cell Graphics

The first of rudimentary in-cell graphics became capable with the totally reworked conditional formatting tools (in the form of data bars, color scales, or icon sets) in Excel 2007. Excel 2010 refined the conditional formatting, allowing several improvements on the previous implementation, and also added sparklines, a concept pioneered by Edward Tufte (n.d.) and up to then only available via third-party add-ins. These two developments, seemingly small, allow a profound intermingling of data and graphics in cells, creating small visuals with high information density, one of Tufte's requirements for graphical excellence (1983, p. 13).

Specialized Tools for Data Visualization

Excel has included PivotCharts since Excel 2000, but these charts have seen numerous improvements over the years. The chief distinction between a standard chart and

PivotChart is that PivotCharts are based on an underlying PivotTable (which can be created when the PivotChart itself is created) while standard charts must draw their data from a range of worksheet cells. This means that PivotCharts can access larger datasets external to the workbook itself. Furthermore, PivotCharts are interactive, allowing users to modify the display of the chart without having to manipulate the underlying data. However, PivotCharts do also have liabilities, in that they are bound to their data source (they update as it updates, but also cannot exclude part of the data, or include data from other sources). Also, certain chart types (scatter, stock, bubble) cannot be used, and certain formatting is lost when PivotCharts are updated (Microsoft, 2010a; Peltier, 2008a; Treacy, 2016a). PivotCharts are, however, crucially important for the visualization of big data in Excel, as they allow access to potentially much larger datasets via Get and Transform.

One of the most common components of big data, after its temporal elements, is its geospatial nature. This information is often only properly understood when examined in its geographical context, and as such, data of this nature also need to be represented in Excel if Excel is to be a big data visualization tool. Since Office 97, Excel has been accompanied by the adjunct Microsoft Map program (Microsoft, 1997). This was eventually discontinued, and Excel 2013 had, for the highest-priced subscription versions, a new program called Power Map (Microsoft, 2013a). This was again rebranded and included in all versions of Excel 2016 as 3D Maps (Microsoft, 2016g).

A DEMONSTRATION OF EXCEL AS A TOOL FOR DATA ANALYSIS AND DATA VISUALIZATION

Data visualization is difficult, as it appears to be equal parts art and science. The important aim is to create a visual display of the data that gives insight to and/or summarizes the data effectively, in such a way that insights are gained which would not be obtained simply from examining the data values individually. The aim, then, is very much to see the finery of the forest, and not be misled by the intertwining of the trees.

The biggest limitation of any program used to analyze data was traditionally that the data had to "fit" into that program for it to be able to work with it. Data were thus imported into the program, and then analyzed and visualized, placing a limit on the amount of data a user could work with (Jacobs, 2009). Big data, however, requires a different, distributed, approach (Fisher, DeLine, Czerwinski, & Drucker, 2012). This led to "trite proclamations that Big Data consists of datasets too large to fit in an Excel spreadsheet or be stored on a single machine" (Kitchin, 2014, p. 1). When the dataset becomes too big for the workspace of the analysis tool (e.g., too big for a worksheet), difficulties are encountered, leading to tactics such as that employed by de Rosa (2016): Sample the dataset to obtain a representative sampling of the data that will fit into the worksheet, and then analyze that.

However, with developments in the storage formats of data, that boundary has long been crossed, and Microsoft has enabled Excel to capitalize on that. Even with the vast increase in worksheet size—and the fact that the number of worksheets in a single workbook is limited only by the available memory (Microsoft, 2016f)—Excel actually simply cannot efficiently deal with a worksheet full of data—it slows to a complete crawl. But with the introduction of Power Query and Power Pivot, Excel can leave the data in the data file, accessing it as needed, and present only the analysis and visualization of the data in the workbook. In fact, Excel can function as a fully relational database engine, creating (sometimes even automatically) relationships between datasets, and then presenting the combined analysis of that data. Microsoft (2016e) lists the limit for Excel's data model as a staggering 1 999 999 997 rows of data, although it should be remembered that the data model is still stored within an Excel workbook which is still limited to a file size of 2 GB for the 32-bit version of Excel (workbook file size for the 64-bit version is limited only by the capacity—RAM and disk space—of the system on which it is running).

An Analysis of US Traffic Fatalities in Excel

In order to demonstrate the practical utility and limitations of Excel for accessing, analyzing and visualizing big data, data from the United States National Highway Traffic Safety Administration's Fatality Analysis Reporting System (http://www.nhtsa.gov/FARS) will be examined. The data files were downloaded from their ftp site: ftp://www.nhtsa.dot.gov/FARS. The idea to use these data originated from a webinar provided by Mynda Treacy (http://www.myonlinetraininghub.com/excelwebinars). The FARS data have been collected since 1975, and are publicly available on the FARS website listed above. Because of large changes made to the structure of the databases in 2010 (which were aimed at synchronizing the FARS data and the National Automotive Sampling System General Estimates System data; cf. National Highway Traffic Safety Administration, 2016, pp. 520–585), this demonstration will use data files only from 2010 to 2015. It should be noted that, although in absolute terms, some might not consider these data to be "big data," the data files do serve the purpose of demonstrating how Excel can be used to access and combine multiple external datasets into a model that can then be analyzed and presented within the program, while demonstrating how Excel can be used to deal with common problems that might be encountered with data of this nature. Even though the individual datasets contain "relatively" few records (<80 000 per data file), the combination of files (four specific data files across six years) represents a sufficiently large model to demonstrate the basic concepts. Furthermore, Excel's ability to handle larger datasets of tens of millions of rows has already been noted (cf. Jelen, 2010, pp. 1–2). It should also be pointed out that the demonstration analysis will be kept relatively simple, as the author is a biostatistician, not a traffic data analyst—the aim is not an in-depth study of traffic fatalities, but rather an analysis of one single example that can serve as a demonstration of the underlying principles.

Because changes to the user interface can quickly lead to this chapter becoming dated, only key points of the analysis will be shown using screen captures, more to illustrate the process than to the demonstrate the method.

Background to the Analysis

For simplicity, only four files will be used from the total data collection, viz., Accident_*, Person_*, Vehicle_*, and Distract_* (where one file is created for each year, which is indicated in the asterisk portion of the file name—for example, the Person files are Person_2010.csv, Person_2011.csv, etc.). These files contain information on each accident incident that resulted in one or more fatalities, as well as information on the vehicles and persons involved, as well as any driver distractions noted (more information can be found in National Highway Traffic Safety Administration, 2016, pp. 31–284). What makes the use of these data sets interesting is that three data elements identify (and thus link) the records in the various files, viz. ST_CASE (in the accident files), VEH_NO (in the vehicle files), and PER_NO (in the person files). Relationships between datasets can thus be constructed and used in analysis on the basis of these unique identifiers. This analysis will examine only driver-related information, and thus only the subset of drivers from the distract* files (on the basis of the field PER_TYP=1) will be extracted. Figure 1 shows the variables which link the different files. Each successive level requires the primary fields from all preceding levels to be linked (i.e., while the Vehicle file is linked to the Accident file on the basis of only ST_CASE, the Person and Distract files are linked to the Vehicle file on the basis of both ST_CASE and VEH_NO).

Figure 1. Primary field variables which link data files

The first principle to keep in mind when dealing with large datasets is to know the context of the data. The FARS data embody Laney's (2001) challenges of volume (data has been recorded yearly since 1975), velocity (more data is continually added and the nature of the data is continually expanded) and variety (data definitions, variables captured, and even the location [file] in which some variables are stored, constantly change). The data cannot simply be downloaded and "plugged" into whatever analysis program one might want to use. Rather, the data analyst has to gain an understanding of the nature of the data, how datasets relate to each other, and how items change over time. The FARS user guide (National Highway Traffic Safety Administration, 2016) is indispensable in this regard. As such, the data files were downloaded by this author from the FARS website, the relevant individual files were extracted and renamed (one file for each year) and then saved as Comma-Separated Value (CSV) files, as Excel itself can open the FARS dBASE (DBF) files, but Power Query does not.

The context of the data also extends beyond changes to its structure and content. In this instance, for example, it should always be remembered that the FARS data are recorded only for accidents in which fatalities occurred. It would be incorrect, for example, if the majority of these accidents involved drunk drivers, to conclude that drunken driving led to accidents in which fatalities occurred, without first confirming that significantly lower proportions of non-fatal accidents involved drunken drivers.

A short summary of the data files is displayed in Table 4. Looking at the fields, it is apparent that the data files have changed considerably even only over the last six years, but that there appears to have been more stability in the years 2013–2016. The records per file show that the number of accidents are relatively stable (e.g., the largest discrepancy is for the vehicles involved in accidents, where the smallest number, from 2011, is less than 10% smaller than the largest number, from 2015).

The second principle to keep in mind when dealing with large datasets is that one may need to sift through larger datasets to extract only the variables needed for the current analysis. When dealing with small datasets, having extraneous data will not affect the analysis, but when the volume of the data increases by orders of magnitude, extraneous data can make the difference between the hardware and software being able to analyze the data or not. Even working with only the four files from only the six years shown in Table 4, the total number of data points equals 82 667 019. One sifting method could simply be sampling the larger dataset, as suggested by de Rosa (2016), which would reduce the number of records to analyze. The method used here is to keep only the fields needed for the analysis, which retains all the records, but reduces the number of variables. The art then becomes not including extraneous information, while not excluding necessary information. Thus, as the variables are imported into Excel via Power Query, extraneous variables are discarded. This is also relevant in terms of the variability of the data, because data files from successive

Table 4. Summary of FARS data files used in analysis

	Year	Accident	Vehicle	Person	Distract
Fields	2010	47	82	116	4
	2011	50	93	127	4
	2012	50	92	126	4
	2013	50	68	102	4
	2014	50	68	102	4
	2015	52	68	102	4
Records	2010	30 296	44 862	74 863	46 048
	2011	29 867	44 119	73 364	44 187
	2012	31 006	45 960	76 436	45 995
	2013	30 202	45 101	74 331	45 129
	2014	30 056	44 950	73 711	44 977
	2015	32 166	48 923	80 587	48 962
	Totals	**183 593**	**273 915**	**453 292**	**275 298**

years cannot simply be appended, as the actual number of variables (and in certain cases even the definitions of the variables) differ from year to year. Selecting only the relevant variables allows for the creation of data-subsets that can be appended. Nonetheless, it should also always be remembered that the records must be uniquely identified if any meaningful analysis is to be performed (i.e., they must contain the database equivalent of a primary key). This is complicated in the process of appending data from multiple years of FARS files, as the ST_CASE variable is reset each year. Thus, ST_CASE uniquely identifies records *within* one year, but as soon as multiple years are appended, repetitive ST_CASE values will be found. It is thus necessary to combine the year with ST_CASE to identify each record uniquely. The Accident file, however, is the only file used in this analysis which contains the YEAR variable (all the files used contain the ST_CASE variable), and it thus has to be added to the remaining files.

Adding and Manipulating Data

It is beyond the scope of this demonstration to display all the techniques listed in Table 2. Figure 2 shows that Power Query (Get & Transform) allows access to a wide variety of data file types and data file manipulations (e.g., merging and appending data).

Figure 2. Loading and transforming data files with power query

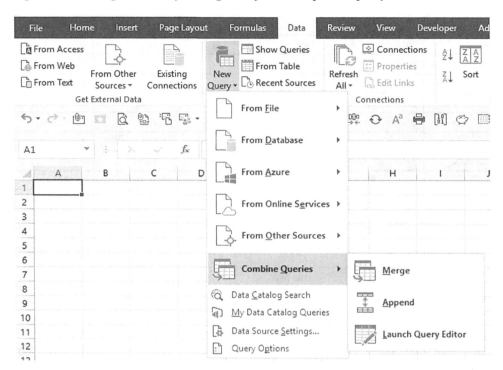

For this analysis, each data file was added to the Query editor, and then modified as needed for the analysis. The first step involved removing any unneeded columns, and then adding columns to create data fields needed for the analysis. The advantage to these added fields is that they add very little overhead in terms of storage, although they do add a little in terms of processing. The PQL language was used to create new data fields, and, very usefully, a syntax check is computed as an expression is created, which helps avoid delays when a query is applied to a large dataset only to return an error.

Table 5 shows some of the PQL expressions used to create the columns in various queries (one such query was created for each file type for each of the six years). The examples show how PQL can perform date and time manipulation, text manipulation, and also how PQL expressions can be nested—the latter being used to replace the null categories of 8 and 9 for gender with blank cells, for example.

The next important concept to understand for the analysis of big data in Excel is that of the Excel data model (Microsoft, 2016b, 2016e). Each Excel workbook may contain one data model, which embeds and stores data from multiple tables in a compressed, relational format, within the workbook file for use in data analysis

Table 5. PQL expressions used

Data Files	Name of Column	PQL Expression
Accident	DateOfAccident	= #date([YEAR], [MONTH], [DAY])
Accident	TimeOfAccident	= #time([HOUR],[MINUTE],0)
Person	AGEofPERSON	= Replacer.ReplaceValue(Replacer.ReplaceValue([AGE],998,""),999,"")
Person	SEXofPERSON	= Replacer.ReplaceValue(Replacer.ReplaceValue([SEX],8,""),9,"")
Vehicle,Person,Distract	YEAR	= 201x (where x represents the precise year)
Accident &Vehicle	YEAR_ST_CASE	= Text.From([YEAR]) & Text.From([ST_CASE])
Vehicle,Person,Distract	YEAR_ST_CASE_VEH_NO	= Text.From([YEAR]) & Text.From([ST_CASE]) & Text.From([VEH_NO])

and visualization tools such as PivotTables. Single tables of data can be stored in a worksheet and can be analyzed without employing the data model, but as soon as multiple tables which are related by one or more fields are used in an analysis, the data model allows for very efficient analysis and modelling of the data through its ability to create relationships between tables. Also, thanks to the high compression, large volumes of data can be stored in the model, allowing Excel to overcome the row limit of the worksheet.

Once the queries were defined as needed for the analysis, the Close & Load To… option was chosen to specify how the query should be loaded (the default creates a table in a new worksheet, which can quickly become burdensome when working with large amounts of data). For maximum efficiency with large data, each query was loaded only as a connection, and the queries for each year were not loaded to the data model. Once the queries for the data files for all years of a specific file type were loaded, Append queries were created to build one dataset from the trimmed-down files for each year (e.g., all the accident_201x.csv files were combined into one file named Accident). This stacked data table was then added to the data model, allowing Excel to access the data without creating an overly large workbook—in this example, 205 MB of CSV files were loaded to a workbook data model of 57 MB, which included the additional columns added and the appended queries discussed next.

When a query is created in this manner, Excel displays a pane showing all the workbook queries, and from this pane, a preview of the data and the nature of the query can be seen (Figure 3). An outstanding feature of the Power Query editor is that every step performed in the process is recorded in a pane adjacent to the query fields. This allows the user to return and edit or remove any step, or even to insert additional steps in between existing steps. Furthermore, a query can be duplicated

Figure 3. Query preview

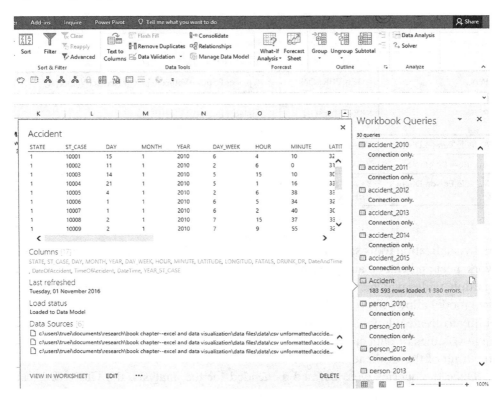

and then its steps can be modified. In this way, instead of recreating each query for every year, the first query was duplicated and then modified (e.g., the name of the source file was changed to the correct file for the next year, etc.).

One additional step, which also helped reduce the size of the final model, was that the author was only interested in driver information from the Person file for the purposes of the analysis. Thus, when creating the queries for the various Person year files, a filter was added in the Query Editor to include only the PER_NO of 1 (indicated in the FARS user guide as the driver).

Defining Data Relationships

Once all the queries had been created, the various elements had to be connected in meaningful ways so as to allow analysis of the interconnected relationships. This is done in Power Pivot, but it should be noted that Power Pivot is not a relational database tool in the conventional sense. Firstly, until very recently, only one-to-many relationships could be created, but Power Pivot for Excel 2016 now has the ability to also create one-to-one relationships. Secondly, while multiple relationships can be created between two tables, only one of those relationships can be active (i.e., can be referenced directly) at any given time. This is the reason for the concatenation of YEAR, ST_CASE and VEH_NO in the last row of Table 5—to create a single field which represents up to three index columns so that different queries can be meaningfully joined.

The Power Pivot tool also contains a very helpful diagram view in which relationships between various tables can be viewed, created, and edited (Figure 4).

Analyzing the Data

Once the data model has been created, a standard PivotTable can be added, using the data model as its data source. The immediately noticeable difference to such a PivotTable (as seen in Figure 5) is that the fields list displays all the tables from the data model, and any field from any table can be used in the analysis, provided the tables are correctly linked.

Figure 4. Diagram view of table relationships in power pivot

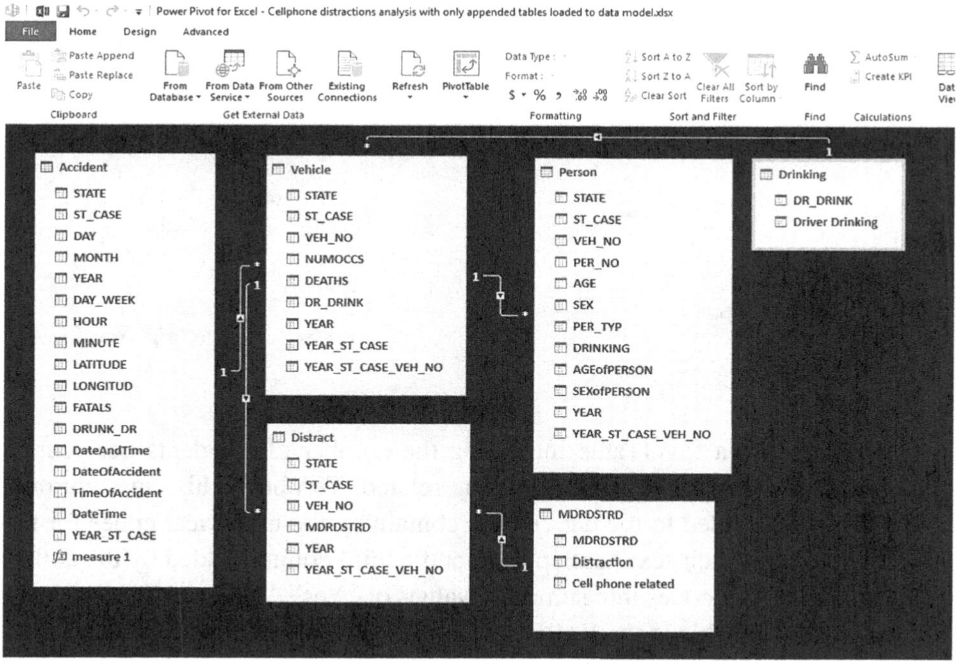

Figure 5. PivotTable (cellphone related distractions by year) showing all tables in the data model

Figure 5 shows a PivotTable indicating the number of accidents per year in which the driver distraction was cellphone related. To obtain this, an additional lookup table was added to the data model containing the numerical codes for the driver distractions, their text descriptions, and a third column added by the author grouping the various codes into summary values of "Yes", "No" and "n/a"—detail on the codes is available in the FARS user guide (National Highway Traffic Safety Administration, 2016, p. 455). This new column was then used in the PivotTable, as seen in Figure 5. The result, however, is dubious—the PivotTable shows that a very small number of accidents were cellphone related, which may very well be the case, but the large number of indeterminate (n/a) cases precludes the making of any conclusive deductions from this. Clearly, further detailed investigation will be required to attempt an answer to this question.

Visualizing the Data

Once the data model has been constructed, analyses using Power Pivot such as that shown in Figure 5 are easy to construct. But very often it may be useful to visualize the data rather than looking only at a table of figures. Figure 6 shows this in practice, where the number of fatalities from accidents in which drunk drivers (the field shows the actual number of drunk drivers involved in the accident) is compared to the day of the week (day 1 being Sunday) on which the accident took place (National Highway Traffic Safety Administration, 2016, pp. 41, 72). Examining the table of values only does not readily reveal the trend, as the amount of information tends to clutter the reader's perception. This is further hindered by the small number of accidents in which two, three, or even four drunk drivers were involved. But once the data is plotted as a proportionate bar chart (in Excel, 100% stacked bar chart), the small values for >1 drunk drivers occupy proportionately small areas of the chart (and thus no longer clutter the display), and the trend of more drunk drivers being involved on days 1 and 7 (i.e., the weekend days), becomes readily apparent. Furthermore, there is a noticeable increase on day 6 (Fridays), which, presumably, would indicate Friday nights. Since the data files contain the date and time of the accident, even this hypothesis (that more drunk driving accidents occur from Friday night through to Sunday) could be investigated. Figure 6 also shows a Slicer, which would allow the user to focus on any individual day of the week, or any combination of days.

Mapping the Data

The data used in Excel data models can also be mapped geospatially using the 3D Maps feature (in Excel 2016, or its Power Map equivalent in Excel 2013). The FARS Accident data files contain the fields LATITUDE and LONGITUD which allow the number of fatalities to be plotted on a map of the US by location. Figure 7 shows two of the possible displays provided by 3D Maps: A bar chart and a heat map. A glance at the chart reveals that, as could be expected, more fatalities occur in more densely populated areas, presumably because these areas also experience more accidents.

Figure 6. PivotChart (drunk drivers by day of week) with slicer on pivot table

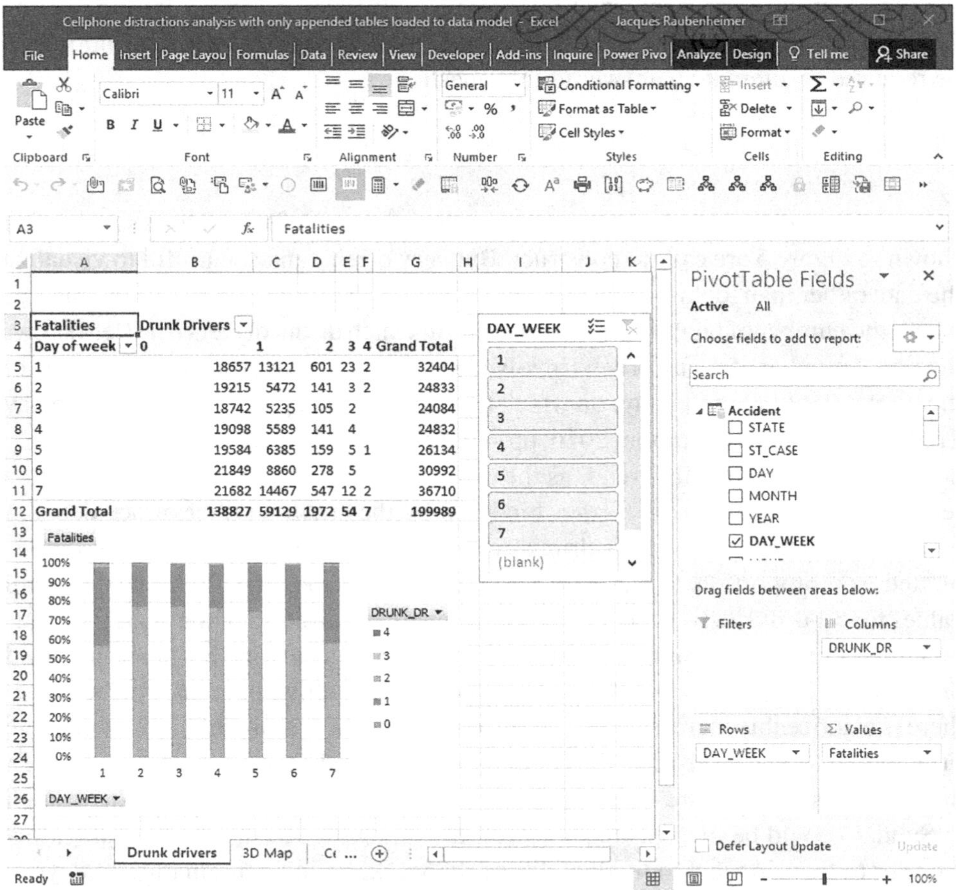

DATA VISUALIZATION IN THE 21ST CENTURY: THE POPULARITY OF DASHBOARDS

A concept that has steadily gained traction in the business world in the latter part of the 20th century, and even more so in the 21st (Few, 2013, pp. 3–5), is that of a dashboard: A summary tool that provides analysis and interpretation of multiple sources of data, often in an interactive manner that allows further investigation or action. Few's (Few, 2013, p. 26) simple definition is that "a dashboard is a visual display of the most important information needed to achieve one or more objectives, consolidated and arranged on a single screen so the information can be monitored at a glance." Alexander and Walkenbach (2013, p. 12) distinguish dashboards from reports by noting that dashboards contain graphic visualization of data, limit the

Figure 7. Number of fatalities plotted geospatially using Excel 3D Maps (bar chart and heat map)

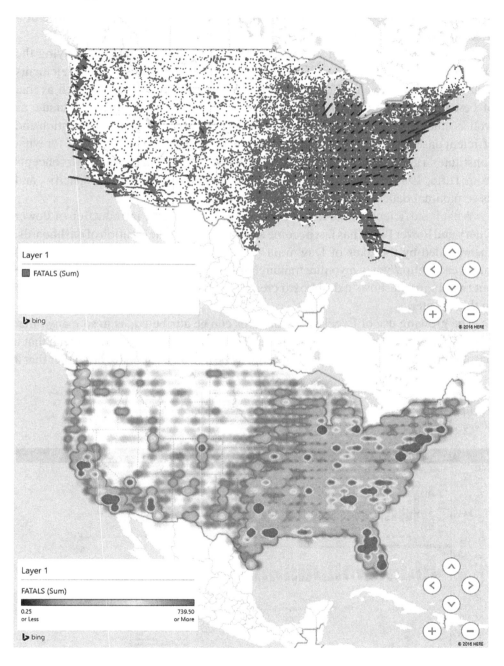

display to only the relevant data, and present "predefined conclusions relevant to the goal of the dashboard." Furthermore, they note that dashboards often are linked to Key Performance Indicators (KPIs) which show "the level of performance of a task deemed to be essential to daily operations or processes" (p. 14).

It is beyond the scope of this chapter to discuss the principles underlying the creation of dashboards, as well as to delve into the specifics of what elements contribute to effective dashboards, and readers are referred to works such as that of Few (2013), who discusses examples of what to avoid and what to pursue, as well as elucidating clearly the principles underlying effective data visualization and efficient dashboard design. A summary of the principles Few puts forward for what constitutes a good dashboard (Few, 2013, p. 94; melded by this author with concepts from Tufte, 1983) is that a good dashboard is organized, condensed, specific, and uses maximal data density while remaining sensible.

What is sufficient to note is that Excel, doubly so with the introduction of Power Query and Power Pivot, has fast become a favorite tool for the creation of dashboards, spearheaded by the likes of Duggirala (http://chandoo.org/wp/excel-dashboards/) and Treacy (http://www.myonlinetraininghub.com/excel-dashboard-course), to name but two. Figure 8 shows a dashboard created by Treacy on data similar to that used in this chapter.

The growing use of Excel for dashboards can be attributed, as in so many other cases, to its ubiquitous availability and its flexibility. But that does not mean that a dashboard created with Excel will necessarily be a good dashboard, but rather that it

Figure 8. Car crash analysis dashboard
(Treacy, 2016b)

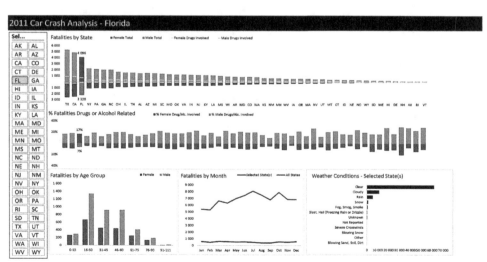

is a tool that, when used with skill, can be used to create very effective dashboards. In fact, in Few's (2013) penultimate chapter in which he showcases good dashboard design, several examples are pointed out as being created in Excel, and he states (p. 233) that "even though Excel was not created for the development of dashboards and lacks some of the functionality that is common in other products, we can, if we know a few tricks, use it to create dashboards that exhibit exceptional visual design."

A WORD OF CAUTION

This chapter has demonstrated that Excel can, in fact, be used for the analysis and visualization of big data. However, significant hurdles exist as well. As Bovey, Wallentin, Bullen and Green (2009, p. 9) point out, a very significant problem in the world of Excel is that not all users upgrade immediately, choosing, for reasons related to personal preference, cost, or otherwise, to remain with a specific version. This chapter has demonstrated the principles of the analysis of big data with the latest version of Excel available at present, but the danger is that as Excel is updated, this chapter will become dated. Furthermore, even using the principles discussed in this chapter on different versions of Excel could lead to slight variations in results (witness the updates to Excel's statistical functions and the changes in the display of conditional formatting between Excel 2007 and later versions of Excel, as select examples).

Moreover, users themselves are one of the biggest threats to the correct use of spreadsheets, and users should proceed with caution. One of the biggest problems with spreadsheets remains that while the tools are functional, users are not always competent, and are prone to make errors (Bradley & McDaid, 2009; Hesse & Scerno, 2009), either through lack of knowledge, lack of care, or both (Croll, 2009; Lawson, Baker, Powell, & Foster-Johnson, 2009; Panko, 2006; Panko & Ordway, 2005; Powell, Baker, & Lawson, 2009a; Powell, Baker, & Lawson, 2009b). These concerns remain when analyzing big data, but should not be limited to spreadsheets. Users can make errors, apparently with similar ease, using the simplest or the most complex software tools. However, this problem appears to be one not readily solvable (Panko, 2007), as many are of the opinion that users naturally gravitate to programs such as Excel because of their simplicity to use. At the same time, Chambers and Scaffidi (2010) report that "the complexity of Excel" is a significant barrier to using more advanced features of the program. This would seem to indicate that users, generally, use the simplest programs they feel they can master, but that they simultaneously overestimate their ability to master those programs. Even agreeing on what best practices should be is extremely difficult (Colver, 2004). Perhaps the best way to address the problem would be to train users to "debug" their spreadsheets by reviewing them for errors regularly (e.g., Croll, 2008; Goswami, Chan, & Kim, 2008; Leon, Kalbers, Coster, & Abraham, 2012), although even that may prove difficult when users overestimate their abilities (and thus feel that they do not need training). Training and experience, though, remain key components of the quality of spreadsheets and data analysis with spreadsheets (Lawson et al., 2009).

CONCLUSION

Microsoft Excel has come a long way since it was first released. Clearly, Microsoft has, through the years, endeavored to adapt Excel to meet the continuously evolving needs of spreadsheet users, and it thus remains a popular and widely-used tool. In the early 21st century Microsoft has, accordingly, aligned its strategy to making Excel a powerful and accepted tool for the analysis of big data in a suite of complementary tools. Excel can meet the three core challenges of big data: Volume, velocity and variety (as defined by Laney, 2001). It is capable of accessing (through Power Pivot and Power Query), analyzing, and visualizing, data of the scale any comparable systems can handle; it can store an analysis model that can be updated as new data are added, and it provides a set of tools for the effective visualization and/or analysis of that data, both through standard charts as well as through geospatial mapping (through 3D Maps). However, the world of data analysis and data visualization is, in keeping with its subject, evolving. Excel will have to continue to evolve in corresponding fashion in order to maintain its utility to big data analysts. The addition of new chart types in Excel 2016 is one example of how Microsoft is seeking to do this. But even there, scope for improvement remains. The new box plots and waterfall charts, while simple to implement, remain relatively inflexible and somewhat limited, and third party solutions still provide much greater functionality for these chart types. Also, while new charts have been added, others (e.g., tornado charts, slopegraphs, etc.) are still lacking, although these can be created in Excel with a little skill and imagination.

Two factors count in Excel's favor as a tool for the analysis and visualization of big data. Firstly, it is precisely Excel's flexibility and customizability, evident in both the way that third party vendors can create solutions that leverage Excel's capabilities to create new analysis and visualization tools, as well as in the way in which Excel users can customize existing Excel tools to create visualizations not possible by conventional means, that makes Excel such an adept tool for the data analyst. Secondly, Excel remains ubiquitous. The very ubiquity of Excel means that there is value in showing how it can be used for the needs of Big Data. It is for these reasons that this author believes that Excel will still remain a viable choice for the analysis and visualization of big data for large numbers of analysts for many years to come.

DISCLAIMER

No support or funding was provided by Microsoft, but the author is a Microsoft Certified Trainer and holds the Microsoft Office Specialist Expert certification for Microsoft Excel, as well as the Microsoft Office Specialist Master Instructor certification. This chapter appears to advertise Excel only to the extent that Excel is, as noted in the introduction, the spreadsheet application used by the vast majority of spreadsheet users.

ACKNOWLEDGMENT

Dr. Daleen Struwig, Medical Editor, Faculty of Health Sciences, University of the Free State, is gratefully acknowledged for the editorial preparation of the chapter.

REFERENCES

Alexander, M., & Walkenbach, J. (2013). *Microsoft Excel Dashboards and Reports.* Hoboken, NJ: Wiley.

Allington, M. (2016). *What is Power Query.* Retrieved October 20, 2016, from http://exceleratorbi.com.au/what-is-power-query

Almiron, M. G., Lopes, B., & Oliveira, A. L. C. (2010). On the numerical accuracy of spreadsheets. *Journal of Statistical Software, 34*(4). Retrieved from http://physics.usyd.edu.au/~wheat/teaching/cscp/resources/almiron_etal.pdf

Apigian, C. H., & Gambill, S. E. (2004). Is Microsoft Excel 2003 ready for the statistics classroom? *Journal of Computer Information Systems, 45*(2), 27–35.

Berger, R. (2007). Nonstandard operator precedence in Excel. *Computational Statistics & Data Analysis, 51*(6), 2788–2791. Retrieved from http://www.sciencedirect.com/science/article/pii/S0167947306003641

Bovey, R., Wallentin, D., Bullen, S., & Green, J. (2009). *Professional Excel development: The definitive guide to developing applications using Microsoft Excel, VBA, and. Net* (2nd ed.). Upper Saddle River, NJ: Addison-Wesley.

Bradley, L., & McDaid, K. (2009). Using Bayesian statistical methods to determine the level of error in large spreadsheets. In *Software Engineering-Companion Volume. 31st International Conference on Software Engineering* (pp. 351–354). IEEE. Retrieved from http://ieeexplore.ieee.org/xpls/abs_all.jsp?arnumber=5071019

Brandel, M. (1999). PC Software transforms the PC. *Computerword*, 62.

Bricklin, D. (2006). *When The Long Tail Wags The Dog*. Retrieved September 23, 2016, from http://danbricklin.com/log/2012_11_18.htm#lotus30

Bricklin, D. (2009a). *About Dan Bricklin's special short paper for the Harvard Business School advertising course*. Retrieved from http://www.bricklin.com/anonymous/bricklin-1978-visicalc-paper.pdf

Bricklin, D. (2009b). *The Idea*. Retrieved September 21, 2016, from http://www.bricklin.com/history/saiidea.htm

Bricklin, D. (2013). *30 years since Lotus 1-2-3*. Retrieved September 15, 2016, from http://danbricklin.com/log/2012_11_18.htm#lotus30

Bricklin, D. (2015). *Was VisiCalc the "first" spreadsheet?* Retrieved September 21, 2016, from http://www.bricklin.com/firstspreadsheetquestion.htm

Campbell, M. (2007). Number crunching without programming: The evolution of spreadsheet usability. *IEEE Annals of the History of Computing*. doi:10.1109/MAHC.2007.4338438

Chambers, C., & Scaffidi, C. (2010). Struggling to excel: A field study of challenges faced by spreadsheet users. In *2010 IEEE Symposium on Visual Languages and Human-Centric Computing*. Retrieved from http://ieeexplore.ieee.org/xpls/abs_all.jsp?arnumber=5635221

Colver, D. (2004). Spreadsheet good practice: is there any such thing? In *European Spreadsheet Risk Interest Group*. Retrieved from http://arxiv.org/abs/1001.3967

Courtland, R. (2015). *Gordon Moore: The Man Whose Name Means Progress: The visionary engineer reflects on 50 years of Moore's Law*. Retrieved September 15, 2016, from http://spectrum.ieee.org/computing/hardware/gordon-moore-the-man-whose-name-means-progress

Croll, G. J. (2008). In Pursuit of Spreadsheet Excellence. In *European Spreadsheet Risk Interest Group*. Retrieved from http://arxiv.org/abs/0806.3536

Croll, G. J. (2009). Spreadsheets and the financial collapse. In *European Spreadsheet Risk Interest Group*. Retrieved from http://arxiv.org/abs/0908.4420

de Rosa, M. (2016). *How to Analyze Big Data with Excel*. Retrieved September 22, 2016, from http://www.datasciencecentral.com/profiles/blogs/how-to-analyze-big-data-with-excel

Duggirala, P. (2011, January 13). *A Brief History of Microsoft Excel – Timeline Visualization*. Retrieved October 17, 2016, from http://chandoo.org/wp/2010/01/13/history-of-excel-timeline/

Few, S. (2004). *Show Me the Numbers: Designing Tables and Graphs to Enlighten*. Oakland: Analytics Press.

Few, S. (2006). *Information Dashboard Design: The Effective Visual Communication of Data*. Sebastopol: O'Reilly Media.

Few, S. (2009). *Now You See It: Simple Visualization Techniques for Quantitative Analysis*. Oakland: Analytics Press.

Few, S. (2013). *Information dashboard design: Displaying data for at-a-glance monitoring* (2nd ed.). Burlingame: Analytics Press.

Fisher, D., DeLine, R., Czerwinski, M., & Drucker, S. (2012). Interactions with big data analytics. *Interactions*, 50–59. doi:10.1145/2168931.2168943

Frankston, B. (1999). *RE: VisiCalc history*. Retrieved from http://dssresources.com/history/frankston4151999a.html

Fylstra, D. (2016). *Frontline Systems company history*. Retrieved September 22, 2016, from http://www.solver.com/frontline-systems-company-history

Fylstra, D., Lasdon, L., Watson, J., & Waren, A. (1998). Design and use of the Microsoft Excel Solver. *Interfaces, 28*(5), 29–55. doi:10.1287/inte.28.5.29

Garfinkel, S. L. (n.d.). *Improv*. Retrieved September 22, 2016, from https://simson.net/clips/1991/1991.NW.Improv.html

Goswami, S., Chan, H. C., & Kim, H. W. (2008). The role of visualization tools in spreadsheet error correction from a cognitive fit perspective. *Journal of the Association for Information Systems, 9*(6), 321–343. Retrieved from http://165.132.10.17/dslab/Journal/JAIS 2008.pdf

Grad, B. (2007). The creation and the demise of VisiCalc. *IEEE Annals of the History of Computing, 3*, 20–31. doi:10.1109/MAHC.2007.4338439

Graves, S. (1997). *Maximum Likelihood Regression on Censored, Experimental Data Using a Spreadsheet Program* (No. 164). Retrieved from http://cqpi.engr.wisc.edu/system/files/r164.pdf

Great Speculations. (2013). *An Overview Why Microsoft's Worth $42*. Retrieved September 15, 2016, from http://www.forbes.com/sites/greatspeculations/2013/01/09/an-overview-why-microsofts-worth-42/

Heiberger, R., & Neuwirth, E. (2009). *R through Excel: A spreadsheet interface for statistics, data analysis, and graphics.* Dordrecht: Springer. doi:10.1007/978-1-4419-0052-4

Hesse, R., & Scerno, D. (2009). How Electronic Spreadsheets Changed the World. *Interfaces, 39*(2), 159–167. doi:10.1287/inte.1080.0376

Hilbert, M. (2012). How much information is there in the "information society"? *Significance, 9*(4), 8–12. doi:10.1111/j.1740.2012.00584.x

Hilbert, M., & López, P. (2012a). How to measure the world's technological capacity to communicate, store, and compute information, part I: Results and scope. *International Journal of Communication, 6*(1), 956–979.

Hilbert, M., & López, P. (2012b). How to Measure the World's Technological Capacity to Communicate, Store, and Compute Information Part II: Measurement Unit and Conclusions 1. *International Journal of Communication, 6*, 936–955. Retrieved from http://ijoc.org/index.php/ijoc/article/view/1563/741

Jacobs, A. (2009). The Pathologies of Big Data. *Queue, 7*(6), 36–44. doi:10.1145/1563821.1563874

Jelen, B. (2010). *PowerPivot for the data analyst: Microsoft Excel 2010.* Indianapolis, IN: Que.

Kapor, M. (2007). Recollections on Lotus 1-2-3: Benchmark for spreadsheet software. *IEEE Annals of the History of Computing.* doi:10.1109/MAHC.2007.4338440

Keeling, K. B., & Pavur, R. J. (2004). Numerical accuracy issues in using excel for simulation studies. *Proceedings of the 2004 Winter Simulation Conference.* doi:10.1109/WSC.2004.1371492

Kitchin, R. (2014). Big Data, new epistemologies and paradigm shifts. *Big Data & Society, 1*(1), 1–12. doi:10.1177/2053951714528481

Knüsel, L. (1998). On the accuracy of statistical distributions in Microsoft Excel 97. *Computational Statistics & Data Analysis, 26*, 375–377. Retrieved from http://www.sciencedirect.com/science/article/pii/S0167947397817562

Knüsel, L. (2005). On the accuracy of statistical distributions in Microsoft Excel 2003. *Computational Statistics & Data Analysis.* Retrieved from http://www.sciencedirect.com/science/article/pii/S0167947304000337

Knüsel, L. (2011). *On the Accuracy of Statistical Distributions in Microsoft Excel 2010.* Retrieved from http://www.csdassn.org/software_reports/Excel2011.pdf

Kwak, J. (2013). *The Importance of Excel*. Retrieved September 16, 2016, from https://baselinescenario.com/2013/02/09/the-importance-of-excel/

Laney, D. (2001). 3D data Management: Controlling data volume, velocity, and variety. *Application Delivery Strategies, 949*, 4. Retrieved from http://blogs.gartner.com/doug-laney/files/2012/01/ad949-3D-Data-Management-Controlling-Data-Volume-Velocity-and-Variety.pdf

Laverty, W. H., Miket, M. J., & Kelly, I. W. (2002). Simulation of hidden Markov models with EXCEL. *Journal of the Royal Statistical Society Series D: The Statistician, 51*(1), 31–40. doi:10.1111/1467-9884.00296

Lawson, B., Baker, K., Powell, S., & Foster-Johnson, L. (2009). A comparison of spreadsheet users with different levels of experience. *Omega, 37*(3), 579–590. doi:10.1016/j.omega.2007.12.004

Leon, L., Kalbers, L., Coster, N., & Abraham, D. (2012). A spreadsheet life cycle analysis and the impact of Sarbanes–Oxley. *Decision Support Systems, 54*(1), 452–460. doi:10.1016/j.dss.2012.06.006

Lynn, J. (2016). *Healthcare Analytics Biggest Competitor – Excel Posted*. Retrieved April 10, 2016, from http://www.hospitalemrandehr.com/2016/03/16/healthcare-analytics-biggest-competitor-excel/

Mattessich, R. (1961). Budgeting Models and System Simulation Author. *Accounting Review*, *36*(3), 384–397. Retrieved from http://www.jstor.org/stable/242869

Mattessich, R. (1964). *Simulation of the firm through a budget computer program*. Homewood, IL: Irwin.

Mattessich, R. (n.d.). *Spreadsheet: Its First Computerization (19611964)*. Retrieved September 15, 2016, from http://dssresources.com/history/mattessichspreadsheet.htm

McCullough, B. D. (2008). Microsoft Excel's "Not The Wichmann–Hill" random number generators. *Computational Statistics & Data Analysis, 52*(10), 4587–4593. doi:10.1016/j.csda.2008.03.006

McCullough, B. D., & Wilson, B. (1999). On the accuracy of statistical procedures in Microsoft Excel 97. *Computational Statistics & Data Analysis, 31*, 27–37. Retrieved from http://www.sciencedirect.com/science/article/pii/S0167947308001606

McCullough, B. D., & Wilson, B. (2002). On the accuracy of statistical procedures in Microsoft Excel 2000 and Excel XP. *Computational Statistics & Data Analysis, 40*, 713–721. 10.1016/S0167-9473(02)00095-6

Mélard, G. (2014). On the accuracy of statistical procedures in Microsoft Excel 2010. *Computational Statistics, 29*(5), 1095–1128. doi: 10.1007/s00180-014-0482-5

Meyer, D. Z., & Avery, L. M. (2008). Excel as a Qualitative Data Analysis Tool. *Field Methods, 21*(1), 91–112. doi:10.1177/1525822X08323985

Microsoft. (1994). *Visual Basic User's Guide*. Redmond: Microsoft.

Microsoft. (1997). *Getting results with Microsoft Office 97*. Microsoft.

Microsoft. (2004). *Description of improvements in the statistical functions in Excel 2003 and in Excel 2004 for Mac*. Retrieved September 28, 2016, from https://support.microsoft.com/en-us/kb/828888

Microsoft. (2010a). *Overview of PivotTable and PivotChart reports*. Retrieved September 26, 2016, from https://support.office.com/en-US/article/Overview-of-PivotTable-and-PivotChart-reports-00a5bf71-65cb-49f9-b321-85bb7b0b06c2

Microsoft. (2010b). *What's new in Excel 2010*. Retrieved August 28, 2013, from https://support.office.com/en-US/article/What-s-New-in-Excel-2010-44316790-A115-4780-83DB-D003E4A2B329

Microsoft. (2013a). *Power Map for Excel*. Retrieved September 26, 2016, from https://support.office.com/en-US/article/Power-Map-for-Excel-82D65BD7-70C9-48A3-8356-6B0E82472D74

Microsoft. (2013b). *What's new in Excel 2013*. Retrieved June 4, 2013, from https://support.office.com/en-US/article/What-s-new-in-Excel-2013-1CBC42CD-BFAF-43D7-9031-5688EF1392FD

Microsoft. (2015). *Days of the week before March 1, 1900 are incorrect in Excel*. Retrieved September 21, 2016, from https://support.microsoft.com/en-za/kb/214058

Microsoft. (2016a). *Access 2016 specifications*. Retrieved September 23, 2016, from https://support.office.com/en-US/article/Access-2016-specifications-0cf3c66f-9cf2-4e32-9568-98c1025bb47c

Microsoft. (2016b). *Create a Data Model in Excel*. Retrieved September 22, 2016, from https://blogs.office.com/2012/08/23/introduction-to-the-data-model-and-relationships-in-excel-2013/

Microsoft. (2016c). *Create a forecast in Excel 2016 for Windows*. Retrieved September 23, 2016, from https://support.office.com/en-US/article/Create-a-forecast-in-Excel-2016-for-Windows-22c500da-6da7-45e5-bfdc-60a7062329fd

Microsoft. (2016d). *Create a funnel chart*. Retrieved September 26, 2016, from https://support.office.com/en-us/article/Create-a-funnel-chart-ba21bcba-f325-4d9f-93df-97074589a70e?ui=en-US&rs=en-US&ad=US

Microsoft. (2016e). *Data Model specification and limits*. Retrieved October 21, 2016, from https://support.office.com/en-US/article/Data-Model-specification-and-limits-19AA79F8-E6E8-45A8-9BE2-B58778FD68EF

Microsoft. (2016f). *Excel specifications and limits*. Retrieved September 23, 2016, from https://support.office.com/en-US/article/Excel-specifications-and-limits-CA36E2DC-1F09-4620-B726-67C00B05040F

Microsoft. (2016g). *Get started with 3D Maps*. Retrieved September 22, 2016, from https://support.office.com/en-us/article/Get-started-with-3D-Maps-6b56a50d-3c3e-4a9e-a527-eea62a387030?ui=en-US&rs=en-US&ad=US

Microsoft. (2016h). *Large Address Aware capability change for Excel*. Retrieved October 15, 2016, from https://support.microsoft.com/en-us/kb/3160741

Microsoft. (2016i). *Power Query (informally known as " M ") formula categories*. Retrieved October 20, 2016, from https://msdn.microsoft.com/library/mt253322

Microsoft. (2016j). *Switch between various sets of values by using scenarios*. Retrieved September 23, 2016, from https://support.office.com/en-US/article/switch-between-various-sets-of-values-by-using-scenarios-2068afb1-ecdf-4956-9822-19ec479f55a2

Microsoft. (2016k). *Use Goal Seek to find the result you want by adjusting an input value*. Retrieved September 23, 2016, from https://support.office.com/en-US/article/Use-Goal-Seek-to-find-the-result-you-want-by-adjusting-an-input-value-320cb99e-f4a4-417f-b1c3-4f369d6e66c7

Microsoft. (2016l). *Use the Analysis ToolPak to perform complex data analysis*. Retrieved September 23, 2016, from https://support.office.com/en-US/article/use-the-analysis-toolpak-to-perform-complex-data-analysis-f77cbd44-fdce-4c4e-872b-898f4c90c007

Microsoft. (2016m). *What's new in Excel 2016 for Windows*. Retrieved September 22, 2016, from https://support.office.com/en-US/article/What-s-new-in-Excel-2016-for-Windows-5fdb9208-ff33-45b6-9e08-1f5cdb3a6c73

Microsoft. (2016n). *What's the difference between Office 365 and Office 2016?* Retrieved September 26, 2016, from https://support.office.com/en-us/article/What-s-the-difference-between-Office-365-and-Office-2016-ed447ebf-6060-46f9-9e90-a239bd27eb96?ui=en-US&rs=en-US&ad=US

Miles, J. N. V. (2005). Confirmatory factor analysis using Microsoft Excel. *Behaviour Research Methods, 37*(4), 672–676. Retrieved from http://www.jeremymiles.co.uk/mestuff/publications/p36.pdf

Moore, G. E. (1965). Cramming more components onto integrated circuits. *Electronics, 38*(8), 114–117. doi:10.1109/N.2006.4785860

Nash, J. (2006). Spreadsheets in statistical practice—another look. *The American Statistician, 60*(3), 287–289. doi:10.1198/000313006X126585

National Highway Traffic Safety Administration. (2016). *Fatality Analysis Reporting System (FARS): Analytical User's Manual 1975-2015* (No. DOT HS 812 315). Retrieved from ftp://ftp.nhtsa.dot.gov/FARS/FARS-DOC/Analytical User Guide/USERGUIDE-2015.pdf

Neyeloff, J. L., Fuchs, S. C., & Moreira, L. B. (2012). Meta-analyses and Forest plots using a Microsoft Excel spreadsheet: Step-by-step guide focusing on descriptive data analysis. *BMC Research Notes, 5*, 52. doi:10.1186/1756

Ose, S. O. (2016). Using Excel and Word to Structure Qualitative Data. *Journal of Applied Social Science, 10*(2), 147–162. doi:10.1177/1936724416664948

Panko, R. R. (2006). *Spreadsheets and Sarbanes-Oxley: Regulations, risks, and control frameworks*. San Jose. Retrieved from http://citeseerx.ist.psu.edu/viewdoc/download?doi=10.1.1.87.101&rep=rep1&type=pdf

Panko, R. R. (2007). Thinking is Bad: Implications of Human Error Research for Spreadsheet Research and Practice. In *European Spreadsheet Risk Interest Group*. Retrieved from http://arxiv.org/abs/0801.3114

Panko, R. R., & Ordway, N. (2005). Sarbanes-Oxley: What about all the spreadsheets? In *European Spreadsheet Risk Interest Group*. Retrieved from http://arxiv.org/abs/0804.0797

Pardo, R. (2000). *The world's first electronic spreadsheet*. Retrieved September 15, 2016, from http://www.renepardo.com/articles/spreadsheet.pdf

Peltier, J. (2008a). *Making Regular Charts from Pivot Tables*. Retrieved September 26, 2016, from https://support.office.com/en-US/article/Overview-of-PivotTable-and-PivotChart-reports-00a5bf71-65cb-49f9-b321-85bb7b0b06c2

Peltier, J. (2008b). *Why I don't like Excel 2007 charts*. Retrieved September 26, 2016, from http://peltiertech.com/why-i-dont-like-excel-2007-charts/

Peltier, J. (2011a). *Excel box and whisker diagrams (Box plots)*. Retrieved September 2, 2013, http://peltiertech.com/excel-box-and-whisker-diagrams-box-plots/

Peltier, J. (2011b). *Excel waterfall charts (Bridge charts)*. Retrieved September 2, 2013, from http://peltiertech.com/excel-waterfall-charts-bridge-charts/

Peltier, J. (2016a). *Microsoft Excel Charting Survey*. Retrieved from http://peltiertech.com/microsoft-excel-charting-survey/

Peltier, J. (2016b). *PeltierTech charts for Excel 3.0. Shrewsbury: PeltierTech*. Retrieved from http://peltiertech.com/Utility30/

Powell, S., Baker, K., & Lawson, B. (2009a). Impact of errors in operational spreadsheets. *Decision Support Systems, 47*, 126–132. doi:10.1016/j.dss.2009.02.002

Powell, S. G., Baker, K. R., & Lawson, B. (2009b). Errors in Operational Spreadsheets. *Journal of Organizational and End User Computing, 21*(3), 24–36. doi:10.4018/joeuc.2009070102

Power, D. J. (2004). *A Brief History of Spreadsheets*. Retrieved September 15, 2016, from http://dssresources.com/history/sshistory.html

Ripley, B. D. (2002). Statistical methods need software: A view of statistical computing. In *Opening lecture of Royal Statistical Society*. Retrieved from http://www.stats.ox.ac.uk/~ripley/RSS2002.pdf

Seila, A. F. (2004). Spreadsheet simulation. In *Proceedings - Winter Simulation Conference* (pp. 41–48). doi:10.1109/WSC.2006.323034

Sharma, A., & Ellis, C. (2016). *Excel and big data*. Retrieved September 21, 2016, from https://blogs.office.com/2016/06/23/excel-and-big-data/?Ocid=Excel Editorial_Social_FBPAGE_MicrosoftExcel-microsoftexcel_20160726_527474728

Tan, V. (2009). *The leap year 1900 "bug" in Excel*. Retrieved September 21, 2016, from http://polymathprogrammer.com/2009/10/26/the-leap-year-1900-bug-in-excel/

Treacy, M. (2016a). *Create Regular Excel Charts from PivotTables*. Retrieved June 7, 2016, from http://www.myonlinetraininghub.com/create-regular-excel-charts-from-pivottables

Treacy, M. (2016b). *Webinar 2: Dashboards with Power Query and Power Pivot*. Retrieved February 16, 2016, from http://www.myonlinetraininghub.com/excel-webinars

Tufte, E. R. (1983). *The visual display of quantitative information*. Cheshire: Graphics Press.

Tufte, E. R. (1990). *Envisioning Information*. Cheshire: Graphics Press.

Tufte, E. R. (1997). *Visual Explanations: Images and quantities, evidence and narrative*. Cheshire: Graphics Press.

Tufte, E. R. (2006). *Beautiful Evidence*. Cheshire: Graphics Press.

Tufte, E. R. (n.d.). *Sparkline theory and practice*. Retrieved September 23, 2016, from http://www.edwardtufte.com/bboard/q-and-a-fetch-msg?msg_id=0001OR&topic_id=1

Wainer, H. (1997). *Visual revelations: Graphical tales of fate and deception from Napoleon Bonaparte to Ross Perot*. New York: Copernicus. doi:10.1007/978-1-4612-2282-8

Wainer, H. (2005). *Graphic discovery: A trout in the milk and other visual adventures*. Princeton, NJ: Princeton University Press.

Wainer, H. (2009). *Picturing the uncertain world: How to understand, communicate, and control uncertainty through graphical display*. Princeton, NJ: Princeton University Press.

Walkenbach, J. (2010). *Excel 2010 power programming with VBA*. Indianapolis, IN: Wiley. doi:10.1002/9781118257616

Walkenbach, J. (n.d.). *Microsoft Excel*. Retrieved August 7, 2007, from http://j-walk.com/ss/excel/index.htm

Weber, T. E. (2010). *Microsoft Excel: Software That Changed the World*. Retrieved May 3, 2011, from http://www.thedailybeast.com/articles/2010/12/27/microsoft-excel-the-programs-designer-reveals-the-secrets-behind-the-software-that-changed-the-world-25-years-ago.html

Zaiontz, C. (2015). *Real Statistics Resource Pack*. Retrieved from http://www.real-statistics.com

KEY TERMS AND DEFINITIONS

Data Visualization: The graphical display of data in such a way as to efficiently summarize the data and lead to an understanding of the data that would not be readily apparent from an examination of the values only.

Information Dashboard: A dynamic and interactive graphical summary of data intended to aid understanding and decision making.

PivotTable: Interactive tool for the summary and analysis of underlying relationships in a set of data.

Sparkline: A miniature graphic, often consisting of nothing more than a simple charted line, sans axes or labels, envisioned by Edward Tufte for the maximal display of information in a minimal amount of space.

Spreadsheet Application: Software program characterized by a tabular row-by-column layout for the organization of data so that it can then be computed on and analyzed in the same grid.

Chapter 8

Teachers Analyzing Sampling With *TinkerPlots*:
Insights for Teacher Education

Maria Niedja Pereira Martins
University of Lisbon, Portugal

Carlos Eduardo Ferreira Monteiro
Federal University of Pernambuco, Brazil

Theodosia Prodromou
University of New England, Australia

ABSTRACT

The teaching of statistics at the secondary level should provide statistical literacy for students who interact with data in several everyday situations. Therefore, it is crucial that the teacher education can provide a wider variety of situations in which teachers can learn how to improve students' statistical literacy. The conceptualization of sampling is crucial to understand statistical data. However, this topic is not generally emphasized in school curriculum or in teacher education programs. This chapter discusses a study on how primary school teachers understand issues of size and representativeness of samples using TinkerPlots 2.0 software. The participants were four teachers from a public school in Brazil. The research protocol followed three phases: interviews to identify the teacher's profile and their statistical knowledge; a familiarization session with TinkerPlots; and a session to use the software to solve tasks involving sampling. The results showed that the teachers began to consider aspects of data variation to determine when representative samples were presented using TinkerPlots. The ability to select samples and analyze them seemed to contribute to improve their understanding about sample size and representativeness. Since the purpose of the study was to explore teacher education activities that could support

DOI: 10.4018/978-1-5225-2512-7.ch008

development of aspects of statistical literacy, further analysis of findings from the study offered insights into design of tasks to help teachers teach sampling as part of statistical literacy. For example, the analysis suggested that the questions asked during the research sections should not only explore the participants' knowledge on the sample size or the confidence level, but should also promote reflection on the meanings assigned to tasks, leading to discussion of the skills required for statistical literacy in the Big Data era.

INTRODUCTION

Statistical education is related to the demand to develop capable citizens to interpret and to argue about statistical information presented in daily situations (North, Gal & Zewotir, 2014). People should be able to understand the processing of statistical data and make decisions based on their conscious analysis. Therefore, statistical knowledge is essential for critical reflective and participatory citizenship (Carvalho & Solomon, 2012).

An important area of knowledge that enables citizens to understand statistical data critically is related to conceptualization of samples and sampling. Bolfarine and Bussab (2005) conceptualize a sample as any subset of a given population, and sampling as a technique of selection of such subsets. Innabi (2006) argues that in order to analyze the representativeness of a sample it is necessary to know whether the sample is large enough and has the variety present in the population. In general, larger sample sizes ensure that the variety of the population will be represented in a sample, but with homogenous populations with less variability, smaller samples will be effective.

Crucial in understanding any sampling process is knowledge of how the data were chosen, what methods were employed for the selection of these cases, and what features and prioritized variables, so we can understand other contexts in which the information can be applied (Saldanha & Thompson, 2002; 2007).

Although samples and sampling are fundamental to the practice of statistics, they need to be more emphasized in school curriculum (Watson, 2004). Recently, several studies investigated the conceptualization of samples and sampling among students from different levels (Meletiou-Mavrotheris & Paparistodemou, 2015; Noll & Hancock, 2015; Phannkuch, Arnold & Wild, 2015). However, it is also important to investigate such situations among teachers who are going to approach such curriculum content (Martins, Monteiro & Queiroz, 2013).

Several studies have investigated the development of understanding about samples and sampling using computer-based tasks. For example, Manor, Ben-Zvi and Aridor (2013) conducted a study that engaged students in designed instructional activities using computer modeling and simulations of drawing many samples. According to those authors, the research tasks enabled the students to think about sampling as a process when analyses are associated with samples.

Simulation has been considered an interesting resource in the teaching and learning of statistics for different school levels since it can allow the use of a set of interrelated actions to achieve a specific educational purpose (Garfield & Ben-Zvi, 2007). Therefore, simulations can be useful for helping students understand important concepts and, more generally, to get them involved with Information and Communication Technologies (ICT).

Batanero et al. (2005) emphasize the possibility of using technological simulators to facilitate the ability to build models, to display random phenomena in a way that allows the realization of long-term forecasts, and to interpret the frequency of these phenomena.

Studies suggest that the use of simulators can be an effective strategy to improve statistical literacy (Batanero & Diaz, 2010, Batanero, Godino, & Cañizares, 2005; Carvalho, 2008; Gattuso, 2008; Lopes, 2003; Shi, He, & Tao, 2009), since the simulation requires direct action of those who manipulate the technological tool rather than simply offering a set of right or wrong answers that follow a limited and predetermined interaction. In addition, the simulators might promote more meaningful pedagogical contexts to motivate students to learn statistics.

In order to produce an impact on learning situations, it is necessary to develop a simulation process, which is in line with the most current assumptions for the teaching of statistics and probability. Souza and Lopes (2011) consider that technological resources may be useful for the construction of knowledge in statistics and probability since they are related to practical problems, and they need teachers' frequent interventions.

Baker, Derry, and Konold (2006) involved young students in two experiments about center and variation. In one of the experiments they used *TinkerPlots* (Konold & Miller, 2011) to develop a task in which students can get engaged in an inferential game. According to these authors "the inferential approach acknowledges that students with their teachers have to take part in the social practice of reasoning" (p. 2).

Inferences about distributions necessitate the coordination among practices and fundamental statistical concepts (Lehrer, Jones, & Kim, 2014; Prodromou, 2014), such as average, spread of data around the average, number of data cases in each bar, variability of the data, while they reason about the spread of data across a range of values, from which the probability distribution can be determined (Prodromou, 2008). When students compare two distributions, they compare the notions of average (mean) and spread and the shape of the distribution to reach a conclusion whether the distributions were different or not (Prodromou, 2014).

These studies suggest the importance of the selection of several samples. *TinkerPlots* offers the possibility to explore the relationships between data and chance (Konold & Kazak, 2008), since it is possible to perform simulations of sampling from populations. Prodromou (2014), researched year 10 students' interactions with the tools of *TinkerPlots*2 in particular the "Data Factory" feature to generate individual "virtual students" to populate a "virtual secondary school" with each virtual student created using the student-defined probability distributions for each of the different variables (e.g., gender, name, height) necessary to identify one of the virtual students. As the simulation ran, the students observed the generation of data sampled from the populations and the distribution of the attributes of data. When the students compared the generated data to the curves they created in the sample, they could not recognize the absolute resemblance of the distributions because of (1) messiness caused by variation among many variables, (2) relationship between signal and noise; and (3) knowledge of events/situations to be simulated.

Ponte (2012) argues that the teacher is the main agent of his/her initial and continuing education. This perspective implies the responsibility of statistics educators in finding appropriate ways to promote the processes of professional development, whether through collaboration with other colleagues, taking their practice as a starting point, or considering research on the practice as a fundamental element for the construction of knowledge of curriculum, classroom structure, tasks, materials, management of time, organizing students work and assessment planning, knowledge of ways in which classroom processes of communication are handled; and reflection, which is the ability to self-assess one's classroom teaching. Therefore, we clarify that the agenda of this paper emerges from the possibilities which teachers have to reflect on their knowledge specific statistical concepts such as samples and sampling, as well as to discuss the possibility of promoting challenges related to development of statistical literacy.

Teacher's professional development need to be about helping teachers to identify appropriate theory and to reorganize, revise, and reconstruct their knowledge (Imbernón, 2010). According to Imbernón argument, the Teacher Professional Development Cycle (TPDC) model for teacher development in statistics education that was developed by Souza, Lopes and Phannkuch (2015), is based on the principle that "teacher development should be managed as time for reflection and innovation, instead of time for updating, with the aim of preparing teachers to create new teaching approaches and also identify and face new problems" (Souza, Lopes, & Phannkuch,

2015). This TPDC model involves five phases: orientation, exploration, application, analysis and reflection.

The design of these five phases aimed to enhance teachers' professional practice, including their statistical, investigative and pedagogical knowledge.

The orientation phase (Makar, 2010; Makar & Fielding-Wells, 2011) must have at its base the experience and needs that teachers bring to the discussion. This phase is focused on supporting teachers to analyze and adapt their own practice, including lesson content within the spirit of statistical inquiry. Facilitators need to take into consideration teachers' practices and content knowledge (Ponte, 2011) in order to improve teachers' pedagogical approaches, understanding, and educational theory, providing teachers with opportunities to learn following the different steps of the inquiry process and to resolve any problems related to teaching statistics.

The exploration phase is the phase during which the teachers and facilitators reflect about how to enhance the planning of their statistical lessons, and the way of data collection from and for their lessons.

While teachers are trying to make connections between their planning of inquiry lessons and the curriculum, they can ask the facilitator questions. The questions might result in the facilitator reflecting on how to help teachers to link their practice knowledge with the theory. Or when teachers are predicting during lesson planning, they may resolve their own questions. The facilitator should act like a partner and be involved in this process by assisting teachers to produce better materials, assessments, and teaching techniques and by building on the diverse backgrounds and experiences of the teachers in the group. While the teachers and the facilitator reflect on the planning inquiry lessons, teachers draw connections among their planning of their inquiry lessons and the curriculum and ask the facilitator questions. The facilitators reflect on how to enhance teachers' association of their practice knowledge with the statistical theory supporting teachers to improve their teaching materials, assessments, and teaching techniques, by capitalizing on the different backgrounds and experiences of the teachers in the group.

The phase of application is grounded by collaboration between teachers and facilitators who help teachers to make appropriate changes to their lesson plans and critically reflect on these changes.

The phase of reporting and analysis in the TPDC model encompasses formative assessment, analysis of data drawing inferences from data and conclusions, and reflecting on those conclusions (Wild & Pfannkuch, 1999). During this reporting phase, both the facilitators and the other school teachers contribute with their own experiences, advising the teacher to reformulate concepts and make changes to the lesson or validating the process and the lesson.

The reporting phase requires that teachers self-assess their lesson and analyze their students' performance, providing feedback on students' learning of the target material and on how they might make modifications of instruction if necessary.

In the reporting phase, the facilitators are concerned with promoting teachers' reflective practice during the reflection phase of the cycle that allows time to reflect, and evaluate the process of teacher professional development, and begin a new cycle (Zaslavsky, 2009).

Statistical Literacy and Sampling

An important definition of statistical literacy was presented by Wallman: 'the ability to understand and critically evaluate statistical results that permeate our daily lives – coupled with the ability to appreciate the contributions that statistical thinking can make in public and private, professional and personal decisions" (1993, p. 1). Wallman´s perspective emphasizes the importance of statistical literacy for adults, although her statements also inspire the process of teaching statistical literacy to children and youths in different school levels.

Watson and Callingham (2003, p. 5) argue that: "Although the building blocks for statistical literacy are found within the mathematics, chance, data, and literacy components of the school curriculum, for students to become statistically literate they also need to interact with a variety of contexts as they take their place as consumers of information in the adult world". These authors understand that statistical literacy is important for society as a whole, but is also relevant in the context of individual decisions that a person makes based on information from different sources.

Gal (2002) argues that the term literacy increasingly suggests a wide range of factual knowledge and certain formal and informal skills, but also beliefs, habits and attitudes, as well as general awareness and a critical stance. Gal discusses the need for statistical literacy as an essential element to an adult person living in an industrialized society and facing different social and labor challenges. Gal (2002, p. 10) lists five basic skills so that the subject can considered statistically literate: "1) Knowing why data are needed and how data can be produced; 2) Familiarity with basic terms and ideas related to descriptive statistics; 3) Familiarity with basic terms and ideas related to graphical and tabular displays; 4) Understanding basic notions of probability; 5) Knowing how statistical conclusions or inferences are reached".

In this sense, when students build their own statistical knowledge, they may be able to question the validity of representations, interpretations based on data, and generalizations made from a single study and/or small samples (Garfield & Gal, 1999). Therefore, thinking about sampling can be an important element in the formation of statistically literate individuals, since the skills and knowledge associated with the questioning of the data necessarily pervade the understanding of the sample, the degree of representativeness, among other aspects.

Big Data and Tasks About Sampling

According to Caldas and Silva (2016)*Big Data* comes on the basis of information that is generated continuously by various means and becomes a wide range of jumbled data, but that can be analyzed, processed and used in the solution of various problems.

Among the key concepts associated with Big Data is Data Mining. As explained Caldas and Silva (2016, p. 69) Data Mining refers to "an analytic process designed to explore (typically related to business, market or scientific research), in search of consistent patterns and / or systematic relationships between variables to then validate them by applying the detected patterns to new subsets of data". Thus, using statistical techniques, it is possible to explore a set of data through data mining that can help identify patterns, thus favoring data-based decision-making.

Big Data also allows the use of different management technologies related to the generation of data ranging from paid packages and specific data analysis software, to, for example, available tools in social networks. Therefore, data mining is a view associated with the exploration of databases.

At the secondary and tertiary school levels, concerns for Big Data are not based on how to manage a lot of data, but in finding ways to prepare students to deal with this data. When discussing a definition of Big Data in Statistics Education, Ainley, Gould, and Pratt (2015, p. 409) state that "data are not big because of the size of the data file, but because they belong to a new class of data that differ in structure and source from traditional data that have inspired institutional changes in how we learn from data".

Therefore, thinking of ways to help students learn from the data necessarily requires that the teacher emphasize the most relevant content for this new context, as well as the strategies and materials most significant for this learning.

With regard to materials, Ben-Zvi and Friedlander (1996) argue that the introduction of students to computerized environments can encourage them to become smart consumers. The authors emphasize that in computer-based activities students are "forced" to choose the tools and options available. The authors also argue that the large databases to represent real-world situations are difficult to handle without appropriate technological training.

In order to use Big Data in primary school settings, the teacher can make use of a technological artifact with a more accessible language, enabling students to experience tools that lead them to explore data processing. It is not, therefore, to introduce complex tools, but to offer a viable way for young students to experience artifacts that lead them to think about data.

From the point of view of content necessary for learning to think about the data, Ainley, Gould and Pratt (2015) state that the description of the data is an important subject in the era of Big Data. Thus, among the various skills needed to work in a world full of technology, the students can understand the limits of data if they learn concepts associated with representativity of sample, the relationship between sample and population, and the sampling variability.

However, bringing sampling problems into classrooms can be difficult for teachers, since such problems are complex and the problems that may be easily understood by students sound artificial and disconnected from real-world contexts, while real-world contexts are too complex to be understood by less advanced students. The concern for the importance of sampling tasks in the classroom depends on the assumption that sampling is a crucial idea in teaching statistical concepts, at the same time that the concept is generally difficult for students. This aspect is very important because, as emphasized by Gal & Garfield (1997), generally the statistical data are seen as numbers with a context.

Ainley, Pratt, and Hansen (2006) develop the notion of utility in task design. These authors argue an important dimension of learning about a statistical idea is understanding what it is useful for, and the degree of confidence that can be attached to it. Ainley, Gould and Pratt (2015, p. 405) suggest that "one question we would wish to ask in analysing any task design is does this task give learners opportunities to appreciate the utility of the ideas they are learning?" Therefore, an important aspect in the introduction of sampling tasks in school is to understand how useful this task is to students. This is because often the idea of analyzing a sample instead of analyzing the entire population is not always perceived as necessary in many situations of everyday life.

These authors state that there are two different situations in which selection of samples inspired by real data can be used in the classroom: 1) situations in which the population is material, finite, and countable; and 2) situations in which the population is described by a mathematical formula. For each type of scenario in these situations, we can imagine different reasons for whether the samples are useful or not useful. For example, in situations related to A, in which a possible scenario is market research, where the population is finite but considerably large. In these cases, the extraction of samples is required because otherwise it would take a long time to reach the entire population. On the other hand, in situations related to type B, in which a possible scenario is to play a die or toss a coin, where the population is a probability distribution and does not have a material existence, it is possible to reach the conclusion that all that can be known about the population as a whole is described by the theoretical/mathematical model, and therefore further sampling becomes unnecessary.

Given these different possibilities, teachers may have to deal with different pedagogical conflicts by choosing the sampling tasks they try to replicate with their students. Based on the premise that the statistical investigations necessary to classroom situations must make particular sense to the students, the tasks of type B can still be used with the pedagogical sense to engage students to discover how to draw a sample that is not biased in these scenarios.

Therefore, Ainley, Gould, and Pratt (2015) argued for the importance of teachers using a variety of sampling activities to ensure that students are able to recognize situations where sampling is useful and when it becomes unnecessary. This also requires the teacher's ability to identify the initial intuitions, understandings, and reasoning of students facing such situations to intervene in the construction of statistical knowledge in students.

Rubin, Bruce, and Tenney (1991) argue that students who are beginning to work with random samples can present two main types of intuitions. One type of intuition refers to those students who believe that a random sample is a true picture of the population, and therefore, any sample taken shall be representative of the population. Another intuition type is related to students with little confidence in the inference based on random samples because it is only a subset of the population. These two types of intuitions might cause conflicts on student's analyses about the samples. Rubin, Bruce, and Tenney (1991) suggest that when students are solving sample selection tasks, some of them experience a conflict between the idea of variability and sample representativeness. A belief in the representativeness of the sample induces the perception that it tells us everything about the population to which it belongs. On the other hand, a belief in the variability of the samples induces the perception that the sample does not present useful information about the population to which it belongs.

In order to help students to overcome this dilemma, the Guidelines for Assessment and Instruction in Statistics Education (GAISE, 2005) suggest that such students be given tasks in which they draw different samples of the same size; analyze the variation of the same statistical measure; and compare that measure with the parameter of the respective population. This is because such a task design could help them realize that random samples of the same population may vary slightly and may not necessarily present an accurate picture of the population, but even so, a representative sample can be used to establish inferences for the population.

Ben-Zvi, Bakker, and Makar (2015) understand that by allowing students repeatedly take samples from a simulator, the individual can progressively reach clearer conclusions about the reason that sample is or is not representative.

METHODOLOGY

This chapter presents a qualitative exploratory study that used an interpretative approach. The research was conducted in a rural public school located in a municipality of the Metropolitan Region of Recife (RMR), Brazil.

The choice for this school was based on a survey conducted by GPEME - Research Group on Mathematics and Statistics Education (Carvalho & Monteiro, 2012), which identified 85 public schools in the RMR which had computer labs, and investigated how those labs were used.

The researcher contacted all seven teachers who belonged to that school during the school year of 2013. Four female primary school teachers agreed to participate.

The data collection was comprised of two research sessions with each teacher. The first session included an individual semi-structured interview in order to have a profile of each teacher (Table 1).

The data presented in Table 1 show some of the participants' different characteristics with respect to their pedagogical training. However, all of them knew about sampling prior to their participation in the study teacher education and none of them were familiar with *TinkerPlots* software.

The interview during the first session also aimed to identify participants' levels of understanding about the concept of sampling. The interview items were based on the translation into Brazilian Portuguese of a questionnaire about sample (Figure 1), and sampling items from written surveys (Figure 2), which were used in the studies to explore knowledge of sample, representativeness of small and large samples, sampling, and media news about sample surveys with inadequate statistical basis by Watson, Collis and Moritz (1995) and Watson and Moritz (2000), see Figure 1 and 2.

The first research session also included some familiarization with the *TinkerPlots* 2.0 program. The researcher presented different functions of *TinkerPlots* to each teacher, including those to handle the database and produce graphs. The familiarization

Table 1. Profile of study participants

Teachers	Suzy	Adrianne	Lorraine	Josenir
Age	30	37	45	48
University course (conclusion/situation)	Pedagogy (2012)	Pedagogy (Attending)	Portuguese Language (2004)	Pedagogy (2005)
Experience as teacher (years)	5	9	9	27
Computer use	everyday	4 times per week	3 times per week	Rarely
Statistical teaching topics	Graphing	graphing	Data interpretation	Graphing

Figure 1. Items from the interview protocol for sampling
(Watson, 2004, p. 281)

1. (a) Have you heard of the word *sample* before?
Where? What does it mean?

   (b) A newsperson on TV says:
"In a research study on the weight of Grade 5 children, some researchers interviewed a *sample* of Grade 5 children in the state."
What does the word *sample* mean in this sentence?

2. (a) Why do you think the researchers used a *sample* of Grade 5 children, instead of studying all the Grade 5 children in the state?

   (b) Do you think they used a sample of about 10 children? Why or why not? How many children should they choose for their sample? Why?

   (c) How should they choose the children for their sample? Why?

3. The researchers went to 2 schools:
One school in the center of the city and 1 school in the country.
Each school had about half girls and half boys.

   The researchers took a random sample from each school:
   50 children from the city school
   20 children from the country school

   One of these samples was unusual: It had more than 80% boys.

   Is it more likely to have come from
   the large sample of 50 from the city school, or
   the small sample of 20 from the country school, or
   are both samples equally likely to have been the unusual sample?
   Please explain your answer.

was carried out to ensure that they would be able to use *TinkerPlots* without guidance during the second research session.

The second session was comprised of three tasks using *TinkerPlots*. These tasks were about representativeness, size and type of sample. Tasks 1 and 2 were adapted from *TinkerPlots* databases.

Task 1 used a database entitled Fish Population. The aim of this task was to see whether the participants understood that increasing the size of a sample would lead to better accuracy of inferences about the population, since the characteristics of the population would be better represented.

Figure 3 shows a copy of screen with 625 cases (fish) randomly selected from a *TinkerPlots* database called Fish Population. Each case had a numerical code, and information about the type and size of fish.

We asked the participant to read the following situation, which was based on the *TinkerPlots* resources:

Figure 2. Sampling items from written surveys
(*Watson, 2004, p. 280*).

> ABOUT six in 10 United States high school students say they could get a handgun if they wanted one, a third of them within an hour, a survey shows. The poll of 2508 junior and senior high school students in Chicago also found 15 per cent had actually carried a handgun within the past 30 days, with 4 per cent taking one to school.

(a) Would you make any criticisms of the claims in this article?

(b) If you were a high school teacher, would this report make you refuse a job offer somewhere else in the United States, say Colorado or Arizona? Why or why not?

Decriminalise drug use: poll

SOME 96 percent of callers to youth radio station Triple J have said marijuana use should be decriminalised in Australia.

The phone-in listener poll, which closed yesterday, showed 9924 - out of the 10,000-plus callers - favoured decriminalisation, the station said.

Only 389 believed possession of the drug should remain a criminal offence.

Many callers stressed they did not smoke marijuana but still believed in decriminalising its use, a Triple J statement said.

(a) What was the size of the sample in this article?

(b) Is the sample reported here a reliable way of finding out public support for the decriminalisation of marijuana? Why or why not?

A certain fish farmer bought some genetically modified fish of a company with the promise that they would grow more than the non-GM fish. In order to check whether GM fish grow more, the fish farmer joined GM fish with other fish that he used to have in a tank in which totalized 625 fish. After the total growth time of fish, the fish farmer gradually withdrew each fish from tank, and measured each one. From the data analysis in *TinkerPlots*, indicate which type of fish had greater length. Did the fish farmer make a good deal?

During participants' analyses of task 1, we initially took samples of 10 cases, and then sample size was increased based on their indications. The participants should infer which population had bigger fish interpreting a graph similar to the Figure 4.

For each new inclusion of cases in the sample, we asked the participant to informally rate her confidence level in a scale from 0 to 10, with 10 as the teacher's maximum confidence. This procedure aimed to make explicit their understanding about changes on their own analyses, a strategy also used by Prodromou (2011) to conduct an investigation with young Australian students, using *TinkerPlots* 1.0.

Figure 3. TinkerPlots screen with 625 cases of fish population database

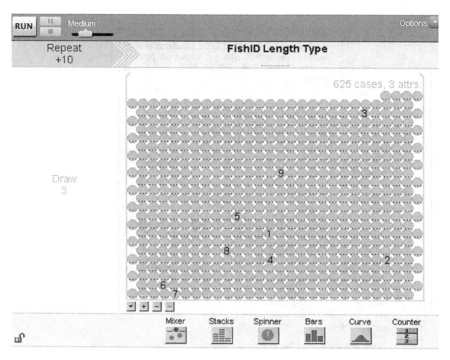

Figure 4. TinkerPlots screen with fish population database, n = 10

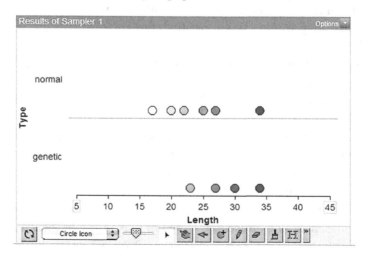

The participants were asked to determine, from the selection of growing samples, which types of fish tend to be larger in a population comprised of genetically modified fish and normal fish. The purpose of this task was to identify whether the teachers could understand that increasing the sample size could lead to better accuracy of inferences about the population.

The second task was based two TinkerPlots databases contained a fixed set of 500 cases of *number*, ranging rom 1 to 100—"balls"—each of which is assigned a different number. The distribution of both databases was unknown to the participants, who where asked to infer the distribution of population only by taking samples. Each database contained 500 "balls" and each one had registered numbers ranging from 1 to 100, so some values repeated themselves, allowing a tendency to be found and the distribution was not uniform across the numbers from 1 to 100.

The participant should determine the cluster distribution of a population of real integers between 1 and 100 from the selection of the smallest sample possible.

Figure 5. TinkerPlots screen with MysteryMixer1 database N = 500

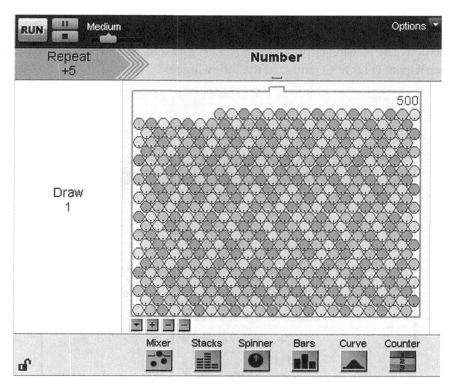

This second task aimed to identify whether the teachers could reach a conclusion on a small sample. Therefore, the participants were encouraged to identify clusters of samples and infer the population distribution from them, using the smallest possible sample. To ensure this, we engaged the participants in a fictional situation that included a cost for sample surveys:

You have a limited amount of money to conduct survey on numbers. Each selection of five cases of this survey you should pay R$1,00. Your task is to identify a range in which all numerical values are repeated. You need to spend the least amount of money possible, but you need to be quite sure about your answer.

In each task, the first author, acted as researcher asking questions to make more explicit the teachers' considerations about the data, and assisting the participants in the selection and manipulation of the *TinkerPlots* tools.

The purpose of this problem situation was to identify whether the teachers realized that in populations with little variation between the data, it is possible to select a small and representative sample.

Task 3 aimed to investigate whether teachers could choose a suitable sampling technique to select a representative sample of a heterogeneous population.

The database associated with Task 3 simulated a classroom of 40 students (30 females and 10 males). The participant should draw a representative sample of this population. The researcher presented a *TinkerPlots* screen showing the database to the participant (Figure 6), and read the following text:

Figure 6. TinkerPlots screen which represents the database of task 3

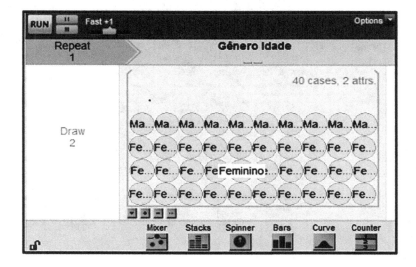

Trying to identify the average age of the groups presented in a classroom, take a sample that best represents the average age of each gender, knowing that: - The average age of all men in the room is 3 years greater than the average for women.

The piece of information about the average age of the male group aimed to be a clue for the participant to identify at which point it would be possible to select the most representative sample.

During the exploration of the task 3 database, the researcher asked the participants if the random selection of these cases could be efficient in choosing a sample that was representative of the population, since the number of female cases was higher than male cases. The teachers should recognize that the heterogeneous and proportional characteristics of the data required another type of selection and consider a reorganization of the Sampler tool, as shown in Figure 7:

The challenge of this task was to identify whether the teachers were aware of the data collection process, relating the representativeness of the sample to the chosen sampling process.

Camtasia Studio 7.1 software was used to record on video the participants' speeches, their gestures and work developed in the computer screen while they solved the tasks. The transcriptions of audio records were organized in protocols, which were used for the data analysis.

Figure 7. The configuration of TinkerPlots for task 3 database that allowed the extraction of proportional random samples

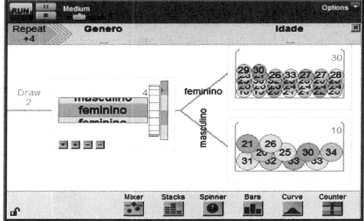

RESULTS

In this section we present teachers' speech excerpts to discuss aspects of how the participants understood the selected samples as well as the dynamic representations produced in *TinkerPlots* which supported their explanations.

When responding to the semi-structured interview, as part of the first research session, all teachers presented their notions about samples and sampling. They provided examples that emphasized the purpose of using sampling elements in data handling processes. These notions seemed to be related to teachers' everyday experiences or their knowledge about research studies in education.

For example, when asked what the sample was, Lorraine and Josenir gave examples, but Adrianne did not. However, when asked about the reason to do sampling in a survey with students, all teachers commented on how important sampling is in these situations, as the following interview excerpts demonstrate:

Lorraine: *When you will do a survey, and it is labeled "by sampling"... The person cannot interview all. Let's say it is 100,000 inhabitants, I think they got a number and interviewed them, because they cannot interview all of them. I do not know if that's right. Is it? (...) Because it is not feasible, right? For you to gather all would take longer, the number of people to survey would be greater. (...) So, it would take much longer to perform the survey. Like during the census, when they go another time to carry out the survey with a person [who was absent].*

Josenir: *I've seen in a different context, right? As a small fragment of something... a fragrance, a cream, a piece of text. (...) I do not know, I believe that because of the demand that is too large [a large total population]. At first glance it seems a waste of time [if collect data from the total population].*

Adrianne: *What I understand by sample, it is a small part of something. (...) I think because would not have how, right? Because it would be a huge amount of students. They would not have time to do, right? And usually when somebody is doing research, it is done with samples, right?*

Suzy: *So I think the sample is a part that can represent the whole. Because there will contain all the information. A sample for me is this. (...) There is the information that can be generalized to a group.*

Lorraine stated a definition based on a social context. Similarly, Josenir defined sample correctly and gave examples connected to market products. On the other hand, Adrianne did not endorse her definition with any example. She was able to give an opinion about sample only when the researcher gave an example of a social situation. The excerpts also suggest that the teachers recognize the utility of sampling. However, when they explain their views on this concept, some teachers have seemed to have doubts as to their answers. For example, sometimes they requested the researcher´s opinion.

Our analyses suggested that comparing different situations of the use of samples could help teachers to understand sampling's utility. For example, they could analyze contexts in which the selection of samples could be useful as well as those in which sampling was not necessary.

The participants did not have formal teaching about sampling, and their responses suggested that their knowledge about this topic was based on their social experiences. As statistical literacy is comprised of formal and dispositional elements, it is possible that this lack of knowledge influenced their responses. Therefore, when they were responding the questions from studies of Watson and her colleagues (Figure 1 and 2), some teachers could not identify biased samples in social research contexts.

For instance, the participants´ responses to the question about the decriminalization of drug use: *Is the sample reported here a reliable way of finding out public support for the decriminalization of marijuana? Why or why not?* Three of the four teachers could not express any criticism about bias in this study. It was common among the teachers to accept the results presented in the statement, even when they were opposed to the decriminalization of marijuana, as we can observe this in this excerpt from Josenir's interview protocol:

Josenir: *It is a critical moment, well... (...) I very particularly, I get those 389 who do not believe... Because, you see, marijuana is not a healthy thing, because it has been proven that it affects several areas of the brain. The first, the second time, right? It goes much of each... It is not only in marijuana, goes in search of other things... And the worst, the worst of it is... The person who becomes addicted to such a thing, he has a big change of behavior. So it's hard to deal with this. There is no love... you'll excuse me frankness. I already said to my son.*

In this part of the interview, the researchers were concerned to recognize the perspectives of each teacher about the concepts of samples and sampling, and how they recognized and selected samples.

In terms of relationships between size and representativeness in task 1, it was observed that all the teachers used the strategy to look for patterns to analyze the distribution of data and trends in the larger samples. The utilization of this strategy seemed to influence the levels of confidence of teachers about their inferences, since they were able to confirm in each sample the trend of the population. The conclusions of the teachers seem to be based on dynamic representations built with the help of software. Software tools that allow the use of the mean and the identification of data variance also seemed to generate more confidence in the teachers' answers.

The purpose of task 2 was to see if the participants could recognize that smaller samples are sufficient in some contexts. The results suggest the participants were sophisticated enough to recognize that smaller samples were all that was needed. They understood that, in certain cases, smaller samples also provide notions about the population. All teachers explained that the fact that in task 2 the data presented were more homogeneous, which allowed better inferences even with small samples. Therefore, these results suggest that it was easier for participants to consider the little variability of the sample elements as important for representativeness.

For example, when developing task 1, Suzy seemed to understand that a factor that enabled to offer a more assertive response on the fact that the sample was or not representative, it was to observe if the trend of the sample remained similar when more cases were included in the sample:

Researcher: *Why was it easy to tell a response with fewer cases?*

Suzy: *I think due to that issue of group that I told you... because it is concentrated in the group... and... I do not know.*

Researcher: *Concentrated in the group? What do you mean?*

Suzy: *So... let me say... do not know. I thought so.., as we were taking... I thought, should have 50%, and then I was putting down, 25%. And with that there, I did much less than the percentage that I thought at first. And as I was pulling (removing cases from the simulator); I was doing, and then the concentration was remaining constant. So I would not need to use all this data, to study with a higher percentage... I believe that this is because the information is contained so, in that group.*

Although, they did not use formal language to explain their findings, the teachers demonstrated their realization that when the variability of cases is higher, you need to collect more cases. On the other hand, they also realized that when the sample offers a trend that is confirmed in the search for more cases, it is possible to generalize to the population with a smaller sample. The excerpt from the interview with Josenir illustrates:

Josenir: *Yeah... I think so. And through the graph you will confirm, right?*

Researcher: *Why do you think that with a sample of 30, only, you have already achieved gives an answer?*

Josenir: *Because it had much.*

Researcher: *It had much? What do you mean?*

Josenir: *It is. Because, to reach here (end of the scale) came only one... two, it seems. And here (beginning of scale) he concentrated more. It is concentrating, so there is no logic of do not come more. If it had spread that amount equal... three, four, three... four... then, it would be difficult. I would have more possibilities of uncertainty, is not it?*

Researcher: *And to resolve a situation so, you would have to do what?*

Josenir: *Search more samples. Search, search, search.*

Researcher: *Then, if there is a possibility of very different cases...*

Josenir:*...It would have to have a larger sample. And this bigger, it needs to seek.*

Figure 8. Case selection made by Adrianne from the MisteryMixer2 database

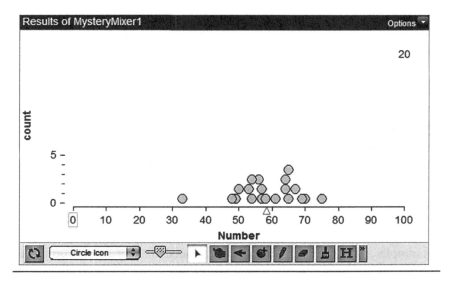

In addition to analyzing the concentration of cases in increasing samples, a factor that seems to contribute to the determination of a sample size of this task was the context of the problem presented to the teachers. As described in the methodology section, the teachers were asked to consider controlling spending when selecting cases for the sample. The following excerpt from Adrianne's interview and Figure 8 illustrate:

Adrianne: *I want to get, just that.*

Researcher: *Only 20? Do you think that 20 then, already it is possible to say where the concentration of 500 is? [refering to the size of total population]*

Adrianne: *Can I take up to how much?*

Researcher: *It is up to you to say. You spent 4 Reals. [Real is the Brazilian monetary unit]*

Adrianne: *I just do not want to spend too much. The case is that here already we can see that will be from here to there [using the mouse cursor to point the cases between 50 and 60 on Figure 8].*

Researcher: *Right.*

The issues the teachers considered in order to determine the size of a sample in *TinkerPlots* are equally relevant in the context of real-world sampling. It seems that the tasks encouraged teachers' reflections, even though the task situations were designed to be simple. We believe that if the purpose of tasks would focus on the exploration of the utility idea of the sampling, teachers would make broader analyses, which would be important to develop their statistical literacy.

The identification of clusters through dynamic representations also was not a complicated task to teachers. It is possible that the type of problem seemed to be easier reading to teachers, since it was asked to identify only the range of a single variable.

The results from task 3 suggested that three of the four teachers realized the implications of a specific sampling procedure for the representativeness of a sample of heterogeneous variables. Therefore, three teachers began to test out using simple random samples. Afterwards, they identified the need to select a proportional random sample. The simulation tool was essential to make possible these tests. Consequently, the simulation tool helped teachers to understand about the differences in the samples while comparing the results for both types of procedures.

These results are interesting to reflect on the limits and possibilities of using a technological tool to improve teachers' statistical knowledge in teacher education contexts.

By allowing teachers to reflect on the design of tasks and its purpose, they could be more aware of what that led them to conclude about the representativeness of samples, which in this case, meant understanding that with increasing sample size, the variability of the population could be better visualized. A possible alternative is to explore other *TinkerPlots* tools, such as the Text feature that provide a blank space in order to the user writes comments. This feature could be used to record conclusions throughout the entire analysis process of samples, allowing a more organized way of resuming the comparison of statistics and distributions of each extracted sample.

CONCLUSION

The importance of using technology in the form of software like *TinkerPlots* that provides students with contexts that support possibilities to explore data and produce different graphical representations. The use of *TinkerPlots* technological tool for dynamic data handling at the school level, seemed to facilitate the teachers' observations about data variations and the implication of these variations for the selection of samples and representativeness.

In certain situations, the representations of the samples by means of graphical displays produced by *TinkerPlots* and the successive increase of cases were important to interpret the samples and make conclusions about the representativeness of the same. These results corroborate the considerations of Ben-Zvi, Bakker, and Makar (2015) about the context of increasing samples and the possibility that the subjects identify patterns in samples in order to recognize them as representative.

In this study the participants did not have much time to explore freely and autonomously the *TinkerPlots* features in order to develop more experiences and knowledge about the sample and sampling. Further studies should be conducted to understand how teachers could utilize *TinkerPlots tools*, including utilization aspects, which promote reflections about the teaching and learning of sampling and samples in classroom activities. The examples discussed in this chapter show that the opportunities for using the appropriate technology to visualize data taking on the challenge of developing statistical literacy about data variations and the implication of these variations for the selection of samples and representativeness. Therefore, further research needs to be developed in order to propose pedagogical situations that can improve teachers' knowledge about sampling, the concepts of sample representations, the relation of samples to population, sampling variability and bias that are important to understand the "algorithmically collected data" (Ainley et al., 2015, p. 411). An example of algorithmically collected data is data collected by a personal sensor or a mobile. That data might be representative of the owner's phone calls or text messages for the last few weeks or it might have dismissed a great number of text messages if, for instance, the owner was on vacations for two weeks and could not use his mobile. However, the total number of text messages sent by one person is not representative of another person's number of text messages. And the collection of all citizens of one country is not representative of all citizens of one continent. Nevertheless, a random sample is representative of its population, even though the size of the sample might have a high sample variability that would make difficult to make any useful inferences. The Big Data being generated by everything around us at all times, such as sensors and mobile devices etc., not only create the need of optimal processing power, analytics capabilities and skills, they also create new challenges for students and teachers in relation to their understanding of how and when we can make inferences to a larger population. Teachers with better knowledge about statistical notions such as sampling might promote better levels of statistical literacy of students.

The data discussed in this chapter are "objects in the formal context of the classroom" (Gould 2010). Big "data, however, is potentially a large and diverse category of data types and might include data accumulated on smartphones, data collected by the students using smartphones, data presented in HTML format on websites, data from personal health sensors, government web sites, etc." (Ainley et al., 2015, p. 410). According to Ainley et al. (2015) and others propose that preparing students to understand these data during the school years, require students to identify and describe trends in data that might represent a population. Konold, Higgins, Russell and Khalil (2015) pointed out that students need careful scaffolding to interpret data visualizations, a central skill for the era of bid data, as big data are understood through complex data visualisation portals, such as Google Maps, GapMinder World etc.

In the era of integrating Big Data, secondary and tertiary school levels are concerned with finding ways to prepare students to deal with the complexities of learning to make sense of Big Data, and providing opportunities for visualizing this Data under investigation. The teachers are faced with challenges to provide their students with rich experiences and data visualizations to develop solid understandings of statistical concepts and procedures that may appear counter-intuitive or false. As Big Data leads to reconsideration of the teaching of traditional statistical concepts, a range of new experiences for teaching students to make sense of data, including exploiting technology to support new visualizations of Big Data, are essential tools for our Big Data world.

REFERENCES

Ainley, J., Gould, R., & Pratt, D. (2015). Learning to reason from samples: Commentary from the perspectives of task design and the emergence of big data. *Educational Studies in Mathematics*, *88*(3), 405–412. doi:10.1007/s10649-015-9592-4

Ainley, J., Pratt, D., & Hansen, A. (2006). Connecting Engagement and Focus in Pedagogic Task Design. *British Educational Research Journal*, *32*(1), 23–38. doi:10.1080/01411920500401971

Bakker, A., Derry, J., & Konold, C. (2006). Using technology to support diagrammatic reasoning about center and variation. In A. Rossman & B. Chance (Eds.), *International Conference on Teaching of Statistics*, (vol. 7, pp. 1–6). Voorburg: International Statistical Institute.

Batanero, C., Biehler, R., Maxara, C., Engel, J., & Vogel, M. (2005b). *Using simulation to bridge teachers content and pedagogical knowledge in probability.* Paper presented at the 15th ICMI study conference: the professional education and development of teachers of mathematics, Aguas de Lindoia, Brazil.

Batanero, C., Burrill, G., Reading, C., & Rossman, A. (Eds.). (2008). *Joint ICMI/IASE Study: Teaching Statistics in School Mathematics. Challenges for Teaching and Teacher Education. Proceedings of the ICMI Study 18 and 2008 IASE Round Table Conference.* Monterrey, Mexico: International Commission on Mathematical Instruction and International Association for Statistical Education.

Batanero, C., & Diaz, C. (2010). Training teachers to teach statistics: What can we learn from research? *Statistique et Enseignement*, *1*(1), 5–20.

Batanero, C., Godino, J. D., & Cañizares, M. J. (2005). Simulation as a tool to train Pre-service School Teachers. In J. Addler (Ed.), *Proceedings of ICMI First African Regional Conference* [CD]. Johannesburg, South Africa: International Commission on Mathematical Instruction. Retrieved from http://www.ugr.es/~batanero/ARTICULOS/CMIRCr.pdf

Ben-Zvi, D., Bakker, A., & Makar, K. (2015). Learning to reason from samples. *Educational Studies in Mathematics*, *88*(3), 291–303. doi:10.1007/s10649-015-9593-3

Ben-Zvi, D., & Friedlander, A. (1997). Statistical thinking in a technological environment. In J. Garfield & G. Burrill (Eds.), *Research on the role of technology in teaching and learning statistics* (pp. 45–55). Voorburg, The Netherlands: International Statistical Institute.

Bolfarine, H., & Bussab, W. O. (2005). *Elementos de Amostragem*. São Paulo: Edgar Blücher.

Caldas, M.S., & Silva, E.C. (2016). Fundamentos e aplicação do Big Data: como tratar informações em uma sociedade de yottabytes. *Bibl. Univ., Belo Horizonte, 3*(1), 65-85.

Carvalho, C., & Solomon, Y. (2012). Supporting statistical literacy: What do culturally relevant/realistic tasks show us about the nature of pupil engagement with statistics? *International Journal of Educational Research, 55*, 57–65. doi:10.1016/j. ijer.2012.06.006

Carvalho, L. M. T., & Monteiro, C. E. F. (2012). Reflexões sobre implementação e uso de laboratório de informática na escola pública. *Roteiro, 37*, 343–360.

GAISE Report. (2005). Guidelines for Assessment and Instruction in Statistics Education (GAISE) Report, A Pre-K-12 curriculum framework, August 2005 – American Statistical Association. Retrieved Out, 30, 2016, from http://it.stlawu. edu/~rlock/gaise/

Gal, I. (2002). Adults statistical literacy: Meanings, components, responsibilities. *International Statistical Review, 70*(1), 1–51. doi:10.1111/j.1751-5823.2002. tb00336.x

Gal, I., & Garfield, J. (Eds.). (1997). *The Assessment Challenge in Statistics Education*. Amsterdam: IOS Press and the International Statistical Institute.

Garfield, J., & Ben-Zvi, D. (2007). How students learn statistics revisited: A current review of research on teaching and learning statistics. *International Statistical Review, 75*(3), 372–396. doi:10.1111/j.1751-5823.2007.00029.x

Garfield, J., & Gal, I. (1999). Teaching and Assessing Statistical Reasoning. In L. Stiff (Ed.), *Developing Mathematical Reasoning in Grades K-12* (pp. 207–219). Reston, VA: National Council Teachers of Mathematics.

Gattuso, L. (2008). Mathematics in a statistical context? In C. Batanero, G. Burrill, C. Reading, & A. Rossman (Eds.), *Teaching statistics in school mathematics. Challenges for teaching and teacher education.Proceedings of the Joint ICMI Study 18 and 2008 IASE Round Table Conference.*

Gould, R. (2010). Statitics and the modern student. *International Statistical Review, 78*(2), 297–315. doi:10.1111/j.1751-5823.2010.00117.x

Imbernón, F. (2010). *Formação continuada de professores*. Porto Alegre, Brazil: Artmed.

Innabi, H. (2006). Factors considered by secondary students when judging the validity of a given statistical generalization. In A. Rossman & B. Chance (Eds.), *Proceedings of the Seventh International Conference on Teachings Statistics* (ICOTS 7) (pp. 1-6). Retrieved October 13, 2016, from https://www.stat.auckland.ac.nz/~iase/publications/17/2B1_INNA.pdf

Konold, C., Higgins, T., Russell, S. J., & Khalil, K. (2015). Data seen through different lenses. *Educational Studies in Mathematics*, *88*(3), 305–325. doi:10.1007/s10649-013-9529-8

Konold, C., & Kazak, S. (2008). Reconnecting data and chance. *Technology Innovations in Statistics Education*, *2*, 1–37.

Konold, C., & Miller, C. D. (2011). *TinkerPlots: Dynamic data exploration* [Computer software, Version 2.2]. Emeryville, CA: Key Curriculum Press.

Lehrer, R., Jones, R. S., & Kim, M. J. (2014). Model-based informal inference. In K. Makar, B. de Sousa, & R. Gould (Eds.), Sustainability in statistics education. Proceedings of the Ninth International Conference on Teaching Statistics (ICOTS9, July, 2014), Flagstaff, Arizona, USA. Voorburg, The Netherlands: International Statistical Institute. Available at http://icots.info/9/proceedings/pdfs/ICOTS9_6E3_PRODROMOU.pdf

Lopes, C. E. (2003). *O conhecimento profissional dos professores e suas relações com Estatística e Probabilidade na Educação Infantil* (Doctoral dissertation). Faculdade de Educação, Universidade Estadual de Campinas, Campinas, Brasil.

Makar, K. (2010). Teaching primary teachers to teach statistical inquiry: The uniqueness of initial experiences. In C. Reading (Ed.), *Data and context in statistics education: Towards an evidence-based society. Proceedings of the Eighth International Conference on Teaching Statistics (ICOTS-8, July, 2010), Ljubljana, Slovenia.* Voorburg, The Netherlands: International Statistical Institute.

Makar, K., & Fielding-Wells, J. (2011). Teaching teachers to teach statistical investigations. In C. Batanero, G. Burrill, & C. Reading (Eds.), *Teaching statistics in school mathematics – Challenges for teaching and teacher education: A Joint ICMI/IASE Study* (pp. 347–358). New York: Springer. doi:10.1007/978-94-007-1131-0_33

Manor, H., Ben-Zvi, D., & Aridor, K. (2013). Students' emergent reasoning about uncertainty exploring sampling distributions in an "integrated approach". In J. Garfield (Ed.), *Proceedings of the Eighth International Research Forum on Statistical Reasoning, Thinking, and Literacy* (SRTL8) (pp. 18–33). Minneapolis, MN: University of Minnesota.

Martins, M. N. P., Monteiro, C. E. F., & Queiroz, T. N. (2013). Compreensões sobre amostra ao manipular dados no software *TinkerPlots*: Um caso de uma professora polivalente. *Revista Eletrônica de Educação, 7*(2), 317–342. doi:10.14244/19827199763

Meletiou-Mavrotheris, M., & Paparistodemou, E. (2015). Developing students reasoning about samples and sampling in the context of informal inferences. *Educational Studies in Mathematics, 88*(3), 385–404. doi:10.1007/s10649-014-9551-5

Noll, J., & Hancock, S. (2015). Proper and paradigmatic metonymy as a lens for characterizing student conceptions of distributions and sampling. *Educational Studies in Mathematics, 88*(3), 361–383. doi:10.1007/s10649-014-9547-1

North, D., Gal, I., & Zewotir, T. (2014). Building capacity for developing statistical literacy in a developing country: Lessons learned from an intervention. *Statistics Education Research Journal, 13*(2), 15–27.

Phannkuch, M., Arnold, P., & Wild, C. J. (2015). What I see is not quite the way it really is: Students' emergent reasoning about sampling variability. *Statistics Education Research Journal, 13*(2), 343–360.

Ponte, J. (2011). Preparing teachers to meet the challenges of statistics education. In C. Batanero, G. Burrill, & C. Reading (Eds.), *Teaching statistics in school mathematics – Challenges for teaching and teacher education: A joint ICMI/IASE study* (pp. 299–309). New York: Springer. doi:10.1007/978-94-007-1131-0_29

Ponte, J. P. (2012). Estudando o conhecimento e o desenvolvimento profissional do professor de matemática. In *Teoria, crítica y prática de laeducación matemática* (pp. 83–98). Barcelona: GRAO.

Prodromou, T. (2008). *Connecting Thinking About Distribution* (Unpublished Doctoral Dissertation). University of Warwick, UK.

Prodromou, T. (2011). Students' emerging inferential reasoning about samples and sampling. In *Biennial Conference of the Australian Association of Mathematics Teachers AAMT Proceedings*. Retrieved December 30, 2016, from http://www.merga.net.au/documents/RP_PRODROMOU_MERGA34-AAMT.pdf

Prodromou, T. (2014). Developing a modelling approach to probability using computer-based simulations. In E. J. Shernoff & B. Sriraman (Eds.), *Probabilistic Thinking: Presenting Plural Perspectives* (pp. 417–439). New York, NY: Springer; doi:10.1007/978-94-007-7155-0_22

Rubin, A., Bruce, B., & Tenney, Y. (1991). Learning about sampling: Trouble at the core of statistics. In D. Vere-Jones (Ed.), *Proceedings of the Third International Conference on Teaching Statistics* (vol. 1, pp. 314–319). Voorburg: International Statistical Institute.

Saldanha, L., & Thompson, P. (2002). Conception of sample and their relationship to statistical inference. *Educational Studies in Mathematics, 51*(3), 257–270. doi:10.1023/A:1023692604014

Saldanha, L., & Thompson, P. (2007). Exploring connections between sampling distributions and Statistical inference: An analysis of students' engagement and Thinking in the context of instruction involving repeated Sampling. *International Electronic Journal of Mathematics Education, 2*(3), 270–297.

Shi, N., He, X., & Tao, J. (2009). Understanding statistics and statistics education: A Chinese perspective. *Journal of Statistics Education, 17*(3), 1–8. PMID:21603584

Souza, L. O., & Lopes, C. E. (2011). O Uso de Simuladores e a Tecnologia no Ensino da Estocástica. *Boletim de Educação Matemática, 24*(40), 659–677. Retrieved February 16, 2016, from http://www.redalyc.org/pdf/2912/291222113003.pdf

Souza, L.O., Lopes, C.E., & Phannkuch, M. (2015). Collaborative profesional development for statistics teaching: A case study of two middle-school mathematics teachers. *Statistics Education Research Journal, 14*(1), 112–134.

Wallman, K. K. (1993). Enhancing statistical literacy: Enriching our society. *Journal of the American Statistical Association, 88*(421), 1–8.

Watson, J., Collis, K. F., & Moritz, J. B. (1995). The development of concepts Associated with sampling in grades 3, 5, 7 and 9. In *Annual Conference of the Australian Association for Research in Education*. Retrieved Jan, 18, 2014, from: http://www.aare.edu.au/data/publications/1995/watsj95475.pdf

Watson, J. M. (2004). Developing reasoning about samples. In *The challenge of developing statistical literacy, reasoning and thinking* (pp. 277–294). Dordrecht, The Netherlands: Kluwer Academic Publishers. doi:10.1007/1-4020-2278-6_12

Watson, J. M., & Callingham, A. R. (2003). Statistical literacy: a complex hierarchical construct. *Statistical Education Research Journal, 2*(2), 3–46. Retrieved October 29, 2016, from http://citeseerx.ist.psu.edu/viewdoc/download?doi=10.1.1.144.96 17&rep=rep1&type=pdf

Watson, J. M., & Moritz, J. B. (2000). Developing concepts of sampling. *Journal for Research in Mathematics Education, 31*(1), 44–70. doi:10.2307/749819

Wild, C. J., & Pfannkuch, M. (1999). Statistical thinking in empirical enquiry. *International Statistical Review, 67*(3), 223–265. doi:10.1111/j.1751-5823.1999.tb00442.x

Zaslavsky, O. (2009). Mathematics educators' knowledge and development. In R. Even & D. L. Ball (Eds.), *The professional education and development of teachers* (pp. 105–111). New York: Springer. doi:10.1007/978-0-387-09601-8_12

Section 3
Gathering and Processing Big Data

Chapter 9
Visualising Big Data for Official Statistics:
The ABS Experience

Frederic Clarke
Australian Bureau of Statistics, Australia

Chien-Hung Chien
Australian Bureau of Statistics, Australia

ABSTRACT

This chapter outlines recent ABS research in applying data visualisation to the analysis of big data for official statistics. Examples are presented from the application of a prototype analytical platform created by the ABS to two significant big data use cases. This platform – the Graphically Linked Information Discovery Environment (GLIDE) – demonstrates a new approach to representing, integrating and exploring complex information from diverse sources. This chapter discusses the role of data visualisation in meeting the analytical challenges of big data and describes the entity-relationship network model and data visualisation features implemented in GLIDE, together with examples drawn from two recent projects. It concludes and outlines future directions.

INTRODUCTION[1]

National statistics agencies like the Australian Bureau of Statistics (ABS) typically produce a comprehensive set of statistical products, such as key economic indicators, population estimates, and measures of social, cultural, and environmental conditions and progress. Traditionally, the ABS has relied on data collected from surveys and the

DOI: 10.4018/978-1-5225-2512-7.ch009

administrative programs of government to meet its statistical compilation needs. With the emergence of the Internet as a unified global platform for digital connectivity, diverse new sources of human- and machine-generated data are now available for use in statistical production. These sources are often collectively referred to under the rubric of *big data*, and include commercial transactions, remote imagery, sensor measurements, geospatial positioning, web content, and online user activity.

The ABS strategy (ABS, 2015) (ABS, 2014) is to systematically combine complementary information derived from big data sources and traditional data sets, in order to create a richer, more dynamic and better focused statistical picture of Australian society, the economy and the environment. This is intended not only to reduce the cost and time-to-market of existing statistical products, but also to deliver innovative solutions that meet the evolving information needs of statistical consumers. Moreover, it leverages a groundswell of support for open data in government, industry and academia, as a way of making public services more efficient, generating new economic value, and reducing the distance between governments and citizens. Recent open data initiatives in Australia (Turnbull, 2014) and around the world (United Nations, 2014) are changing the data landscape for statistical analysis, the ways in which data is captured and presented, and the necessary level of statistical literacy to analyse and interpret data.

Statistical literacy is considered a vital skill for prospective data users, since it facilitates the interpretation and critical evaluation of statistical information and data-based arguments in the context of intended use (Gal, 2000). For example, the advent of big data accentuates the need to understand the impact of non-sampling bias, and the possible conflation of correlation and causality (Ridgway, 2015). The ABS has a transformative role in the growth of statistical literacy in government and the broader community, in line with its broader vision of supporting "informed and increased use of statistics". Contemporary data visualisation methods and tools provide a powerful enabler of accessible and informative statistics, since they assist users of varied statistical literacy to extract, interpret and communicate analytical insights from statistical data.

This chapter outlines recent ABS research in applying *dynamic visualisation* to the analysis of big data for official statistics. Examples are presented from the application of a prototype analytical platform created by the ABS to two significant big data use cases. This platform – the *Graphically Linked Information Discovery Environment (GLIDE)* – demonstrates a new approach to representing, integrating and exploring complex information from diverse sources. Section 2 discusses the role of data visualisation in meeting the analytical challenges of big data. Section 3 describes the entity-relationship network model and data visualisation features implemented in GLIDE, presents example visualisations from two recent projects. Section 4 concludes and outlines future directions.

ROLE OF DATA VISUALISATION

Big data offers fresh analytical insights for policy development, regulatory compliance and service delivery, particularly when combined in a problem-specific way with survey and administrative data sets. This is of particular value to governments in tackling "wicked problems" (APSC, 2012), such as indigenous disadvantage, obesity, climate change, and land degradation. Wicked problems are *intrinsically complex, dynamic* and *difficult to objectively define* – they are characterised by many contributing time-dependent factors of varying effect that interact in subtle and sometimes surprising ways. To identify the important causal factors and understand their interactions over time, analysis needs to incorporate diverse economic, demographic, social and environmental data, and to move iteratively between the *exploration* and *explanation* of data.

It is the view of the authors that the synergistic interplay of exploration and explanation underpins the delivery of purposive, focused and timely information solutions by statistical agencies in the Information Age. Exploratory analysis is intended to describe the structural and statistical features of data to identify significant correlations among the variables, to detect anomalies and outliers, and to check assumptions on which subsequent statistical inference will be based. From these insights and relevant background knowledge, explanatory analysis can then formulate models of the underlying system to confirm hypotheses about the observed data and predict its future state.

Visualisation as a Cognitive Lever

Visualisation can enhance the utilisation of data by exposing its statistical characteristics and information content in a perceptual form that is more efficiently and meaningfully decoded by information users. Translating complex data into an appropriate visual form condenses and simplifies its information content, and assists user interpretation by exposing relevant features in a more intuitive way. Given an appropriate representation, human perception is highly attuned to the visual recognition of structure, correlation and change in data. Thus visualisation enables the user to discern relationships within and across data sets that would not be visible in tabular or simple graphical form. Visualisation also amplifies human cognition by using visual resources to expand human working memory (Card, Mackinlay, & Shneiderman, 1999).

Figure 1. Location of business and people

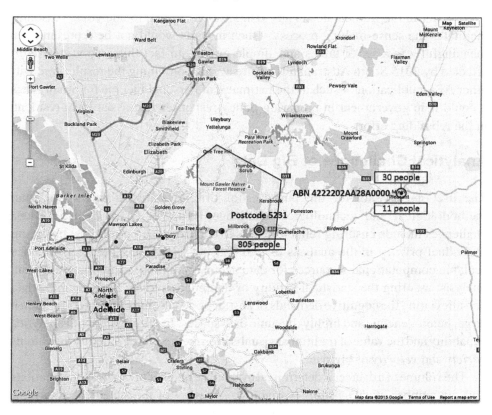

As an example, consider the information drawn from synthetic data that is conveyed visually in Figure 1. It shows a geographic region of South Australia northeast of Adelaide. The area framed by the blue boundary contains five postcode centroids, each of which has been overlaid with a red bubble whose size indicates the number of people residing in the area associated with that postcode. There are also a number of blue bubbles that represent the locations of medium-sized businesses that have employees who reside at one of the five postcodes. It is clear that these businesses are distributed throughout the Adelaide region.

The postcode 5231 (indicated by a red circle) is shown to have 805 people. The business with the Australian Business Number (ABN) identifier of 4222202AA28A0000 (indicated with the blue circle) employs 30 people, 11 of which reside at postcode 5231. Since more than one third of the workforce of this business resides at postcode 5231, any event affecting people in the framed area would be expected to have a substantial impact on its operation – even though the business itself is not in the framed area. Thus visualisation applied to analytical reasoning facilitates the sense-making process – such insights would not be represented as meaningfully in a set of tables and simple graphs. In fact this area was severely affected by 2015 South Australian Bushfire event. Combining the results here with other ABS publications – such as the Estimates of Personal Income for Small Areas – could help government in preparing policy responses that assist local residents in the rebuilding effort.

Analytical Challenges of Big Data

The use of big data for the purposes of official statistics raises important methodological and technological challenges (Tam & Clarke, 2015). These challenges include ensuring reliable access to enduring sources of data; protecting individual privacy in the analysis of rich data sets; providing high-performance, scalable computational resources for data acquisition, processing, integration and analysis; assuring the statistical validity of inferences derived from sampled data; and alleviating the cognitive demands of abstraction, reasoning and interpretation in large, heterogeneous and highly dynamic data spaces. In this regard, both analytical capability and the value of traditional visualisation methods are eroded by the *volume*, *variety* and *velocity* of big data.

The volume of a data set is determined by both the number of *records* (observations) and the number of *dimensions* (variables). As many of the statistical algorithms used routinely in data integration and analysis do not scale linearly with the number of variables, they cannot be easily applied to hyperdimensional data with existing computational resources. High dimensionality is also the source of spurious correlations in data, which may lead to incidental endogeneity in explanatory models. This in turn produces erroneous inferences.

In fact, the dimensionality of data is as much a problem for effective visualisation as it is for analytical routines, even when the number of observations is relatively small. The reason is that processing visual information in more than three dimensions is challenging for human perception. This is complicated by the fact that beyond three or four dimensions, it is increasingly difficult to find a mutually orthogonal set of informative visual properties (such as position, size, colour, and so on), and few established conventions to ensure consistent user interpretation (Iliinsky & Steele, 2011).

It has therefore become standard practice to reduce the dimensionality of the data space using techniques such as principal component analysis (PCA). This is based on the assumption that only a limited subset of variables is actually significant for analysis or visualisation. However, these techniques are computationally demanding, and their success depends on certain assumptions that do not necessarily hold for observations on complex systems. For example, PCA is based on the assumptions that the dimensionality of the data set can be efficiently reduced by a linear transformation of the original variables to a smaller set of components, and that most information of analytical value is captured in relatively few components where the statistical variability is greatest.

Moreover, such dimensionality reduction is not necessarily desirable. Since it is not known a priori which variables are significant to the underlying problem, exploratory analysis is usually best performed at a high level of granularity and covering as broad a span of records and dimensions as possible. The more dimensions visualised in a cognitively accessible way, the greater the chances of recognising potentially important features in data (Wang, Wang, & Alexander, 2015) (Chen & Zhang, 2014). On the other hand, the pattern of data access associated with data exploration aligns poorly with the way that data is represented and stored in traditional databases. These issues are discussed further in the subsequent section.

The variety of data refers to the range of possible data sources (commercial transactions, remote imagery, sensor measurements, spatial positioning, web content, and online user activity), data types (numeric, text, image, sound, video, binary) and data formats (files, streams) available for analytical purposes. The heterogeneity of big data adds significant complexity to its acquisition, storage, integration and analysis. This is particularly the case for unstructured data such as text and imagery, which do not conform to the relational database model, and require new techniques for extracting and leveraging the underlying information content. Data variety also undermines assumptions about what constitutes a "data set". For example, sensors produce a continuous stream of observations rather than a discrete data file in the conventional sense.

Data velocity describes the rate at which data items are produced, changed, transmitted, received, processed and understood. With the advent of the *Internet of Things* (IoT), a network of connected digital devices (or "things") is emerging that operates independently of human intervention. These devices have embedded sensors, software and communication components, enabling them to continuously collect and exchange data about the state of the ambient environment, or the condition of things with which they are associated. Examples include satellite and ground sensors, smart energy meters, point-of-sale scanners, and vehicle telematics units. The IoT has led to a proliferation of fast, disaggregated and potentially volatile data streams that can only be properly exploited by real-time automated analytical systems. The main issue is that many analytical routines are intended for data in batch form, which can be processed through random access over several passes of the data set.

Creating static data files by sampling chunks from a data stream is infeasible for high rate data streams (Stolpe, 2016).

From Static to Dynamic Visualisation

Static visualisation – which provides a fixed snapshot of a data set for a printed or online document – is still the most common presentation model in use for official statistics. Most static graphs are easily created by users using readily accessible tools, which offer simplicity and clarity of purpose. However, recent technological innovations in the field of data science – coupled with a greater understanding of how humans process and synthesise information – has produced a new generation of sophisticated, interactive visualisation methods and applications (Forbes, Ralphs, Goodyear, & Pihama, 2011).

We use the term *dynamic visualisation* to refer to the adaptive, navigable and context-specific depiction of data for the purposes of analysis and communication. It is the essential characteristic of an emerging scientific discipline – *visual analytics* – in which analytical reasoning is facilitated by interactive visual interfaces (Wong & Thomas, 2004) It is intended to address problems whose size, complexity and need for closely coupled human and machine analysis may make them otherwise intractable (Keim, Mansmann, Schneidewind, Thomas, & Ziegler, 2008). Dynamic visualisation is an iterative process that combines machine-oriented data representation, capture, processing and analysis with human-oriented data interaction and decision making.

Analytical systems that employ a dynamic visualisation model significantly enhance the visual discrimination and interpretation of data structure, correlation and change. They enable users to present the data in a variety of visual forms that expose important characteristics and changes in a meaningful way; to iteratively drill down or roll up the granularity of the view, to re-project the view for different subsets of variables; and to focus on particular subsets of records. In particular, the emergence of interactive geospatial visualisation has created unparalleled opportunities for the exploration of geocoded statistical data sets (de Róiste, Gahagen, Morrison, Ralphs, & Bucknall, 2009).

Dynamic visualisation involves two distinct types of operations: *interaction* and *presentation*. Interaction enables the user to specify the *visual form* in which the information content will be encoded (such as a spatial map showing the geographic distribution of an observed variable), set the *perceptual context* (such as geographic area and the level of aggregation), select the data items that will be mapped to this visual form (such as the subset of variables), and adjust the characteristics of *visual elements* to maximise perceptual clarity (such as to expand the view). Presentation accesses the selected data elements, translates them into the specified visual form for the context of use, and composes, organises and renders the visual elements for display on the user device.

Common visual forms (and their specific types) for analytical and communication purposes (DUL, 2017) include *tables*, *two-dimensional spatial maps* (choropleth, cartogram, dot distribution map, proportional symbol map, geospatial data map), *multidimensional charts* (histogram, line chart, bar chart, pie chart, area chart, scatter plot, box and whisker plot, bubble chart, word or concept cloud), *temporal diagrams* (timeline, stream graph, sankey diagram), *hierarchical diagrams* (tree diagram, dendrogram, tree map) and *network diagrams* (node-link diagram, dependency graph). In static visualisation media, the visual elements are presented once and fixed thereafter. Dynamic visualisation enables user interaction to change the context, so the presentation of visual elements is updated as needed. It may also automatically refresh the view in response to an event that changes the values of the selected data items.

Representing Data as a Network

Big data provides rich information about the way that *entities* of different kind (persons, families, businesses, jobs, industries, products, markets, places, events and so on) interact in economic, social and environmental systems of statistical interest. These interactions are typically mediated by a diverse, complex and evolving set of inter-entity *relationships* (such as kinship, friendship, business association, organisational membership, location). It is therefore natural to represent such systems in the form of a *network* (or graph), in which the nodes (or vertices) represent the

Figure 2. Entity-relationship network

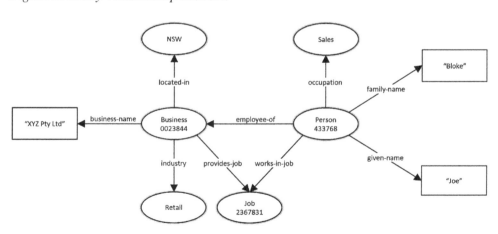

entities contained in one or more data sets, and the links (or edges) between nodes are the relationships that have been observed to exist among them (Clarke & Chien, 2015). A simple example of such a network is given in Figure 2.

The entity-relationship networks described here are somewhat similar to sociograms used in social network analysis (SNA) to visually depict the structure of interpersonal relations in groups. The difference is that sociograms are a static representation of social network structure, and typically involve a single type of entity (person), and small number of possible relationship types. Entity-relationship networks can contain any type of entity and relationship that is of analytical utility; the entities may be multiply connected. Such networks are intrinsically dynamic – entity-relationships characteristics may evolve over time and the network topology itself may undergo change as nodes and links appear and disappear (Windhagera, Zenka, & Federico, 2010).

Since the definitions of entity and relationship type in such network structures are user-defined and purpose-specific, they can form the basis of *conceptual schemata* for modelling complex systems, summarising data, and representing abstract concepts in a clear and intuitive way (Chu & Wipfi, 2013). Such schemata are derived from the mental model that underlies user understanding of the problem domain. Hence they influence (either explicitly or implicitly) the perspective through which data is interpreted (Bertini & Lalanne, 2004). Applying schemata to the way that data is visually presented therefore promotes coherence in the conceptual and perceptual aspects of analysis. An example of a schema is shown in Figure 3.

Representing heterogeneous multisource data in the form of a network shifts the mental model from records and fields (dimensions) in traditional data sets to the entities and relationships of statistical interest that are the real focus of analytical

Figure 3. Conceptual schema

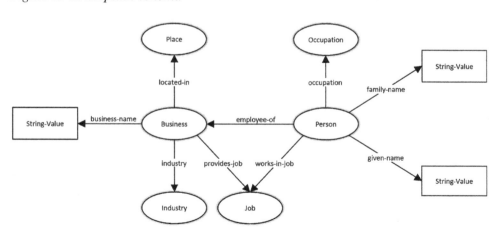

attention. This approach essentially "deconstructs" the boundaries of individual *data containers*, whether those containers are relational database tables, text documents, binary image files, or data streams. All entity-relationship patterns contained in the content of structured and unstructured data are treated in the exactly the same way – they are extracted from their respective data containers and brought together in a network structure according to the entity and relationship type definitions of the underlying schema. Where required, links back to the source data can be embedded in the network.

Information represented and stored in the form of an entity-relationship network is *entity-centric* rather than *record-centric*. Thus the performance scalability problem encountered for the exploratory analysis of multidimensional tabular data does not arise. Interrogation of the network to retrieve relational information involves *traversing the paths between entities*. This pattern of data access is congruent with the structure of the network and does not require a complex sequence of join operations across multiple tables in relational databases. For the human analyst, this path traversal approach is also natural way to conceptualise the patterns of association in complex systems.

GLIDE

GLIDE is a prototype application platform developed by the ABS for the integration and analysis of heterogeneous data from diverse sources, including surveys, administrative collections, and big data. It provides a proof-of-concept implementation of the methods and technology components needed to represent and integrate information in the form of an entity-relationship network; to capture and describe the statistical concepts to which these entities are aligned; and to explore, manipulate and visualise entity-level and aggregate data. It can handle large volumes of both structured and unstructured content, but is not yet able to analyse stream data in real time. This will be implemented in a later version.

GLIDE draws on the now well-established technical framework developed by the World Wide Web Consortium (W3C) for the *Semantic Web* (or Web 3.0) – the global "web of data" for advanced *machine-to-machine interaction* that forms the next stage of evolution of the traditional "web of documents" (W3C, 2017). In the Semantic Web, the *Resource Description Framework* (RDF) is the framework for connecting multiple data sets together in a network of entities and relationships. Content analysis techniques automatically extract entities and relationships of analytical interest from structured and unstructured data. The *Web Ontology Language* (OWL) provides a way to precisely specify the logical properties of the network in a machine-interpretable form. These specifications are captured in a

Figure 4. Functional elements of GLIDE

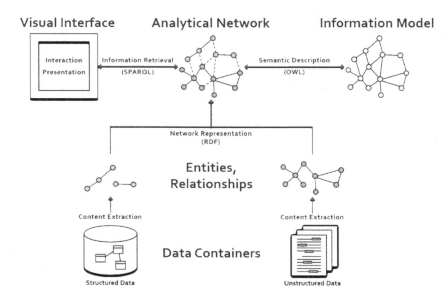

formal semantic information model called an *ontology*. Finally, the *SPARQL query language* provides the mechanism for retrieving information from the network for analysis and visualisation. This is shown in Figure 4.

GLIDE is being used to create and analyse entity-relationship networks – what we call *data pools* – for a range of pathfinder projects. These data pools are composed of many connected "triples" and are stored in an RDF-specific container called a "triplestore". Each triple consists of a pair of entities linked by a specific relationship, and so represents a *known fact* such as "person-x employee-of firm-y". Analysts access the data pool either interactively through a web browser, or programmatically through an R interface. In either case, analytical operations dynamically invoke SPARQL queries that retrieve connected facts for visualisation or statistical computation. SPARQL has a set of aggregation functions (COUNT, SUM, AVG, MIN, MAX, and so on) that allow query results to be enumerated in various ways.

A key design principle for GLIDE is that dynamic visualisation should be embedded within a developing *analytical storyline*, which moves iteratively between exploration and explanation in response to the emerging information needs of the user. Such needs often rely on combining heterogeneous data sets in *problem-specific ways*, and integrating new sources of potential value as data gaps are exposed in the analytical process. Thus in the GLIDE model, *data integration and data analysis are interwoven*.

The usage scenarios underpinning two pathfinder projects will be described below to highlight the visualisation framework implemented in GLIDE and its role in the analytical process. They are:

- **Labour Market Dynamics:** Analysis of multiple administrative data sets containing business and employment information to understand firm entry and exit, job flows, multiple job holders, and employment tenure.
- **Road Freight Performance:** Analysis of telematics and road infrastructure data to understand the movement of road freight vehicles and identify bottlenecks in the national road network.

Labour Market Dynamics

Labour market dynamics refers to changes over time in the activity status of persons in the labour market (employed, unemployed and inactive), and the changes in jobs of employed persons. It covers a broad range of issues that are of significant policy interest to federal and state governments, such as *firm entry and exit* (the impact of true firm birth and death on economic activity); *job flows* (industries in which are jobs being created and destroyed); *multiple job holders* (the characteristics of people who hold multiple jobs); *job tenure* (the industries and job types characterised by short-term employment); and *life-stage transitions* (movement into and out of work associated with finishing education, retirement, and family commitments) (Stibbard, 1999).

To support policy analysis of these labour market issues, the ABS has created a prototype *Labour Market Data Pool* from multiple administrative data sets containing business and employment information. The source data sets contain three years (2009-10 – 2011-12) of taxation records (business, personal and 'pay as you go'), business activity statements, and business characteristics data from ABS Business Register. The data pool currently contains about 2.5 billion triples. Analytical concepts of interest in labour market dynamics include *persons*, *jobs*, *firms*, *events* (e.g. employee separation and hiring, firm entry and exit), *households*, *industries*, *occupations* and *places*. These are connected by rich set of relationships that capture the employment, business and personal information needed for labour market analysis.

The following storyline illustrates the visualisation features in GLIDE for a typical labour market analysis scenario. The analytical scenario is concerned with understanding the changes in the manufacturing industry after the Global Financial Crisis (GFC) of 2007-08, and investigates the impact of firm closure on employment outcomes. *(Note that for confidentiality reasons the diagrams below have been created using a very much smaller data pool created from synthetic source data sets. The two firms mentioned in the scenario – Essential Envelopes and True Blue Offices Supplies – are fictitious and used only for the purposes of the example).*

Which States Were Adversely Affected by the GFC?

Step 1: Present a Macro-Level View of the Manufacturing Industry After 2008

Figure 5 shows a GLIDE interactive dashboard summarising relevant information about all manufacturing firms (industry C) in the Australian economy. It contains separate bar charts of the number of firms by state and industry respectively (with manufacturing selected), a pie chart indicating the years of available data (2009-10, 2010-11 and 2011-12), and separate bubble charts of the number of firms by the total turnover and the number of employees respectively. These results are grouped by state and year. Note that all the visual elements are colour-coded and the size of the bubbles in the second bubble chart are an indication of the number of firms in the state-level aggregation. Such visual dimensions provide additional information to be encoded in the two-dimensional chart representation.

Figure 5. Macro-level view of the manufacturing industry (Australia)

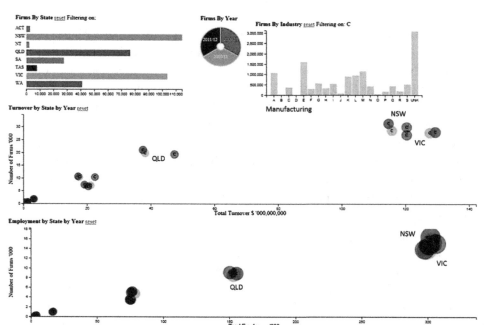

Interaction with any of the visual elements triggers a change in the view, which may invoke a SPARQL query to retrieve new information from the data pool, or simply change/augment the perspective of current information. For example, hovering over any of the bubbles creates a pop-up with additional numerical or contextual information, such as the state to which a particular bubble refers. Selecting the green area in the pie chart would restrict the view to 2011-12. Such changes of perspective assist in exploring the data. The current Australia-wide view suggests that there has been an economic rebound in all states except Victoria. By selecting the bar for Victoria (VIC) in the bar chart of firms by state, the view focuses on Victorian data as shown in Figure 6.

It can be seen that that both the total industry turnover and the number of firms has fallen in Victoria, even though the total employment count has remained about the same and the number of employing firms has not declined as much. It is possible that some industry consolidation has occurred in Victoria, with smaller non-employing firms dropping out – a hypothesis that can form the basis of subsequent explanatory

Figure 6. Macro-level view of the manufacturing industry (Victoria)

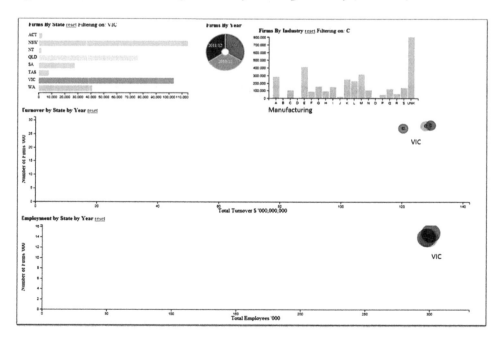

analysis. GLIDE provides an interactive environment for exploring the underlying

ABS social and economic data to validate and explain such macro-level effects. This enables researchers to better understand the drivers in the economic patterns.

Which Manufacturing Were Operating in the Period After the GFC?

Step 2: Present a Micro-Level View of the Manufacturing Sector in Victoria after 2008

Continuing the scenario, GLIDE is now used to determine whether industry consolidation has occurred in Victoria by investigating micro-level changes in the manufacturing sector in Victoria, and their effect on the macro-level picture. Figure 7 shows one possible launching point in GLIDE for this kind of interactive micro-level analysis. It contains a rescalable geographic canvas that allows a specific area to be selected by framing, and over which information about the distribution of persons or firms can be overlaid. This information is retrieved from the data pool using a SPARQL query that is generated automatically from the specifications selected in a set of focus controls – the type of unit, visualisation form, year, industry (or sector), and firm size.

Figure 7. Micro-level view of firms in the Melbourne CBD

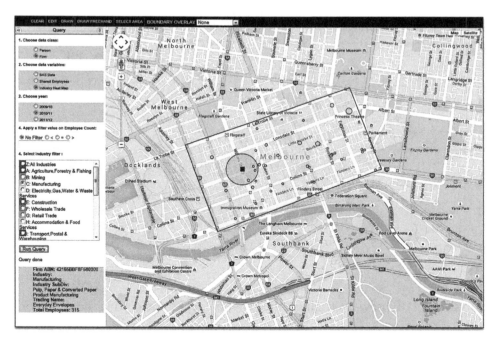

In the example, the geographic view has been focused on inner Melbourne, and the framed area has selected the Melbourne Central Business District (CBD). The focus controls have been to set to retrieve information about manufacturing firms with headquarters in the framed area during 2010-11. This information is depicted in the form of a proportional symbol overlay in which firms are represented by bubbles; the locus of each bubble represents the geographic location of the firm headquarters (which is the only firm location information available from the source data), and its size the number of employees. Hovering over a bubble reveals basic information about the associated firm in the grey box below the selection controls – such as its Australian Business Number (ABN), industry, trading name and number of employees. In this case (shown by the bubble with a black square), it is a firm within the paper manufacturing industry identified as Essential Envelopes.

Selecting Essential Envelopes (by clicking on the bubble) changes the GLIDE view to a rescalable map showing the postcode-level geographic location of the firm (black square) and its employees (blue bubbles, with size indicating employee number) in each of the years for which data exists. Figure 8 presents this information for 2010-11. The firm location here is set to headquarters location, highlighting a data gap that would need to be addressed by integrating other source data sets. Employee location is derived from residential address, another limitation in the source data. Nonetheless, it is clear from where its employees are situated that Essential Envelopes has operations in Brisbane, Sydney, Adelaide and Perth, as well as in Melbourne. Selecting the firm (by clicking on the black square) creates a pop-up histogram of the age and sex profile of Essential Envelopes employees. In the example, this reveals that Essential Envelopes has a large proportion of employees in the 40-50 year age bracket, and more males than females.

The slider control in the employee location map allows the geographic view to be scaled up to focus on Victoria, as shown in Figure 9. Selecting an employee location (by clicking a blue bubble) pops up a sortable table showing the characteristics of the individual employees of the firm at that location. In the example, the location centred on the postcode 3977 (shown with a red circle) has been selected, providing information on the occupation, sex and age of nine employees of Essential Envelopes.

Which Firms Exited the Manufacturing Industry and What Happened to Their Employees?

Step 3: Present a Network View of Specific Firm Transitions between 2009-10 and 2011-12

GLIDE may be used to detect complex labour market events, such firm entry and exit. Firms can enter and exit the economy for a variety of reasons – administrative,

Figure 8. Employee location map

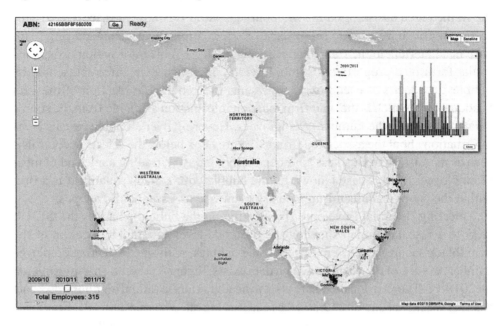

Figure 9. Employee details by location

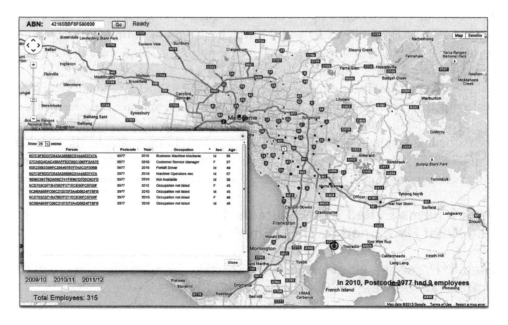

financial and structural changes – but not all entries reflect the true births of new enterprises, nor all exits the deaths of old enterprises. A firm can change its visible characteristics due to a merger or takeover, including its Australian Business Number (ABN) identifier. By contrast, employee characteristics (such as employer) are considerably less volatile. If the majority of employees of a deregistered firm are working for the same new firm in the following year, then this is likely to reflect continuing economic activity. Conversely, if the employees are dispersed among other firms then this is likely to reflect a true firm death (Chien & Mayer, 2015).

In this example scenario, it observed that no employee information for Essential Envelopes exists for 2011-12. This may be due to a firm exit event – it is possible that Essential Envelopes has closed or been taken over. The hypothesis is that the macro-level statistics on the Victorian manufacturing can be explained by industry consolidation. This can be tested in GLIDE by examining transitions in the Essential Envelopes work force from 2010-11 to 2011-12. Figure 10 shows the pattern of employee connections to Essential Envelopes in 2010-11 and 2011-12 respectively in the form of an entity-relationship network (where the squares are persons, the coloured circles firms of 4 or more employees in various industries and the links are employment relationships). Note that all of the employee connections in 2010-11

Figure 10. Everyday envelopes – Connections in 2010-11 and 2011-12

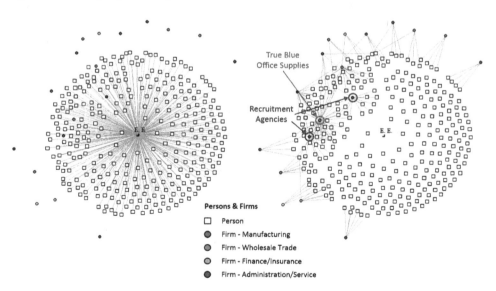

have been cut in 2011-12, confirming the firm exit hypothesis, and indicating that Essential Envelopes has closed rather than been taken over.

Step 4: Present a Network View of the Impact of Firm Transitions on Employment Outcomes

From the example post-closure network in Figure 10 it can be seen that a number of employees displaced by the closure of Essential Envelopes have connected to other firms. Information about these firms can be easily extracted from the data pool. One of them – True Blue Office Supplies – has taken on about 50 of the 315 Essential Envelopes employees, leaving the rest to find another job. A number of former employees have connected to recruitment firms (which is not strictly an employee-of relationship). It can also be seen from the connection network that about 30 employees have not been able to find a job after Essential Envelopes closed down. This may provide an important insight for the development of policy intended to facilitate the transition of displaced workers back into the labour market. It also highlights the natural synergy of exploratory and explanatory analysis in understanding complex economic and social systems. In this case, visualising the connection network of people and firms reveals specific events that are important for subsequent statistical analysis.

GLIDE provides a number of mechanisms for investigating the impact of firm closure on employment outcomes. One is to present the post-event characteristics of displaced workers in the form of a connection network, using visual dimensions to highlight any significant shifts. Figure 11 shows two such characteristics – occupation and income – in the year after the closure of Essential Envelopes.

In the left-hand diagram, former employees of Essential Envelopes who have changed their occupation in finding a new job are indicated by a different colour from those with the same occupation afterwards (yellow for different, green for the same). This provides information on the demand for particular occupations in the labour market. With the addition of source data on educational attainment to the data pool, it would be possible to determine whether some of these people had upskilled to find new work.

The right-hand indicates by colour whether the overall income of displaced workers changed by more than 10% (where blue means increased, purple is the same, and red is decreased) in the year after Essential Envelopes closed down. In this example, it can be seen that many of them – including those unable to find work again – have experienced a reduction in their income. Note that simply merging the two diagrams in Figure 11 would require additional visual dimensions to properly encode the relationships, and so result in greater symbolic complexity. We are currently investigating options for how such joint correlations might be best represented.

Figure 11. Everyday envelopes – Post-closure employee outcomes

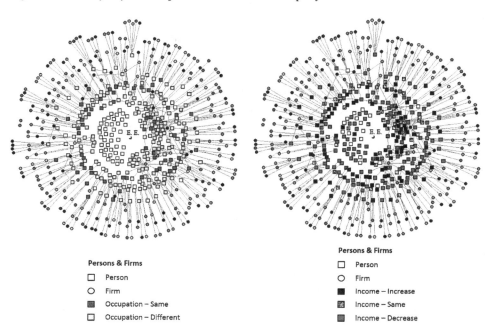

Persons & Firms

☐ Person
○ Firm
▦ Occupation – Same
☐ Occupation – Different

Persons & Firms

☐ Person
○ Firm
■ Income – Increase
▩ Income – Same
■ Income – Decrease

Road Freight Performance

Road freight performance measurement aims to provide policy makers and industry with fine-grained and timely statistics on the efficacy of freight movement in Australia's road network. This supports improved policy development and informed investment decisions in critical transport infrastructure. The ABS and the Bureau of Infrastructure, Transport and Regional Economics (BITRE) have demonstrated the feasibility of using new data sources, methods and technologies for the delivery of detailed and timely road freight performance measurements (ABS, 2016).

Important road freight performance measures include *vehicle movement measures* (speed, route, travel time, idle time, fuel use, and pollutant emissions) and *freight movement measures* (origin, destination, commodity, mass/volume) for the major intercity transport corridors; and *traffic flow and congestion measures* (origin-destination node connectivity, flow convergence and divergence characteristics, congestion location and dynamics) for the national road freight network. In order to assist cognitive uptake, it is important for summary "at a glance" compilations of performance measurement to be linked to more detailed "drill down" performance information (TRB, 2011).

The ABS has produced a prototype *Freight Performance Data Pool* containing data generated by in-vehicle telematics units, combined with government and commercial road infrastructure datasets. The telematics data consists of freight vehicle status information – such as its geolocation (GPS coordinates), speed, weight, and engine characteristics – transmitted in frequent bursts (typically 6 to 20 per minute). Road infrastructure data provides information on the designation, type and condition of roads (e.g. national highway identifier, number and direction of lanes, grade, sealed or unsealed), and the location of traffic control structures (e.g. traffic lights, stop signs) and public or private transport facilities (e.g. service centres, rest stops, weighbridges, inspection points, freight depots).

The prototype data pool contains telematics data sourced from 10 separate freight operators, either directly in a variety of formats – such as Microsoft Excel files, comma-separated variable (CSV) format files and Java Script Object Notation (JSON) format objects – or as extracts from telematics service provider data streams via provider-published Application Programming Interfaces (APIs). This data covers around 18 million separate data bursts from 1500 vehicles over 104,000 trips for the month of May 2016. Each burst contains a minimal set of data fields (dimensions) – vehicle identifier, geolocation (latitude-longitude), date-time and speed. When integrated with road infrastructure datasets, this produced about 241 million triples in the data pool. This is indicative of the complexity that big data sources bring to the analytical domain.

The analytical concepts of interest in road freight performance include *roads*, *vehicles*, *operators*, *commodities*, *corridors*, *trajectories*, *routes*, *trips*, *segments*, *events* (e.g. vehicle stop, road closure), and *places*. These are connected by a variety of relationships that capture spatial location and movement, commerce and regulatory information. Since road transport is inherently a network phenomenon, it is well suited to the data representation and exploration methods implemented in GLIDE.

The following analytical scenario is concerned with identifying parts of the national road infrastructure that might be prioritised for investment by government in order to improve freight movement.

What Routes Are Important for Freight Movement in Australia?

Step 1: Present a National View of Freight Vehicle Movement in the Road Network

Note that we are concerned here with routes that are heavily used by the freight and logistics industry, and the high capacity roads associated with them. Figure 12 shows a GLIDE geographic view of the number and average speed of freight vehicles travelling along major mainland Australian highways.

Figure 12. Freight vehicle movement on major Australian highways

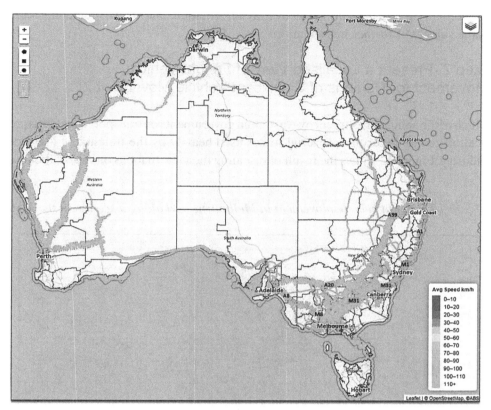

This information is derived from geolocation data produced by the in-vehicle telematics transmission from the sample of freight vehicles available for May 2016. It is depicted in the form of a proportional symbol overlay in which the movement trajectories are represented by lines of varying width (wider means more vehicles) and colour (green indicates that the average speed is close to the designated "free flow" speed of the road segment, usually 110 km/h for national highways). The information retrieved from the data pool using a SPARQL query that is generated automatically for this view. Hovering over a movement trajectory creates a pop-up with additional information.

As expected, the national highways that service the key intercity transport corridors of south-eastern Australia are all heavily utilised, such as the M31 (Melbourne-Sydney), M1/A1 and M1/A39 (Sydney-Brisbane), M31/A39 (Melbourne-Brisbane), M8/A8 (Melbourne-Adelaide), and M31/A20 (Sydney-Adelaide). However, it is not possible to discern detailed road utilisation information at this level of spatial granularity, and the map is visually cluttered. GLIDE has a number of mechanisms for computing and presenting the overlay information, and the best default option is the subject of further investigation.

Step 2. Present a Localised View of Freight Vehicle Movement for Regions of Significant Vehicle Movement

Much of the annual investment by Australian governments on transport infrastructure is allocated to the primary arterial routes used heavily by the freight and logistics industry. Figure 13 shows the result of rescaling the view to focus on the Melbourne

Figure 13. Freight vehicle movement in Melbourne and along a section of the M80

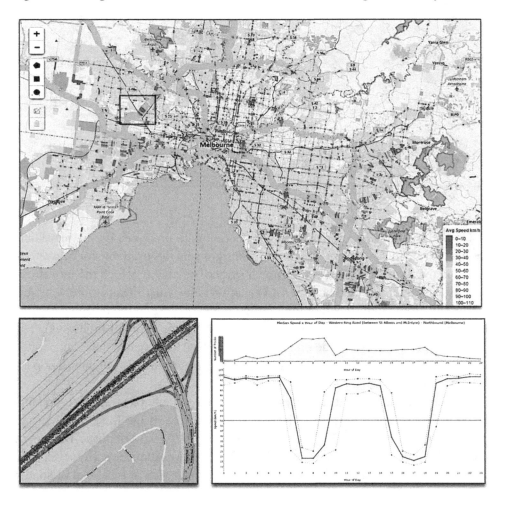

metropolitan area (indicated by the blue box in the national-level map), and further to a specific section of the M80 Ring Road (blue box in the local-level map). The red and yellow sections of the major highways indicate road segments in which the average vehicle speed is significantly lower than the posted limit (where the free flow speed is typically between 80 and 110 km/h, depending on the road status). We take this as a simple indicator of congestion.

The road-specific view of the M80 is sufficiently fine-grained to show the geolocation readings of individual telematics bursts as distinct map points (red dots in the left hand panel of Figure 13). Selecting a road section (indicated by the blue box) creates a popup line chart of the number of vehicles and median speed at that location over a 24-hour period. This shows significant congestion in the periods 0700 to 0900 (the morning peak) and 1500 to 1800 (afternoon peak), with average vehicle speeds around 15-25 km/h. This also coincides with peak heavy vehicle usage in the sample, with 371–378 vehicles per hour in those time windows.

How Does Observed Road Utilisation for Freight Vehicle Movement Align With National Priorities?

Step 3: Present a Localised View That Compares the Network of Key Freight Routes With Freight Vehicle Movement

National Key Freight Routes (NKFRs) are the road and rail routes connecting Australia's nationally significant places for freight, including ports, airports and intermodal terminals. An interactive map of designated NKFRs has been published online to support planning and investment decisions, regulatory purposes and customer service features for the transport and logistics industry. This is expected to facilitate a greater understanding of the national land freight system and allow users to overlay other base-maps and datasets, and zoom into a high level of detail (DIRD, 2015). When a NKFR is heavily utilised, there are likely to be important network-wide effects on vehicle congestion.

In Figure 14, the road freight component of the NKFRs has been overlaid as a set of blue lines on the map of observed freight vehicle movements in south-eastern Australia. The green movement trajectories show the routes traversed by freight vehicles in the Melbourne-Sydney transport corridor during May 2016, based on spatial positioning data from the sample of the pilot project. The inset map shows that the section of the M80 previously identified as a congestion point is indeed part of a NKFR.

However, it is also immediately apparent from even a cursory visual examination of the data that a significant proportion of freight vehicles do not follow the designated NKFRs. Further investigation of the data is of course needed to develop and test

Figure 14. Road vehicle movement on the national key freight routes

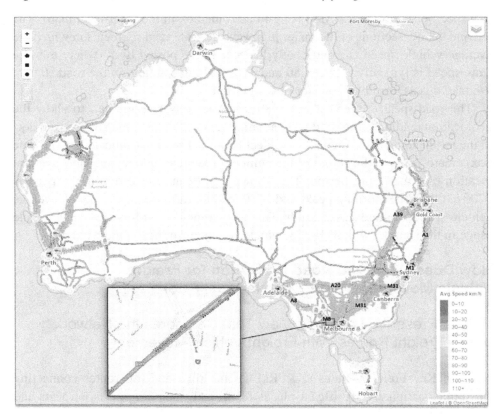

hypotheses about the cause of this observed effect – taking into account factors such as the size of the vehicles, the type of freight carried, the location of depots and fuel centres, the condition of the roads, and the impact of congestion. As in the case of data exploration, such explanatory analysis is greatly assisted by effective visual assimilation and reinforcement.

Step 4: Present a Targeted View of Route Divergence in High Volume Intercity Transport Corridors

While freight impeding congestion in the national road network is a significant impetus for major infrastructure investment, traffic flow and congestion is a complex analytical problem. Congestion can be measured in several ways, and may be temporary or prolonged. As is clear from the map in Figure 14, the major intercity transport corridors typically contain multiple alternative routes, so the patterns of flow can change as freight vehicles actively circumvent known or emerging congestion points. Moreover, other factors influence individual vehicle route selection decisions.

As a way of delving into this issue, GLIDE can be used to drill down into the national-level NKFR road utilisation. As an example, Figure 15 shows that freight traffic on the A39 route of the Melbourne-Brisbane transport corridor diverges into two tributaries at the New South Wales border – one stream continues to follow A39 (Gore and Warrego Highways); the other takes a more southerly route using 42/15 (Cunningham Highway) between Goondiwindi and Brisbane. In this view, important summary statistics are displayed in a pop-up chart by selecting an available route. As the map in the lower right panel of Figure 15 shows, the section of the 42/15 route from Goondiwindi to Warwick is not an NKFR. This has infrastructure investment implications, given the potential volume of freight traffic carried by this tributary.

CONCLUSION AND FUTURE DIRECTIONS

This chapter describes application of advanced visualisation approaches by the ABS to analysis of big data in statistical production. It can be seen from the examples provided that contemporary dynamic visualisation is a powerful enabler of inductive reasoning in both exploratory and explanatory analysis for complex problems and data. GILDE is intended to provide the ABS with a technology platform for the

Figure 15. Road vehicle movement in the Melbourne-Brisbane transport corridor

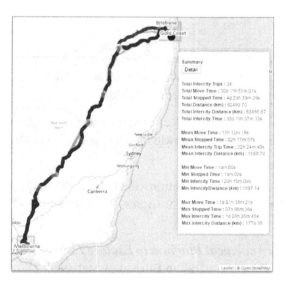
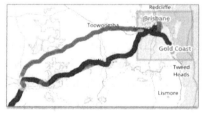

development and evaluation of new methods for knowledge discovery and model building for statistical purposes. Future work will focus on improving data navigability across different analytical perspectives and integrating interactive visually-oriented modelling with traditional automated statistical techniques.

ACKNOWLEDGMENT

We gratefully acknowledge several people who provided inputs for this chapter: Jenny Myers, Chris Conran, Laurent Lefort, Rory Tarnow-Mordi, Nick Husek and Andreas Mayer for their contributions to the development of GLIDE. We also thank Amanda Clark and Jon Williams for providing critical subject matter guidance in the freight project.

REFERENCES

ABS. (2014). *Big Data For Informed Decisions.* Australian Bureau of Statistics. Unpublished.

ABS. (2015). *Special Report: Big Data Plays a Big Role in the Future of Statistics.* Annual Report, 2014-15, Australian Bureau of Statistics. Retrieved from http://www.abs.gov.au/

ABS. (2016). *Freight Performance Measurement Project - Phase 2 Final Report.* Unpublished report submitted to Secretaries Data Group, December 2016, Australian Bureau of Statistics.

APSC. (2012). *Tackling wicked problems: A public policy perspective.* Australian Public Service Commission. Retrieved from http://www.apsc.gov.au/publications-and-media/archive/publications-archive/tackling-wicked-problems

Bertini, E., & Lalanne, D. (2004). Investigating and Reflecting on the Integration of Automatic Data Analysis and Visualization in Knowledge Discovery. *SIGKDD Explorations, 11*(2).

Chen, C., & Zhang, C.-Y. (2014). Data-intensive applications, challenges, techniques and technologies: A survey on Big Data. *Information Sciences, 275*(10), 314–347. doi:10.1016/j.ins.2014.01.015

Chien, C., & Mayer, A. (2015). *A New Analytical Platform to Explore Linked Data. Methodological Advisory Committee Paper.* Australian Bureau of Statistics.

Chu, K.-H., & Wipfi, H. (2013). Using Visualizations to Explore Network Dynamics. *Journal of Social Structure, 14.*

Clarke, F., & Chien, C.-H. (2015). Connectedness and Meaning: New Analytical Directions for Official Statistics. *Proceedings of the 3rd International Workshop on Semantic Statistics.* Bethlehem, PA: CEUR Workshop Proceedings. Retrieved from http://ceur-ws.org/Vol-1551/#article-02

de Róiste, M., Gahagen, M., Morrison, P., Ralphs, M., & Bucknall, P. (2009). *Geovisualisation and policy: exploring the links.* Official Statistics Research Project Report, Statistics New Zealand.

DIRD. (2015, December). *National Key Freight Routes Map.* Retrieved from Department of Infrastructure and Regional Development: http://maps.infrastructure. gov.au/KeyFreightRoute/

DUL. (2017). *Introduction to Data Visualization: Visualization Types.* Retrieved from Duke University Libraries: http://guides.library.duke.edu/datavis/vis_types

Forbes, S., Ralphs, M., Goodyear, R., & Pihama, N. (2011). *Visualising official statistics.* Statistics New Zealand.

Gal, Y. (2000). *Adult Numeracy Development: Theory, Research, Practice.* Cresskill, NJ: Hampton Press.

Iliinsky, N., & Steele, J. (2011). *Designing Data Visualizations.* Sebastopol, CA: O'Reilly Media, Inc.

Keim, D., Mansmann, F., Schneidewind, J., Thomas, J., & Ziegler, H. (2008). Visual Analytics: Scope and Challenges. In *Visual Data Mining* (pp. 76–90). Berlin: Springer. doi:10.1007/978-3-540-71080-6_6

Ridgway, J. (2015, December). Implications of the Data Revolution for Statistics Education. *International Statistical Review, 84*(3), 528–549. doi:10.1111/insr.12110

Stibbard, P. (1999). *Labour market dynamics: a global survey of statistical activity.* International Labour Organization. Retrieved from http://www.ilo.org/employment/ Whatwedo/Publications/WCMS_120366/lang--en/index.htm

Stolpe, M. (2016). The Internet of Things: Opportunities. *ACM SIGKDD Explorations Newsletter, 8*(1), 15–34. doi:10.1145/2980765.2980768

Tam, S.-M., & Clarke, F. (2015). Big Data, Official Statistics and Some Initiatives by the Australian Bureau of Statistics. *International Statistical Review, 83*(3), 436–448. doi:10.1111/insr.12105

TRB. (2011). *Performance Measures for Freight Transportation. Transportation Research Board.* Washington, DC: National Academy of Sciences. doi:10.17226/14520

Turnbull, M. (2014). *National Map Open Data initiative to boost innovation.* Retrieved from Ministers for the Department of Communications and the Arts: http://www. minister.communications.gov.au/malcolm_turnbull/news/national_map_open_data_ initiati ve_to_boost_innovation#.WIRcoFN96Hs

United Nations. (2014). *Open Government and Data Services.* Retrieved from Public Administration and Development Management: https://publicadministration. un.org/en/ogd

W3C. (2017). *Semantic Web.* Retrieved 2017, from World Wide Web Consortium (W3C): https://www.w3.org/standards/semanticweb/

Wang, L., Wang, G., & Alexander, C. (2015). Big Data and Visualization: Methods, Challenges and Technology Progress. *Digital Technologies, 1*(1), 33–38. doi:10.12691/dt-1-1-7

Windhagera, F., Zenka, L., & Federico, P. (2010). Visual Enterprise Network Analytics – Visualizing Organizational Change. *7th Conference on Applications of Social Network Analysis.*

Wong, P., & Thomas, J. (2004). Visual Analytics. *IEEE Computer Graphics and Applications, 24*(5), 20–21. doi:10.1109/MCG.2004.39 PMID:15628096

ENDNOTE

[1] Views expressed in this paper are those of the authors and do not necessarily represent those of the Australian Bureau of Statistics. Where quoted or used, they should be attributed clearly to the authors. Note that the examples presented in this chapter use synthetic data and are intended for demonstration purposes.

Chapter 10
Big Data Techniques for Supporting Official Statistics:
The Use of Web Scraping for Collecting Price Data

Antonino Virgillito
Istituto Nazionale di Statistica (ISTAT), Italy

Federico Polidoro
Istituto Nazionale di Statistica (ISTAT), Italy

ABSTRACT

Following the advent of Big Data, statistical offices have been largely exploring the use of Internet as data source for modernizing their data collection process. Particularly, prices are collected online in several statistical institutes through a technique known as web scraping. The objective of the chapter is to discuss the challenges of web scraping for setting up a continuous data collection process, exploring and classifying the more widespread techniques and presenting how they are used in practical cases. The main technical notions behind web scraping are presented and explained in order to give also to readers with no background in IT the sufficient elements to fully comprehend scraping techniques, promoting the building of mixed skills that is at the core of the spirit of modern data science. Challenges for official statistics deriving from the use of web scraping are briefly sketched. Finally, research ideas for overcoming the limitations of current techniques are presented and discussed.

DOI: 10.4018/978-1-5225-2512-7.ch010

INTRODUCTION

The use of Big Data in official statistics is a major topic that in recent years has been the subject of several initiatives both at the level of single National Institutes of Statistics and in the form of international collaboration projects. Among all the possible types of Big Data sources that have been tested for supporting the production of statistical indicators, the "Internet as a data source" is a highly popular one, which was subject of several experimentations in various domains, since the idea of exploiting the huge amount of information available on the web is largely appealing for researchers. However, despite the apparent high accessibility of Internet data, the task of setting up a collection of web data with a level of quality that is sufficient to produce correct statistical indicators over a medium-long period of time is still an open issue.

The consumer price survey is an interesting test bed in this sense because automated collection of Internet data can replace that part of the current data collection based on repetitive centralized activities, at the same time improving the representation of modern consumption habits, more and more biased towards the use of e-commerce.

In general, various challenges have emerged for statisticians in terms of the use of Big Data for statistical purposes in this field. First of all the use of web scraping techniques as a tool to achieve big data for inflation measurement has directly to do with one of the three V's of big data, i.e., velocity. "Velocity" implies the possibility of improving timeliness in the production of statistical indicators. This is clearly true for a phenomenon, like inflation, that is characterized by temporal evolution but also for other phenomena, as unemployment, touristic flows, telecommunication, that are investigated through traditional data collection tools. Secondly web scraping techniques are widely available and Internet as data source is at disposal of all: in particular for topics for which the information are largely available on the web (and this is typically the case of consumer prices) this is a major "threat" to the monopoly of the National Statistical Institutes over data and information, currently derived by their official status. Last but not least, web scraping techniques applied to consumer prices as well as to other phenomena could offer access to a bigger amount of data compared to that accessed by the current data collection with the potential of improving the quality of the derived indicators.

In this chapter we extensively review the techniques that have been setup for collecting price data from the Internet relatively to different kinds of products. The objective is to automatically retrieve and make recognizable the information off the web page, writing it in local database/data-store/files, eliminating the use of "copy and paste" activity, currently used to collect price data. We will present and classify scraping implementation techniques that have been used in practice in different National Statistical Institutes and comment their effectiveness in the light of their application to different kinds of products, as a result of tests carried out in the Italian National Institute of Statistics.

The general problem of web scraping is to extract from semi-structured documents (i.e., web pages) some structured pieces of information that are contained in it. However, the languages that are used to implement web pages (e.g., HTML, CSS etc.) mostly constitute a syntax for describing stylistic aspects of the pages themselves, with no indication of the semantics of data they represent, which on the contrary is the specific focus of the scraping activity. This conceptual mismatch is at the basis of all the difficulties in the use of Internet as a data source, that are common to all the techniques used to implement scraping. Moreover, once a scraping process has been set up it has to be constantly monitored and maintained, in order to respond to changes in the structure of the web sites that may disrupt the correct execution of the collection process. This is an additional problem in a context such as that of an NSI, where IT resources for conducting surveys are generally scarce and survey statisticians do not have the skills to carry out such activity.

We will present the specific technical aspects of each solution and comment on the results of experimentation carried out in various National Institutes of Statistics, highlighting that although each technique provides some benefits with respect to a specific category of product, there is still no such a thing as a "one-stop-shop" solution for web scraping, that is a tool or technique that at the same time is easy to setup and maintain, preferably for non-technical users, and is not very sensitive to changes in the structure of the page. For this reason, large-scale approaches, like the Billion Prices Project (Cavallo & Rigobon, 2016), are based on the intense work of a large number of dedicated resources, a solution that cannot be considered feasible for a National Institute of Statistics.

In the final part of the chapter we propose a novel technique that is currently being developed at Istat, intended to meet all the above-mentioned requirements. The idea is to use a machine learning approach, by exploiting simplified text mining techniques to detect price data on the page. Differently from a general text mining problem, where a generic text has to be analyzed in order to determine the significant semantic elements which is a priori unknown, the extraction of price data can rely on the assumption that the information of interest is normally inserted into a structure (such as a table) and is easily recognizable from its syntactic characteristics (e.g., the presence of the Euro sign or the number format). For these reasons, we believe that an unassisted approach can be implemented that, with little or no training and maintenance required, can be applied to a large number of pages and web sites, finally leading to a real collection of Big Data, that can highly improve the quality of the estimation of the inflation.

BACKGROUND

"Web Scraping" is the generic term that is used for techniques for accessing the information contained in unstructured/semistructured form within web pages and convert it to treatable data that can be stored and analyzed. There are different approaches to implement web scraping according to the kind of application and data to extract. The general problem can be decomposed in two phases: the *Selection* of the set of web sites and pages to scrape and the *Extraction* of information from such pages. In the following we try to identify the purpose of each phase:

Selection Phase

The target of web scraping can range from a single web page to a large set of entire web sites. Deciding the target set of pages to scrape and getting their URLs is the first problem to solve. In this sense, the simplest form of scraping starts from a fixed set of links to the target pages but this is obviously feasible only for limited sets of pages/sites. The term *web crawling* (Pinkerton, 1994) is used to identify those techniques that are used to access a possibly large set of web pages via a software process that automatically browses web sites through an extensive navigation of all the pages. The basic crawling algorithm starts from an initial page and follows recursively all the links included in it, keeping track of all the visited pages to avoid loops (Liu, 2011, p. 312). It is obvious that the number of pages that can be returned can be very high, so several techniques have been developed to restrict the search, for example constraining the crawl within the parent web site.

In its most general form the crawling process may not even start with a URL, because a list of initial links may be unavailable. In this case solutions for identifying and retrieving web sites of interest must be developed. An example is presented in Barcaroli et al. (2015), where a large number of web sites of enterprises are scraped starting only from a list of enterprise names, without the associated URLs. Thus, before the actual scraping is done, a preliminary activity is performed in order to try to detect an enterprise URL by querying a search engine for its name.

It often occurs in practice that even crawling an entire web site is not sufficient to obtain the data of interest. In many situations the content of a web site is not accessible through browsing, normally because of the amount of the underlying data. The best examples of this are airline web sites, where the number of variations for air fares and the number of available flights make it impossible to organize the content in a navigation menu. In such cases, selection of the desired content of the web site is made by injecting (manually or through an automated process) values into a web form that once submitted returns only filtered content. For the airline site example, one must first select flight dates, origins and destinations before consulting – and extracting – prices.

Extraction Phase

Once pages are selected, the real core operation of web scraping consists in the extraction of information from it. A web page is simply a text file consisting in a set of tags delimiting text blocks and indicating the general appearance that the text should have on the page (organized in table, links, etc.). In substance, the technologies used to implement the majority of web sites completely ignore the actual semantics of the page elements, which is the main interest of web scraping. A formulation of the problem of web scraping is how to obtain semantics (i.e., information) from unstructured content, only exploiting hints given by the tags and style features.

A primary distinction should be made about the kind of data to be extracted. In the case of unstructured data, the extracted content is considered as simple text. Text mining techniques are applied to classify the elements of text present on the page with the aim of retrieving information from the text, as in Barcaroli et al. 2015, where the scraped enterprise web sites are used to infer responses to questions in the survey about the use of ICT from enterprises. If on the contrary the target of the extraction is structured data, the idea is to aim for obtaining data organized in tabular structures on the page and reconstructing the inner relationships within an organized data set. In the following of the chapter we will focus on the collection of online price data that belong to the latter category.

WEB SCRAPING TO COLLECT DATA FOR OFFICIAL STATISTICS

The advent of so-called "Big Data" in recent years has suggested a novel approach to the use of data gathered from multiple sources and used as a source both for gaining insights of aspects of business, society and individual behavior that were previously difficult or impossible to represent (Manyika et al., 2011).

Among the various sources of Big Data, the Internet is always mentioned as one of the major ones in terms of potential scale of data that can be gathered and coverage of possibly any field of human activity. The Official Statistics Community, both at international and national level, has started discussing the possibility of using Big Data sources and in particular the Internet, in the context of the production of official statistical indicators, with the aims of replacing the traditional tools of data collection and producing indicators coherent with the qualitative requirements of the Official Statistics (ESCC, 2013). The use of Big Data is the subject of a number of initiatives at international level involving statistical organizations worldwide, discussing the best ways to incorporate novel sources into statistical production processes and carrying out experiments and pilots.

In particular, the High-Level Group (HLG) for the Modernization of Statistical Production and Services, an initiative promoted by the United Nations Economic Commission for Europe (UNECE), developed a deep debate about the role of Big Data for the production of official statistics. The results within this HLG initiative included a SWOT (Strength, Weaknesses, Opportunities, Threats) and a risk/benefit analysis for Official Statistics in using Big Data (UNECE, 2014a), a Big Data quality framework (UNECE, 2014b), and an inventory of Big Data projects (UNECE, 2014c).

The first result is an interesting framework of the risks that potentially could derive to official statistics from the use of Big Data. This framework offers a synthesis of the tools to deal with the quality management of statistics derived from Big Data and groups risks into six main categories (Wirthmann et al., 2015): 1) lack of access to data; 2) loss of access to data; 3) risks related to the legal environment; 4) Risks related to confidentiality and data security; 5) Adverse Public Perception of Big Data usage by official statistics; 6) Risks related to skills.

As for the quality management, an extension of the existing statistical data quality frameworks was defined. The extended framework uses a hierarchical structure with three hyper-dimensions: the source, the metadata and the data. Source is associated with the type of data, the characteristics of the entity from which the data is obtained, and the governance under which it is administered and regulated. Metadata is associated to information describing the concepts, the contents of the data sets, and the processes applied to it.

All these analyses, as well as several projects listed in the inventory, focus on the use of Internet as a data source, mostly because the apparent lack of barriers to access to data with respect to other sources makes it an attractive option, with most popular examples of domains involved in collections being online prices (Polidoro et al., 2015; Ten, Bosch, & Griffioen, 2016; Radzikowski & Śmietanka, 2016) and job vacancies (Nikić et al., 2015).

However, collecting data for the production of official statistical indicators presents significant differences with their use for analysis or application development. Statistical data collection requires a high level of control on the sources, that should guarantee quality of the data and representativeness with respect to the universe of interest. Hence, it is natural to use the Internet as a replacement for manual data collection, which means using web scraping, automating operations that are traditionally made by human operators.

Nevertheless, these methods represent mostly a change in the tools used for data collection, which does not necessary imply the shift in the paradigm that could be enabled by the full potential of the Internet as a data source. The attempt in the remainder of this chapter is to approach the problem in more general terms, by identifying two desirable characteristics for statistical online data collection:

Scale

The huge quantity of data potentially available on the Internet could trigger a real Big Data approach, where the volume and variety of the sources can expand the representativeness and coverage of the data and possibly overcome some of the inherent limitations of traditional sources. Collection on large scale may result in a radical improvement in the quality of the collection for some specific topics, such as online prices (Cavallo, 2016) where the variety of data and its rapid variation is difficult to represent with traditional collection techniques.

Repeatability

Statistical processes are typically reproduced over time at regular frequencies that range from monthly to yearly according to the particular process, involving a well-identified and solid set of sources. Particularly for some statistical domains (e.g., prices) the stability of the sample is a crucial feature in order to preserve the correctness of the computed indicators. Nowadays, expectations from the general public are targeted toward statistical information that is more timely and frequently updated. Thus, a scraping process used for statistical data collection should be solid enough to be repeated regularly and possibly allow higher collection frequencies than traditional methods, in order to expand the time sampling and better represent the rapid fluctuations that characterize Internet data. The main challenge with repeatability is how to cope with the frequent changes that are made on web sites, such as changes in the structure of the pages, URLs and general organization of the content. This inherent instability of web sites may disrupt the initial setup of the extraction phase, making it necessary to constantly monitor scraped pages.

A large scale of collection and stable and frequent repetition are the ideal characteristics to achieve comprehensive and consistent data collection for statistical purposes. However, scale and repeatability are conflicting requirements, since the higher the number of sites and pages that are involved, the higher the probability of a change that interrupts data collection.

WEB SCRAPING TECHNIQUES

In this section we present the main techniques that can be used for collecting data from the web, introducing the core technical details behind them. Although this chapter is not targeted to a technical audience, we believe that a basic understanding of the technological issues of web scraping is necessary in order to understand the implications of setting up data collection based on scraped data in a statistical production process and to provide the complete decisional elements for correctly organizing all the related activities.

Furthermore, we present the various techniques under the light of the dimensions introduced in previous sections, explaining on one hand how they can be used to implement the extraction and selection phases and on the other how they are fit to reach scale and repeatability.

Technical Background

The World Wide Web at its core is based on the transmission of pages containing mixed content, such as text, images and links to other pages. A page and all its related content are stored in a web server. When a user types a URL in a web browser, the page associated is downloaded to the local computer and presented to the user. The HTTP protocol is the way a browser and a web server use to establish a conversation, articulated in two type of messages: a request for the page and each file attached to it and a response, that contains the actual content if the request is correct or an error message in the other cases.

Any web page is basically a text file that, besides the actual human-readable content, also contains machine-readable code interpreted by the browser to render the page correctly. This code is written in a language called HTML. HTML defines a set of markup codes that are used to denote the constructive elements of the page, such as images, tables, boxes, lists, etc. Each element may contain text or other elements – for example a table contains elements defining the rows, which include an element for each table cell. All elements descend from a common one, the <body> element, indicating the beginning of the page. An HTML page can thus be represented by a tree (the so-called DOM – Document Object Model – W3C, 2005) where each element is a node, with the root being the <body> element. Figure 1 shows an example of a web page and an excerpt of the corresponding HTML code. The representation on the right shows clearly the hierarchical structure of the DOM, where one can note the repeating elements corresponding to the products on the page, which are the data items of interest for the extraction.

Each element can be enhanced with attributes determining its unique name in the page (id) and/or its formatting features. The latter are expressed through the *class* or *style* attributes that refer to a group of formatting characteristics (font, color, border, etc.) defined in what is called a Cascading Style Sheet (CSS).

So, the DOM can be used to access elements within a page. The enabler for this is a language called XPath, that allows to extract portions of a web page by issuing query expressions such as "Return all the elements inside a table" or "return all the elements with the id 'price'" or "return all the element with the style 'discount'". We will provide a practical example in the following.

Figure 1. A page in the IKEA web site (left) and an excerpt of the corresponding HTML code (right)

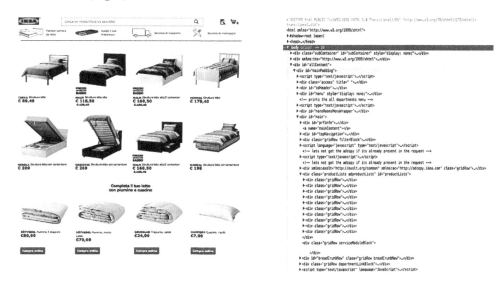

Basics of Web Scraping

Extracting information from a web page basically means accessing the elements corresponding to the data item inside the page, and this is possible only through the definition of correct XPath query expressions.

However, defining such expressions requires a deep knowledge about how a page is structured and coded. In order to allow in-depth analysis of web pages, mainly for testing purposes, all modern browsers make available a feature called "inspector" that once enabled allows a user to click to a portion of the page and visualize all the details related to its position in the DOM and its defining attributes. In the worst case, this is a process that must be repeated for every data item in the page, although it becomes immediately obvious that patterns are normally present in the page in correspondence of the regions containing structured data.

Figure 2 shows again a portion of the page of the Ikea site highlighting the result of the use of the inspector over a single data cell (price of a product). The inspector returns the description of the HTML element associated to the data cell (a div element of class "price regularPrice"), which can be used to extract the corresponding XPath rule. Since all data cells share a common layout, the application of the XPath rule returns the prices of all the products in the page.

This example shows how with only a basic knowledge of web technologies it is possible to access potentially all the data shown in a web page. Moreover, it is

Figure 2. Use of the inspector function of the browser (left) to obtain the HTML element associated to a data item and application of the corresponding XPath rule to extract the data (right)

interesting to point out how the HTML code, although difficult to decipher as a whole, often contains hints about the single elements of the page, as in the example where the elements containing prices are tagged as "price regularPrice". Unfortunately this is not a general rule: in real-world web sites the possible variations in terms of layout and implementation are endless and may lead to situations where the rules are much more difficult to detect than in this simple example. In such cases, more in-depth IT skills are required to comprehend the page structure and design the extraction method.

In a nutshell, implementing data extraction is largely a reverse engineering activity whose objective is to connect the conceptual characteristics of the data (records, attributes, etc.) with their counterparts on the rendered page, expressed through a set of XPath expressions.

In the remainder of this section it is shown how all the various solutions used for scraping start from this very concept, differentiating themselves in aspects such as the way the scraping technique is implemented and, more importantly, the different level of technical skill involved in realizing and maintaining the whole process.

However, some conclusions can already be drawn, also backed up by experience in the field, which could be considered relevant for understanding the use of scraping for data collection:

1. Knowledge of web technology is required in some amount to develop and maintain a web scraper. In many cases the basic extraction techniques do not need an IT specialist.
2. Advanced IT skills are required mainly to deal with those situations where the XPath rule for extracting the data is more complex to determine, and in general to write programs that carry out an organized data collection
3. Implementations of extractors are in general strictly tied to every single page and are very difficult to generalize. The range of possibilities is as broad as are the ways a developer can choose to implement a web site, so there is no standard solution. Collecting data on a large scale is a really difficult task.

Implementing Web Scraping: Custom Programs

The most natural and common solution for scraping is to write a dedicated program in a general-purpose programming language. Java, Python and R are commonly used for this aim, offering plenty of dedicated libraries and reusable solutions that can help reducing the amount of code to be written, such as libraries to automate browser behavior (to be used in the selection phase) and to rapidly access the DOM (to be used in the extraction phase). Examples are JSoup, ScraPY and ScrapeR. Developing a program for scraping allows the maximum level of control because every detail of the extraction and selection processes can be customized and controlled at the maximum depth, allowing the program to cope with even the most complex cases.

Basically, implementing an extractor in general involves following these steps:

- Reconstructing the patterns of the data elements in the page in terms of style, id, DOM path, through manual reverse engineering (e.g., using the inspector function of the browser)
- Defining the XPath expressions that access the data elements
- Writing a program that issues the XPath expressions, collects the attached data and constructs the output data structures

The main drawbacks of this solution when applied to data collection are evident: the scraping program must be tailored to each page being scraped, thus requiring a significant effort for development and, more significantly, for maintenance. It is clear that scale is really hard to achieve under these conditions because targeting a large number of sites requires a corresponding number of programs to be developed. Given the fact that programming skills are required, the adoption of this solution creates a total dependence from IT resources, creating an obstacle to achieving repeatability.

Implementing Web Scraping: Browser Automation Tools

Browser automation tools, often referred to as "Robots", are software tools that can record a sequence of manual operations carried out by a human operator on a web browser and are able to repeat it automatically upon request. Typically used for testing web sites by emulating user behavior over the entire site, enabling detection of errors and measurement of response performance, robots are also largely employed for collecting data from the web. Starting from an initial page, a user can identify the elements of the page that should be extracted and those that correspond to page navigation. Through browser automation it is also easy to fill up forms for providing input.

When a sequence of operations is recorded, a script is generated, normally expressed in a dedicated, high-level language that can be learned also by users with no programming skills. Scripts can be edited to cope with changes in web sites without the need for recording the sequence from scratch. Moreover, it is usually possible to feed a parametric input so that the same sequence of operations can be used for different kinds of data (for example with different product types).

The main advantage of robots is that they can simplify the definition of the scraping procedure with respect to custom programs and as a consequence in principle they do not need constant assistance from IT specialists. There are a number of free products available, although the advanced features useful for data collection are normally available only in paid-for versions. Robots are not particularly fit to scale because they should be programmed for every different web site. As for repeatability, non-technical users are potentially able to write and maintain automation script but in practice more complex cases might require thorough knowledge of web technologies in order to understand how the page is composed. However, if well organized, the use of a robot can lead to significant gains in productivity and help especially during the development phase.

Implementing Web Scraping: Point-and-Click

The most recent evolution of tools for scraping are the point-and-click scraping tools (also known as "visual scrapers"). The principle is that users can extract a data table from a web site by simply clicking on the elements of the page that they need to scrape, associating them to a column in the output table. For example a user tags the product description, price and image respectively by clicking on some of their occurrences on the page. Typically, after tagging the first few occurrences, the tool can automatically detect where they are repeated on the page and can recognize all the remaining elements.

Normally additional features are included to automate pagination, for example by clicking on the "next page" button, or by indicating a pattern on the URL. The output of the extraction is a data set containing all the scraped data, organized in columns, that can be downloaded in CSV or JSON format or also queried directly from a program by specifying a URL associated to the data set. Figure 3 shows two screenshots from one of the most popular point-and-click scraping tool, import. io: on the left the training phase is shown, relative to the "product name" column. The user tagged some of the product names (in pink) and the tool detected all the others on the page (green). Note that the products highlighted in yellow were not recognized by the tool and required further manual training. On the right is the output data table obtained by executing the training on all the other columns, such as price, description and also image.

Figure 3. The training phase of a point-and-click training tool (left) and the resulting output data table (right)

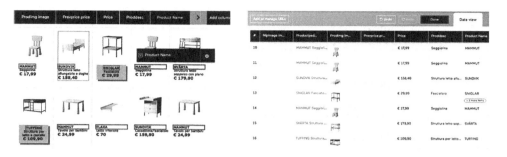

The way these tools work in technical terms is based on the following idea: when the user clicks on an element on the page, the tool extracts automatically the XPath expression associated to it, without the need for manual inspection through the browser, and associates that XPath expression with a column of a data table. Some of the more modern incarnations of this concept are able to automatically detect the whole data region in a page and infer all the columns, even without manual training.

These tools allow non-technical users to build their scrapers with no coding at all. So ideally no knowledge about web technologies like HTML, CSS and XPath is required for setting up the extraction, and scrapers can be setup in a much shorter time than with other techniques. For these reasons, they are being developed and tested for replacing custom coding for collecting prices in NSIs (Breton et al. 2016; Nygaar, 2016). The approach is particularly successful when stable patterns can be identified on the data elements. However, its application in general cases depends on the capability of the specific tool to adapt to the variations to such patterns and to implement effectively the mechanisms of interaction for crawling. In summary, scale and repeatability can be achieved more easily with respect to the other solutions, although there is still a high variability of success.

One final aspect that should be mentioned is the "volatility" of tools, especially the possibility of a product being suddenly discontinued. Currently many different tools exist in this area whose main functionality and price largely overlap, making it difficult to choose and commit to a single one. In such a very competitive market, the probability of a product's long-term success is not easy to predict, regardless of its quality. Indeed, we have direct experience of testing one such product that appeared promising and solid in terms of quality, functionality and support but ended up being shut down after only a few years.

EXPERIENCES OF WEB SCRAPING IN STATISTICAL INSTITUTES

In this Section, some of the main experiences in the practical use of web scraping for price collection in National Statistical Institutes are presented. As already mentioned, the use of web scraping has been largely investigated initially for experimentation and currently for production.

Polidoro et al. 2015 presents the work made at the Italian NSI, Istat, in recent years, focusing on the collection of consumer electronic product prices and airfares. The main aim of the work is to test if web scraping, implemented through a browser automation tool - namely iMacros, would reduce the workload required for collecting data with respect to manual collection via direct cut&paste of data from web sites. Collection of consumer electronic product prices involved 9 online stores, where 10 different kinds of products where considered for a total of 24,000 quotes collected per month. The results indicated a saving of 30% of the time required for collection, allowing an increase the amount of elementary quotes collected. Surprisingly, a similar result was not confirmed by experimentation with airfares, where a couple of web sites of low cost carriers plus 3 web agencies were involved in the collection, considering 960 elementary quotes per month: the improvements in terms of time saving were relatively small in this case, due to the time spent in preparing the complex input files and the relatively low number of quotes involved. Moreover, the time spent to prepare the scraping program was significant because of the complexity and the variety of the web sites. To the latter issue one of the risks mentioned earlier (Web Scraping to collect data for official statistics) emerged clearly and concerned the lack and the loss of access to the data. As a matter of fact, two web search engines raised a block to Istat robots set up to collect airfare prices. This was a big issue to be dealt with and it was not easily solved. An official communication was sent to the companies that manage the two web search engines and a request to include IP Istat address in their "white list" was necessary. Therefore, for consumer electronic product prices it was decided to start the regular use of the web scraping techniques in the production process, whereas for airfares, the adoption of this approach to the data collection was limited to a single low cost carrier.

Web scraping has been used since 2010 (Hoekstra et al., 2012) in the Dutch Institute of Statistics (CBS). Ten Bosch and Windmeijer (2014) describe experimentation carried out on housing markets, air fares and clothing prices Currently CBS has several active scrapers in production. As detailed in ten Bosch and Griffioen (2016), the approach followed is twofold, treating in a different way the collection of data from internet sites with many items (e.g., clothing prices on one hand and on the other the collection of data from many data sources with only few items (e.g. the price of a cinema ticket from a cinema website). In the first case, 3 retailers are involved, with 500,000 quotes gathered per day. The collection mainly focuses on clothing prices, because for such prices online collection can easily replace on-field collection, producing an evident advantage in terms of cost reduction. The second case follows an interesting approach based on a custom-coded tool that does not continuously collect the prices but only signals variations of the prices. This is based on the observation that many prices do not vary frequently so the work of the CPI experts in production is aided by the tool that focuses on those prices that actually changed, resulting in a reduction of the working time.

In the UK a large pilot project to compile Consumer Price Indices from web scraped data has been in progress since June 2014 (Breton et al., 2016). Since that month, the project has collected 5000 quotes per day (150,000 per month) of consumer price data web scraped from 3 chains (Tesco, Sainsbury and Waitrose, who account for about 50% share of the grocery market), for 35 CPI items. The project was started to overcome the difficulties found with the retail trade market chains to provide the Office for National Statistics (ONS) with scanner data. The most important difficulties found by ONS researchers were due to two aspects: 1) missing data in October 2015 caused by structural changes implemented by the retailers in their websites, which necessitated some adjustments in the scrapers developed taking into account the original structure of the web page; 2) classification issues, because each chain uses its own classification system. At the beginning, the approach was a simple search and exclusion terms. It was based on checking the alphabetic description of each elementary item creating "filter words" for each item, in order to exclude the elementary items that present in their description one of these "filter words". The example reported concerns "toffee apples": the word "apples" links the elementary item to "Apples", but the word "toffee" is a filter word that correctly excludes it. This method was very time consuming, in particular for the manual drafting and maintaining of the list of filter words. Therefore it was abandoned in favor of a supervised machine learning algorithm that learns from training data and creates filtering rules automatically (the algorithm chosen was Support Vector Machine, SVM). The CPI that was calculated by ONS on the basis of the web scraped data, even if not comparable with the CPI produced using the data traditionally collected, presented similar trends with the official CPI (for Food and non-alcoholic beverages) with relevant differences in the short-term movements.

The experiments and the practices (some of which are mentioned above) carried out by NSIs showed a lot of problems for the use of web scraping techniques within an Official Statistics environment. All the risks listed in theory emerged in the field. None of them seem insurmountable, but all of them need to be dealt with, adopting a combined strategy. Moreover statistical issues became clearer with particular reference to consequences for the traditional sampling scheme of the web scraping as tool to collect Big Data from the Internet. In the following paragraph an approach is presented to achieve the objective of using web scraping in the field of consumer price statistics, not only as a tool to replace the human intervention in the data collection, but to overcome the constraints in the statistical approach to the data collection due to the limited amount of resources previously and currently available. In particular the proposal is aimed at collecting and then treating big amount of data, trying to cover all the dimensions of the phenomenon of interest without using (or completely changing) the traditional sampling schemes adopted for consumer price survey.

UNASSISTED SCRAPING TECHNIQUES FOR COLLECTING PRICE DATA

It should be clear at this point that a web scraping method for easily collecting data achieving both scale and repeatability is not available with the current state of technology. A certain level of manual intervention for setting up the tools is always required, as is frequent regular monitoring of the scraped web sites. For these reasons all the current attempts at using web scraping for statistical data collection, although with all their differences, start from a common assumption: the quotes are selected and classified with the objective of making them fit within the traditional framework of the CPI survey, based on the notion of a basket of products whose price quotes are accurately cleaned before being aggregated in the computation of the index. In other words, web scraping is basically used as a tool to replace manual collection, aiming at reducing the time required for collection and increasing the size of the basket and the frequency of the collection, but still preserving the full methodological framework of price statistics.

The objective of this section is to suggest and discuss a possible alternative approach, based on the idea of carrying out a data collection process on a massive scale, that aims at scraping the *entire* content of a web site in order to ideally extract all the prices contained in it. The price indexes could be computed through the massive aggregation of all the scraped prices, obtaining a more comprehensive representation of the prices at the cost of a possible loss of control on every single elementary quote.

This idea raises several new research questions:

- On the methodological side, the question is whether it would be possible to switch to a real Big Data approach, where the amount of data involved do not allow the fine-grained control over quality of the source, but which could be compensated by the volume of data that makes the overall dynamic of the price emerge anyway. This quality issue is at the core of the mismatch in the application of Big Data to official statistics with respect to other kinds of business, where the focus of Big Data is precisely on the use of a large amount of data to drive new insights that are impossible through detailed analysis. A discussion on this can be found in UNECE, 2016, where it is suggested that statistics based on Big Data sources should accept "a different notion of quality", to cope with the inherent instability of the source and devise new methods to exploit the data volume to preserve soundness and quality of the output. Methodological issues in the use of Big Data are also presented and discussed in Daas et al., 2015 and Scannapieco et al., 2013.

- In technical terms, aiming at a radically larger volume of data collection would be unfeasible using the techniques that we presented in previous Sections, all depending on a form of training needing a human operator and repeated for every page. New solutions should be developed for the automatic unassisted selection and extraction of price data from web sites.

An ideal automated selection process would start from the initial page of the site and follow all the links, extracting data only from those pages that actually contain prices. Current tools for crawling such as Nutch already implement such features. Obviously this approach could be possible only for small to medium sites, excluding the largest ones such as Amazon, whose catalog has a size that defies any reasonable possibility of succeeding with IT architectures normally available in NSIs. More pragmatically though, the selection process could be marginally assisted, for example by providing the URLs of the initial pages of the product catalog of an e-commerce site.

Unassisted techniques for extracting data from the web are not novel in literature. A general method for developing an automatic extractor is described in Liu (2011, p. 363). In a nutshell, the idea is to detect automatically the portion of the page containing data, by detecting the recurring elements in it. This is what is done "behind the scenes" by the automatic data recognition function of point-and-click tools. However, the fact that the algorithm should focus on price collection largely simplifies the problem: price data is easy to recognize automatically, for example by checking the format of the strings and the presence of the currency sign, and product description and identification can be attached to it by using several heuristic approaches, such as the presence of certain keywords in the class attributes of the HTML elements (e.g., "product", "description", etc.) or, again, the format of the string (plain text, different from one row to another). In general, the large body of work already developed in the context of automatic classification of web tables (Yakout et al., 2012; Braunschweig et al., 2015) can be effectively reused, applied to a context that would represent a special simplified case of a problem already solved under less restrictive hypothesis.

This approach is being tested in Istat for improving the collection of air fares. A new scraper for air ticket web sites has been developed, covering both online travel agencies and low-cost carriers, that improves on the first version in terms of the ability to extract data more rapidly. The whole web page is downloaded beside single prices and all the prices contained in the page are considered. The scraper can then adapt more easily to a wider range of web sites without training and better respond to changes (that are frequent in that domain). While there is a potential loss in quality, it is planned that this will be compensated by a larger amount of scraped data.

RECOMMENDATIONS AND CONCLUSION

Big Data represent a challenge for the Official Statistics Community. Their potential availability has triggered radical change in the statistical approaches to data collection and data treatment compared to the traditional methods. The Internet is one of the main sources of Big Data and web scraping techniques are the tools available to explore Internet in order to extract a huge amount of information. This is true in particular for some variables of high statistical and economic interest, such as consumer prices. The work of data collectors visiting thousands of shops, selected on the basis of probabilistic or purposive samples, collecting prices once a month to provide NSIs with the information necessary to calculate inflation could be partially replaced by robots acting on web pages, downloading continuously prices to use for measuring the evolution of consumer prices over time. To what extent this scenario will be possible depends on a lot of factors: transformation of distribution channels and their relative weights (with a growing importance of the online retail trade), coherence between prices in online shops and prices in physical shops, changes in consumer behavior, and last but not least the capability of official statistics to evolve towards a safe and reliable use of modern techniques to capture the wide variety of information available on the Internet.

It is about the latter topic that the debate about the use of web scraping should be aimed at overcoming the bottlenecks that until now statisticians have been forced to face when they had to design how to collect the information necessary to measure economic, social and other kinds of phenomena. Web scraping as a key to Big Data on the Internet proposes to move the attention to data science, focusing on the nature and treatment of data, instead of on defining a small portion of the universe to save resources in the statistical surveys, thereby changing the traditional approaches to sampling currently used to understand the reference population.

It is within this theoretical framework for official statistics that the comparative analysis and the debate about the use of different web scraping techniques have to be posed.

The choice should fall on the web scraping instruments that adapt better to the nature of the variables observed. In general the choice should be addressed to techniques that allow extracting a big amount of data covering all the dimensions that characterize the phenomenon of interest, limiting the use of those techniques mainly aimed at replacing the work of human resources in downloading information from the web. A typical example is proposed by the case of prices referred to products (such as airfares) for which temporal changes are highly frequent and need to be detected. In this case, the "simple" substitution of the human intervention in the data collection appears of little use. Together with the criterion of choosing the best approach to web scraping on the basis of the phenomena observed, the exigence of adopting friendly techniques is relevant. In this sense it is advisable to use point & click tools whenever possible because they are fast to set up and involve IT only for more difficult tasks, given that the use of different tools is not conflicting.

In the future, implementing web scraping methods for easily collecting data achieving both scale and repeatability is the issue to be dealt with in order to obtain consistent results in accessing Big Data on the Internet. The development of such a method could fulfill the need to cover both spatial and temporal dimensions of data and to gain efficiency in the production process of statistical indicators.

REFERENCES

Barcaroli, G., Nurra, A., Salamone, S., Scannapieco, M., Scarnò, M., & Summa, D. (2015). Internet as a Data Source in the Istat Survey on ICT in Enterprises. *Austrian Journal of Statistics*, *44*(2), 31. doi:10.17713/ajs.v44i2.53

Braunschweig, K., Thiele, M., Eberius, J., & Lehner, W. (2015) Column-specific Context Extraction for Web Tables. *Proceedings of The 30th ACM/SIGAPP Symposium On Applied Computing*. doi:10.1145/2695664.2695794

Breton, R., Clews, G., Metcalfe, L., Milliken, N., Payne, C., Winton, J., & Woods, A. (2016). *Research indices using web scraped data*. Paper presented at the UNECE Meeting of the Group of Experts on Consumer Price Indices, Geneva, Switzerland.

Cavallo, A., & Rigobon, R. (2016). The Billion Prices Project: Using Online Prices for Measurement and Research. *Journal of Economic Perspectives, 30*(2),151–178.

Daas, P. J. H., Puts, M. J., Buelens, B., & van den Hurk, P. A. M. (2015). Big Data and Official Statistics. *Journal of Official Statistics*, *31*(2), 249–262. doi:10.1515/jos-2015-0016

European Statistical System Committee (ESCC). (2013). *Scheveningen Memorandum on Big Data and Official Statistics*. Available at: http://ec.europa.eu/eurostat/documents/42577/43315/Scheveningen-memorandum-27-09-13

Hammer, J., Garcia-Molina, H., Cho, J., Crespo, A., & Aranha, R. (1997) Extracting Semistructured Information from the Web.*Proceedings of the Workshop on Management of Semistructured Data held in conjunction with ACM SIGMOD'97*, 18-25.

Hoekstra, R., ten Bosh, O., & Harteveld, F. (2012). Automated data collection from web sources for official statistics: First experiences. *Journal of the International Association for Official Statistics*, *28*(3-4), 99–111.

Liu, B. (2011). *Web Data Mining: Exploring Hyperlinks, Contents and Usage Data* (2nd ed.). Springer-Verlag. doi:10.1007/978-3-642-19460-3

Manyika, J., Chui, M., Brown, B., Bughin, J., Dobbs, R., Roxburgh, C., & Hung Byers, A. (2011). *Big Data: The Next Frontier for Innovation, Competition, and Productivity. Report of the McKinsey Global Institute*. McKinsey & Company.

Nikić, B., Špeh, T., & Klun, Z. (2015). Usage of new data sources at SURS.*UNECE Workshop on Statistical Data Collection: Riding the Data Deluge*.

Nygaard, R. (2016). *Alternative data collection methods - focus on online data*. Paper presented at the UNECE Meeting of the Group of Experts on Consumer Price Indices.

Pinkerton, B. (1994). Finding what people want: Experiences with the web crawler. *Proceedings of the Second World-Wide Web Conference*.

Polidoro, F., Giannini, R., Lo Conte, R., Mosca, S., & Rossetti, F. (2015). Web scraping techniques to collect data on consumer electronics and airfares for Italian HICP compilation. *Statistical Journal of the IAOS*, *31*(2), 165–176. doi:10.3233/sji-150901

Radzikowski, B., & Śmietanka, A. (2016). Online CASE CPI.*First International Conference on Advanced Research Methods and Analytics, CARMA2016*. doi:10.4995/CARMA2016.2016.3133

Scannapieco, M., Virgillito, A., & Zardetto, D. (2013). *Placing Big Data in Official Statistics: A Big Challenge?* Paper presented at the conference on New Techniques and Technologies for Statistics, NTTS 2013, Bruxelles, Belgium.

ten Bosch, O., & Griffioen, R. (2016). *On the use of Internet data for the Dutch CPI*. Paper presented at the UNECE Meeting of the Group of Experts on Consumer Price Indices, Geneva, Switzerland.

ten Bosh, O., & Windmeijer, D. (2014). On the Use of Internet Robots for Official Statistics. MSIS-2014.

UNECE, Statistical Division of the United Nations Economic Commission for Europe. (2014a). *A suggested Framework for the Quality of Big Data, Deliverables of the UNECE Big Data Quality Task Team*. Retrieved from http://www1.unece. org/stat/platform/download/attachments/108102944/Big%20Data%20Quality%20 Framework%20-%20final-%20Jan08-2015.pdf?version=1&modificationDate=14 20725063663&api=v2

UNECE, Statistical Division of the United Nations Economic Commission for Europe. (2014b). *How big is Big Data? Exploring the role of Big Data in Official Statistics*. Retrieved from http://www1.unece.org/stat/platform/download/ attachments/99484307/Virtual%20Sprint%20Big%20Data%20paper.docx?version =1&modificationDate=1395217470975&api=v2

UNECE, Statistical Division of the United Nations Economic Commission for Europe. (2014c). *Big Data Inventory*. Available at: http://www1.unece.org/stat/ platform/display/BDI/UNECE+Big+Data+Inventory+Home

UNECE, Statistical Division of the United Nations Economic Commission for Europe. (2016). *Outcomes of the UNECE Project on Using Big Data for Official Statistics*. Available at: http://www1.unece.org/stat/platform/display/bigdata/Big+ Data+in+Official+Statistics

W3C - The World Wide Web Consortium. (2005). *Document Object Model (DOM)*. Retrieved from https://www.w3.org/DOM/

Wirthmann, A., Karlberg, M., Kovachev, B., & Reis, F. (2015). Structuring risks and solutions in the use of big data sources for producing official statistics – Analysis based on a risk and quality framework. *Eurostat*. Retrieved from: https://ec.europa. eu/eurostat/cros/system/files/Big%20Data%20Risk%20Paper%20Version1.pdf

Yakout, M., Ganjam, K., Chakrabarti, K., & Chaudhuri, S. (2012). InfoGather: Entity Augmentation and Attribute Discovery by Holistic Matching with Web Tables. *Proceedings of SIGMOD 2012*.

Chapter 11
Big Data in Official Statistics

Kees Zeelenberg
Statistics Netherlands, The Netherlands

Barteld Braaksma
Statistics Netherlands, The Netherlands

ABSTRACT

Big data come in high volume, high velocity and high variety. Their high volume may lead to better accuracy and more details, their high velocity may lead to more frequent and more timely statistical estimates, and their high variety may give opportunities for statistics in new areas. But there are also many challenges: there are uncontrolled changes in sources that threaten continuity and comparability, and data that refer only indirectly to phenomena of statistical interest. Furthermore, big data may be highly volatile and selective: the coverage of the population to which they refer, may change from day to day, leading to inexplicable jumps in time-series. And very often, the individual observations in these big data sets lack variables that allow them to be linked to other datasets or population frames. This severely limits the possibilities for correction of selectivity and volatility. In this chapter, we describe and discuss opportunities for big data in official statistics.

INTRODUCTION

Big data come in high volume, high velocity and high variety; examples are web scraping, Twitter and Facebook messages, mobile-phone records, traffic-loop data, and banking transactions. This leads to opportunities for new statistics or redesign of existing statistics. The potential of big data for official statistics lies in the immense amount of information contained. For example, the sheer size might make it possible

DOI: 10.4018/978-1-5225-2512-7.ch011

to add more details to official statistics. Also, big data sources may cover areas of society for which official statistics do not yet exist. Their high volume may lead to better accuracy and more details, their high velocity may lead to more frequent and timelier statistical estimates, and their high variety may give rise to statistics in new areas.

There are various challenges with the use of big data in official statistics, such as legal, technological, financial, methodological, and privacy-related ones; see e.g., Struijs, Braaksma, and Daas (2014), UN-ECE (2013), and Vaccari (2016). This paper focuses on methodological challenges, in particular on the question of how official statistics may be produced from big data. Specifically, we look at the question: what are the best strategies for using big data in official statistics?

From a methodological perspective, big data also poses many challenges. Big data may be highly volatile and selective: the coverage of the population to which they refer may change from day to day, leading to inexplicable jumps in time-series. And very often, the individual observations in big data sets lack linking variables and so cannot be linked to other datasets or population frames. This severely limits the possibilities for correction of selectivity and volatility. The use of big data in official statistics therefore requires other approaches. We discuss two such approaches.

In the first place, we may accept big data just for what they are: an imperfect, yet very timely, indicator of developments in society. In a sense, this is what national statistical institutes (NSIs) often do: we collect data that have been assembled by the respondents and the reason why, and even just the fact that they have been assembled is very much the same reason why they are interesting for society and thus for an NSI to collect.

Secondly, we may extend this approach in a more formal way by modelling these data explicitly. In recent years, many new methods for dealing with big data have been developed by mathematical and applied statisticians.

The structure of this chapter is as follows. In section 2, we briefly describe big data sources and possible uses. In section 3, we look at statistics from big data as they are collected or assembled, i.e., as statistics in their own right; we describe several examples of big data as official statistics. In section 4, we discuss how models may be useful for creating information from big data sources, and under what conditions NSIs may be using models for creating official statistics; we also describe several examples of statistics derived through modelling big data. We look at how to create representative estimates and how to make the most of big data when this is difficult or impossible. We show how big data may be useful in solving several of the major challenges to official statistics, in particular the quality of national accounts (rate of growth of gross national product or GNP), the timeliness of official statistics, and the statistical analysis of complex and coherent phenomena. We also look at disclosure control of official statistical data now that open data and big data have become so widely available.

BIG DATA AND OFFICIAL STATISTICS

There are nowadays three types of sources for official statistics:

- **Survey Data:** Data collected by interviewing persons, households and enterprises,
- **Administrative Data:** Data from official registrations, such as the population register and the tax registrations,
- **Big Data:** Data generated by digital activities, e.g., activities on the internet, communications between devices or between devices and their operators (*internet of things*).

Traditionally, producers of official statistics have relied on their own data collection, using paper questionnaires, face-to-face and telephone interviews, or, in recent years, web surveys. The classical approach originates from the era of data scarcity, when official statistical institutes were among the few organizations that were able to gather data and disseminate information. A main advantage of the survey-based approach is that it gives full control over questions asked and populations studied. A big disadvantage is that it is costly and burdensome, both for the surveying organization and the respondents.

More recently, statistical institutes have started to use administrative registers, usually assembled by government agencies as sources for official statistics. This reduces control over the data and leads to overcoverage or undercoverage of the population as well as to errors. For example, the official population register contains no data about homeless persons or illegal persons; additionally, people may not actually live at their registered address, so that the administrative population often does not exactly match the statistical one. However, these data are cheaper to obtain than survey data. In some countries, the access and use of secondary sources has even been regulated by law, so that statistical institutes have easy and free access.

Big data sources offer even less control. They typically consist of *organic* data (Groves, 2011) collected by others, who have a non-statistical purpose for their data. For example, a statistical organization might want to use retail transaction data to provide prices for their Consumer Price Index statistics, while the original purpose of the data collector, e.g., a supermarket chain, is to track inventories and sales.

EXAMPLES OF BIG DATA IN OFFICIAL STATISTICS

In this section, we will look at three examples of big data in official statistics: social media messages, traffic-loop data, and mobile phone data. Other examples, which we will not discuss here, include web scraping, scanner data, satellite images and banking transactions.

Traffic-Loop Data (Van Ruth, 2014; Daas et al., 2013)

In the Netherlands, approximately 100 million traffic detection loop records are generated a day. More specifically, for more than 12 thousand detection loops on Dutch roads, the number of passing cars is available on a minute-by-minute basis. The data are collected and stored by the National Data Warehouse for Traffic Information (NDW) (http://www.ndw.nu/en), a government agency which provides the data to Statistics Netherlands. The detection loops discern length classes, enabling the differentiation between, e.g., cars and trucks. Their profiles clearly reveal differences in driving behaviour.

Harvesting the vast amount of data is a major challenge for statistics; but it could result in speedier and more robust traffic statistics, including more detailed information on regional levels and increased resolution in temporal patterns. This is also likely indicative of changes in economic activity in a broader sense.

Unfortunately, at present this source suffers from under-coverage and selectivity. The number of vehicles detected is not available for every minute due to system failures and many Dutch roads, including some important ones, lack detection loops. Fortunately, the first problem can be corrected by smoothing, e.g., by imputing the absent data with data that is reported by the same loop during a 5-minute interval before or after that minute. And coverage is improving over time, as gradually more and more roads have detection loops, enabling a more complete coverage of the most important Dutch roads and reducing selectivity. In one year, more than two thousand loops were added.

Some detection loops are linked to weigh-in-motion stations, which automatically measure the weight of the vehicle while driving and which are combined with cameras that record the license plate. One very important weigh station is in the highway connecting the port of Rotterdam to the rest of the Netherlands. In the future, these measurements may be used to estimate the weight of the transported goods. Statistical applications may then be very rapid estimates of goods transported from ports or exported and imported across land boundaries. Or they may even be used to create a rough indicator of economic activity (Van Ruth, 2017).

Social Media Messages (Daas & Puts, 2014)

Social media is a data source where people voluntarily share information, discuss topics of interest, and contact family and friends. More than three million public social media messages are produced on a daily basis in the Netherlands. These messages are available to anyone with internet access, but collecting them all is obviously a huge task. The social media data analysed by Statistics Netherlands were provided by the company Coosto (https://www.coosto.com/en), which routinely collects all Dutch social media messages. In addition, they provide some extra information, like assigning a sentiment score to individual messages or adding information about the place of origin of a message.

To find out whether social media is a useful data source for statistics, Dutch social media messages were studied from two perspectives: content and sentiment. Studies of the content of Dutch Twitter messages, which was the predominant public social media message in the Netherlands at the time, revealed that nearly 50% of those messages were composed of "pointless babble." The remainder predominantly discussed spare time activities (10%), work (7%), media (5%) and politics (3%). Use of these, more serious, messages was hampered by the less serious "babble" messages. The latter also negatively affected text mining studies.

The sentiment in Dutch social media messages was found to be highly correlated with Dutch consumer confidence (Daas and Puts, 2014). Facebook gave the best overall results. The observed sentiment was stable on a monthly and weekly basis, but daily figures displayed highly volatile behaviour. Thus, it might become possible to produce useful weekly sentiment indicators, even on the first working day after the week studied.

Mobile Phone Data (De Jonge, Van Pelt, & Roos, 2012)

Nowadays, people carry mobile phones with them everywhere and use their phones throughout the day. To manage the phone traffic, a lot of data needs to be processed by mobile phone companies. This data is very closely associated with behaviour of people; behaviour that is of interest for official statistics. For example, the phone traffic is relayed through geographically distributed phone masts, which enables determination of the location of phone users. The relaying mast, however, may change several times during a call: nontrivial location algorithms are needed.

Several uses for official statistics may be envisaged, including inbound tourism (Heerschap et al, 2014) and daytime population (Tennekes and Offermans, 2014). The 'daytime whereabouts' is a topic about which so far very little is known due to lack of sources; in contrast to the 'night-time population' based on official (residence) registers. Obviously, we have to take into account several issues when considering statistical uses of mobile phone data. For example, the group of mobile phone users is selective when compared with the population: young children do not usually carry a mobile phone, approximately 40 percent of the people over 65 do not have a mobile phone, whereas more than 95 percent of the young people (12 – 30 years) have a mobile phone (Telecompaper, 2015). Also, we may not have the data from all mobile-phone providers, which will create additional selectivity. This means that we have to be careful when interpreting the data or when developing processing methods.

A FRAMEWORK FOR ASSESSING THE QUALITY OF BIG DATA STATISTICS

The framework we use for evaluating big data is, following the EU Statistical Law, that of statistical quality (relevance, accuracy, timeliness, accessibility, comparability, and coherence) and statistical principles (independence, impartiality, objectivity, reliability, confidentiality, and cost effectiveness). In particular, we focus on

- Accuracy, objectivity, and reliability, since these are fundamental for official statistics: if statistics do not describe society accurately enough or are not objective or reliable, they are essentially useless;
- Relevance, timeliness, accessibility, comparability, and coherence.

In the discussion below we distinguish between survey data (data based on a probability sample from a well-defined population), census data (data based on a complete enumeration of a population), administrative data (data from official sources, for a well-defined population), and big data (large datasets from other sources than the other three categories).

Accuracy

The accuracy of any statistic is measured by its variance and its bias. To judge these, we have to know the process by which the data have been generated. For surveys based on probability sampling, the bias is approximately zero, but the variance is positive, whereas for censuses (complete enumerations of the population), both are approximately zero. For data not based on surveys or censuses, the variance of statistics may be small, even approximately zero, if the dataset is sufficiently large, but the bias may be large, even if the size of the dataset is very large. For example, for a dataset of 150 million persons, the bias may be so large that its accuracy is the same as that of a probability sample of 500 persons. In a certain sense, there is a paradox here: the bigger the data, the bigger the chance that the statistical results are wrong. So, without further information, big data are useless, since bias cannot be ascertained, but may be large.

Big data may be highly volatile and selective: the coverage of the population to which they refer may change from day to day, leading to inexplicable jumps in time-series. And very often, the individual observations in these big data sets lack linking variables and so cannot be linked to other datasets or population frames. This severely limits the possibilities for correction of selectivity and volatility using traditional methods.

For example, phone calls usually relate to persons, but how to interpret their signals is far from obvious. People may carry multiple phones or none, children use phones registered to their parents, phones may be switched off, etcetera. Moreover, the way people use their phones may change over time, depending on changes in billing, technical advances, and preferences for alternative communication tools, among other things. For social media messages, similar issues may arise when trying to identify characteristics of their authors.

Many big data sources are composed of event-driven observational data which are not designed for data analysis. These "fuzzy" big data are often collected through some intermediary ("aggregator") such as Google, Facebook and Coosto. They lack well-defined target populations, data structures and quality guarantees. This makes it hard to apply traditional statistical methods that are based on sampling theory. In fact, statistical applications of these big data, such as the Google Flu index and the Billion Prices Project, always refer to, and will always have to refer to, official statistical series to establish their validity.

It is therefore necessary to use additional information, either from the big data source itself, or from other data sources. The additional information must be sufficient for correction of the bias, not completely of course but such that the statistic will be relevant to users. This information may consist of characteristics of the individuals in the dataset that make post-stratification possible. However, if some important part of the population that is important is completely missing, correction will be impossible.

Models in Official Statistics

Use of additional information, requires the use of models that specify the relations between the statistics of interest and the additional information.

We follow here the well-known distinction between design-based methods, model-assisted methods and model-based methods. Design-based methods are the methods that strictly conform to a survey model, where respondents are sampled according to known probabilities, and the statistician uses these probabilities to compute an unbiased estimator of some population characteristics, such as average income. Model-assisted methods use a model that captures some prior information about the population to increase the precision of the estimates; however, if the model is incorrect, then the estimates are still unbiased when taking only the design into account. The examples of big data in official statistics given above, rely mostly on the data as collected supplemented with obvious corrections for probabilities of observation, and thus fall in the categories of design-based or model-assisted methods.

Model-based methods, however, rely on the correctness of the model: the estimates are biased if the model does not hold. As an example, suppose we want to estimate consumer confidence in a certain period, and that we have a traditional survey sample for which consumer confidence according to the correct statistical concept is observed, but also a social media source where a sentiment score can be attached to individual messages by applying a certain algorithm. A model-assisted approach would be to use the social media source data as auxiliary variables in a regression estimator. Even if the model that relates consumer confidence to sentiment scores does not hold perfectly, the resulting estimator is still approximately unbiased under the sampling design. A simple example of a model-based estimator would be to aggregate all the individual sentiment scores in the social media source, and use this as an estimate for consumer confidence. The implicit model here is that sentiment in the social media source is equal to consumer confidence in the statistical sense. If this model does not hold, then the resulting estimate will be biased. Of course, if we actually do have both types of data, the sample and the social media data, it would not be efficient to use only the latter data in a model-based estimator. But it may be much cheaper to not sample at all and to use only the big data source. The response burden on persons in the sample may also be a barrier to maintain a survey if a suitable alternative is available.

National statistical institutes have always been reluctant to use model-based methods in official statistics. They have relied on censuses and surveys, using mostly design-based and model-assisted methods. Yet, in specific statistical areas, NSIs have used model-based methods, e.g., in making small-area estimates, in correcting for non-response and selectivity, in computing seasonally-adjusted time series, and in making preliminary macro-economic estimates. And, in fact, common techniques like imputation of missing data often rely on some model assumptions. So, in a sense, models are already being used in official statistics. But very often, these models remain implicit and are not being emphasized in the documentation and the dissemination. Therefore, in general NSIs should not be scared to use model-based methods for treating big data sources. In the next subsections we will look at how this might be done.

Based on these principles, Statistics Netherlands has developed guidelines (Buelens, De Wolf and Zeelenberg, 2017) for the use of models in the production of official statistics. Many, if not most, examples in official statistics where models have been used, conform to these guidelines. So, despite the above warnings, we believe that there is room for using models also in the production of official statistics from big data.

Objectivity and Reliability

NSIs must, as producers of official statistics, be careful in the application of model-based methods. The public should not have to worry about the quality of official statistics, as formulated in the mission statement of the European Statistical System:

We provide the European Union, the world and the public with independent high quality information on the economy and society on European, national and regional levels and make the information available to everyone for decision-making purposes, research and debate.

Objectivity and *Reliability* are among the principles of official statistics in the European Statistical Law (EU, 2009) "... meaning that statistics must be developed, produced and disseminated in a systematic, reliable and unbiased manner". And the European Statistics Code of Practice (EU, 2005) says: "European Statistics accurately and reliably portray reality." Other international declarations, such as those of the ISI (1985) and the UN (1991), but also national statistical laws such as those of the Netherlands, have similar principles.

When using models, we can interpret these two principles as follows. The principle of objectivity means that the data being used to estimate the model should refer to the phenomenon that one is describing; in other words, the objects and the populations for the model correspond to the statistical phenomenon at hand. Data from the past may be used to estimate the model, but official statistical estimates based on the model never go beyond the present time period; so, for an NSI now-casting is allowed, but not forecasting and policy analyses. Of course, this is different for a forecasting agency or a policy-evaluation agency, whose purpose is exactly to go beyond the present period or present context. We believe that even if official statistics and policy evaluation are combined, for example in one report or even as is the case with some NSIs in one organization, it is always desirable to distinguish official statistics, which describe what has actually happened, from policy evaluation which deals with "what-if" situations.

The principle of reliability means that we must prevent having to revise official statistical data just because the model changes, e.g., because it breaks down (*model failure*). In particular for time-series models we must be on guard, because model failure may lead to an incorrect identification of turning points in the series.

Also, we should refrain from using behavioural models, because these are prone to model failure: it is almost certain that at some time in the future, any behavioural model will fail because behaviour of economic and social agents has changed. An additional reason to avoid behavioural models is that we must prevent situations where an external researcher finds good results when fitting a certain model, but, unknown to the researcher, that same model had been used by the NSI to create the very data that have been used by the external researcher. Again, this is different for a forecasting agency or a policy-evaluation agency.

In addition, models are not to be used indiscriminately: we have to remember that the primary purpose of an NSI is to describe, and not to prescribe or judge. So, we should refrain from making forecasts and from making purely behavioural models. Also, we should be careful to avoid model failure when the assumptions underlying it break down. Therefore, any model should rely on actually observed data for the period under consideration, which relates to the economic and social phenomena we are trying to describe by statistical estimates; and model building should be accompanied by extensive specification tests.

The principles of objectivity and reliability lead to some methodological principles for model-based methods. In particular, model building should be accompanied by extensive specification tests, in order to ensure that the model is robust. And any use of models must be made explicit: it should be documented and made transparent to users.

Relevance

Even if we know that a big data source covers the whole population, the statistical information that can be extracted, may be limited. For example, with traffic sensors one can observe that a car is passing, but we don't know who is in the car, who owns the car, and why he or she is driving at that spot. So, these data can be used for statistics on traffic intensity, but the relevance and the coherence with other statistics remain limited.

BIG DATA AS STATISTICS

One way to implement big data in official statistics is to regard big data aggregates as statistics in their own right. We may accept the big data just for what they are: an imperfect, yet very timely, indicator of developments in society. In a general sense, this is what NSIs often do: we collect data that have been assembled by the respondents and the reason why, and even just the fact that they have been assembled, is very much the same reason why they are interesting for society and thus for an NSI to collect.

This is perhaps most obvious with social media messages, and indicators derived from them. Opinions expressed on Twitter or Facebook already play a role, and sometimes an important role, in public debates. For example, the website (http://www.nos.nl) of the Dutch public radio and television system often adds Twitter messages from the public to its news items, and so these Twitter messages become part of the news and of public discussion.

Also, the sentiment indicator based on social media messages, discussed in the previous section, is an example. It has been shown that this indicator is highly correlated with more traditional estimates of consumer confidence. Therefore, we may conclude that this indicator is relevant. However, the social media-based sentiment indicator does not track exactly the traditional indicator. On the other hand, as the traditional way of making consumer-confidence statistics is by means of a telephone survey, these statistics can contain sampling errors, and also, perhaps worse, non-sampling errors. The important point here is that the traditional consumer-confidence indicator is not an exact measure of consumer confidence because of sampling errors, and possibly even has a bias because of non-sampling errors. Thus, it would be more appropriate to say that the social media sentiment indicator and the traditional indicator both are estimates of 'the mood of the nation', and we should not consider one of these to be the exact and undisputable truth.

Further, in addition to accuracy, quality has other aspects: relevance, timeliness, accessibility, comparability and coherence (EU, 2005, 2009). Since the social media indicator clearly can be produced much more frequently, it scores higher on the aspect of timeliness. On the other hand, comparability may be much harder to maintain, since participation in social media may change or even show large fluctuations over time; and methods similar to non-response correction methods in surveys may have to be used to correct for this. Still, even if the social-media sentiment indicator might score lower on relevance or accuracy, it may because of its timeliness still be useful for society if an NSI produces it as an official statistic.

The other examples of big data presented above can also be judged according to the usual quality dimensions.

For example, traffic-loop data may be used to produce very rapid estimates of traffic intensity and possibly also of the quantity of goods transported, exported and imported. Since quantities will be based on the weight of the transported goods, the bias component of its accuracy may be lower than that of the traditional estimate derived from a survey among transport companies, but because its coverage will be nearly complete, the variance component will be nearly zero. And such a very rapid estimate may be highly relevant.

With mobile-phone data, there may be more problems of representativeness: some persons carry more than one mobile phone, some phones may be switched off, and background characteristics are not known or imperfect because of prepaid phones, company phones, and children's phones registered to parents. There can also be accuracy issues when mapping phone masts to statistically relevant geographical areas: often they do not overlap perfectly. This problem becomes more pronounced when going to higher levels of detail, where to some extent model-based decisions need to be made for assigning phone calls to areas.

INTEGRATION OF BIG DATA WITH OTHER STATISTICAL SOURCES

Big Data as Auxiliary Data

Big data may be used as auxiliary data for statistics; in this approach, they are combined with other statistical data from surveys or from administrative sources. We may distinguish two cases:

- The big data source may be linked to the statistical data at the individual level. This is very much like the situation described in the previous section, and in general there are limited possibilities for linking.
- The big data may be linked to the statistical data at some intermediate level of aggregation, for example at the level of regions or industries. This looks very much like integration of statistical sources as in the National Accounts. For example, if a series derived from big data appears to be co-integrated with a statistical series, we may use the big data series to add more details to a statistical series or to increase its frequency or its timeliness; and thereby we increase its relevance and its timeliness. This is potentially a very promising route. It may also have an important impact on the timeliness of the National Accounts.

Coverage and Selectivity

Big data may be highly volatile and selective: the coverage of the population to which they refer may change from day to day, leading to inexplicable jumps in time-series. And very often, the individual observations in these big data sets lack linking variables and so cannot be linked to other datasets or population frames. This severely limits the possibilities for correction of selectivity and volatility.

In other words, with big data there is often insufficient information about the relations of the data source to the statistical phenomena we want to describe. This is often caused by lack of information about the data-generating process itself. Models are then useful to formulate explicit assumptions about these relations, and to estimate selectivity or coverage issues. For example, one way to reduce possible selectivity in a social media source could be to profile individual accounts in order to find out more about background characteristics. If we can determine whether an account belongs to a man or a woman, we should be able to better deal with gender bias in sentiment. Techniques to do this have already been developed and are becoming increasingly sophisticated. The same applies to age distribution, education level and geographical location. Coverage issues with individual social media sources can be reduced by combining multiple sources; and the sensible way to do this is through using a model, for example a multiple regression model or a logit model if we have information about the composition of the various sources. Another example is the use of a Bayesian filter to reduce volatility.

On the other hand, for many phenomena where we have big data, we also have other information, such as survey data for a small part of the population, and prior information from other sources. One way to go then is to use big data together with such additional information and see whether we can model the phenomenon that we want to describe. In recent years, there has been a surge in mathematical statistics in developing advanced new methods for big data. They come in various flavours, such as high-dimensional regression, machine-learning techniques, graphical modelling, data science, and Bayesian networks (Belloni, Chernozhukov, & Hansen, 2014; Choi & Varian, 2011; Gelman et al, 2013; Nickerson & Rogers, 2014; Varian, 2014). Also, more traditional methods, such as Bayesian techniques, filtering algorithms and multi-level (hierarchical) models have appeared to be useful (Gelman et al, 2013).

Another strategy is to take inspiration from the way National accounts are commonly compiled. Many sources which are in themselves incomplete, imperfect and/or partly overlapping are integrated, using a conceptual reference frame to obtain a comprehensive picture of the whole economy, while applying many checks and balances. In the same way, big data and other sources that in themselves are incomplete or biased may be combined together to yield a complete and unbiased picture pertaining to a certain phenomenon.

Disclosure Control With Big Data

Traditionally, statistical disclosure control by national statistical institutes (NSIs) has focused on tables and microdata collected and produced by the NSI itself. However, big data have made it possible for private data companies to assemble databases with very detailed information on individuals and enterprises, with data coming from many sources, and linked sometimes deterministically but often also probabilistically.

This abundance of data poses new problems for statistical disclosure control, both strategic and ethical problems as well as methodological problems, which need to be addressed but for which there are at present no clear-cut solutions. For example, should NSIs, when protecting tables or data files against disclosure, take into account the possibility that government agencies and private companies will use the NSI data to enrich their own databases and so get to know more about their citizens or customers? And what if these enriched data are used to profile citizens so that they may come under suspicion or are denied access to certain services such as loans? Should we use another methodological paradigm than we have used so far? Should we consider different disclosure scenarios? Does the changing attitude towards privacy influence the way we should treat our published data? How much existing as well as future data should we take into account when assessing disclosure risks?

As mentioned in the Introduction, big data are often characterized by the *three V's*: volume (amount of data), velocity (speed of data in and out), and variety (range of data types and sources). Each V poses several questions and issues related to statistical disclosure control (SDC):

Volume

How will NSIs deal with huge amounts of data? In general they will continue to publish aggregated information. In that case the current SDC techniques might still be applicable. However, when big data (or excerpts from them) are released as microdata, the current SDC techniques no longer apply: identity disclosure is almost certain. Then methods producing synthetic data may be preferable: use the big data sets to estimate a model and use that model to generate a synthetic dataset that resembles the original big data. Or other techniques that mask the true values of sensitive variables: just create enough uncertainty about the exact values to make it less sensitive.

Velocity

When data become available more quickly, the processing of the data also needs to be done in less time. The current SDC techniques can be time consuming when the underlying datasets increase in size and number. Streaming data might lead to streaming statistics, but then we should be able to protect those statistics in real time.

Variety

With big data we might have unstructured data, distributed over different places, indirect observations (events instead of units), unclear underlying population, selectivity, etc. Current SDC methods rely on masking characteristics of individuals so that it seems as if there are more than one similar unit in the population. For example, information about the characteristic zip code might be replaced by information about the region of residence, so that there will be many more individuals with that characteristic, and identification of individuals in the dataset becomes much more difficult. But when the underlying population is not known, this is not a valid option. Uncertainty should then be attained by introducing uncertainty on the sensitive information directly, for example by rounding.

Examples of model-based and integrated approaches using big data

Size of the Internet Economy[1]

The internet is clearly an important technology that acts as both a driver and a means for changes in the economy. There are four main ways in which the internet influences the economy:

1. Means of communication: online presence on the internet with a website;
2. Online stores (e-commerce), e.g., Amazon and Zalando;
3. Online services, e.g., AirBnB, eBay, Booking.com, and dating sites;
4. Internet-related information and communication technology (ICT) such as web design, hosting, and internet marketing.

Estimating the size of the internet economy is not easy. Only the last group, internet-related ICT, is to some extent distinguished as a separate industry in statistical surveys. Online stores are, according to European rules, grouped in a single industry, so that there is hardly any information about the type of their activities. Online services are subsumed in the industries corresponding to their output, so that, again, there is hardly any information about the type of their activities. And about the internet as means of business communication there is no regular statistical information at all. By combining big data, administrative data and survey data, Statistics Netherlands (Oostrom, 2016) has succeeded in estimating the size of the internet economy for each of these four classes. The data consisted of:

*   **Big Data**
    *   List of all Dutch websites, including business name, company-registration number, size of site traffic, and other data. The list contains 2½ million websites and is maintained by Dataprovider (https://www.

dataprovider.com). When a website is owned by a company, it is legally obliged to publish its company-registration number.

- **Administrative Data**
  - ○ General Business Register (GBR): a comprehensive list of all enterprises in the Netherlands and their ownership relations, based on administrative data from the company register and the tax registers.[2] There are 1½ million enterprises in the GBR. Addresses and telephone numbers are also included in the GBR; for many enterprises, a hostname of the website is included.
  - ○ Short-term statistics (STS): turnover of enterprises based on the VAT (value added tax) register, giving a nearly complete census of enterprises.
- **Survey Data**
  - ○ Structural Business Statistics (SBS): annual survey of enterprises on employment and financial data; all enterprises with more than 50 employed are included, smaller enterprises are sampled.
  - ○ Several other surveys such as on ICT and wages.

Several keys were used in linking all these databases: the company-registration number, address and telephone number, and hostname.

The statistical results were remarkable. About two thirds of all enterprises have no website; most of these are self-employed persons. Online stores, online services, and internet-related ICT, are in size about 5 per cent of the economy, comparable to construction and transportation. So the internet economy is important, but its size is not very large, much smaller than for example health services and education services. On the other hand, the use of ICT and internet is probably very extensive, since most enterprises use computers and the internet.

Big Data and the Quality of GNP Estimates

Big data may also contribute to the improving the quality of gross national product (GNP) estimates. This is important, because there is a need to improve the quality of the first estimate of quarterly GNP, 45 days after the quarter (Zeelenberg, 2017). Also, in many countries users need an even more timely first estimate, preferably 30 days after the end of the quarter.

There are four possible big data sources, here:

1. **Tax Databases:** These are mainly for taxes on wages and on sales. These are not yet rapid enough. They lag about two months: one month for reporting taxes and one month for filling the databases.

2. **Company Accounts:** It will become possible within the next few years to have direct access to company accounts. Direct access in the sense that reporting modules for taxation and statistics will have been built in the accounting software. But this is not yet possible, and even when it will have been implemented, then only for annual accounts.

3. **Banking Transactions of Enterprises and Households:** This is clearly the most promising. There is only one clearing-house for banks in the Netherlands, and it is very rapid. Also, banks have to report daily, weekly and monthly to the central bank. But there are of course very strong privacy concerns here. So it will be very, very difficult, and will take a long time before even the first steps will be taken and even longer before it will be implemented.

4. **Model-Based Estimates Based on Big Data:** Not a big data source as such, of course, but a way to use big data. At the moment, this appears to be the best option.

An example of what model-based estimates from big data may have to offer, is given by Van Ruth (2015) who analysed the relation between traffic intensity and economic activity in an important region of the Netherlands, around the city of Eindhoven. Traffic intensity is measured from traffic sensors in the road surfaces, and economic activity is measured by expected output, taken from the monthly Manufacturing Sentiment Survey. The traffic intensity indicator tracks that of expected output amazingly well. Peaks and troughs coincide, meaning that the traffic intensity index should be able to signal important turning points in economic activity. Statistically, the series appear to be coincident, and possibly seasonal adjustment and a trend-cycle decomposition may remove some noise and further improve the model. Now, traffic intensity data becomes available with a much shorter time lag than traditional survey data. From the model that relates output to traffic intensity, we may then make a preliminary estimate of output, which in turn may be used to improve the first estimate of GNP. So, this and similar models, might be useful in making better first and preliminary estimates of GNP.

Google Trends for Nowcasting

Choi and Varian (2011) show how to use search engine data from Google Trends to 'predict the present', also known as nowcasting. They present various examples of economic indicators including automobile sales, unemployment claims, travel destination planning, and consumer confidence.

In most cases, they apply simple autoregressive models incorporating appropriate Google Trends search terms as predictors. For nowcasting consumer confidence, they use a Bayesian regression model, since in that case it is not so clear in advance which search terms to use.

They found that even their simple models that include relevant Google Trends variables tend to outperform models that exclude these predictors by 5% to 20%. No claims to perfection or exhaustiveness are made, but these preliminary results indicate that it is worthwhile to pursue this model-based path further.

On the other hand, we should be cautious with interpreting search-term based results. A couple of years ago, there was a lot of enthusiasm concerning Google Flu, but more recently the nowcasting performance of Google Flu has decreased significantly (Lazer et al, 2014). Google have also been criticized for not being transparent: they have not revealed the search terms used in Google Flu, which inhibits a sound scientific debate and cross-validation by peers.

In fact, this last point has more general significance. One of the items in the European Code of Practice (EU, 2005), is that NSIs should warn the public and policy makers when statistical results are being used inappropriately or are being misrepresented. As emphasized by Reimsbach-Kounatze (2015) and Fan, Han and Liu (2014), with big data it is easy to find spurious results, and there is a role for NSIs as *statistical authorities* to offer best practices for analysing big data.

ANALYTICAL USE OF BIG DATA

In recent years, new techniques, usually grouped under the heading machine-learning techniques, have been developed that may be used to analyse big data. These techniques have been developed for high-dimensional data (i.e., data with a large number of variables per record), whereas the big data we have discussed above often have a low, sometimes even very low, dimension. However, some experiments have suggested that within official statistics, they may be useful also for low-dimensional data, for example to correct for selectivity.

Also, for statistical analysis, i.e., for answering what-if questions, it is not always necessary to have representative data, and so big data might be useful for analysis. But insight into the data quality and the data-generating process is always necessary, and, as we have seen above, this is a problem for many big data from intermediaries.

It is crucial to remember that any use of models must be made explicit. It should be documented and made transparent to users. Also, models are not to be used indiscriminately: we should not forget that the primary purpose of an NSI is to describe, and not to prescribe or judge. So, we should refrain from making forecasts and from making purely behavioural models. Also, we should be careful to avoid model failure when the assumptions underlying it break down. Therefore, any model should rely on actually observed data for the period under consideration, which relates to the economic and social phenomena we are trying to describe by statistical estimates; and model building should be accompanied by extensive specification tests.

DISCUSSION

There are three main conclusions.

First, big data come in high volume, high velocity and high variety. This leads to new opportunities for new statistics or redesign of existing statistics:

- Their high volume may lead to better accuracy and more details,
- Their high velocity may lead to more frequent and more timely statistical estimates,
- Their high variety may give opportunities for statistics in new areas.

Secondly, at least in some cases, statistics based on big data are useful in their own right, for example because they are being used in policy making or play a role in public discussion. An important caveat is that often a big data source does not cover the entire target population that is interesting from a statistics user's perspective. This may introduce selectivity in statistical estimates which limits the usefulness of big data from a statistical perspective. A number of possible solutions and workarounds have been discussed in this chapter but more work should be done in this important area.

Thirdly, in general NSIs should not be scared to use models in producing official statistics, as they have apparently done this before, provided these models and methods are adequately documented. So, we should look more closely at how models may be used to produce official statistics from big data. In particular Bayesian methods and multilevel models seem promising.

It is crucial that NSIs continue to actively explore opportunities of big data. Many more sources will emerge, and may become available for production of statistics. In the near future, biological data, e.g., on genomes, and medical data, on health and care of individuals, will become available for scientific research and for linking with social data on income, crime, jobs, etc.[3] The *internet of things*, consisting of all kinds of large and small devices, is expected to generate a tremendous amount of data from which e.g., information on personal behaviour can be derived: movement patterns, health aspects, energy consumption, and much more. Sensors in the public space will provide information on the environment like air quality or noise pollution, contributing to the concept of a smart city. Smart manufacturing and smart agriculture refer to industries that take advantage of intensive generation and analysis of large amounts of data. And in addition to physical space, virtual or cyber space becomes an increasingly important study object in itself, giving rise to new phenomena like cybercrime or the internet economy. The exploration of opportunities will be accompanied by non-trivial challenges as argued in this chapter, but NSIs are in an excellent position to use their traditional experience and high quality standards in innovative ways.

REFERENCES

Belloni, A., Chernozhukov, V., & Hansen, C. (2014). High-dimensional methods and inference on structural and treatment effects. *The Journal of Economic Perspectives*, *28*(2), 29–50. doi:10.1257/jep.28.2.29

Braaksma, B., & Zeelenberg, K. (2015). Re-make/Re-model: Should big data change the modelling paradigm in official statistics? *Statistical Journal of the IAOS*, *31*(2), 193–202. doi:10.3233/sji-150892

Buelens, B., de Wolf, P.-P., & Zeelenberg, K. (2017). *Model-based estimation at Statistics Netherlands*. Discussion Paper, Statistics Netherlands, The Hague.

Choi, H., & Varian, H. R. (2011). *Predicting the present with Google trends*. Retrieved from http://people.ischool.berkeley.edu/~hal/Papers/2011/ptp.pdf

Daas, P. J. H., & Puts, M. J. (2014). *Social media sentiment and consumer confidence*. Paper presented at the Workshop on using big data for Forecasting and Statistics, Frankfurt, Germany. Retrieved from https://www.ecb.europa.eu/events/pdf/conferences/140407/Daas_Puts_Sociale_media_cons_conf_Stat_Neth.pdf?40 9d61b733fc259971ee5beec7cedc61

Daas, P. J. H., Puts, M. J., Buelens, B., & van den Hurk, P. A. M. (2013). *big data and Official Statistics*. Paper presented at the Conference on New Techniques and Technologies for Statistics, Brussels, Belgium. Retrieved from http://www.cros-portal.eu/sites/default/files/NTTS2013fullPaper_76.pdf

De Jonge, E., van Pelt, M., & Roos, M. (2012). *Time patterns, geospatial clustering and mobility statistics based on mobile phone network data*. Discussion paper 2012-14, Statistics Netherlands. Retrieved from http://www.cbs.nl/NR/rdonlyres/010F11EC-AF2F-4138-8201-2583D461D2B6/0/201214x10pub.pdf

De Meersman, F., Seynaeve, G., Debusschere, M., Lusyne, P., Dewitte, P., Baeyens, Y.,... Reuter, H. I. (2016). *Assessing the Quality of Mobile Phone Data as a Source of Statistics*. Paper presented at the European Conference on Quality in Official Statistics, Madrid, Spain. Retrieved from http://www.ine.es/q2016/docs/q2016Final00163.pdf

De Wolf, P.-P., & Zeelenberg, K. (2015). *Challenges for statistical disclosure control in a world with big data and open data*. Invited paper for the 60th World Statistics Congress. Retrieved from http://www.isi2015.org

EU (European Union). (2009, March31). Regulation on European statistics, 2009. *Official Journal of the European Union, L, 87*, 164–173. Retrieved from http://data.europa.eu/eli/reg/2009/223/2015-06-08

EU (European Union). (2005). *Code of Practice for European Statistics*. Retrieved from http://epp.eurostat.ec.europa.eu/portal/page/portal/quality/code_of_practice

Eurostat. (2016). *Statistics Explained - Glossary: Enterprise*. Retrieved from http://ec.europa.eu/eurostat/statistics-explained/index.php/Glossary:Enterprise

Fan, J., Han, F., & Liu, H. (2014). Challenges of big data analysis. *National Science Review, 1*(2), 293–314. doi:10.1093/nsr/nwt032 PMID:25419469

Gelman, A., Carlin, J. B., Stern, H. S., Dunson, D. B., Vehtari, A., & Rubin, D. B. (2013). *Bayesian Data Analysis (3rd ed.)*. Chapman and Hall/CRC.

Groves, R. M. (2011). 2011, Three eras of survey research. *Public Opinion Quarterly, 75*(5), 861–871. doi:10.1093/poq/nfr057

Heerschap, N. M., Ortega Azurduy, S. A., Priem, A. H., & Offermans, M. P. W. (2014). *Innovation of tourism statistics through the use of new big data sources*. Paper prepared for the Global Forum on Tourism Statistics, Prague, Czech Republic. Retrieved from http://www.tsf2014prague.cz/assets/downloads/Paper%20 1.2_Nicolaes%20Heerschap_NL.pdf

ISI (International Statistical Institute). (1985). *Declaration on Professional Ethics*. Retrieved from http://www.isi-web.org/about-isi/professional-ethics

KNAW (Koninklijke Nederlandse Akademie van Wetenschappen: Royal Netherlands Academy of Arts and Sciences). (2016). *Thirteen selected facilities and three honourable mentions*. Retrieved from https://www.knaw.nl/en/advisory-work/copy_of_knaw-agenda-grootschalige-onderzoeksfaciliteiten-13-geselecteerde-faciliteiten?set_language=en

Lazer, D., Kennedy, R., King, G., & Vespignani, A. (2014). The parable of Google flu: Traps in big data analysis. *Science*, *343*(14), 1203–1205. doi:10.1126/science.1248506 PMID:24626916

Nickerson, D. W., & Rogers, T. (2014). Political campaigns and big data. *The Journal of Economic Perspectives*, *28*(2), 51–74. doi:10.1257/jep.28.2.51

Oostrom, L., Walker, A. N., Staats, B., Slootbeek-Van Laar, M., Ortega Azurduy, S., & Rooijakkers, B. (2016). *Measuring the internet economy in The Netherlands: a big data analysis*. Discussion Paper 2016-14, Statistics Netherlands, Heerlen. Retrieved from https://www.cbs.nl/nl-nl/achtergrond/2016/41/measuring-the-internet-economy-in-the-netherlands

Reimsbach-Kounatze, C. (2015). *The proliferation of "big data" and implications for official statistics and statistical agencies: a preliminary analysis*. OECD Digital Economy Papers 245. Paris: OECD; doi:10.1787/20716826

Struijs, P., Braaksma, B., & Daas, P. J. H. (2014, April). Official statistics and big data. *Big Data & Society*, 1–6. doi: 10.1177/2053951714538417

Telecompaper. (2015). *Majority of the elderly in the Netherlands has a smartphone*. Retrieved from https://www.telecompaper.com/pressrelease/majority-of-the-elderly-in-the-netherlands-has-a-smartphone--1088067

Tennekes, M., & Offermans, M. P. W. (2014). *Daytime population estimations based on mobile phone metadata*. Paper prepared for the Joint Statistical Meetings, Boston, MA. Retrieved from http://www.amstat.org/meetings/jsm/2014/onlineprogram/AbstractDetails.cfm?abstractid=311959

UN-ECE High-Level Group for the Modernisation of Statistical Production and Services. (2013). *What does "big data" mean for official statistics?* Retrieved from http://www1.unece.org/stat/platform/pages/viewpage.action?pageId=77170622

UN (Statistical Commission of the United Nations). (1991). *Fundamental Principles of Official Statistics*. Retrieved from http://unstats.un.org/unsd/dnss/gp/fundprinciples.aspx

Vaccari, C. (2016). *Big Data in Official Statistics*. Saarbrücken: Lambert.

Van Ruth, F. J. (2014). *Traffic intensity as indicator of regional economic activity*. Discussion paper 2014-21, Statistics Netherlands.

Varian, H. R. (2014). Big data: New tricks for econometrics. *The Journal of Economic Perspectives*, 28(2), 3–28. doi:10.1257/jep.28.2.3

Zeelenberg, K. (2016). *Challenges to Methodological Research in Official Statistics*. Presentation at the 2016 International Methodology Symposium, Gatineau. Retrieved from http://www.statcan.gc.ca/eng/conferences/symposium2016/program

ENDNOTES

[1]   This subsection in based on Oostrom et al (2016).
[2]   An enterprise in official statistics is more or less the same as a business unit, and a legal unit is an entity officially registered as an economically active unit, such as a corporation and a self-employed person, whereas an enterprise group (a set of enterprises controlled by the same owner) is more or less the same as a company. See Eurostat (2016) for more details and references to implementation rules.
[3]   The Royal Netherlands Academy of Arts and Sciences has placed a proposal for such a database by universities and Statistics on its *Academy Agenda for Large-scale Research Facilities* which need to be in place by 2025. This Agenda lists research facilities that could produce new scientific breakthroughs (KNAW, 2016).

Chapter 12
Linked Open Statistical Metadata

Franck Cotton
National Institute of Statistics and Economic Studies (INSEE), France

Daniel Gillman
U.S. Bureau of Labor Statistics (BLS), USA

ABSTRACT

Linked Open Statistical Metadata (LOSM) is Linked Open Data (LOD) applied to statistical metadata. LOD is a model for identifying, structuring, interlinking, and querying data published directly on the web. It builds on the standards of the semantic web defined by the W3C. LOD uses the Resource Description Framework (RDF), a simple data model expressing content as predicates linking resources between them or with literal properties. The simplicity of the model makes it able to represent any data, including metadata. We define statistical data as data produced through some statistical process or intended for statistical analyses, and statistical metadata as metadata describing statistical data. LOSM promotes discovery and the meaning and structure of statistical data in an automated way. Consequently, it helps with understanding and interpreting data and preventing inadequate or flawed visualizations for statistical data. This enhances statistical literacy and efforts at visualizing statistics.

INTRODUCTION

Linked Open Data (LOD) (Linked Data, n.d.) is a method for identifying, structuring, interlinking, and querying data published directly on the World Wide Web (hereinafter abbreviated as the Web). It builds on the standards of the Semantic Web defined by the World Wide Web Consortium (W3C) and on the contributions of a vibrant

DOI: 10.4018/978-1-5225-2512-7.ch012

and enthusiastic community W3, 2015; W3C, 2017). LOD can be used in private contexts, for example to organize a business information system, but most often the content published is open. The results of using LOD techniques are supposed to be published on the Web. Tim Berners-Lee (2006) defines LOD as the highest-quality form of open data. LOD methodology makes use of some W3C and Internet standards. This provides a uniform way to represent and query data that are linked under LOD principles. The most important of these standards is the Resource Description Framework (RDF) (W3, 2014), a data model based on a very simple logic using a triple comprising a subject – predicate – object sentence structure. Subjects are Web resources, linked through Predicates to Objects, which are either other Web resources (and thus can serve as Subjects for new triples) or contain literal content, such as data. The simplicity of the model makes it able to represent any kind of information, for example statistical data, but also any kind of "meta-information": how the data is modeled, how it is structured, who publishes it, what is its quality, etc. This is the concept of Linked (Open) Metadata. Since the RDF model is so basic, it is also extremely powerful because it formalizes all information in a uniform way. This facilitates the linking between resources both within a data set and across data provided by different publishers. The ultimate logic is that each resource is uniquely identified on a global scale and referenced rather that copied in a specific context. The RDF model is also built on a simple but strong logical background, which allows for semantic query and inference of new facts. This chapter addresses the consequences of applying LOD principles to statistical data. As first described and promoted by Berners-Lee, the aim of LOD was to link all data, datum by datum. Not only does this approach not scale, but for much statistical data the need to maintain the privacy of individual responses trumps any other benefit.

The solution is to link the metadata describing each datum instead. The reasoning behind the approach and some efforts to achieve it are described. In particular, the effort to represent several statistical metadata standards in RDF are included.

In this chapter, we describe RDF, statistical data, statistical surveys, confidentiality, and statistical metadata. From these, we arrive at a framework for assessing statistical literacy and applying visualization techniques. We then describe Linked Open Statistical Metadata, two important statistical metadata models, and the efforts to represent them as LOD. We then discuss how these enhance efforts to understand and visualize statistical data.

SEMANTIC WEB AND RESOURCE DESCRIPTION FRAMEWORK

This section gives a brief primer on RDF, a W3C standard that facilitates the exchange of structured data on the Internet. Based on a simple subject-predicate-object model commonly referred to as "triples", it allows for a generic, standardized structuring of resources that can be used to model and disseminate everything from taxonomies to statistical observations to metadata records. The model used by RDF is also commonly referred to as a "graph model" consisting of "nodes" (which are vertices) and "edges" or "arcs". See the Figure 1 below for an example.

The Web Ontology Language (OWL) (W3, 2013) is part of the Semantic Web technology stack in which RDF also resides. It is a logic-based language intended to represent formal knowledge of things on the Web. Though OWL is not the subject of this section, it is in wide use and can be used in situations for which RDF is not expressive enough to account for all the knowledge a system demands.

The RDF model, which by itself contains only the barest set of classes (subjects and objects) and properties (predicates), is extended using RDF Schema, another fairly limited set of classes and properties that together with RDF form the foundation of the framework which can then be endlessly extended and specialized as needed (Brickley & Guha, 2014). Each extension is known as a *vocabulary*, which is bounded by a *namespace*. Namespaces allow implementers to specify the *set* of classes and properties that belong to a vocabulary and give a strong assurance of uniqueness even in the open waters of the World Wide Web (WWW). This is a concept that will be quite common to those familiar with XML schemas.

The other very important aspect of RDF is that as with its namespaces, all of its classes and properties are also uniquely identified using the underpinning naming

Figure 1. RDF graph

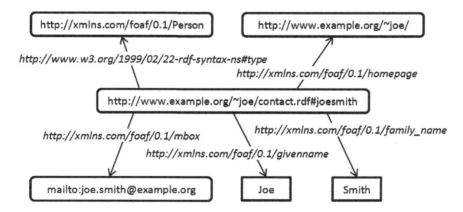

mechanism of the internet, the URI (Uniform Resource Identifier) (Berners-Lee, Fielding & Masinter, 2005). In the same way that all web pages are uniquely identified by a URI (web pages actually use the familiar URL used by web pages is, a subset of the URI specification), all RDF classes and properties are uniquely identified by a URI (Berners-Lee, Masinter, & McCahill, 1994). In practice this enables a powerful, standardized method for uniquely identifying information of all kinds with great certainty that they will remain unique not only within the closed context of an internal database, but also across the WWW.

As mentioned before, each vocabulary uses a namespace to scope its set of classes and properties. This namespace is known by a URI, and by common convention the unique identifiers for the classes and properties are appended to this common namespace URI with an intervening hash or forward slash. For example, the commonly used Friend of a Friend (FOAF) vocabulary, designed to link instances of people and information, uses the common namespace http://xmlns.com/foaf/0.1/ (Brickley & Miller, 2014). All of the FOAF classes and properties are then appended to this namespace, *e.g.* the FOAF class *Person* is uniquely identified by its URI as http://xmlns.com/foaf/0.1/Person.

Just as in an XML schema, one can define a *namespace prefix* to act as a shortcut for the entire namespace (W3, n.d.). Thus in a group of FOAF statements (written in XML syntax) one will commonly find a statement such as *xmlns:foaf*=http://xmlns.com/foaf/0.1/. This simply means that once this *foaf* shortcut has been defined, one can now refer to the URI that uniquely identifies the class FOAF Person more compactly as *foaf:Person*.

One of the other important aspects of RDF is that it does not rely on a particular syntax for its expression. Thus, there are a handful of interchangeable syntaxes that can be and are used depending on a variety of requirements that one may have such as brevity or readability. This paper uses the popular Turtle (Terse RDF Triple Language) syntax, prized for its readability (Beckett & Berners-Lee, 2011).

Returning to the FOAF example, here is how one might make the simple *triple* statement that one of the authors of this paper is a thing known as a person (with a web page to provide an identifier for the actual person):

```
<http://aims.fao.org/community/profiles/Franck-
Cotton><http://www.w3.org/1999/02/22-rdf-syntax-ns#type>
<http://xmlns.com/foaf/0.1/Person>.
```

So to recap, we have a subject "Franck-Cotton" a "type" predicate (defined in RDFS) and an object *foaf:Person*.

To put it in another way, "Franck-Cotton" is an *instance* of the *class* "Person". In RDF "type" gets used so often that Turtle lets you simply use "a" for convenience:

```
        <http://aims.fao.org/community/profiles/Franck-Cotton>
a
<http://xmlns.com/foaf/0.1/Person>.
```

Let's say we want to get our statement a little shorter, we can define namespace prefixes one time and then use the shortcut for all the other triples in our graph:

```
@prefix foaf: <http://xmlns.com/foaf/0.1/>.
@prefix rdf: <http://www.w3.org/1999/02/22-rdf-syntax-ns#>.
@prefix aims: <http://aims.fao.org/community/profiles/>.
```

So with those shortcuts defined, we can now write the same statement as (putting the triple on a single line this time:

```
aims:Franck-Cotton rdf:type foaf:Person.
```

Or using the Turtle shortcut for *rdf:type*:

```
aims:Franck-Cotton a foaf:Person.
```

Let's say we want to put a few triples together so we can say a little bit more:

```
aims:Franck-Cotton
a foaf:Person ;
        foaf:name "Franck Cotton".
```

So here we are seeing the short-hand Turtle notation for two sets of triples. In words, these triples are

```
"The Franck-Cotton AIMS profile web page is a person."
        "The person is named Franck Cotton."
```

This illustrates another feature of RDF. The triples may be linked together to tell a story. The object in the first triple is then used as the subject in the next (possibly many) triple(s).

To think about what RDF looks like graphically, here is a nice diagram courtesy of Marek Obitko (2007). The round-cornered boxes are classes or instances of classes (subjects/objects), the arrows are properties (predicates) and the square boxes are *literals*. Literals are typically used to represent simple numeric values, dates or labels. Literals can also have a datatype and language, powerful mechanisms to enforce restrictions on permissible values.

And here is the corresponding Turtle (note the use of the empty namespace shortcut):

```
@prefix: <http://www.example.org/~joe/contact.rdf#>.
@prefix foaf: <http://xmlns.com/foaf/0.1/>.
@prefix rdf: <http://www.w3.org/1999/02/22-rdf-syntax-ns#>.
:joesmith a foaf:Person ;
      foaf:givenname "Joe" ;
      foaf:family_name "Smith" ;
      foaf:homepage <http://www.example.org/~joe/> ;
      foaf:mbox <mailto:joe.smith@example.org>.
```

To briefly recap, RDF is a framework that is designed to organize structured data about resources and their relationships over the Internet in a standard way. It is designed from the ground-up to be endlessly extensible and able to maintain the uniqueness of the things it represents even in the radically decentralized WWW.

STATISTICS

Statistical Data

We can define statistical data as data that is produced through some statistical process or intended for statistical analyses. For socio-economic statistics, data are either microdata (those data whose records correspond to individual units from a population) or macrodata, data that are generated from other data.

Microdata are respondent level data or data from administrative sources, which might include Big Data. Each microdata record corresponds to some individual unit, often people, patients, households, business establishments, hospitals, etc. Microdata files are often fixed format files set up for statistical packages, such as R, SAS, SPSS, or Stata. Sometimes they are delivered as CSV files or as Excel spreadsheets.

Macrodata may be multi-dimensional cross-tabulations, which are referred to as "n-cubes". A kind of example are the tables that are generated from a statistical program, such as the Summary Files (SF1 and SF2) that are generated for the Decennial Census of the United States. Leading economic indicators, such as a national unemployment rate or consumer price index are other examples of aggregated macrodata.

Time is a very important factor for statistical data. So, a time series is a collection of the same measurement taken over some time interval. This technique allows for comparisons over time, uncovering trends and relationships. Leading demographic and economic indicators are a large component of what is known as official statistics. These are the statistical data produced by governments that reflect the state of the population or economy. They are designed to be amenable to time series analyses.

Roughly speaking, statistical literacy includes knowing enough to use statistical data in a defensible way. This is necessarily broad, because there are many ways to use statistical data. However, it is through metadata (described below in section 4) that the necessary understanding of the specifics of some data are conveyed. It is easy to misuse data, and the metadata help the user understand the limits of the data they describe.

Visualization, again roughly speaking, is a set of technologies for turning the relationships among data into visual representations. These include graphs, pie and bar charts, bubble plots, scatter plots, and many more. It is the job of the person creating the visualizations to understand what aspects of the data to plot and how that might be achieved with the data at hand. If, for instance, one wanted to convey income quintiles in a bar chart for some data set on income, yet the data were reported as quartiles, the desire to show quintiles is not feasible. The metadata should indicate if income data are provided in quartiles or quintiles. So, the design of the data at hand has a large impact on the potential ways it can be visualized.

A basic understanding of any data is a pre-condition for literacy and visualization. This understanding is derived through metadata. In what follows, we will go deeper into this. The main point to realize is that metadata is the driver behind teaching how to use and visualize data.

Statistical Surveys

Sample surveys were developed during the 20th century as a means to make socio-economic estimates based on a small sample of a population of interest (Lohr, 2010). Sampling was developed to solve the problem of making estimates without having to collect data from every person, a so-called census. As it turned out, applying the theories of probability and statistics aided in this development. A sample selected by knowing the probability of selection for every unit in a population simultaneously provides a means to build estimates (say, a total for the population) and know their standard error, or variance, which is known as the sampling error. The sampling error provides a range within which an estimate is expected to fall. The reliability of an estimate increases as the range narrows.

Statistical data are produced under a process model that is well understood, broadly used, and flexible. Statistical surveys and other statistical activities of a wide variety are all described in this framework. There is even a standard process model for statistics, the Generic Statistical Business Process Model (GSBPM). This will be described further below. But, the model is divided into sections based on broad phases of the statistical life-cycle. These phases are called Specify Needs, Design, Build, Collect, Process, Analyze, Disseminate, and Evaluate.

Many of the processes defined in GSBPM, including design steps, are based in statistics, and they have an impact on the estimates (values produced) and estimations (processes applied). For example, using a probability sampling technique other than simple random sampling requires building a design effect, a ratio of how estimates under the new design differ from those applied in the simple random sampling case. Sampling also produces a sampling error, often reported as a "survey error". This error is inherent to the sampling process, and it is often expressed as the variance or standard error.

Errors can be associated with any of the processes under GSBPM, and all the error from all sources is known as total survey error. This is a subject of current research. However, the main point is how the process affects the quality, interpretation, and usage of the data produced. This means that the process is important for describing statistical data produced, and this must be accounted for. One is interested in knowing which processes were applied, what error or quality assessments were made, and how these might impact the quality and usage of the data.

The error in surveys that is not related to sampling is called non-sampling error. Sources for non-sampling error, as alluded to above, are interviewing, design of an answer form or questionnaire, or the construction of a frame (the set from which a sample is drawn). This names but a few of the sources of non-sampling error, and the total of all the non-sampling error is called the bias. Total survey error is (approximately) the variance plus the bias.

Estimates are built by assigning weights to each unit selected in a sample, the weights are roughly the inverse of the probability of selection. These weights are calculated to match estimates to totals for some known variable from a "gold standard", usually a census, from which the true population values may be taken. The weights are used as multipliers for each collected value from a variable of interest. By the use of weights, it is possible to get an estimate for an entire population by interviewing just a sample of that population.

So, for instance, a means to measure the total employment of people living in some country at a fixed time is to take a sample, collect data about the employment status of each person in the sample, and use that data to estimate the total for all people in the country by applying weights to the values associated with the variables of interest.

One area that is poorly understood by the general data-using public is the idea of representation of a sample. Samples are selected for the purposes of the design of the survey, and reliable estimates rely on that. However, there may be sampling units in geographical areas that are not representative of the specific are yet are part of the design of the survey. Is it OK to go ahead and make these estimates anyway? In general, the answer is NO, but sometimes it might be defensible. This depends on variance (sampling error) estimates.

Another important area of design and processing is the design of questionnaires and the process of data collection: questions, their order, the mode in which they are used, and the way an interviewer asked questions. Surveys can often be made to provide pre-arranged results if the questionnaire is designed in a peculiar way. So, questionnaire design and data collection are crucial aspects of data quality and total survey error.

It turns out the specific wording of questions, the order in which they are asked, and the mode in which they are asked all have an impact on data quality. An example is the question "How many sexual partners have you had in the past year?" First, the question must be asked in private, since the presence of a significant other will materially affect response. Second, the wording itself may be subject to interpretation. A "sexual partner" might be limited to those with whom intercourse occurred, or might include others. Finally, the order might affect a response if the question follows another about morality, such as "Do you attend church or other religious ceremonies on a regular basis?

If an interviewer asks questions with bias in her voice, this can affect answers to questions. More generally, survey managers want to understand as many aspects of the data collection process they can, such as why and where the process bogs down, and feedback to see how changes might be improving the process. Data collection process improvements are geared towards improving data quality.

Confidentiality

Statistical data are collected under a promise that the respondent, the person or company responding to a survey, will remain anonymous. This is the promise of confidentiality, and the responses will be used for statistical purposes only. The confidentiality promise will apply to administrative record data sources as well.

The promise of confidentiality means that the responses tied to individuals will not be released. With this pledge, it is possible to collect private or sensitive information from individuals and businesses. Without this promise, or if the promise is breached, most official statistics would be impossible to produce. Businesses and people will be unwilling to provide any data about themselves if they know those data will be made public.

Even though microdata is data about each individual unit, many official statistical offices release some anonymized data of this kind. These are called public use microdata files (PUMD). They are specially sanitized so the units the data represent are protected. If a mistake is made and some unit is uncovered, this is called a disclosure. Confidentiality controls are applied to reduce the risk of disclosures.

Cells in tables are also subject to disclosure control. If a cell represents a small number of units, then it may be possible to infer individuals and responses, especially if that individual is an outlier – providing an unusual response. Therefore, thresholds on the number of units represented are imposed on table cells before values are published. Several techniques have been developed to perturb or suppress cell values in cases where there are not enough units.

So, a big concern with the use of LOD techniques to statistical data is the chance that confidentiality will be compromised through combining statistical data with others. There are no known techniques for insuring that confidentiality is maintained after some data sets are combined. Further, application of LOD to PUMD cannot use the actual subject (respondent) in an RDF triple leading to some data. The question is whether there is value in using RDF in this instance.

STATISTICAL METADATA

Originally, metadata was defined as data about data. However, the usage of metadata expanded during the early years of the public use of the Internet. Efforts such as the Dublin Core Metadata Initiative forced a revision to the original view. Now, more comprehensively, metadata is defined as data used to describe some objects. So, data become metadata when the describing role is revealed. A few years ago the US National Security Agency tried to justify a campaign to collect data about all US telephone calls by saying the collected data were just metadata. However, this does not meet the definition given here, because the data around each telephone call were being used in their own right. They were the data being scrutinized. Yes, they describe telephone calls, but that was not their purpose. Their purpose was to map which telephone numbers were connected through calls placed among them. As a result, because the data are analyzed in their own right and are not being used to describe telephone calls, they should not be called metadata. The term metadata is applied when a descriptive relationship is the focus.

A very important feature of metadata is re-use, the idea that one writes down a description one time and uses it whenever and wherever needed to describe other objects. This is achieved through the use of pointers and relationships, and it is the basic power behind metadata management. For reuse provides the efficiency for metadata management and usage. This is similar to the idea of normalization in relational databases, and it increases the power of metadata, promotes discovery, uncovers similarities, and reduces the burdens of metadata management.

Since metadata are data, they can be organized into databases for efficient storage and manipulation. The schemas used to design such databases are metadata models. Models are designed to maximize reuse. Among the many purposes of metadata is to provide meaning to data and categories. By themselves, metadata can't provide all the meaning for some data; other resources are needed as well, such as ontologies, glossaries, and thesauri. However, metadata are a necessary part of these descriptions and definitions.

For a statistical office that conducts many surveys on an on-going basis, this means a statistical metadata specification is needed to handle all the metadata for each survey and all the iterations of each one. For instance, the data sets produced by each iteration of a survey share the same questionnaire, data dictionary, and data formats, among others. An obvious consequence of this is that much statistical metadata is shared across surveys and survey iterations, i.e., re-use is an important aspect of statistical metadata. An effective statistical metadata specification is designed to take this into account. This means that traditional database designs (e.g., the relational model) are appropriate for organizing statistical metadata.

Another important aspect of statistical metadata is to define concepts. Concepts appear in many parts of survey design: over-arching survey concepts, such as what the survey is trying to measure, e.g., employment; concepts in classifications for stratifying, or sub-setting, measures, e.g., industries; measures or variables themselves, such as "average hourly wage" or "employment cost index". From the perspective of a data user or survey manager, it is important to have good definitions of these concepts. No definition of a socio-economic concept will be so good we can be sure of all instances that correspond, we should strive for the best possible. In any case, though, the statistical metadata system can serve as an authoritative source for all the definitions.

The design and production of statistical data have an impact on the understanding and use of that data. Understanding that a sample was used to collect some statistical data leads to knowing that weights are needed to make any estimates based on that data. How those weights are determined provides a clue as to how and when to use them in making estimates. Knowing how to estimate the variance, the sampling error, provides the means to show how accurate a resulting estimate might be. Therefore, the design of a survey is vital for understanding how to use the data the survey produced.

Likewise, the production process for a statistical survey is important for understanding the data. Sometimes, people asked to participate in a survey refuse outright to answer any questions or refuse to answer some questions. This is called non-response. It is important to account for that missing data, and much effort is expended to try to get reluctant people to respond anyway. If the missing data cannot be collected or otherwise derived (through techniques called imputation), this means that the sample as designed and the set of respondents don't coincide. The weights derived by the sample design cannot be right, and one has to know how to adjust the weights for the missing data. Therefore, aspects of the actual implementation of a survey are important to know for the proper use of the data.

Obviously, the meaning and descriptions of variables, metadata for the data themselves, are important for understanding data, too. The conclusion is that statistical metadata is a broad subject, and much information is necessary for the proper understanding and use of statistical data.

The work to develop comprehensive models for statistical metadata is an active area of research and collaboration among national statistical offices throughout the world. Already, several important statistical metadata models have been or are under development. Some of these are:

- **GSBPM:** Generic Statistical Business Process Model – A business process model for official statistics.
- **GSIM:** Generic Statistical Information Model – A conceptual model for statistical design, production, and dissemination.
- **SDMX:** Statistical Data and Metadata eXchange – A model for the description and exchange of dimensional statistical data and metadata.
- **DDI:** Data Documentation Initiative – An implementable, logical version of GSIM. An RDF binding to this model will be produced.
- **XKOS:** eXtended Knowledge Organization System, an extension of SKOS (Simple Knowledge Organization System) – An RDF vocabulary for describing statistical classifications.
- **RDF Data Cube Vocabulary:** An RDF vocabulary of the SDMX data model for dimensional data.

In this chapter, we will discuss GSBPM and GSIM in more detail. GSIM and GSBPM are dual models for the production and management of statistical data. The duality between an information model and the related process model is that the processes defined in the process model are the relationships between classes (representing the information objects) in the information model. GSBPM models the statistical production process and identifies the activities undertaken by producers of statistics that result in information outputs. GSIM describes the information objects important for documenting statistical design, production, and data. It helps describe GSBPM sub-processes by defining objects that flow between them (the inputs and outputs) to produce statistics.

STATISTICAL LITERACY AND VISUALIZATION

For our purposes, statistical literacy is achieved through an understanding of statistical data. This is realized one data set at a time, and it requires a thorough understanding of the data and how they are produced. This is why metadata are important. Metadata convey the information needed to understand data.

As we described above, to understand statistical data much about the design and processes that produced that data must be known to use them correctly. A typical example is misunderstandings about the use of data based on a sample. Samples for surveys used to make national estimates sometimes include a few cases scattered around the country. The areas from where these isolated cases come might be the focus of estimates themselves. But, if the cases in an area are not representative of it, then estimates describing a population in the area are not reliable. Sampling error will be very large, rendering the estimates useless.

This is but one of many examples where lack of knowledge can get the user of data into trouble. Throughout the statistical life cycle pitfalls arise that can severely impact the use of statistical data. This includes the use of data to communicate ideas, often by using visualization techniques. Lack of knowledge of basic statistical ideas and lack of knowledge of the data each and in combination can make communication problematic. The literature is rich with examples of how and when to use particular kinds of charts and graphs for describing data. However, the data themselves can cause problems. For instance, data collected over a wide time interval should not be used for a point in time estimate. Another kind of example includes displaying statistics about categories labelled with numeric codes. Satisfaction ratings are often labelled this way, and averages are produced, yet these are mostly meaningless.

LINKED OPEN STATISTICAL METADATA

Statistical metadata can also be used to discover and differentiate among various data sets that are candidates for use in some analyses. This is where LOD becomes important. However, in the previous sections we laid out important considerations for why linking statistical data to each other is not practical. The way to find data is through a description of that data. This means data must be linked to the metadata that describes them. This is where linking metadata plays a role.

Linked Open Statistical Metadata (LOSM) is a means to structure and expose statistical data and metadata in a standard, universally understandable, linkable, and actionable fashion. LOSM, as a part of LOD, is represented in RDF or more formal languages such the Web ontology language (OWL). LOSM also improves semantic interoperability, which is very beneficial to the data economy. For example, one can relate separate data sets through semantically linked concepts or articulated code lists or classifications.

By providing an "intelligent path" to data, LOSM can enhance statistical data discovery and access on a global scale, and thus facilitate reuse of data and avoid data duplication with its associated risks of errors and loss of relevance. Since LOSM provides paths to knowledge about the data and attaches that directly to the data, it can enrich approaches such as machine learning where the knowledge is more *ad hoc* or *a posteriori*. Further, in official statistics, it facilitates the discovery and analyses of leading national indicators, both demographic and economic.

It is also interesting to note that most LOD standard vocabularies and models relate to metadata, and so a lot of organized knowledge is already available as Linked Metadata and LOSM (for statistics) – in particular structured classifications, thesauri or taxonomies, geographic information infrastructures, etc. More knowledge can be derived through linking of concepts, inferring on semantic models, etc. LOSM helps discover, even without accessing the data itself, its meaning and structure in an automated way, and to select adequate discovery or representation techniques. Consequently, it helps preventing erroneous interpretations and inadequate or even flawed visualizations. This enhances statistical literacy.

As we described above, the design behind the collection of statistical data is important to know to use the data correctly. This includes the sampling scheme, the means by which data are collected, and the concepts that define the data and variables that are used. The means to describe these designs is with metadata through a metadata model.

In the next section, we describe two metadata models from the statistical domain, and in the following section, we describe work that has been done to represent these as LOD.

STATISTICAL METADATA MODELS

Generic Statistical Business Process Model (GSBPM)

The effort to build the Generic Statistical Business Process Model (GSBPM started around 2005 under the United Nations Economic Commission for Europe (UNECE) Statistical Metadata Working (METIS) Group within its project known as the Common Metadata Framework (CMF). By 2008, the first draft was completed, and GSBPM became the major deliverable of Part C of the CMF. Revisions have been produced periodically since. Around 2011, refinements to the GSBPM are being managed under the MCS. The fifth version of GSBPM was released in late 2013.

GSBPM will be described in more detail in the next section, but it is built as a set of major process steps with additional detail under each. The terminology used to name and describe each step is generic, and the terms do not necessarily correspond to the terminology used in any country. Further, the standard is written in English, so most countries have to translate GSBPM to their own language to make it most useful locally. However, many countries have adopted GSBPM, and it is being used in many novel ways. One common use is to classify statistical processing software, and this provides a means to manage and uncover areas where statistical offices are unnecessarily duplicating software development activities.

GSBPM has also spawned two other newer standards under HLG/MCS, and these are the Generic Activity Model for Statistical Organizations (GAMSO) and the Generic Statistical Information Model (GSIM). GAMSO, first produced in 2016, extends GSBPM to include non-statistical activities common to all statistical offices. These include many management activities such as needs for computing infrastructure. GSIM, first released in 2012, is an information model describing the statistical information objects necessary for statistical activities. GSIM and GSBPM are duals of each other in the sense that GSBPM names activities and GSIM names the inputs and outputs of those activities. In this way, GSIM and GSBPM are intertwined.

The GSBPM is not really a business process model. The flow is not described, even if there is a timeline broadly going right and down. It is centered on the naming of the different statistical activities that constitute the statistical process. In fact, it is rather a taxonomy.

GSBPM is called a business process model. Typically, process models include the flows among all the processes, but GSBPM does not go to that detail. In fact, the statistical process is fluid enough, that the order of many processes is not that important. Sometimes, steps can be conducted in any order with the same results. Therefore, the higher level taxonomy is the lowest level of detail the model can provide and still be useful world-wide.

Figure 2 contains the top two levels of the GSBPM.

There are eight main process steps, which are labeled in the blue boxes at the tops of each of the columns. The items below each of the blue boxes are the sub-processes under the main process labels. Provided across the top are two over-arching steps, quality and metadata – as these are important activities that go along with every process in the model. In other words, every process generates metadata needed to describe that process and describe its usage; and every process has a quality component attached to it.

The main processes, or phases, are defined as follows:

Figure 2. Generic statistical business process model

Quality Management / Metadata Management							
Specify Needs	**Design**	**Build**	**Collect**	**Process**	**Analyse**	**Disseminate**	**Evaluate**
1.1 Identify needs	2.1 Design outputs	3.1 Build collection instrument	4.1 Create frame & select sample	5.1 Integrate data	6.1 Prepare draft outputs	7.1 Update output systems	8.1 Gather evaluation inputs
1.2 Consult & confirm needs	2.2 Design variable descriptions	3.2 Build or enhance process components	4.2 Set up collection	5.2 Classify & code	6.2 Validate outputs	7.2 Produce dissemination products	8.2 Conduct evaluation
1.3 Establish output objectives	2.3 Design collection	3.3 Build or enhance dissemination components	4.3 Run collection	5.3 Review & validate	6.3 Interpret & explain outputs	7.3 Manage release of dissemination products	8.3 Agree an action plan
1.4 Identify concepts	2.4 Design frame & sample	3.4 Configure workflows	4.4 Finalise collection	5.4 Edit & impute	6.4 Apply disclosure control	7.4 Promote dissemination products	
1.5 Check data availability	2.5 Design processing & analysis	3.5 Test production system		5.5 Derive new variables & units	6.5 Finalise outputs	7.5 Manage user support	
1.6 Prepare business case	2.6 Design production systems & workflow	3.6 Test statistical business process		5.6 Calculate weights			
		3.7 Finalise production system		5.7 Calculate aggregates			
				5.8 Finalise data files			

- **Specify Needs:** The initial investigation and identification of what statistics are needed and what is needed of the statistics.
- **Design:** The development and design activities, and any associated practical research work needed to define the statistical outputs, concepts, methodologies, collection instruments, and operational processes.
- **Build:** Build and test the production solution to the point where it is ready for use in the "live" environment.
- **Collect:** Collects or gathers all necessary information (data and metadata), using different collection modes (including extractions from statistical, administrative and other non-statistical registers and databases), and loads them into the appropriate environment for further processing.
- **Process:** The cleaning of data and their preparation for analysis.
- **Analyze:** Statistical outputs are produced, examined in detail and made ready for dissemination.
- **Disseminate:** Manage the release of the statistical products to customers.
- **Evaluate:** Manages the evaluation of a specific instance of a statistical business process.

Under each main process are defined several sub-processes. These define specific kinds of processes under each of the main headings. Further detail can be described, but at this level those details are probably institute specific.

The main result of the GSBPM is a taxonomy of business production activities for official statistics. This is made possible in part by the acceptance of common practices across the official statistical community world-wide.

Generic Statistical Information Model (GSIM)

The text and figures in this section are adapted from the GSIM Communication Paper on the Generic Statistical Information Model (GSIM) website (Lohr, 2010) under the UNECE (United Nations Economic Commission for Europe) (Cotton & Gillman, 2016).

GSIM provides a set of standardized, consistently described classes, which are the inputs and outputs in the design and production of statistics. The design and production processes for which GSIM defined objects are the inputs and outputs are themselves defined in GSBPM [4].

In general, information and process models describing the same domain are duals of each other in the sense that the classes in one model are the relationships in the other. Though GSIM and GSBPM are not designed to directly convey this connectedness, as GSBPM is more of an outline than a model, they nevertheless imply it. More details about how GSIM and GSBPM are inter-connected follow below.

GSIM does not include classes related to business functions within an organization such as human resources, finance, or legal functions, except to the extent that this information is used directly in statistical production.

At the highest level, GSIM is designed and was developed in four main sections. These four top-level groups are described below:

- The Business group is used to capture the designs and plans of statistical programs, and the processes undertaken to deliver those programs. This includes the identification of a Statistical Need, the Business Processes that compose the Statistical Program, and the evaluations of them.
- The Exchange group is used to catalogue the information that comes in and out of a statistical organization via Exchange Channels. It includes classes that describe the collection and dissemination of information.
- The Concepts group is used to define the meaning of data, providing an understanding of what the data are measuring.
- The Structures group is used to describe and define the terms used in relation to structures for organizing data.

Figure 3 gives an example of GSIM classes that tell a story about some of the information that is important in a statistical organization. In particular:

- "A statistical organization initiates a *Statistical Program*. The *Statistical Program* corresponds to an ongoing activity such as a survey or an output series and has a *Statistical Program Cycle* (for example it repeats quarterly or annually).
- The *Statistical Program Cycle* will include a set of *Business Processes*. The *Business Processes* consist of a number of *Process Steps* which are specified by a *Process Design*. These *Process Designs* have *Process Input Specifications* and *Process Output Specifications*.
- The specifications will often be pieces of information that refer to Concepts and Structures (for example, *Statistical Classification, Variable, Population, Data Structure,* and *Data Set*). If, for example, the *Business Process* is related to the collection of data, there will be an *Information Provider* who agrees to provide the statistical organisation with data (via a *Provision Agreement*). This *Provision Agreement* specifies an agreed *Data Structure* and governs the *Exchange Channel* used for the incoming information. The *Exchange*

Figure 3. GSIM information objects

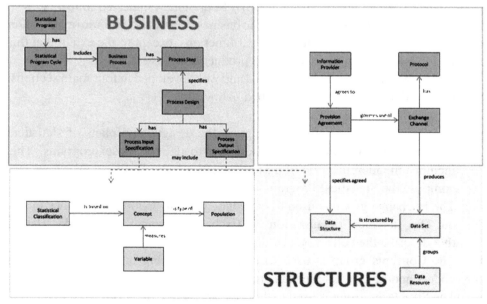

Channel could be a *Questionnaire* or an *Administrative Register*. It will receive the information via a particular mechanism (*Protocol*) such as an interview or a data file exchange.

• The *Data Set* produced by the *Exchange Channel* will be stored in a *Data Resource* and structured by a *Data Structure*."

As described above, GSIM and GSBPM are dual models for the production and management of statistical data. GSBPM models the statistical production process and identifies the activities undertaken by producers of official statistics that result in information outputs. These activities are broken down into sub-processes, such as "Impute" and "Calculate aggregates". As shown in Figure 4, GSIM helps describe GSBPM sub-processes by defining the objects that flow between them, that are created in them, and that are used by them to produce official statistics.

Greater value will be obtained from GSIM if it is applied in conjunction with GSBPM. Likewise, greater value will be obtained from GSBPM if it is applied in conjunction with GSIM. Nevertheless, it is possible (although not ideal) to apply one without the other. In the same way that individual statistical business processes do not use all of the sub-processes described within GSBPM, it is very unlikely that all classes in the GSIM will be needed in any specific statistical business process.

Good metadata management is essential for the efficient operation of statistical business processes. Metadata are present in every phase of GSBPM, either created, updated, or carried forward unchanged from a previous phase. In the context of GSBPM, the emphasis of the over-arching process of metadata management is on the creation, updating, use, and reuse of metadata. Metadata management strategies and systems are therefore vital to the operation of GSBPM, and are facilitated by GSIM.

Applying GSIM together with GSBPM (or an organization-specific equivalent) can facilitate the building of efficient metadata driven collection, processing, and dissemination systems, and help harmonize statistical computing infrastructures.

GSIM supports a consistent approach to metadata, facilitating the primary role for metadata envisaged in Part A of the Common Metadata Framework "Statistical Metadata in a Corporate Context" [5], that is, metadata should uniquely and formally define the content and links between objects and processes in the information system.

Figure 4. GSIM and GSBPM

GSBPM AND GSIM AS LOD

We saw in the previous sections that the GSIM and the GSBPM are the fundamental models for the description of the statistical process. Together, they are used to specify statistical services that can be shared between institutes (http://www1.unece.org/stat/platform/display/CSPA/), and the GSBPM serves as a common framework to which more and more works are linked, like quality indicators, definitions of skills, business capabilities, etc.

In order to allow the two models to fully play their central role, they were recently re-expressed as RDF vocabularies. The general benefits of this approach were described previously, and in this specific case the important feature expected were:

- Unique global naming of the GSBPM processes and GSIM objects, so they can be referred to unambiguously.
- Coherent formalization of the two models.
- Link to existing vocabularies, particularly in the case of the GSBPM.

Expressing the GSBPM as OWL (Cotton & Gillman, 2016) was quite straightforward. As already mentioned, the model is rather a taxonomy of statistical activities than a business model. This observation leads to the idea of reusing two important models available for the semantic web: SKOS and PROV-O, both W3C recommendations. SKOS (https://www.w3.org/TR/skos-reference/) is a model for expressing the structure and content of controlled vocabularies, thesauri, taxonomies and other concept schemes. PROV-O (https://www.w3.org/TR/prov-o/) is an OWL expression of a model about provenance metadata ("Provenance is information about entities, activities, and people involved in producing a piece of data or thing, which can be used to form assessments about its quality, reliability or trustworthiness"[1]).

The connection between PROV and the GSBPM is the notion of statistical activity, which can be seen as a special case of the general concept of activity defined in PROV. Consequently, we define (the prefix declarations are omitted for brevity):

```
gsbpm:StatisticalProductionActivity
        a rdfs:Class, owl:Class ;
        rdfs:label "Statistical production activity"@en ;
        rdfs:subClassOf prov:Activity.
```

This class is further specialized into *gsbpm:Phase* and *gsbpm:SubProcess*, which are also defined as sub-classes of *skos:Concept*, so that the actual instances (all GSBPM classes and sub-processes) can be organized as a *skos:ConceptScheme* (the GSBPM itself) using the usual SKOS properties. In particular, the hierarchies between classes and sub-processes is represented with standard *skos:broader/ skos:narrower* properties.

With this simple modeling, we can benefit from all the possibilities offered by SKOS and PROV-O: add labels and notes to our GSBPM components, attach provenance information to our statistical activities, etc. This is an illustration of how easy reusing is in LOD and how rewarding it is.

Expressing the GSIM as OWL (Dreyer, Duffes, Gillman, Scannapieco, & Tosco, 2016) proved more challenging, and can still be considered as work in progress.

First, the GSIM is much bigger than the GSBPM: it contains nearly 150 classes, and 600 properties. Second, the GSIM was initially formalized as a UML model (ref.). UML models do not have the same constraints regarding the naming of the properties of classes or relations between classes. For example, different UML classes may have identically named attributes, but that does not imply that these attributes have the same type or semantics. Even if the two UML properties are the same, they can have different cardinality constraints in the two classes. In OWL, properties are "first-class citizens" and their name is not scoped by a class where they would be defined.

OWL properties can be restricted on their domain (the "subject" class) or their range (the "object" class), as well as in terms of cardinalities, and this is also usually done globally, and not in a specific class context like in UML.

The main problem for translating the GSIM to OWL was thus to deal with the cases of UML properties or relations with identical names in order to determine if they were really the same property from the semantic point of view. Two approaches were used for that. The first one was manual, and served mainly as a proof of concept and a learning phase. The second approach aimed at creating an automated procedure for better auditability and reproducibility. This was obtained by writing an XSLT transformation operating on an UML exchange format known as XMI, incorporating a complex decision tree which is detailed in Dreyer et al. (2016).

Regarding the classes, the process was more direct: each UML class gave birth to an OWL class, and additional classes were created to materialize the packages described before (*gsim:Business*, *gsim:Exchange*, etc.). An overall *gsim:GSIMObject* was also added as the mother of all GSIM object classes.

It should be noted that translating GSIM in OWL allowed the discovery and repair of a few inconsistencies in the model, which is an interesting by-product in itself.

IMPACT ON LITERACY AND VISUALIZATION

LOSM provides a systematic and standard approach to implementing and querying a metadata scheme. As we have seen, metadata are critical for the understanding necessary to know enough to use data wisely (literacy) and the knowledge to apply techniques to tell a story using the data (visualization). So, to achieve literacy and promote good visualizations, a standard way to provide the necessary metadata is a critical step.

SPARQL is a W3C standard for querying RDF graphs (Prud'hommeaux & Seaborne, 2013). With statistical metadata presented as LOSM, the application of SPARQL to query statistical metadata provides a standard way to ask questions of the metadata for any statistical data set. The use of GSIM and GSBPM for specifying the underlying models of the metadata gives the users the language and relationships necessary to make meaningful queries.

This represents an advance in the use of metadata in statistics. Previously, each organization disseminating statistical data and metadata organized its metadata in its own way. Now, GSIM and GSBPM provide a standard means for organizing the metadata, LOSM provides a standard means to implement it, and SPARQL provides a standard means to query it.

This standard and comprehensive approach to statistical metadata should go far in promoting literacy and supporting the various means of visualizing statistical data.

CONCLUSION

In this chapter we described the concept of Linked Open Statistical Metadata (LOSM). LOSM follows both from the precepts on Linked Open Data and from considerations of statistical metadata from the statistical data community. The marriage of the two ideas provides the means to use semantic technologies from the W3C to the problem of discovering and describing statistical data. The discovery capability of the Web makes this approach particularly inviting.

Statistical visualization and literacy, the subject of this volume, are enhanced by the LOSM approach. Since metadata is a basic requirement and foundation for any educated use of data, LOSM technology is one way to achieve those. Educated use of statistical data is the goal of statistical literacy, and statistical visualization requires a thorough understanding of the data being presented.

REFERENCES

Beckett, D., & Berners-Lee, T. (2011). Turtle – terse RDF triple language. *W3*. Retrieved from: http://www.w3.org/TeamSubmission/turtle/

Berners-Lee, T. (2006). Linked data. *W3*. Retrieved from: http://www.w3.org/DesignIssues/LinkedData.html

Berners-Lee, T., Fielding, R., & Masinter, L. (2005). Uniform Resource Identifier (URI) Generic Syntax. *Network Working Group*. Retrieved from: http://tools.ietf.org/html/rfc3986

Berners-Lee, T., Masinter, L., & McCahill, M. (1994). Uniform resource locators (URL). *Network Working Group*. Retrieved from: http://www.ietf.org/rfc/rfc1738.txt

Brickley, D., & Guha, R. V. (2014). RDF schema 1.1. *W3C*. Retrieved from: http://www.w3.org/TR/rdf-schema/

Brickley, D., & Miller, L. (2014). FOAF vocabulary specification 0.99. *XMLNS*. Retrieved from: http://xmlns.com/foaf/spec/

Cotton, F., & Gillman, D. (2015). Modeling the Statistical Process with Linked Metadata. In S. Capadisli, F. Cotton, A. Haller, E. Calambokis, M. Scannapieco, & R. Troncy (Eds.), *Proceedings of the 3rd International Workshop on Semantic Statistics co-located with 14th International Semantic Web Conference* (vol. 1551). Retrieved December 19, 2016, from http://ceur-ws.org/Vol-1551/article-06.pdf

Dreyer, A., Duffes, G., Gillman, D., Scannapieco, M., & Tosco, L. (2016). An OWL Ontology for the Generic Statistical Information Model (GSIM) - Design and Implementation. In S. Capadisli, F. Cotton, A. Haller, E. Calambokis, M. Scannapieco, & R. Troncy (Eds.), *Proceedings of the 4th International Workshop on Semantic Statistics co-located with 15th International Semantic Web Conference* (vol. 1654). Retrieved December 19, 2016, from http://ceur-ws.org/Vol-1654/article-03.pdf

Linked Data. (n.d.). Linked data-connect distributed data accorss the Web. *Linked Data*. Retrieved from: http://linkeddata.org/

Lohr, S. (2010). *Sampling: Design and Analysis* (2nd ed.). Boston: Brooks/Cole Cengage Learning.

Obitko. (2007). RDF graph and syntax. *Obitko*. Retrieved from: http://www.obitko.com/tutorials/ontologies-semantic-web/rdf-graph-and-syntax.html

Prud'hommeaux, E., & Seaborne, A. (2013). SPARQL query language for RDF. *W3*. Retrieved from: http://www.w3.org/TR/rdf-sparql-query/

W3. (2013). Web ontology language (OWL). *W3C*. Retrieved from: https://www.w3.org/OWL/

W3. (2014). Resource description framework (RDF). *W3C*. Retrieved from: https://www.w3.org/RDF/

W3. (2015). Semantic web. *W3*. Retrieved from: http://www.w3.org/standards/semanticweb/

W3. (n.d.). Schema. *W3*. Retrieved from: http://www.w3.org/standards/xml/schema

W3C. (2017). *W3C*. Retrieved from: http://www.w3.org/

ENDNOTE

[1]   https://www.w3.org/TR/prov-dm/_

Compilation of References

ABS. (2014). *Big Data For Informed Decisions.* Australian Bureau of Statistics. Unpublished.

ABS. (2015). *Special Report: Big Data Plays a Big Role in the Future of Statistics.* Annual Report, 2014-15, Australian Bureau of Statistics. Retrieved from http://www.abs.gov.au/

ABS. (2016). *Freight Performance Measurement Project - Phase 2 Final Report.* Unpublished report submitted to Secretaries Data Group, December 2016, Australian Bureau of Statistics.

Ainley, J., Gould, R., & Pratt, D. (2015). Learning to reason from samples: Commentary from the perspectives of task design and the emergence of big data. *Educational Studies in Mathematics, 88*(3), 405–412. doi:10.1007/s10649-015-9592-4

Ainley, J., Pratt, D., & Hansen, A. (2006). Connecting Engagement and Focus in Pedagogic Task Design. *British Educational Research Journal, 32*(1), 23–38. doi:10.1080/01411920500401971

Alexa. (2017). *Site Overview: fao.org Traffic Statistics.* Alexa.

Alexander, M., & Walkenbach, J. (2013). *Microsoft Excel Dashboards and Reports.* Hoboken, NJ: Wiley.

Allington, M. (2016). *What is Power Query.* Retrieved October 20, 2016, from http://exceleratorbi.com.au/what-is-power-query

Almiron, M. G., Lopes, B., & Oliveira, A. L. C. (2010). On the numerical accuracy of spreadsheets. *Journal of Statistical Software, 34*(4). Retrieved from http://physics.usyd.edu.au/~wheat/teaching/cscp/resources/almiron_etal.pdf

Althausen, J. D., & Mieczkowski, T. M. (2001). The merging of criminology and geography into a course on spatial crime analysis. *Journal of Criminal Justice Education, 12*(2), 367–383. doi:10.1080/10511250100086181

American Statistical Association. (2014). *Curriculum Guidelines for Undergraduate Programs in Statistical Science.* Retrieved March 6, 2015, from http://www.amstat.org/education/pdfs/guidelines2014-11-15.pdf

Anthony, S. (2014). *Facebook's facial recognition software is now as accurate as the human brain, but what now?* ExtremeTech. Retrieved October 12, 2016, from http://www.extremetech.com/extreme/178777-facebooks-facial-recognition-software-is-now-as-accurate-as-the-human-brain-but-what-now

Apigian, C. H., & Gambill, S. E. (2004). Is Microsoft Excel 2003 ready for the statistics classroom? *Journal of Computer Information Systems, 45*(2), 27–35.

APSC. (2012). *Tackling wicked problems: A public policy perspective.* Australian Public Service Commission. Retrieved from http://www.apsc.gov.au/publications-and-media/archive/publications-archive/tackling-wicked-problems

Atif, A., Richards, D., Bilgin, A., & Marrone, M. (2013) Learning Analytics in Higher Education: A Summary of Tools and Approaches. In M. Gosper, J. Hedberg, H. Carter (Eds.), *Electric Dreams. Proceedings of the Australasian Society for Computers in Learning in Tertiary Education* (pp. 68-72).

Australian Curriculum, Assessment and Reporting Authority. (2016). *Australian Curriculum, Version 8.2.* Sydney, NSW: ACARA.

Australian Government, Department of Finance and Deregulation. (2013). *Big Data Strategy - Issues Paper.* Retrieved October 14, 2014 from http://www.finance.gov.au/files/2013/03/Big-Data-Strategy-Issues-Paper1.pdf

Bakker, A., Derry, J., & Konold, C. (2006). Using technology to support diagrammatic reasoning about center and variation. In A. Rossman & B. Chance (Eds.), *International Conference on Teaching of Statistics,* (vol. 7, pp. 1–6). Voorburg: International Statistical Institute.

Bakker, A., Kent, P., Derry, J., Noss, R., & Hoyles, C. (2008). Statistical inference at work: Statistical process control as an example. *Statistics Education Research Journal, 7*(2), 131–146. Retrieved from http://www.stat.auckland.ac.nz/~iase/serj/SERJ7%282%29_Bakker.pdf

Barcaroli, G., Nurra, A., Salamone, S., Scannapieco, M., Scarnò, M., & Summa, D. (2015). Internet as a Data Source in the Istat Survey on ICT in Enterprises. *Austrian Journal of Statistics, 44*(2), 31. doi:10.17713/ajs.v44i2.53

Barclay, E. M. (2017). Rural Crime. In A. Deckert & R. Sarre (Eds.), *The Australian and New Zealand Handbook of Criminology, Crime And Justice.* Palgrave MacMillan.

Barclay, E. M., Donnermeyer, J. F., & Jobes, P. C. (2004). The dark side of gemeinschaft; Criminality within rural communities. *Crime Prevention and Community Safety: An International Journal., 6*(3), 7–22. doi:10.1057/palgrave.cpcs.8140191

Batanero, C., & Diaz, C. (2010). Training teachers to teach statistics: What can we learn from research? *Statistique et Enseignement, 1*(1), 5–20.

Batanero, C., Arteaga, P., & Ruis, B. (2010). Statistical graphs produced by prospective teachers in comparing two distributions. In V. Durand-Guerrier, S. Soury-Lavergne, & F. Arzarello (Eds.), Proceeding of the Sixth Congress of the European Society for Research in Mathematics Education, (pp. 368-377). Lyon: ERME. Retrieved from www.inrp.fr/editions-electroniques/cerme6/

Batanero, C., Biehler, R., Maxara, C., Engel, J., & Vogel, M. (2005b). *Using simulation to bridge teachers content and pedagogical knowledge in probability.* Paper presented at the 15th ICMI study conference: the professional education and development of teachers of mathematics, Aguas de Lindoia, Brazil.

Batanero, C., Burrill, G., Reading, C., & Rossman, A. (Eds.). (2008). *Joint ICMI/IASE Study: Teaching Statistics in School Mathematics. Challenges for Teaching and Teacher Education. Proceedings of the ICMI Study 18 and 2008 IASE Round Table Conference.* Monterrey, Mexico: International Commission on Mathematical Instruction and International Association for Statistical Education.

Batanero, C., Godino, J. D., & Cañizares, M. J. (2005). Simulation as a tool to train Pre-service School Teachers. In J. Addler (Ed.), *Proceedings of ICMI First African Regional Conference* [CD]. Johannesburg, South Africa: International Commission on Mathematical Instruction. Retrieved from http://www.ugr.es/~batanero/ARTICULOS/CMIRCr.pdf

Beckett, D., & Berners-Lee, T. (2011). Turtle – terse RDF triple language. *W3*. Retrieved from: http://www.w3.org/TeamSubmission/turtle/

Belloni, A., Chernozhukov, V., & Hansen, C. (2014). High-dimensional methods and inference on structural and treatment effects. *The Journal of Economic Perspectives*, *28*(2), 29–50. doi:10.1257/jep.28.2.29

Ben-Zvi, D., Bakker, A., & Makar, K. (2015). Learning to reason from samples. *Educational Studies in Mathematics*, *88*(3), 291–303. doi:10.1007/s10649-015-9593-3

Ben-Zvi, D., & Friedlander, A. (1997). Statistical thinking in a technological environment. In J. Garfield & G. Burrill (Eds.), *Research on the role of technology in teaching and learning statistics* (pp. 45–55). Voorburg, The Netherlands: International Statistical Institute.

Ben-Zvi, D. (2006). Using Tinkerplots to scaffold students' informal inference and argumentation. In A. Rossman & B. Chance (Eds.), *Proceedings of the Seventh International Conference on Teaching Statistics*. Voorburg, The Netherlands: International Statistical Institute. Retrieved from http://iase-web.org/Conference_Proceedings.php?p=ICOTS_7_2006

Ben-Zvi, D. (2000). Toward understanding the role of technological tools in statistical learning. *Mathematical Thinking and Learning*, *2*(1 & 2), 127–155. doi:10.1207/S15327833MTL0202_6

Ben-Zvi, D., Aridor, K., Makar, K., & Bakker, A. (2012). Students emergent articulations of uncertainty while making informal statistical inferences. *ZDM Mathematics Education*, *44*(7), 913–925. doi:10.1007/s11858-012-0420-3

Bergen, S. (2016). *Melding Data with Social Justice in Undergraduate Statistics and Data Science Courses*. Paper presented at the IASE 2016 Roundtable Conference: Promoting understanding of statistics about society, Berlin, Germany.

Berger, R. (2007). Nonstandard operator precedence in Excel. *Computational Statistics & Data Analysis, 51*(6), 2788–2791. Retrieved from http://www.sciencedirect.com/science/article/pii/S0167947306003641

Berners-Lee, T. (2006). Linked data. *W3*. Retrieved from: http://www.w3.org/DesignIssues/LinkedData.html

Berners-Lee, T., Fielding, R., & Masinter, L. (2005). Uniform Resource Identifier (URI) Generic Syntax. *Network Working Group*. Retrieved from: http://tools.ietf.org/html/rfc3986

Berners-Lee, T., Masinter, L., & McCahill, M. (1994). Uniform resource locators (URL). *Network Working Group*. Retrieved from: http://www.ietf.org/rfc/rfc1738.txt

Bertin, J. (1967). *Semiology of Graphics: Diagrams, Networks, Maps*. Madison, WI: The University of Wisconsin Press.

Bertini, E., & Lalanne, D. (2004). Investigating and Reflecting on the Integration of Automatic Data Analysis and Visualization in Knowledge Discovery. *SIGKDD Explorations, 11*(2).

Bhutta, Z. A., Ahmed, T., Black, R. E., Cousens, S., Dewey, K., Giugliani, E., & Sachdev, H. et al. (2008). What works? Interventions for maternal and child undernutrition and survival. *Lancet, 371*(9610), 417–440. doi:10.1016/S0140-6736(07)61693-6 PMID:18206226

Bilgin, A. A., Primi, C., Chiesi, F., Lopez, M. V., Fabrizio, M. C., Quinn, V. F., . . . Graham, P. L. (2014). A Comparison of First Year Statistics Units' Content and Contexts in a Multinational Study: With a Case Study for the Validation of ASSIST in Australia. In *Topics from Australian Conferences on Teaching Statistics: OZCOTS 2008-2012* (pp. 189-210). Springer Science+Business Media.

Black, R. E., Allen, L. H., Bhutta, Z. A., Caulfield, L. E., De Onis, M., Ezzati, M., & Rivera, J. et al. (2008). Maternal and child undernutrition: Global and regional exposures and health consequences. *Lancet, 371*(9608), 243–260. doi:10.1016/S0140-6736(07)61690-0 PMID:18207566

Bolfarine, H., & Bussab, W. O. (2005). *Elementos de Amostragem*. São Paulo: Edgar Blücher.

Bovey, R., Wallentin, D., Bullen, S., & Green, J. (2009). *Professional Excel development: The definitive guide to developing applications using Microsoft Excel, VBA, and. Net* (2nd ed.). Upper Saddle River, NJ: Addison-Wesley.

Boyd, D., & Crawford, K. (2011). *Six provocations for big data*. Paper presented at: A Decade in Internet Time: Symposium on the Dynamics of the Internet and Society, Oxford, UK.

Braaksma, B., & Zeelenberg, K. (2015). Re-make/Re-model: Should big data change the modelling paradigm in official statistics? *Statistical Journal of the IAOS, 31*(2), 193–202. doi:10.3233/sji-150892

Bradley, L., & McDaid, K. (2009). Using Bayesian statistical methods to determine the level of error in large spreadsheets. In *Software Engineering-Companion Volume. 31st International Conference on Software Engineering* (pp. 351–354). IEEE. Retrieved from http://ieeexplore.ieee.org/xpls/abs_all.jsp?arnumber=5071019

Bradshaw, L. (2012). Big Data and What it Means. *Business Horizon Q.*, *7*, 32–35.

Braga, A. A., & Bond, B. J. (2008). Policing crime and disorder hot spots: A randomized controlled trial. *Criminology*, *46*(3), 577–608. doi:10.1111/j.1745-9125.2008.00124.x

Brandel, M. (1999). PC Software transforms the PC. *Computerword*, 62.

Brantingham, P. J., & Brantingham, P. L. (1984). *Patterns in crime*. New York: Macmillan.

Brantingham, P. L., & Brantingham, P. J. (1993). Nodes, paths and edges: Considerations on the complexity of crime and the physical environment. *Journal of Environmental Psychology*, *13*(1), 3–28. doi:10.1016/S0272-4944(05)80212-9

Braunschweig, K., Thiele, M., Eberius, J., & Lehner, W. (2015) Column-specific Context Extraction for Web Tables.*Proceedings of The 30th ACM/SIGAPP Symposium On Applied Computing*. doi:10.1145/2695664.2695794

Breton, R., Clews, G., Metcalfe, L., Milliken, N., Payne, C., Winton, J., & Woods, A. (2016). *Research indices using web scraped data*. Paper presented at the UNECE Meeting of the Group of Experts on Consumer Price Indices, Geneva, Switzerland.

Brickley, D., & Guha, R. V. (2014). RDF schema 1.1. *W3C*. Retrieved from: http://www.w3.org/TR/rdf-schema/

Brickley, D., & Miller, L. (2014). FOAF vocabulary specification 0.99. *XMLNS*. Retrieved from: http://xmlns.com/foaf/spec/

Bricklin, D. (2006). *When The Long Tail Wags The Dog*. Retrieved September 23, 2016, from http://danbricklin.com/log/2012_11_18.htm#lotus30

Bricklin, D. (2009a). *About Dan Bricklin's special short paper for the Harvard Business School advertising course*. Retrieved from http://www.bricklin.com/anonymous/bricklin-1978-visicalc-paper.pdf

Bricklin, D. (2009b). *The Idea*. Retrieved September 21, 2016, from http://www.bricklin.com/history/saiidea.htm

Bricklin, D. (2013). *30 years since Lotus 1-2-3*. Retrieved September 15, 2016, from http://danbricklin.com/log/2012_11_18.htm#lotus30

Bricklin, D. (2015). *Was VisiCalc the "first" spreadsheet?* Retrieved September 21, 2016, from http://www.bricklin.com/firstspreadsheetquestion.htm

Bright, D. A., Hughes, C. E., & Chalmers, J. (2012). Illuminating dark networks: A social network analysis of an Australian drug trafficking syndicate. *Crime, Law, and Social Change*, *57*(2), 151–176. doi:10.1007/s10611-011-9336-z

Brown, B., Chui, M., & Manyika, J. (2011). Are you ready for the era of 'big data'. *The McKinsey Quarterly*, *4*, 24–35.

Buelens, B., de Wolf, P.-P., & Zeelenberg, K. (2017). *Model-based estimation at Statistics Netherlands*. Discussion Paper, Statistics Netherlands, The Hague.

Bureau of Crime Statistics and Research (BOCSAR). (2016). *Crime Maps*. NSW Justice, Bureau of Crime Statistics and Research. Retrieved from http://www.bocsar.nsw.gov.au/Pages/bocsar_crime_stats/bocsar_crime_stats.aspx

Byerlee, D. R., Kyaw, D., Thein, U. S., & Kham, L. S. (2014). *Agribusiness models for inclusive growth in Myanmar: Diagnosis and ways forward*. Michigan State University, Department of Agricultural, Food, and Resource Economics.

Cahyadi, A., & Prananto, A. (2015). Reflecting design thinking: A case study of the process of designing dashboards. *Journal of Systems and Information Technology*, *17*(3), 286–306. doi:10.1108/JSIT-03-2015-0018

Caldas, M.S., & Silva, E.C. (2016). Fundamentos e aplicação do Big Data: como tratar informações em uma sociedade de yottabytes. *Bibl. Univ., Belo Horizonte, 3*(1), 65-85.

Callingham, R. (2011). Assessing statistical understanding in middle schools: Emerging issues in a technology-rich environment. *Technology Innovations in Statistics Education, 5*(1). Retrieved from http://escholarship.org/uc/item/3qr2p70t

Callingham, R. A., & Watson, J. M. (2005). Measuring statistical literacy. *Journal of Applied Measurement*, *6*(1), 19–47. PMID:15701942

Campbell, M. (2007). Number crunching without programming: The evolution of spreadsheet usability. *IEEE Annals of the History of Computing*. doi:10.1109/MAHC.2007.4338438

Carvalho, C., & Solomon, Y. (2012). Supporting statistical literacy: What do culturally relevant/realistic tasks show us about the nature of pupil engagement with statistics? *International Journal of Educational Research*, *55*, 57–65. doi:10.1016/j.ijer.2012.06.006

Carvalho, L. M. T., & Monteiro, C. E. F. (2012). Reflexões sobre implementação e uso de laboratório de informática na escola pública. *Roteiro*, *37*, 343–360.

Cavallo, A., & Rigobon, R. (2016). The Billion Prices Project: Using Online Prices for Measurement and Research. *Journal of Economic Perspectives, 30*(2),151–178.

Central Statistical Organization. (2017, February 2). *Welcome to CSO Website: Provider of official statistics of Myanmar*. Retrieved from http://www.csostat.gov.mm/

Chamberlain, J. M. (2013). *Understanding Criminological Research: A Guide to Data Analysis.* London: Sage. doi:10.4135/9781473913837

Chambers, C., & Scaffidi, C. (2010). Struggling to excel: A field study of challenges faced by spreadsheet users. In *2010 IEEE Symposium on Visual Languages and Human-Centric Computing.* Retrieved from http://ieeexplore.ieee.org/xpls/abs_all.jsp?arnumber=5635221

Chen, C., & Zhang, C.-Y. (2014). Data-intensive applications, challenges, techniques and technologies: A survey on Big Data. *Information Sciences, 275*(10), 314–347. doi:10.1016/j.ins.2014.01.015

Chien, C., & Mayer, A. (2015). *A New Analytical Platform to Explore Linked Data. Methodological Advisory Committee Paper.* Australian Bureau of Statistics.

Choi, H., & Varian, H. R. (2011). *Predicting the present with Google trends.* Retrieved from http://people.ischool.berkeley.edu/~hal/Papers/2011/ptp.pdf

Chu, K.-H., & Wipfi, H. (2013). Using Visualizations to Explore Network Dynamics. *Journal of Social Structure, 14.*

Clarke, F., & Chien, C.-H. (2015). Connectedness and Meaning: New Analytical Directions for Official Statistics. *Proceedings of the 3rd International Workshop on Semantic Statistics.* Bethlehem, PA: CEUR Workshop Proceedings. Retrieved from http://ceur-ws.org/Vol-1551/#article-02

Cleveland, W. S., & McGill, R. (1984). Graphical perception: Theory, experimentation and application to the development of graphical methods. *Journal of the American Statistical Association, 79*(387), 531–554. doi:10.1080/01621459.1984.10478080

Colver, D. (2004). Spreadsheet good practice: is there any such thing? In *European Spreadsheet Risk Interest Group.* Retrieved from http://arxiv.org/abs/1001.3967

Commission of the European Communities. (2001). *Making a European Area of Lifelong Learning a Reality.* Retrieved October 18, 2016 from http://aei.pitt.edu/42878/1/com2001_0678.pdf

Connor, D., & Davies, N. (2002). An international resource for learning and teaching. *Teaching Statistics, 24,* 62–65. doi:10.1111/1467-9639.00087

Connor, D., Davies, N., & Holmes, P. (2000). CensusAtSchool 2000. *Teaching Statistics, 22*(3), 66–70. doi:10.1111/1467-9639.00025

Conway, D. (2016). *The data science Venn diagram.* Retrieved October 12, 2016, from https://s3.amazonaws.com/aws.drewconway.com/viz/venn_diagram/data_science.html

Cotton, F., & Gillman, D. (2015). Modeling the Statistical Process with Linked Metadata. In S. Capadisli, F. Cotton, A. Haller, E. Calambokis, M. Scannapieco, & R. Troncy (Eds.), *Proceedings of the 3rd International Workshop on Semantic Statistics co-located with 14th International Semantic Web Conference* (vol. 1551). Retrieved December 19, 2016, from http://ceur-ws.org/Vol-1551/article-06.pdf

Courtland, R. (2015). *Gordon Moore: The Man Whose Name Means Progress: The visionary engineer reflects on 50 years of Moore's Law*. Retrieved September 15, 2016, from http://spectrum. ieee.org/computing/hardware/gordon-moore-the-man-whose-name-means-progress

Croll, G. J. (2008). In Pursuit of Spreadsheet Excellence. In *European Spreadsheet Risk Interest Group*. Retrieved from http://arxiv.org/abs/0806.3536

Croll, G. J. (2009). Spreadsheets and the financial collapse. In *European Spreadsheet Risk Interest Group*. Retrieved from http://arxiv.org/abs/0908.4420

Daas, P. J. H., Puts, M. J., Buelens, B., & van den Hurk, P. A. M. (2015). Big Data and Official Statistics. *Journal of Official Statistics*, *31*(2), 249–262. doi:10.1515/jos-2015-0016

Daas, P. J. H., & Puts, M. J. (2014). *Social media sentiment and consumer confidence*. Paper presented at the Workshop on using big data for Forecasting and Statistics, Frankfurt, Germany. Retrieved from https://www.ecb.europa.eu/events/pdf/conferences/140407/Daas_Puts_Sociale_media_cons_conf_Stat_Neth.pdf?409d61b733fc259971ee5beec7cedc61

Daas, P. J. H., Puts, M. J., Buelens, B., & van den Hurk, P. A. M. (2013). *big data and Official Statistics*. Paper presented at the Conference on New Techniques and Technologies for Statistics, Brussels, Belgium. Retrieved from http://www.cros-portal.eu/sites/default/files/NTTS2013fullPaper_76.pdf

Dangour, A. D., Hawkesworth, S., Shankar, B., Watson, L., Srinivasan, C. S., Morgan, E. H., . . . Waage, J. (2013). Can nutrition be promoted through agriculture-led food price policies? A systematic review. *BMJ Open, 3*(6). doi: 10.1136/bmj.f370310.1136/bmjopen-2013-002937

Davenport, T. H., & Patil, D. J. (2012). Data Scientist: The Sexiest Job Of the 21st Century. *Harvard Business Review*, *90*(10), 70–76. PMID:23074866

Day, L. (2013). Using statistics to explore cross-curricular and social issues opportunities. *Australian Mathematics Teacher*, *69*(4), 3–7.

De Jonge, E., van Pelt, M., & Roos, M. (2012). *Time patterns, geospatial clustering and mobility statistics based on mobile phone network data*. Discussion paper 2012-14, Statistics Netherlands. Retrieved from http://www.cbs.nl/NR/rdonlyres/010F11EC-AF2F-4138-8201-2583D461D2B6/0/201214x10pub.pdf

De Mauro, A., Greco, M., & Grimaldi, M. (2016). A formal definition of Big Data based on its essential features. *Library Review*, *65*(3), 122–135. doi:10.1108/LR-06-2015-0061

De Meersman, F., Seynaeve, G., Debusschere, M., Lusyne, P., Dewitte, P., Baeyens, Y., . . . Reuter, H. I. (2016). *Assessing the Quality of Mobile Phone Data as a Source of Statistics*. Paper presented at the European Conference on Quality in Official Statistics, Madrid, Spain. Retrieved from http://www.ine.es/q2016/docs/q2016Final00163.pdf

de Róiste, M., Gahagen, M., Morrison, P., Ralphs, M., & Bucknall, P. (2009). *Geovisualisation and policy: exploring the links*. Official Statistics Research Project Report, Statistics New Zealand.

de Rosa, M. (2016). *How to Analyze Big Data with Excel*. Retrieved September 22, 2016, from http://www.datasciencecentral.com/profiles/blogs/how-to-analyze-big-data-with-excel

De Veaux, R.D., Hoerl, R.W. & Snee, R. D. (2016, August). Big Data and the Missing Links. *Statistical Analysis and Data Mining: The ASA Data Science Journal*. doi: 10.1002/sam.11303

De Wolf, P.-P., & Zeelenberg, K. (2015). *Challenges for statistical disclosure control in a world with big data and open data*. Invited paper for the 60th World Statistics Congress. Retrieved from http://www.isi2015.org

Delors, J. (1996). *Learning: The treasure within Report to UNESCO of the International Commission on Education for the Twenty-first Century*. UNESCO Publishing.

Denning, G., Baroang, K., & Sandar, T. M. (2013). Rice Productivity Improvement in Myanmar: USAID. Michigan State University, Myanmar Development Resource Institute - Centre for Economic and Social Development (MDRI-CESD).

Diebold, F. X. (2012). *A Personal Perspective on the Origin(s) and Development of "Big Data": The Phenomenon, the Term, and the Discipline*. Retrieved from http://www.ssc.upenn.edu/~fdiebold/papers/paper112/Diebold_Big_Data.pdf

DIRD. (2015, December). *National Key Freight Routes Map*. Retrieved from Department of Infrastructure and Regional Development: http://maps.infrastructure.gov.au/KeyFreightRoute/

Donnermeyer, J. F. (2017). Rural Criminology and Criminological Theory. In The Routledge Companion to Criminological Theory and Concepts. New York: Taylor and Francis.

Dreyer, A., Duffes, G., Gillman, D., Scannapieco, M., & Tosco, L. (2016). An OWL Ontology for the Generic Statistical Information Model (GSIM) - Design and Implementation. In S. Capadisli, F. Cotton, A. Haller, E. Calambokis, M. Scannapieco, & R. Troncy (Eds.), *Proceedings of the 4th International Workshop on Semantic Statistics co-located with 15th International Semantic Web Conference* (vol. 1654). Retrieved December 19, 2016, from http://ceur-ws.org/Vol-1654/article-03.pdf

Duggirala, P. (2011, January 13). *A Brief History of Microsoft Excel – Timeline Visualization*. Retrieved October 17, 2016, from http://chandoo.org/wp/2010/01/13/history-of-excel-timeline/

DUL. (2017). *Introduction to Data Visualization: Visualization Types*. Retrieved from Duke University Libraries: http://guides.library.duke.edu/datavis/vis_types

Eck, J. (2005). Evaluation for lesson learning. In Handbook of Crime Prevention and Community Safety. Willan Publishing.

Eck, J. E., & Weisburd, D. (1995). Crime Places in Crime Theory. In Crime and Place. New York: Willow Tree Press.

Ekbia, H., Mattioli, M., Kouper, I., Arave, G., Ghazinejad, A., Bowman, T., & Sugimoto, C. R. et al. (2015). Big data, bigger dilemmas: A critical review. *Journal of the Association for Information Science and Technology*, *66*(8), 1523–1545. doi:10.1002/asi.23294

Engel, J. (2014). Open data, civil society and monitoring progress: Challenges for statistics education. In K. Makar, B. de Sousa, & R. Gould (Eds.), Sustainability in statistics education (Proceedings of the Ninth International Conference on Teaching Statistics, Flagstaff, USA). Voorburg, The Netherlands: International Association for Statistical Education and the International Statistical Institute. Retrieved from http://iase-web.org/icots/9/proceedings/pdfs/ICOTS9_4F4_ENGEL.pdf

English, L. D. (2014). Statistics at play. *Teaching Children Mathematics, 21,* 37–44.

Espinel, M. C., Bruno, A., & Plasencia, I. (2008). Statistical graphs in the training of teachers. In C. Batanero, G. Burrill, C. Reading, & A. Rossman (Eds.), Joint ICMI/IASE Study: Teaching Statistics in School Mathematics. Challenges for Teaching and Teacher Education. Proceedings of the ICMI Study 18 and 2008 IASE Round Table Conference. Monterrey, Mexico: International Commission on Mathematical Instruction and International Association for Statistical Education. Retrieved from: http://iase-web.org/Conference_Proceedings.php?p=ICME_11_2008.

EU (European Union). (2009, March31). Regulation on European statistics, 2009. *Official Journal of the European Union, L, 87,* 164–173. Retrieved from http://data.europa.eu/eli/reg/2009/223/2015-06-08

EU (European Union). (2005). *Code of Practice for European Statistics.* Retrieved from http://epp.eurostat.ec.europa.eu/portal/page/portal/quality/code_of_practice

European Statistical System Committee (ESCC). (2013). *Scheveningen Memorandum on Big Data and Official Statistics.* Available at: http://ec.europa.eu/eurostat/documents/42577/43315/Scheveningen-memorandum-27-09-13

Eurostat. (2016). *Statistics Explained - Glossary: Enterprise.* Retrieved from http://ec.europa.eu/eurostat/statistics-explained/index.php/Glossary:Enterprise

Fan, J., Han, F., & Liu, H. (2014). Challenges of big data analysis. *National Science Review, 1*(2), 293–314. doi:10.1093/nsr/nwt032 PMID:25419469

Ferrandino, J. (2015). Using GIS to Apply Learning across the Undergraduate Criminal Justice Curriculum. *Journal of Criminal Justice Education, 26*(1), 74–93. doi:10.1080/10511253.2014.925567

Few, S. (2004). *Show Me the Numbers: Designing Tables and Graphs to Enlighten.* Oakland: Analytics Press.

Few, S. (2006). *Information Dashboard Design: The Effective Visual Communication of Data.* Sebastopol: O'Reilly Media.

Few, S. (2009). *Now You See It: Simple Visualization Techniques for Quantitative Analysis.* Oakland: Analytics Press.

Few, S. (2013). *Information dashboard design: Displaying data for at-a-glance monitoring* (2nd ed.). Burlingame: Analytics Press.

Finzer, W. (2001). Fathom: Dynamic Data. Emeryville, CA: Key Curriculum. Retrieved from www.keypress.com/x5656.xml

Finzer, W. (2012). *The data science education dilemma*. Paper presented at the IASE Roundtable Conference: Technology in Statistics Education: Virtualities and Realities, Cebu, The Philippines.

Finzer, W. (2005). *Fathom* [Computer software]. Emeryville, CA: Key Curriculum Press.

Finzer, W., & Erickson, T. (2005). Curriculum innovations based on census microdata: A meeting of statistics, mathematics and social science. In G. Burrill & M. Camden (Eds.), *Curricular development in statistics education. International Association for Statistical Education (IASE) Roundtable, Lund, Sweden, 2004* (pp. 190–203). Voorburg, The Netherlands: International Statistical Institute.

Fisher, D., DeLine, R., Czerwinski, M., & Drucker, S. (2012). Interactions with big data analytics. *Interactions*, 50–59. doi:10.1145/2168931.2168943

Food and Agriculture Organization - Economic and Social Development Department. (2017). *Statistics*. Retrieved from http://www.fao.org/economic/ess/ess-home/ess-about/en/

Food and Agriculture Organization / World Food Programme. (2009). *FAO/WFP Crop and Food Security Assessment Mission to Myanmar*. Rome: Food and Agriculture Organization of the United Nations and World Food Programme.

Food and Agriculture Organization / World Food Programme. (2016). *FAO/WFP Crop Food Security Assessment Mission to Myanmar*. Rome: Food and Agriculture Organization of the United Nations and World Food Programme.

Food and Agriculture Organization Statistics. (2017). *How many visit to FAOSTAT per month?* (T. C. Hlaing, Ed.). FAO.

Food and Agriculture Organization, International Fund for Agricultural Development, & World Food Programme. (2015). The State of Food Insecurity in the World 2015. Meeting the 2015 international hunger targets: Taking stock of uneven progress. Rome: Food and Agriculture Organization of the United Nations, International Fund for Agricultural Development and World Food Programme.

Food and Agriculture Organization. (1996). *Rome Declaration on World Food Security, World Food Summit*. Retrieved from http://www.fao.org/docrep/003/w3613e/w3613e00.HTM

Food and Agriculture Organization. (2006). *Food Security Policy Brief*. FAO.

Food and Agriculture Organization. (2008a). *E-Learning to meet the needs of agriculture and food security professionals*. Retrieved 28.07.2016, from Food and Agriculture Organization of the United Nations and European Unions: http://www.fao.org/elearning/#/elc/en/Course/FC

Food and Agriculture Organization. (2008b). *An Introduction to the Basic Concepts of Food Security*. EC - FAO Food Security Programme. Retrieved from www.foodsec.org/docs/concepts_guide.pdf

Food and Agriculture Organization. (2009). *Declaration of the World Summit on Food Security*. United Nations of Food and Agriculture Organization.

Food and Agriculture Organization. (2016). *Food security indicators*. Retrieved 3.8.2016, from Food and Agriculture Organization of the United Nations, and other international organizations http://www.fao.org/economic/ess/ess-fs/ess-fadata/en/#.V6GrW6J5Lqk

Food and Agriculture Organization. (2017). *Statistics at FAO*. Retrieved from http://www.fao.org/statistics/en/

Food Security Information Network. (2013a). Food Security Information Network. *Food Security Monitoring Bulletin*.

Food Security Information Network. (2013b). *Resilience Measurement*. Paper presented at the Technical Working Group Consultative Meeting, Rome, Italy.

Forbes, S., Ralphs, M., Goodyear, R., & Pihama, N. (2011). *Visualising official statistics*. Statistics New Zealand.

Franklin, C., Kader, G., Mewborn, D., Moreno, J., Peck, R., Perry, M., & Scheaffer, R. (2007). Guidelines for assessment and instruction in statistics education (GAISE) report: A preK-12 curriculum framework. Alexandria, VA: American Statistical Association. Retrieved from http://www.amstat.org/education/gaise/

Frankston, B. (1999). *RE: VisiCalc history*. Retrieved from http://dssresources.com/history/frankston4151999a.html

Friel, S. N., Curcio, F. R., & Bright, G. W. (2001). Making sense of graphs: Critical factors influencing comprehension and instructional implications. *Journal for Research in Mathematics Education, 32*(2), 124–158. doi:10.2307/749671

Fry, H., Kettering, S., & Marshall, S. (1999). *Teaching and Learning in Higher Education: Enhancing Academic Practice*. Kogan Page.

Fujita, K. (2003). Policy-Initiated Expansion of Summer Rice under Constraints of Rural Credit in Myanmar in the 1990s -Perspectives from a Village Study in Ayeyarwaddy Division. The Economic Review, 54(4).

Fylstra, D. (2016). *Frontline Systems company history*. Retrieved September 22, 2016, from http://www.solver.com/frontline-systems-company-history

Fylstra, D., Lasdon, L., Watson, J., & Waren, A. (1998). Design and use of the Microsoft Excel Solver. *Interfaces, 28*(5), 29–55. doi:10.1287/inte.28.5.29

GAISE College Report ASA Revision Committee. (2016). *Guidelines for assessment and instruction in statistics education College Report 2016*. Alexandria, VA: American Statistical Association. Retrieved from http://www.amstat.org/education/gaise/

GAISE Report. (2005). Guidelines for Assessment and Instruction in Statistics Education (GAISE) Report, A Pre-K-12 curriculum framework, August 2005 –American Statistical Association. Retrieved Out, 30, 2016, from http://it.stlawu.edu/~rlock/gaise/

Gal, I., & Garfield, J. (Eds.). (1997). *The Assessment Challenge in Statistics Education.* Amsterdam: IOS Press and the International Statistical Institute.

Gal, I. (2002). Adults' statistical literacy: Meanings, components, responsibilities. *International Statistical Review, 70*(1), 1–25. doi:10.1111/j.1751-5823.2002.tb00336.x

Gal, Y. (2000). *Adult Numeracy Development: Theory, Research, Practice.* Cresskill, NJ: Hampton Press.

Garfield, J., & Ben-Zvi, D. (2007). How students learn statistics revisited: A current review of research on teaching and learning statistics. *International Statistical Review, 75*(3), 372–396. doi:10.1111/j.1751-5823.2007.00029.x

Garfield, J., & Gal, I. (1999). Teaching and Assessing Statistical Reasoning. In L. Stiff (Ed.), *Developing Mathematical Reasoning in Grades K-12* (pp. 207–219). Reston, VA: National Council Teachers of Mathematics.

Garfinkel, S. L. (n.d.). *Improv.* Retrieved September 22, 2016, from https://simson.net/clips/1991/1991.NW.Improv.html

Gartner Orlando (FL). (2012). *Gartner Says Big Data Creates Big Jobs: 4.4 Million IT Jobs Globally to Support Big Data By 2015.* Retrieved February 8, 2015 from http://www.gartner.com/newsroom/id/2207915

Gattuso, L. (2008). Mathematics in a statistical context? In C. Batanero, G. Burrill, C. Reading, & A. Rossman (Eds.), *Teaching statistics in school mathematics. Challenges for teaching and teacher education. Proceedings of the Joint ICMI Study 18 and 2008 IASE Round Table Conference.*

Gelman, A., Carlin, J. B., Stern, H. S., Dunson, D. B., Vehtari, A., & Rubin, D. B. (2013). *Bayesian Data Analysis (3rd ed.).* Chapman and Hall/CRC.

Gelper, S., Wilms, I., & Croux, C. (2015). Identifying demand effects in a large network of product categories. *Journal of Retailing, 92*(1), 25–39. doi:10.1016/j.jretai.2015.05.005

Ghattas, H., Barbour, J. M., Nord, M., Zurayk, R., & Sahyoun, N. R. (2013). Household food security is associated with agricultural livelihoods and diet quality in a marginalized community of rural Bedouins in Lebanon. *The Journal of Nutrition, 143*(10), 1666–1671. doi:10.3945/jn.113.176388 PMID:23946340

Glance, D. (2013). *Solving Big Data's big skills shortage.* Perth: The Conversation. Retrieved February 8, 2015 from http://theconversation.com/solving-big-datas-big-skills-shortage-20352

Gorodov, E. Y., & Gubarev, V. V. (2013). Analytical review of data visualization methods in application to big data. *Journal of Electrical and Computer Engineering, 2013*, 1–7. doi:10.1155/2013/969458

Goswami, S., Chan, H. C., & Kim, H. W. (2008). The role of visualization tools in spreadsheet error correction from a cognitive fit perspective. *Journal of the Association for Information Systems, 9*(6), 321–343. Retrieved from http://165.132.10.17/dslab/Journal/JAIS 2008.pdf

Gould, R. (2010). Statitics and the modern student. *International Statistical Review, 78*(2), 297–315. doi:10.1111/j.1751-5823.2010.00117.x

Gould, R. (2016). *Preparing secondary teachers to teach data science: lessons learned.* Paper presented at the IASE 2016 Roundtable Conference: Promoting understanding of statistics about society, Berlin, Germany.

Grad, B. (2007). The creation and the demise of VisiCalc. *IEEE Annals of the History of Computing, 3*, 20–31. doi:10.1109/MAHC.2007.4338439

Graves, S. (1997). *Maximum Likelihood Regression on Censored, Experimental Data Using a Spreadsheet Program* (No. 164). Retrieved from http://cqpi.engr.wisc.edu/system/files/r164.pdf

Great Speculations. (2013). *An Overview Why Microsoft's Worth $42.* Retrieved September 15, 2016, from http://www.forbes.com/sites/greatspeculations/2013/01/09/an-overview-why-microsofts-worth-42/

Groves, R. M. (2011). 2011, Three eras of survey research. *Public Opinion Quarterly, 75*(5), 861–871. doi:10.1093/poq/nfr057

Haggblade, S., & Boughton, D. (2013). *A Strategic Agricultural Sector and Food Security Diagnostic for Myanmar.* Michigan State University, Department of Agricultural, Food, and Resource Economics.

Haggblade, S., Boughton, D., Cho, K. M., Denning, G., Kloeppinger-Todd, R., Oo, Z., & Wilson, S. et al. (2014). Strategic Choices Shaping Agricultural Performance and Food Security in Myanmar. *Journal of International Affairs, 67*(2), 55.

Hammer, J., Garcia-Molina, H., Cho, J., Crespo, A., & Aranha, R. (1997) Extracting Semistructured Information from the Web. *Proceedings of the Workshop on Management of Semistructured Data held in conjunction with ACM SIGMOD'97*, 18-25.

Hancock, C., Kaput, J. J., & Goldsmith, L. T. (1992). Authentic inquiry with data: Critical barriers to classroom implementation. *Educational Psychologist, 27*(3), 337–364. doi:10.1207/s15326985ep2703_5

Heerschap, N. M., Ortega Azurduy, S. A., Priem, A. H., & Offermans, M. P. W. (2014). *Innovation of tourism statistics through the use of new big data sources.* Paper prepared for the Global Forum on Tourism Statistics, Prague, Czech Republic. Retrieved from http://www.tsf2014prague.cz/assets/downloads/Paper%201.2_Nicolaes%20Heerschap_NL.pdf

Heiberger, R., & Neuwirth, E. (2009). *R through Excel: A spreadsheet interface for statistics, data analysis, and graphics.* Dordrecht: Springer. doi:10.1007/978-1-4419-0052-4

Hesse, R., & Scerno, D. (2009). How Electronic Spreadsheets Changed the World. *Interfaces, 39*(2), 159–167. doi:10.1287/inte.1080.0376

Hilbert, M. (2012). How much information is there in the "information society"? *Significance, 9*(4), 8–12. doi:10.1111/j.1740.2012.00584.x

Hilbert, M., & López, P. (2012b). How to Measure the World's Technological Capacity to Communicate, Store, and Compute Information Part II: Measurement Unit and Conclusions 1. *International Journal of Communication, 6*, 936–955. Retrieved from http://ijoc.org/index.php/ijoc/article/view/1563/741

Hilbert, M., & López, P. (2012a). How to measure the world's technological capacity to communicate, store, and compute information, part I: Results and scope. *International Journal of Communication, 6*(1), 956–979.

Hlaing, T. C., Kuwabara, T., Cuong, N. H., Bounnad, C., Kubo, T., & Ito, S. (2009). International Competitiveness in Rice Exports under High Oil Prices. 農業経営研究, *47*(2), 202-205.

Hoekstra, R., ten Bosh, O., & Harteveld, F. (2012). Automated data collection from web sources for official statistics: First experiences. *Journal of the International Association for Official Statistics, 28*(3-4), 99–111.

Hoerl, R.W., Snee, R. D. & De Veaux, R.D. (2014). Applying Statistical Thinking to 'Big Data' Problems. *Wiley Interdisciplinary Reviews: Computational Statistics, 6*, 222–232. doi: 10.1002/wics.1306

Horton, N., Baumer, B., & Wickham, H. (2014). *Teaching precursors to data science in introductory and second courses in statistics.* Paper presented at the ICOTS-9: Sustainability in statistics education, Flagstaff, AZ.

Huang, T., Fildes, R., & Soopramanien, D. (2014). The value of competitive information in forecasting FMCG retail product sales and the variable selection problem. *European Journal of Operational Research, 237*(2), 738–748. doi:10.1016/j.ejor.2014.02.022

Huff, D. (1954). *How to Lie with Statistics.* New York, NY: W.W. Norton.

Hurwitz, J., Nugent, A., Halper, F., & Kaufman, M. (2013). *Big data for dummies.* Hoboken, NJ: Wiley.

IASE Satellite. (2011). *International Association for Statistical Education: Statistics Education and Outreach.* Dublin, Ireland: Author.

IASE Satellite. (2013). *The Joint IASE/IAOS Satellite Conference on Statistics Education and Outreach: Statistics Education for Progress: Youth and Official Statistics.* Macao, China: Author.

ICOTS-8. (2010). *International Conferences on Teaching Statistics: Data and Context in Statistics Education: Towards an Evidence-Based Society.* Ljubljana, Slovenia: Author.

Iliinsky, N., & Steele, J. (2011). *Designing Data Visualizations*. Sebastopol, CA: O'Reilly Media, Inc.

Imbernón, F. (2010). *Formação continuada de professores*. Porto Alegre, Brazil: Artmed.

Innabi, H. (2006). Factors considered by secondary students when judging the validity of a given statistical generalization. In A. Rossman & B. Chance (Eds.), *Proceedings of the Seventh International Conference on Teachings Statistics* (ICOTS 7) (pp. 1-6). Retrieved October 13, 2016, from https://www.stat.auckland.ac.nz/~iase/publications/17/2B1_INNA.pdf

Institute for Democracy and Electoral Assistance & Integrated Household Living Conditions Assistance. (2007). Integrated Household Living Conditions Assistance Survey in Myanmar: Poverty Profile. Yangon, Myanmar: IDEA International Institute (Canada), IHLCA Project Technical Unit, Ministry of National Planning and Economic Development (MNPED) and United Nations Development Program (UNDP).

Integrated Household Living Conditions Assistance. (2011). Integrated Household Living Conditions Assistance Survey in Myanmar (2009-2010) - Poverty Profile. Yangon, Myanmar: Ministry of National Planning and Economic Development (MNPED), Swedish International Development Cooperation Agency (SIDA), United Nations Children Emergency Fund (UNICEF) and United Nations Development Program (UNDP).

International Food Policy Research Institute. (2016). *Global Nutrition Report 2016: From Promise to Impact: Ending Malnutrition by 2030* [Press release]. Retrieved from http://ebrary.ifpri.org/utils/getfile/collection/p15738coll2/id/130354/filename/130565.pdf

Iram, U., & Butt, M. S. (2004). Determinants of household food security: An empirical analysis for Pakistan. *International Journal of Social Economics*, *31*(7/8), 753–766. doi:10.1108/03068290410546011

ISI (International Statistical Institute). (1985). *Declaration on Professional Ethics*. Retrieved from http://www.isi-web.org/about-isi/professional-ethics

Jacobs, A. (2009). The Pathologies of Big Data. *Queue, 7*(6), 36–44. doi:10.1145/1563821.1563874

James, L. (2013). *Defining Open Data*. Retrieved from http://blog.okfn.org/2013/10/03/defining-open-data/

Jelen, B. (2010). *PowerPivot for the data analyst: Microsoft Excel 2010*. Indianapolis, IN: Que.

Jenkins, J. C., & Scanlan, S. J. (2001). Food security in less developed countries, 1970 to 1990. *American Sociological Review*, *66*(5), 718–744. doi:10.2307/3088955

Jobes, P. C., Donnermeyer, J. F., Barclay, E. M., & Weinand, H. (2004). A Structural Analysis of Social Disorganisation and Crime in Rural Communities in Australia. *Australian and New Zealand Journal of Criminology*, *37*(1), 114–140. doi:10.1375/acri.37.1.114

Jones, N. J., Brown, S. L., Wanamaker, K. A., & Greiner, L. E. (2014). A quantitative exploration of gendered pathways to crime in a sample of male and female juvenile offenders. *Feminist Criminology*, *9*(2), 113–136. doi:10.1177/1557085113501850

Kakuta, S. (2016). Prospect of Open Data on Labor Division of Scientific Research. *MACRO REVIEW*, *28*(1), 39–41.

Kaplan, D., Overvoorde, P., & Shoop, E. (2014). *Integrating big data into the science curriculum.* Paper presented at the ICOTS-9: Sustainability in statistics education, Flagstaff, AZ.

Kapor, M. (2007). Recollections on Lotus 1-2-3: Benchmark for spreadsheet software. *IEEE Annals of the History of Computing*. doi:10.1109/MAHC.2007.4338440

Keeling, K. B., & Pavur, R. J. (2004). Numerical accuracy issues in using excel for simulation studies. *Proceedings of the 2004 Winter Simulation Conference*. doi:10.1109/WSC.2004.1371492

Keim, D., Mansmann, F., Schneidewind, J., Thomas, J., & Ziegler, H. (2008). Visual Analytics: Scope and Challenges. In *Visual Data Mining* (pp. 76–90). Berlin: Springer. doi:10.1007/978-3-540-71080-6_6

Kievit, R. A., Frankenhuis, W. E., Waldorp, L. J., & Borsboom, D. (2013). Simpsons paradox in psychological science: A practical guide. *Frontiers in Psychology*, *4*, 513. doi:10.3389/fpsyg.2013.00513 PMID:23964259

Kitchin, R. (2014). Big Data, new epistemologies and paradigm shifts. *Big Data & Society, 1*(1), 1–12. doi:10.1177/2053951714528481

Kitchin, R. (2014). *The data revolution: Big data, open data, data infrastructures and their consequences.* London: Sage. doi:10.4135/9781473909472

KNAW (Koninklijke Nederlandse Akademie van Wetenschappen: Royal Netherlands Academy of Arts and Sciences). (2016). *Thirteen selected facilities and three honourable mentions.* Retrieved from https://www.knaw.nl/en/advisory-work/copy_of_knaw-agenda-grootschalige-onderzoeksfaciliteiten-13-geselecteerde-faciliteiten?set_language=en

Knüsel, L. (1998). On the accuracy of statistical distributions in Microsoft Excel 97. *Computational Statistics & Data Analysis, 26*, 375–377. Retrieved from http://www.sciencedirect.com/science/article/pii/S0167947397817562

Knüsel, L. (2005). On the accuracy of statistical distributions in Microsoft Excel 2003. *Computational Statistics & Data Analysis.* Retrieved from http://www.sciencedirect.com/science/article/pii/S0167947304000337

Knüsel, L. (2011). *On the Accuracy of Statistical Distributions in Microsoft Excel 2010.* Retrieved from http://www.csdassn.org/software_reports/Excel2011.pdf

Kolb, D. (1984). *Experiential Learning: Experience as the source of Learning and development.* Prentice-Hall.

Konold, C., Higgins, T., Russell, S. J., & Khalil, K. (2015). Data seen through different lenses. *Educational Studies in Mathematics*, *88*(3), 305–325. doi:10.1007/s10649-013-9529-8

Konold, C., & Kazak, S. (2008). Reconnecting data and chance. *Technology Innovations in Statistics Education*, *2*, 1–37.

Konold, C., & Miller, C. (2005). TinkerPlots: Dynamic data exploration. Emeryville, CA: Key Curriculum. Retrieved from www.keypress.com/x5715.xml

Konold, C. (2007). Designing a data analysis tool for learners. In M. C. Lovett & P. Shah (Eds.), *Thinking with data* (pp. 267–291). New York: Lawrence Erlbaum.

Konold, C., & Miller, C. D. (2011). *TinkerPlots: Dynamic data exploration* [Computer software, Version 2.2]. Emeryville, CA: Key Curriculum Press.

Koussoulakou, A., & Kraak, M. J. (1995). Spatio-temporal maps and cartographic communication. *The Cartographic Journal*, *29*(2), 101–108. doi:10.1179/caj.1992.29.2.101

Kudo, T., Yoshihiro Hayashi, Y., Watanabe, M., Morikawa, T., Furutani, T., & Iwasaki, M. (2014). *Challenges and issues in developing real-world curriculum for data scientists in Japan*. Paper presented at the ICOTS-9: Sustainability in statistics education, Flagstaff, AZ.

Kurosaki, T., Okamoto, I., Kurita, K., & Fujita, K. (2004). *Rich Periphery, Poor Center: Myanmar's Rural Economy under Partial Transition to a Market Economy*. Academic Press.

Kwak, J. (2013). *The Importance of Excel*. Retrieved September 16, 2016, from https://baselinescenario.com/2013/02/09/the-importance-of-excel/

Kyaw, D. (2006). *Rural poverty analysis in Myanmar: a micro level study in the dry zone* (Ph. D. dissertation). School of Environment, Resources and Development, Asian Institute of Technology, Bangkok, Thailand.

Kyaw, D. (2009). Rural Households' Food Security Status and Coping Strategies to Food Insecurity in Myanmar. V.R.F. Series, Institute of Developing Economies, Japan External Trade Organization, 444, 83.

Kyaw, D., & Routray, J. K. (2006). Gender and rural poverty in Myanmar: A micro level study in the dry zone. *Journal of Agriculture and Rural Development in the Tropics and Subtropics*, *107*(2), 103–114.

Kyng, T. J., Bilgin, A. A., & Puang-Ngern, B. (2016). *Big Data, Data Science, Computer Science and Statistics Education*. Paper presented at the OZCOTS 2016, Canberra, Australia.

Kyng, T., Bilgin, A., & Puang-Ngern, B. (2015). *Data Science: Is it statistics or computer science? Statistics education in the age of big data*. IASE 2015 Satellite Conference on Advances in statistics education: developments, experiences, and assessments, Rio de Janeiro, Brazil.

LaChance, N. (2016). *Facebook's Facial Recognition Software Is Different From The FBI's. Here's Why*. Retrieved October 12, 2016, from http://www.npr.org/sections/alltechconsidered/2016/05/18/477819617/facebooks-facial-recognition-software-is-different-from-the-fbis-heres-why

Laney, D. (2001). 3D data Management: Controlling data volume, velocity, and variety. *Application Delivery Strategies, 949*, 4. Retrieved from http://blogs.gartner.com/doug-laney/files/2012/01/ad949-3D-Data-Management-Controlling-Data-Volume-Velocity-and-Variety.pdf

Lassinantti, J. (2016). *Re-use of open data from public sector-Towards a definition*. Information Polity.

Laverty, W. H., Miket, M. J., & Kelly, I. W. (2002). Simulation of hidden Markov models with EXCEL. *Journal of the Royal Statistical Society Series D: The Statistician, 51*(1), 31–40. doi:10.1111/1467-9884.00296

Lawson, B., Baker, K., Powell, S., & Foster-Johnson, L. (2009). A comparison of spreadsheet users with different levels of experience. *Omega, 37*(3), 579–590. doi:10.1016/j.omega.2007.12.004

Lazer, D., Kennedy, R., King, G., & Vespignani, A. (2014). The parable of Google flu: Traps in big data analysis. *Science, 343*(14), 1203–1205. doi:10.1126/science.1248506 PMID:24626916

Lehrer, R., Jones, R. S., & Kim, M. J. (2014). Model-based informal inference. In K. Makar, B. de Sousa, & R. Gould (Eds.), Sustainability in statistics education. Proceedings of the Ninth International Conference on Teaching Statistics (ICOTS9, July, 2014), Flagstaff, Arizona, USA. Voorburg, The Netherlands: International Statistical Institute. Available at http://icots.info/9/proceedings/pdfs/ICOTS9_6E3_PRODROMOU.pdf

Leon, L., Kalbers, L., Coster, N., & Abraham, D. (2012). A spreadsheet life cycle analysis and the impact of Sarbanes–Oxley. *Decision Support Systems, 54*(1), 452–460. doi:10.1016/j.dss.2012.06.006

Levy, D., Lee, D., Chen, H., Kauffman, R. J., & Bergen, M. (2011). Price points and price rigidity. *The Review of Economics and Statistics, 93*(4), 1417–1431. doi:10.1162/REST_a_00178

Linked Data. (n.d.). Linked data-connect distributed data accorss the Web. *Linked Data*. Retrieved from: http://linkeddata.org/

Liu, B. (2011). *Web Data Mining: Exploring Hyperlinks, Contents and Usage Data* (2nd ed.). Springer-Verlag. doi:10.1007/978-3-642-19460-3

Liu, Z., Jiangz, B., & Heer, J. (2013). imMens: Real-time Visual Querying of Big Data. *Eurographics Conference on Visualization (EuroVis), 32*(3), 421-430. doi:10.1111/cgf.12129

Livelihoods and Food Security Trust Fund. (2012). *Baseline survey results: July 2012*. Retrieved 16.8.2016, from Livelihoods and Food Security Trust Fund http://www.lift-fund.org/downloads/LIFT%20Baseline%20Survey%20Report%20-%20July%202012.pdf

Livelihoods and Food Security Trust Fund. (2016). Undernutrition in Myanmar, Part 1: A Secondary Analysis of LIFT 2013 Household Survey Data. In *Learn A Consortium of: Save the Children, ACF, Helen Keller International funded by Livelihoods and Food Security Trust Fund (Vol. 1): Livelihoods and Food Security Trust Fund.* Save the Children, ACF, Helen Keller International.

Lohr, S. (2010). *Sampling: Design and Analysis* (2nd ed.). Boston: Brooks/Cole Cengage Learning.

Lohr, S. (2013). The Origins of 'Big Data': An Etymological Detective Story. *The New York Times.* Retrieved from http://bits.blogs.nytimes.com/2013/02/01/the-origins-of-big-data-an-etymological-detective-story/?_r=0

Lopes, C. E. (2003). *O conhecimento profissional dos professores e suas relações com Estatística e Probabilidade na Educação Infantil* (Doctoral dissertation). Faculdade de Educação, Universidade Estadual de Campinas, Campinas, Brasil.

Lutsky, N. (2013). *Connected Worlds: Statistical literacy in art, science, public health, and social issues.* Paper presented at the 59th WSC, Hong Kong.

Lynn, J. (2016). *Healthcare Analytics Biggest Competitor – Excel Posted.* Retrieved April 10, 2016, from http://www.hospitalemrandehr.com/2016/03/16/healthcare-analytics-biggest-competitor-excel/

MacEachren, A. M., & Kraak, M. J. (1997). Exploratory cartographic visualization: Advancing the agenda. *Computers & Geosciences, 23*(4), 335–343. doi:10.1016/S0098-3004(97)00018-6

Mackinlay, J. (1986). Automating the design of graphical presentations of relational information. *ACM Transactions on Graphics, 5*(2), 110–141. doi:10.1145/22949.22950

Makar, K., & Fielding-Wells, J. (2011). Teaching teachers to teach statistical investigations. In C. Batanero, G. Burrill, & C. Reading (Eds.), *Teaching statistics in school mathematics – Challenges for teaching and teacher education: A Joint ICMI/IASE Study* (pp. 347–358). New York: Springer. doi:10.1007/978-94-007-1131-0_33

Makar, K. (2010). Teaching primary teachers to teach statistical inquiry: The uniqueness of initial experiences. In C. Reading (Ed.), *Data and context in statistics education: Towards an evidence-based society. Proceedings of the Eighth International Conference on Teaching Statistics (ICOTS-8, July, 2010), Ljubljana, Slovenia.* Voorburg, The Netherlands: International Statistical Institute.

Makar, K., & Rubin, A. (2009). A framework for thinking about informal statistical inference. *Statistics Education Research Journal, 8*(1), 82–105.

Maltz, M. (1998). Visualizing Homicide: A Research Note. *Journal of Quantitative Criminology, 15*(4), 397–410. doi:10.1023/A:1023081805454

Maltz, M. D. (2010). *Look before you analyze: Visualizing data in criminal justice. In Handbook of Quantitative Criminology* (pp. 25–52). Springer New York.

Mann, M. E. (2013). *The hockey stick and the climate wars: Dispatches from the front lines.* Columbia University Press. doi:10.7312/columbia/9780231152556.001.0001

Manor, H., Ben-Zvi, D., & Aridor, K. (2013). Students' emergent reasoning about uncertainty exploring sampling distributions in an "integrated approach". In J. Garfield (Ed.), *Proceedings of the Eighth International Research Forum on Statistical Reasoning, Thinking, and Literacy* (SRTL8) (pp. 18–33). Minneapolis, MN: University of Minnesota.

Manyika, J., Chui, M., Brown, B., Bughin, J., Dobbs, R., Roxburgh, C., & Hung Byers, A. (2011). *Big Data: The Next Frontier for Innovation, Competition, and Productivity. Report of the McKinsey Global Institute.* McKinsey & Company.

Manyika, J., Chui, M., Brown, B., Bughin, J., Dobbs, R., Roxburgh, C., & Hung Byers, A. (2011). *Big Data: The next frontier for innovation, competition, and Productivity.* San Francisco, CA: McKinsey Global Institute.

Marr, B. (2016). *Big Data: 33 Brilliant And Free Data Sources For 2016.* Academic Press.

Martins, M. N. P., Monteiro, C. E. F., & Queiroz, T. N. (2013). Compreensões sobre amostra ao manipular dados no software *TinkerPlots*: Um caso de uma professora polivalente. *Revista Eletrônica de Educação, 7*(2), 317–342. doi:10.14244/19827199763

Mason, J. B. (2002). *Measuring hunger and malnutrition.* Paper presented at the International Scientific Symposium, Rome, Italy.

Mattessich, R. (n.d.). *Spreadsheet: Its First Computerization (19611964).* Retrieved September 15, 2016, from http://dssresources.com/history/mattessichspreadsheet.htm

Mattessich, R. (1961). Budgeting Models and System Simulation Author. *Accounting Review, 36*(3), 384–397. Retrieved from http://www.jstor.org/stable/242869

Mattessich, R. (1964). *Simulation of the firm through a budget computer program.* Homewood, IL: Irwin.

Mayer-Schonberger, V., & Cukier, K. (2013). *Big Data: A revolution that will transform how we live, work and think.* Boston: Houghton Mifflin Harcourt.

Mayer-Schönberger, V., & Cukier, K. (2013). *Big Data: A Revolution that will transform how we live, work, and think.* New York: Houghton Mifflin Harcourt Publishing Company.

McAfee, A., & Brynjolfsson, E. (2012). Big data: The management revolution. *Harvard Business Review, 90*(10), 60–68. PMID:23074865

McCosker, A., & Wilken, R. (2014). Rethinking big data as visual knowledge: The sublime and the diagrammatic in data visualisation. *Visual Studies, 29*(2), 155–164. doi:10.1080/1472 586X.2014.887268

McCullough, B. D. (2008). Microsoft Excel's "Not The Wichmann–Hill" random number generators. *Computational Statistics & Data Analysis, 52*(10), 4587–4593. doi:10.1016/j. csda.2008.03.006

McCullough, B. D., & Wilson, B. (1999). On the accuracy of statistical procedures in Microsoft Excel 97. *Computational Statistics & Data Analysis, 31*, 27–37. Retrieved from http://www.sciencedirect.com/science/article/pii/S0167947308001606

McCullough, B. D., & Wilson, B. (2002). On the accuracy of statistical procedures in Microsoft Excel 2000 and Excel XP. *Computational Statistics & Data Analysis, 40*, 713–721. 10.1016/S0167-9473(02)00095-6

McNamara, A., & Hansen, M. (2014). *Teaching data science to teenagers*. Paper presented at the ICOTS-9: Sustainability in statistics education, Flagstaff, AZ.

Mélard, G. (2014). On the accuracy of statistical procedures in Microsoft Excel 2010. *Computational Statistics, 29*(5), 1095–1128. doi: 10.1007/s00180-014-0482-5

Meletiou-Mavrotheris, M., & Paparistodemou, E. (2015). Developing students reasoning about samples and sampling in the context of informal inferences. *Educational Studies in Mathematics, 88*(3), 385–404. doi:10.1007/s10649-014-9551-5

Meyer, D. Z., & Avery, L. M. (2008). Excel as a Qualitative Data Analysis Tool. *Field Methods, 21*(1), 91–112. doi:10.1177/1525822X08323985

Michell, M. P. L. (2000). Smoke rings: Social network analysis of friendship groups, smoking and drug-taking. *Drugs Education Prevention & Policy, 7*(1), 21–37. doi:10.1080/dep.7.1.21.37

Microsoft. (1994). *Visual Basic User's Guide*. Redmond: Microsoft.

Microsoft. (1997). *Getting results with Microsoft Office 97*. Microsoft.

Microsoft. (2004). *Description of improvements in the statistical functions in Excel 2003 and in Excel 2004 for Mac*. Retrieved September 28, 2016, from https://support.microsoft.com/en-us/kb/828888

Microsoft. (2010a). *Overview of PivotTable and PivotChart reports*. Retrieved September 26, 2016, from https://support.office.com/en-US/article/Overview-of-PivotTable-and-PivotChart-reports-00a5bf71-65cb-49f9-b321-85bb7b0b06c2

Microsoft. (2010b). *What's new in Excel 2010*. Retrieved August 28, 2013, from https://support.office.com/en-US/article/What-s-New-in-Excel-2010-44316790-A115-4780-83DB-D003E4A2B329

Microsoft. (2013a). *Power Map for Excel*. Retrieved September 26, 2016, from https://support.office.com/en-US/article/Power-Map-for-Excel-82D65BD7-70C9-48A3-8356-6B0E82472D74

Microsoft. (2013b). *What's new in Excel 2013*. Retrieved June 4, 2013, from https://support.office.com/en-US/article/What-s-new-in-Excel-2013-1CBC42CD-BFAF-43D7-9031-5688EF1392FD

Microsoft. (2015). *Days of the week before March 1, 1900 are incorrect in Excel*. Retrieved September 21, 2016, from https://support.microsoft.com/en-za/kb/214058

Microsoft. (2016a). *Access 2016 specifications*. Retrieved September 23, 2016, from https://support. office.com/en-US/article/Access-2016-specifications-0cf3c66f-9cf2-4e32-9568-98c1025bb47c

Microsoft. (2016b). *Create a Data Model in Excel*. Retrieved September 22, 2016, from https:// blogs.office.com/2012/08/23/introduction-to-the-data-model-and-relationships-in-excel-2013/

Microsoft. (2016c). *Create a forecast in Excel 2016 for Windows*. Retrieved September 23, 2016, from https://support.office.com/en-US/article/Create-a-forecast-in-Excel-2016-for-Windows-22c500da-6da7-45e5-bfdc-60a7062329fd

Microsoft. (2016d). *Create a funnel chart*. Retrieved September 26, 2016, from https://support. office.com/en-us/article/Create-a-funnel-chart-ba21bcba-f325-4d9f-93df-97074589a70e?ui=en-US&rs=en-US&ad=US

Microsoft. (2016e). *Data Model specification and limits*. Retrieved October 21, 2016, from https://support.office.com/en-US/article/Data-Model-specification-and-limits-19AA79F8-E6E8-45A8-9BE2-B58778FD68EF

Microsoft. (2016f). *Excel specifications and limits*. Retrieved September 23, 2016, from https:// support.office.com/en-US/article/Excel-specifications-and-limits-CA36E2DC-1F09-4620-B726-67C00B05040F

Microsoft. (2016g). *Get started with 3D Maps*. Retrieved September 22, 2016, from https:// support.office.com/en-us/article/Get-started-with-3D-Maps-6b56a50d-3c3e-4a9e-a527-eea62a387030?ui=en-US&rs=en-US&ad=US

Microsoft. (2016h). *Large Address Aware capability change for Excel*. Retrieved October 15, 2016, from https://support.microsoft.com/en-us/kb/3160741

Microsoft. (2016i). *Power Query (informally known as " M ") formula categories*. Retrieved October 20, 2016, from https://msdn.microsoft.com/library/mt253322

Microsoft. (2016j). *Switch between various sets of values by using scenarios*. Retrieved September 23, 2016, from https://support.office.com/en-US/article/switch-between-various-sets-of-values-by-using-scenarios-2068afb1-ecdf-4956-9822-19ec479f55a2

Microsoft. (2016k). *Use Goal Seek to find the result you want by adjusting an input value*. Retrieved September 23, 2016, from https://support.office.com/en-US/article/Use-Goal-Seek-to-find-the-result-you-want-by-adjusting-an-input-value-320cb99e-f4a4-417f-b1c3-4f369d6e66c7

Microsoft. (2016l). *Use the Analysis ToolPak to perform complex data analysis*. Retrieved September 23, 2016, from https://support.office.com/en-US/article/use-the-analysis-toolpak-to-perform-complex-data-analysis-f77cbd44-fdce-4c4e-872b-898f4c90c007

Microsoft. (2016m). *What's new in Excel 2016 for Windows*. Retrieved September 22, 2016, from https://support.office.com/en-US/article/What-s-new-in-Excel-2016-for-Windows-5fdb9208-ff33-45b6-9e08-1f5cdb3a6c73

Microsoft. (2016n). *What's the difference between Office 365 and Office 2016?* Retrieved September 26, 2016, from https://support.office.com/en-us/article/What-s-the-difference-between-Office-365-and-Office-2016-ed447ebf-6060-46f9-9e90-a239bd27eb96?ui=en-US&rs=en-US&ad=US

Miles, J. N. V. (2005). Confirmatory factor analysis using Microsoft Excel. *Behaviour Research Methods, 37*(4), 672–676. Retrieved from http://www.jeremymiles.co.uk/mestuff/publications/p36.pdf

Miller, S. (2014). Collaborative Approaches Needed to Close the Big Data Skills Gap. *Journal of Organization Design, 3*(1), 26–30. doi:10.7146/jod.9823

MIMU. (2014-2016). *Baseline Datasets-Myanmar Information Management Unit.* Retrieved 27.1.2017, from http://www.themimu.info/baseline-datasets

MMSIS. (2015). *Statistical Database: from Myanmar Statistical Information Service.* Retrieved from http://www.mmsis.gov.mm/

Moore, G. E. (1965). Cramming more components onto integrated circuits. *Electronics, 38*(8), 114–117. doi:10.1109/N.2006.4785860

Morton, K., Bunker, R., Mackinlay, J., Morton, R., & Stolte, C. (2012). Dynamic workload driven data integration in Tableau. In Proceedings of the Special Interest Group on Management of Data Conference (pp. 807-816). Retrieved from https://research.tableau.com/paper/dynamic-workload-driven-data-integration-tableau

Muller, R. (2004). Global warming bombshell. *Technology Review, 15*, 14–15.

Myanmar Census 2014. (2015). *The 2014 Myanmar Population and Housing Census: The Union Report* (Vol. 2). Myanmar: Department of Population, Ministry of Immigration and Population.

Myanmar Times. (2016, December 9). *Myanmar is still the third-most malnourished country in Southeast Asia by ghatt WFP Myanmar.* Retrieved from http://www.mmtimes.com/index.php/national-news/18665-myanmar-is-still-the-third-most-malnourished-country-in-southeast-asia.html

Nash, J. (2006). Spreadsheets in statistical practice—another look. *The American Statistician, 60*(3), 287–289. doi:10.1198/000313006X126585

National Council of Teachers of Mathematics. (2000). Principles and standards for school mathematics. Reston, VA: National Council of teachers of Mathematics.

National Highway Traffic Safety Administration. (2016). *Fatality Analysis Reporting System (FARS): Analytical User's Manual 1975-2015* (No. DOT HS 812 315). Retrieved from ftp://ftp.nhtsa.dot.gov/FARS/FARS-DOC/Analytical User Guide/USERGUIDE-2015.pdf

Neyeloff, J. L., Fuchs, S. C., & Moreira, L. B. (2012). Meta-analyses and Forest plots using a Microsoft Excel spreadsheet: Step-by-step guide focusing on descriptive data analysis. *BMC Research Notes, 5*, 52. doi:10.1186/1756

Nicholson, J., Ridgway, J., & McCusker, S. (2013). Getting real statistics into all curriculum subject areas: Can technology make this a reality? *Technology Innovations in Statistics Education, 7*(2). Retrieved from http://escholarship.org/uc/item/7cz2w089

Nicholson, J., Ridgway, J., & McCusker, S. (2013). *Statistical literacy and multivariate thinking.* Paper presented at the 59th WSC, Hong Kong.

Nickerson, D. W., & Rogers, T. (2014). Political campaigns and big data. *The Journal of Economic Perspectives, 28*(2), 51–74. doi:10.1257/jep.28.2.51

Nikić, B., Špeh, T., & Klun, Z. (2015). Usage of new data sources at SURS. *UNECE Workshop on Statistical Data Collection: Riding the Data Deluge.*

Noll, J., & Hancock, S. (2015). Proper and paradigmatic metonymy as a lens for characterizing student conceptions of distributions and sampling. *Educational Studies in Mathematics, 88*(3), 361–383. doi:10.1007/s10649-014-9547-1

North, D., Gal, I., & Zewotir, T. (2014). Building capacity for developing statistical literacy in a developing country: Lessons learned from an intervention. *Statistics Education Research Journal, 13*(2), 15–27.

Nygaard, R. (2016). *Alternative data collection methods - focus on online data.* Paper presented at the UNECE Meeting of the Group of Experts on Consumer Price Indices.

O*NET Resource Centre. (2016). Retrieved October 12, 2016 from http://www.onetcenter.org/overview.html

Oancea, B., & Dragoecsu, R. M. (2014). Integrating R and Hadoop for big data analysis. *Revista Romana de Statistica, 2*(62), 83–94.

Obitko. (2007). RDF graph and syntax. *Obitko.* Retrieved from: http://www.obitko.com/tutorials/ontologies-semantic-web/rdf-graph-and-syntax.html

OECD. (2001). *Lifelong Learning for All: Policy Directions.* OECD Publishing. Retrieved October 18, 2016 from http://www.oecd.org/officialdocuments/publicdisplaydocumentpdf/?cote=DEELSA/ED/CERI/CD(2000)12/PART1/REV2&docLanguage=En

OECD. (2016). *Equations and Inequalities: Making Mathematics Accessible to All, PISA.* Paris: OECD Publishing. doi:10.1787/9789264258495-en

Okamoto, I. (2009). Transformation of the Rice Marketing System after Market Liberalization in Myanmar. In K. Fujita, F. Mieno & I. Okamoto (Eds.), The economic transition in Myanmar after 1988: Market economy versus state control (Vol. 1, pp. 216-245). NUS Press associated by Kyoto University Press.

Oostrom, L., Walker, A. N., Staats, B., Slootbeek-Van Laar, M., Ortega Azurduy, S., & Rooijakkers, B. (2016). *Measuring the internet economy in The Netherlands: a big data analysis.* Discussion Paper 2016-14, Statistics Netherlands, Heerlen. Retrieved from https://www.cbs.nl/nl-nl/achtergrond/2016/41/measuring-the-internet-economy-in-the-netherlands

Oo, T. H. (2012). Devising a new agricultural strategy to enhance Myanmar's rural economy. In N. Cheesman, M. Skidmore, & T. Wilson (Eds.), *Myanmar's transition: Opening, obstacles and opportunities* (pp. 156–181). Singapore: Institute of Southeast Asian Studies.

Organization for Economic Cooperation and Development. (2016). *Open Government Data-Rebooting Public Service Delivery: How can open government data help to drive innovation? In OECD Comparative Study* (p. 26). OECD.

Ose, S. O. (2016). Using Excel and Word to Structure Qualitative Data. *Journal of Applied Social Science, 10*(2), 147–162. doi:10.1177/1936724416664948

Panko, R. R. (2006). *Spreadsheets and Sarbanes-Oxley: Regulations, risks, and control frameworks.* San Jose. Retrieved from http://citeseerx.ist.psu.edu/viewdoc/download?doi=10.1.1.87.101&rep=rep1&type=pdf

Panko, R. R. (2007). Thinking is Bad: Implications of Human Error Research for Spreadsheet Research and Practice. In *European Spreadsheet Risk Interest Group*. Retrieved from http://arxiv.org/abs/0801.3114

Panko, R. R., & Ordway, N. (2005). Sarbanes-Oxley: What about all the spreadsheets? In *European Spreadsheet Risk Interest Group*. Retrieved from http://arxiv.org/abs/0804.0797

Pardo, R. (2000). *The world's first electronic spreadsheet*. Retrieved September 15, 2016, from http://www.renepardo.com/articles/spreadsheet.pdf

Peltier, J. (2008a). *Making Regular Charts from Pivot Tables*. Retrieved September 26, 2016, from https://support.office.com/en-US/article/Overview-of-PivotTable-and-PivotChart-reports-00a5bf71-65cb-49f9-b321-85bb7b0b06c2

Peltier, J. (2008b). *Why I don't like Excel 2007 charts*. Retrieved September 26, 2016, from http://peltiertech.com/why-i-dont-like-excel-2007-charts/

Peltier, J. (2011a). *Excel box and whisker diagrams (Box plots)*. Retrieved September 2, 2013, http://peltiertech.com/excel-box-and-whisker-diagrams-box-plots/

Peltier, J. (2011b). *Excel waterfall charts (Bridge charts)*. Retrieved September 2, 2013, from http://peltiertech.com/excel-waterfall-charts-bridge-charts/

Peltier, J. (2016a). *Microsoft Excel Charting Survey*. Retrieved from http://peltiertech.com/microsoft-excel-charting-survey/

Peltier, J. (2016b). *PeltierTech charts for Excel 3.0. Shrewsbury: PeltierTech*. Retrieved from http://peltiertech.com/Utility30/

Petkau, J. (2014). President's Message. *SSC Liason, 28*(4), 3–7. PMID:24707580

Pfannkuch, M. (2006). Informal inferential reasoning. In A. Rossman & B. Chance (Eds.), *Working Cooperatively in Statistics Education. Proceedings of the Seventh International Research Conference on Teaching Statistics*. Voorburg, The Netherlands: International Statistical Institute.

Phannkuch, M., Arnold, P., & Wild, C. J. (2015). What I see is not quite the way it really is: Students' emergent reasoning about sampling variability. *Statistics Education Research Journal, 13*(2), 343–360.

Pinkerton, B. (1994). Finding what people want: Experiences with the web crawler.*Proceedings of the Second World-Wide Web Conference.*

Planning Department. (2012). *Monthly Expenditure of Urban and Rural Households by State and Region.* Retrieved 15.09.2015, from Central Statistical Organization, Ministry of Planning and Finance: http://mmsis.gov.mm/statHtml/statHtml.do

Planning Department. (2014). *Statistical Data: Share of Gross Domestic Product (At Current Producers' Prices).* Retrieved 14.09.2015, from Central Statistical Organization, Ministry of Planning and Finance: http://mmsis.gov.mm/statHtml/statHtml.do

Polidoro, F., Giannini, R., Lo Conte, R., Mosca, S., & Rossetti, F. (2015). Web scraping techniques to collect data on consumer electronics and airfares for Italian HICP compilation. *Statistical Journal of the IAOS, 31*(2), 165–176. doi:10.3233/sji-150901

Ponte, J. P. (2012). Estudando o conhecimento e o desenvolvimento profissional do professor de matemática. In *Teoria, crítica y prática de la educación matemática* (pp. 83–98). Barcelona: GRAO.

Ponte, J. (2011). Preparing teachers to meet the challenges of statistics education. In C. Batanero, G. Burrill, & C. Reading (Eds.), *Teaching statistics in school mathematics – Challenges for teaching and teacher education: A joint ICMI/IASE study* (pp. 299–309). New York: Springer. doi:10.1007/978-94-007-1131-0_29

Powell, S. G., Baker, K. R., & Lawson, B. (2009b). Errors in Operational Spreadsheets. *Journal of Organizational and End User Computing, 21*(3), 24–36. doi:10.4018/joeuc.2009070102

Powell, S., Baker, K., & Lawson, B. (2009a). Impact of errors in operational spreadsheets. *Decision Support Systems, 47*, 126–132. doi:10.1016/j.dss.2009.02.002

Power, D. J. (2004). *A Brief History of Spreadsheets.* Retrieved September 15, 2016, from http://dssresources.com/history/sshistory.html

Pratt, D., Davies, N., & Connor, D. (2011). The role of technology in teaching and learning statistics. In C. Batanero, G. Burrill, & C. Reading (Eds.), *Teaching statistics in school mathematics – Challenges for teaching and teacher education: A joint ICMI/IASE study* (pp. 97–107). Dordrecht, The Netherlands: Springer. doi:10.1007/978-94-007-1131-0_13

Prodromou, T. (2014). Developing a modelling approach to probability using computer-based simulations. In E. J. Shernoff & B. Sriraman (Eds.), *Probabilistic Thinking: Presenting Plural Perspectives* (pp. 417–439). New York, NY: Springer; doi:10.1007/978-94-007-7155-0_22

Prodromou, T. (2008). *Connecting Thinking About Distribution* (Unpublished Doctoral Dissertation). University of Warwick, UK.

Prodromou, T. (2011). Students' emerging inferential reasoning about samples and sampling. In *Biennial Conference of the Australian Association of Mathematics Teachers AAMT Proceedings*. Retrieved December 30, 2016, from http://www.merga.net.au/documents/RP_PRODROMOU_ MERGA34-AAMT.pdf

Prodromou, T. (2014). Drawing inferences from data visualisations. *International Journal of Secondary Education, 2*(4), 66-72. Retrieved from http://article.sciencepublishinggroup.com/ pdf/10.11648.j.ijsedu.20140204.12.pdf

Prud'hommeaux, E., & Seaborne, A. (2013). SPARQL query language for RDF. *W3*. Retrieved from: http://www.w3.org/TR/rdf-sparql-query/

Puang-Ngern, B. (2015). *Big data and its implications for the statistics profession and statistics education* (Unpublished Master of Research Thesis). Macquarie University, Sydney, Australia.

Radzikowski, B., & Śmietanka, A. (2016). Online CASE CPI. *First International Conference on Advanced Research Methods and Analytics, CARMA2016*. doi:10.4995/CARMA2016.2016.3133

Rammohan, A., & Pritchard, B. (2014). The role of landholding as a determinant of food and nutrition insecurity in rural Myanmar. *World Development, 64*, 597–608. doi:10.1016/j. worlddev.2014.06.029

Rao, C. R. (1975). Teaching of statistics at the secondary level: An interdisciplinary approach. *International Journal of Mathematical Education in Science and Technology, 6*(2), 151–162. doi:10.1080/0020739750060203

Ratcliffe, J. (2008). *Intelligence-Led Policing*. Cullompton, UK: Willan Publishing.

Reimsbach-Kounatze, C. (2015). *The proliferation of "big data" and implications for official statistics and statistical agencies: a preliminary analysis. OECD Digital Economy Papers 245*. Paris: OECD; doi:10.1787/20716826

Ridgway, J., & Nicholson, J. (2010). Pupils reasoning with information and misinformation. In C. Reading (Ed.), Data and context in statistics education: Towards an evidence-based society. (Proceedings of the Eighth International Conference on the Teaching of Statistics, Ljubljana, Slovenia). Voorburg, The Netherlands: International Statistical Institute. Retrieved from http:// iase-web.org/documents/papers/icots8/ICOTS8_9A3_RIDGWAY.pdf

Ridgway, J., & Smith, A. (2013). Open data, official statistics and statistics education – Threats, and opportunities for collaboration. In S. Forbes & B. Phillips (Eds.), *Proceedings of the Joint IASE/IAOS Satellite Conference*. Macao, China: IASE/IAOS.

Ridgway, J., Nicholson, J., & McCusker, S. (2013). 'Open Data' and the semantic web require a rethink on statistics teaching. *Technology Innovations in Statistics Education, 7*(2). Retrieved from http://escholarship.org/uc/item/6gm8p12m

Ridgway, J., Nicholson, J., & McCusker, S. (2013). 'Open Data' and the Semantic Web Require a Rethink on Statistics Teaching. *Technology Innovations in Statistics Education, 7*(2). Retrieved from: http://escholarship.org/uc/item/6gm8p12m

Ridgway, J., Nicholson, J., & Sean McCusker, S. (2014). *Exploring "white flight" via open data and big data*. Paper presented at the ICOTS-9: Sustainability in statistics education, Flagstaff, AZ.

Ridgway, J. (2015). Implications of the data revolution for statistics education. *International Statistical Review*. doi:10.1111/insr.12110

Ripley, B. D. (2002). Statistical methods need software: A view of statistical computing. In *Opening lecture of Royal Statistical Society*. Retrieved from http://www.stats.ox.ac.uk/~ripley/RSS2002.pdf

Rosegrant, M. W., & Cline, S. A. (2003). Global food security: Challenges and policies. *Science*, *302*(5652), 1917–1919. doi:10.1126/science.1092958 PMID:14671289

Rosling, H. (2010). *Hans Rosling's 200 Countries, 200 Years, 4 Minutes*. Retrieved from https://www.youtube.com/watch?v=jbkSRLYSojo

Royal Flying Doctor Service of Australia. (2009). *Look! Up in the sky. Teacher Handbook. Pilot Version*. Sydney: Author.

Rubin, A., Bruce, B., & Tenney, Y. (1991). Learning about sampling: Trouble at the core of statistics. In D. Vere-Jones (Ed.), *Proceedings of the Third International Conference on Teaching Statistics* (vol. 1, pp. 314–319). Voorburg: International Statistical Institute.

Rubin, A., Hammerman, J. K., & Konold, C. (2006). Exploring informal inference with interactive visualisation software. In A. Rossman & B. Chance (Eds.), *Working Cooperatively in Statistics Education. Proceedings of the Seventh International Research Conference on Teaching Statistics*. Voorburg, The Netherlands: International Statistical Institute.

Russell, S. J., Corwin, R., & Economopoulos, K. (1997). *Sorting and classifying data: Does it walk, crawl, or swim?* Palo Alto, CA: Dale Seymour Publications.

Saldanha, L., & Thompson, P. (2002). Conception of sample and their relationship to statistical inference. *Educational Studies in Mathematics*, *51*(3), 257–270. doi:10.1023/A:1023692604014

Saldanha, L., & Thompson, P. (2007). Exploring connections between sampling distributions and Statistical inference: An analysis of students' engagement and Thinking in the context of instruction involving repeated Sampling. *International Electronic Journal of Mathematics Education*, *2*(3), 270–297.

Sampson, R. J., Raudenbush, S., & Earls, F. (1997). Neighborhoods and Violent Crime: A Multilevel Study of Collective Efficacy. *Science*, *277*(5328), 918–924. doi:10.1126/science.277.5328.918 PMID:9252316

Sampson, R. J., Winship, C., & Knight, C. (2013). Overview of: 'Translating Causal Claims: Principles and Strategies for Policy-Relevant Criminology. *Criminology & Public Policy*, *12*(4), 587–616. doi:10.1111/1745-9133.12027

Samuel, S. (n.d.). History of Data Visualization. *Data Visualization: What it is and why it matters*. Retrieved from http://www.sas.com/en_au/insights/big-data/data-visualization.html

SAS Institute Inc. (2014). *Data visualization techniques: From basics to big data with SAS Visual Analytics* [White Paper]. Retrieved 14 November 2016 from http://www.sas.com/content/ dam/ SAS/en_us/doc/whitepaper1/data-visualization-techniques-106006.pdf

Scannapieco, M., Virgillito, A., & Zardetto, D. (2013). *Placing Big Data in Official Statistics: A Big Challenge?* Paper presented at the conference on New Techniques and Technologies for Statistics, NTTS 2013, Bruxelles, Belgium.

Schwab-McCoy, A. (2016). *Developing A First-Year Seminar Course in Statistics and Data Science.* Paper presented at the IASE 2016 Roundtable Conference: Promoting understanding of statistics about society, Berlin, Germany.

Seila, A. F. (2004). Spreadsheet simulation. In *Proceedings - Winter Simulation Conference* (pp. 41–48). doi:10.1109/WSC.2006.323034

Sharma, A., & Ellis, C. (2016). *Excel and big data.* Retrieved September 21, 2016, from https://blogs. office.com/2016/06/23/excel-and-big-data/?Ocid=Excel Editorial_Social_FBPAGE_Microsoft Excel - microsoftexcel_20160726_527474728

Shaughnessy, J. M., Chance, B., & Kranendonk, H. (2009). *Focus on high school mathematics: Reasoning and sense making in statistics and probability.* Reston, VA: National Council of Teachers of Mathematics.

Shaw, D. J. (2007). *World food security.* Academic Press.

Shaw, C. R., & McKay, H. D. (1942). *Juvenile Delinquency in Urban Areas.* Chicago: University of Chicago Press.

Sherman, L. W. (2013). The rise of evidence-based policing: Targeting, testing, and tracking. *Crime and Justice, 42*(1), 377–451. doi:10.1086/670819

Shi, N., He, X., & Tao, J. (2009). Understanding statistics and statistics education: A Chinese perspective. *Journal of Statistics Education, 17*(3), 1–8. PMID:21603584

Shwe, T. M., & Hlaing, T. C. (2011). *Scoping study on food security and nutrition information in Myanmar. National Consultant's Report of the Project: Support to the EC Programme on Linking Information and Decision-Making to Improve Food Security for Selected Greater Mekong Sub-Regional Countries.* Rome: FAO.

Signoretta, P., Chamberlain, J. M., & Hillier, J. (2014). A Picture Is Worth 10,000 Words: A Module to Test the Visualization Hypothesis in *Quantitative Methods Teaching. Enhancing Learning in the Social Sciences, 6*(2), 90–104. doi:10.11120/elss.2014.00029

Simon, P. (2014). *The visual organization: Data visualization, big data, and the quest for better decisions.* Wiley.

Smith, A. (2013). *Emerging trends in data visualisation: Implications for producers of official statistics.* Paper presented at the 59th WSC, Hong Kong. Retrieved from http://www.statistics. gov.hk/wsc/IPS019-P3-S.pdf

Song, I.-Y., & Zhu, Y. (2015). Big data and data science: What should we teach? *Expert Systems: International Journal of Knowledge Engineering and Neural Networks*. doi:10.1111/exsy.12130

Souza, L. O., & Lopes, C. E. (2011). O Uso de Simuladores e a Tecnologia no Ensino da Estocástica. *Boletim de Educação Matemática, 24*(40), 659–677. Retrieved February 16, 2016, from http://www.redalyc.org/pdf/2912/291222113003.pdf

Souza, L.O., Lopes, C.E., & Phannkuch, M. (2015). Collaborative profesional development for statistics teaching: A case study of two middle-school mathematics teachers. *Statistics Education Research Journal, 14*(1), 112–134.

Stack, S., & Watson, J. (2013). Randomness, sample size, imagination and metacognition: Making judgments about differences in data sets. *Australian Mathematics Teacher, 69*(4), 23–30.

Statistical Analysis System. (n.d.). *Data Visualization: What it is and why it matters*. Retrieved from http://www.sas.com/en_au/insights/big-data/data-visualization.html

Stibbard, P. (1999). *Labour market dynamics: a global survey of statistical activity*. International Labour Organization. Retrieved from http://www.ilo.org/employment/Whatwedo/Publications/WCMS_120366/lang--en/index.htm

Stolpe, M. (2016). The Internet of Things: Opportunities. *ACM SIGKDD Explorations Newsletter, 8*(1), 15–34. doi:10.1145/2980765.2980768

Struijs, P., Braaksma, B., & Daas, P. J. H. (2014, April). Official statistics and big data. *Big Data & Society*, 1–6. doi: 10.1177/2053951714538417

Tammisto, Y., & Lindman, J. (2012). *Definition of open data services in software business*. Paper presented at the International Conference of Software Business. doi:10.1007/978-3-642-30746-1_28

Tam, S.-M., & Clarke, F. (2015). Big Data, Official Statistics and Some Initiatives by the Australian Bureau of Statistics. *International Statistical Review, 83*(3), 436–448. doi:10.1111/insr.12105

Tan, V. (2009). *The leap year 1900 "bug" in Excel*. Retrieved September 21, 2016, from http://polymathprogrammer.com/2009/10/26/the-leap-year-1900-bug-in-excel/

Telecompaper. (2015). *Majority of the elderly in the Netherlands has a smartphone*. Retrieved from https://www.telecompaper.com/pressrelease/majority-of-the-elderly-in-the-netherlands-has-a-smartphone--1088067

ten Bosch, O., & Griffioen, R. (2016). *On the use of Internet data for the Dutch CPI*. Paper presented at the UNECE Meeting of the Group of Experts on Consumer Price Indices, Geneva, Switzerland.

ten Bosh, O., & Windmeijer, D. (2014). On the Use of Internet Robots for Official Statistics. MSIS-2014.

Tennekes, M., & Offermans, M. P. W. (2014). *Daytime population estimations based on mobile phone metadata.* Paper prepared for the Joint Statistical Meetings, Boston, MA. Retrieved from http://www.amstat.org/meetings/jsm/2014/onlineprogram/AbstractDetails.cfm?abstractid=311959

Toro-Gonz'alez, D., McCluskey, J. J., & Mittelhammer, R. C. (2014). Beer snobs do exist: Estimation of beer demand by type. *Journal of Agricultural and Resource Economics, 39*(2), 1–14.

TRB. (2011). *Performance Measures for Freight Transportation. Transportation Research Board.* Washington, DC: National Academy of Sciences. doi:10.17226/14520

Treacy, M. (2016a). *Create Regular Excel Charts from PivotTables.* Retrieved June 7, 2016, from http://www.myonlinetraininghub.com/create-regular-excel-charts-from-pivottables

Treacy, M. (2016b). *Webinar 2: Dashboards with Power Query and Power Pivot.* Retrieved February 16, 2016, from http://www.myonlinetraininghub.com/excel-webinars

Trondheim (NO). (2013). *SINTEF. Big Data, for better or worse: 90% of world's data generated over last two years.* Retrieved February 8, 2015 Feb 8 from http://www.sintef.no/home/corporate-news/Big-Data--for-better-or-worse/

Tufte, E. R. (1983). *The visual display of quantitative information.* Cheshire, CT: Graphics Press.

Tufte, E. R. (n.d.). *Sparkline theory and practice.* Retrieved September 23, 2016, from http://www.edwardtufte.com/bboard/q-and-a-fetch-msg?msg_id=0001OR&topic_id=1

Tufte, E. R. (1990). *Envisioning Information.* Cheshire, CT: Graphics Press.

Tufte, E. R. (1997). *Visual Explanations: Images and Quantities, Evidence and Narrative.* Cheshire, CT: Graphics Press.

Tufte, E. R. (1997). *Visual Explanations: Images and quantities, evidence and narrative.* Cheshire: Graphics Press.

Tufte, E. R. (2001). *The visual display of quantitative information. Cheshire, CT: Graphics Press.*

Tufte, E. R. (2006). *Beautiful Evidence.* Cheshire: Graphics Press.

Tukey, J. W. (1977). *Exploratory Data Analysis.* Addison Wesley Publishing Company.

Turnbull, M. (2014). *National Map Open Data initiative to boost innovation.* Retrieved from Ministers for the Department of Communications and the Arts: http://www.minister.communications.gov.au/malcolm_turnbull/news/national_map_open_data_initiati ve_to_boost_innovation#.WIRcoFN96Hs

Ubaldi, B. (2013). Open Government Data: Towards Empirical Analysis of Open Government Data Initiatives. *OECD Working Papers on Public Governance, 22.*

Uchida, C. D., Swatt, M. L., Solomon, S. E., & Varano, S. (2014). *Data-Driven Crime Prevention: New Tools for Community Involvement and Crime Control.* U.S. Department of Justice. Retrieved 28/11/16 from https://www.ncjrs.gov/pdffiles1/nij/grants/245408.pdf

UN (Statistical Commission of the United Nations). (1991). *Fundamental Principles of Official Statistics*. Retrieved from http://unstats.un.org/unsd/dnss/gp/fundprinciples.aspx

UN-ECE High-Level Group for the Modernisation of Statistical Production and Services. (2013). *What does "big data" mean for official statistics?* Retrieved from http://www1.unece.org/stat/platform/pages/viewpage.action?pageId=77170622

UNECE, Statistical Division of the United Nations Economic Commission for Europe. (2014a). *A suggested Framework for the Quality of Big Data, Deliverables of the UNECE Big Data Quality Task Team*. Retrieved from http://www1.unece.org/stat/platform/download/attachments/108102944/Big%20Data%20Quality%20Framework%20-%20final-%20Jan08-2015.pdf?version=1&modificationDate=1420725063663&api=v2

UNECE, Statistical Division of the United Nations Economic Commission for Europe. (2014b). *How big is Big Data? Exploring the role of Big Data in Official Statistics*. Retrieved from http://www1.unece.org/stat/platform/download/attachments/99484307/Virtual%20Sprint%20Big%20Data%20paper.docx?version=1&modificationDate=1395217470975&api=v2

UNECE, Statistical Division of the United Nations Economic Commission for Europe. (2014c). *Big Data Inventory*. Available at: http://www1.unece.org/stat/platform/display/BDI/UNECE+Big+Data+Inventory+Home

UNECE, Statistical Division of the United Nations Economic Commission for Europe. (2016). *Outcomes of the UNECE Project on Using Big Data for Official Statistics*. Available at: http://www1.unece.org/stat/platform/display/bigdata/Big+Data+in+Official+Statistics

United Nations. (2014). *Open Government and Data Services*. Retrieved from Public Administration and Development Management: https://publicadministration.un.org/en/ogd

Unwin, A., Chen, C., & Hardle, W. (2008). Introduction. In C. Chen, W. Hardle, & A. Unwin (Eds.), *Handbook of Data Visualisation*. New York: Springer-Verlag. doi:10.1007/978-3-540-33037-0_1

US Department of Agriculture. (2016, August 22). *International Markets & Trade*. Retrieved 21 January 2017, from https://www.ers.usda.gov/topics/international-markets-trade/

US Department of Agriculture. (2017, January 25). *Data Products, Economic Research Service, United States Department of Agriculture*. Retrieved 21 January 2017, from https://www.ers.usda.gov/data-products/?topicId=0&sort=UpdateDate&sortdir=desc

Vaccari, C. (2016). *Big Data in Official Statistics*. Saarbrücken: Lambert.

Van Ruth, F. J. (2014). *Traffic intensity as indicator of regional economic activity*. Discussion paper 2014-21, Statistics Netherlands.

Varian, H. R. (2014). Big data: New tricks for econometrics. *The Journal of Economic Perspectives*, *28*(2), 3–28. doi:10.1257/jep.28.2.3

Von Braun, J. (1992). *Improving food security of the poor: Concept, policy, and programs*. Intl Food Policy Res Inst.

Von Braun, J. (1993). *Urban food insecurity and malnutrition in developing countries: Trends, policies, and research implications*. Intl Food Policy Res Inst.

W3. (2013). Web ontology language (OWL). *W3C*. Retrieved from: https://www.w3.org/OWL/

W3. (2014). Resource description framework (RDF). *W3C*. Retrieved from: https://www.w3.org/RDF/

W3. (2015). Semantic web. *W3*. Retrieved from: http://www.w3.org/standards/semanticweb/

W3. (n.d.). Schema. *W3*. Retrieved from: http://www.w3.org/standards/xml/schema

W3C - The World Wide Web Consortium. (2005). *Document Object Model (DOM)*. Retrieved from https://www.w3.org/DOM/

W3C. (2017). *Semantic Web*. Retrieved 2017, from World Wide Web Consortium (W3C): https://www.w3.org/standards/semanticweb/

W3C. (2017). *W3C*. Retrieved from: http://www.w3.org/

Wahlqvist, M. L., Keatinge, J. D. H., Butler, C. D., Friel, S., McKay, J., Easdown, W., & Li, D. et al. (2009). A Food in Health Security (FIHS) platform in the Asia-Pacific Region: The way forward. *Asia Pacific Journal of Clinical Nutrition*, *18*(4), 688–702. PMID:19965367

Wainer, H. (1997). *Visual revelations: Graphical tales of fate and deception from Napoleon Bonaparte to Ross Perot*. New York: Copernicus. doi:10.1007/978-1-4612-2282-8

Wainer, H. (2005). *Graphic discovery: A trout in the milk and other visual adventures*. Princeton, NJ: Princeton University Press.

Wainer, H. (2009). *Picturing the uncertain world: How to understand, communicate, and control uncertainty through graphical display*. Princeton, NJ: Princeton University Press.

Walkenbach, J. (n.d.). *Microsoft Excel*. Retrieved August 7, 2007, from http://j-walk.com/ss/excel/index.htm

Walkenbach, J. (2010). *Excel 2010 power programming with VBA*. Indianapolis, IN: Wiley. doi:10.1002/9781118257616

Wallman, K. K. (1993). Enhancing statistical literacy: Enriching our society. *Journal of the American Statistical Association*, *88*, 1–8.

Wang, L., Wang, G., & Alexander, C. A. (2015). Big data and visualization: Methods, challenges and technology progress. *Digital Technologies*, *1*(1), 33–38.

Wang, L., Wang, G., & Alexander, C. (2015). Big Data and Visualization: Methods, Challenges and Technology Progress. *Digital Technologies*, *1*(1), 33–38. doi:10.12691/dt-1-1-7

Watson, J. M., & Moritz, J. B. (2000). Developing concepts of sampling. *Journal for Research in Mathematics Education*, *31*(1), 44–70. doi:10.2307/749819

Watson, J. M. (2004). Developing reasoning about samples. In *The challenge of developing statistical literacy, reasoning and thinking* (pp. 277–294). Dordrecht, The Netherlands: Kluwer Academic Publishers. doi:10.1007/1-4020-2278-6_12

Watson, J. (2016). Scaffolding statistics understanding in the middle school. In W. Widjaja, E. Y-K. Loong, & L.A. Bragg (Eds.), *MATHS eˣPLOSION 2016 Mathematical Association of Victoria's Annual Conference Proceedings* (pp. 132-139). Melbourne: MAV.

Watson, J. M., & Callingham, A. R. (2003). Statistical literacy: a complex hierarchical construct. *Statistical Education Research Journal, 2*(2), 3–46. Retrieved October 29, 2016, from http://citeseerx.ist.psu.edu/viewdoc/download?doi=10.1.1.144.9617&rep=rep1&type=pdf

Watson, J., & English, L. (2016a). *Eye color and the practice of statistics in grade 6: Comparing two groups*. Manuscript under review.

Watson, J., Collis, K. F., & Moritz, J. B. (1995). The development of concepts Associated with sampling in grades 3, 5, 7 and 9. In *Annual Conference of the Australian Association for Research in Education*. Retrieved Jan, 18, 2014, from: http://www.aare.edu.au/data/publications/1995/watsj95475.pdf

Watson, J. (2008). Eye colour and reaction time: An opportunity for critical statistical reasoning. *Australian Mathematics Teacher, 64*(3), 30–40.

Watson, J. (2014). What is 'typical' for different kinds of data? Examples from the Melbourne Cup. *Australian Mathematics Teacher, 70*(2), 33–40.

Watson, J. M. (2006). *Statistical literacy at school: Growth and goals*. Mahwah, NJ: Lawrence Erlbaum.

Watson, J. M., & Callingham, R. A. (2003). Statistical literacy: A complex hierarchical construct. *Statistics Education Research Journal, 2*(2), 3–46. Retrieved from http://iase-web.org/documents/SERJ/SERJ2(2)_Watson_Callingham.pdf

Watson, J. M., & Kelly, B. A. (2005). The winds are variable: Student intuitions about variation. *School Science and Mathematics, 105*(5), 252–269. doi:10.1111/j.1949-8594.2005.tb18165.x

Watson, J., Beswick, K., Brown, N., Callingham, R., Muir, T., & Wright, S. (2011). *Digging into Australian data with TinkerPlots*. Melbourne: Objective Learning Materials.

Watson, J., & English, L. (2015). Introducing the practice of statistics: Are we environmentally friendly? *Mathematics Education Research Journal, 27*(4), 585–613. doi:10.1007/s13394-015-0153-z

Watson, J., & English, L. (2016b). Repeated random sampling in Year 5. *Journal of Statistics Education, 24*(1), 27–37. doi:10.1080/10691898.2016.1158026

Watson, J., & English, L. (in press). Reaction time in Grade 5: Data collection within the Practice of Statistics. *Statistics Education Research Journal*.

Watson, J., & Fitzallen, N. (2016). Statistical software and mathematics education: Affordances for learning. In L. English & D. Kirshner (Eds.), *Handbook of international research in mathematics education* (3rd ed.; pp. 563–594). New York: Taylor and Francis.

Weber, T. E. (2010). *Microsoft Excel: Software That Changed the World.* Retrieved May 3, 2011, from http://www.thedailybeast.com/articles/2010/12/27/microsoft-excel-the-programs-designer-reveals-the-secrets-behind-the-software-that-changed-the-world-25-years-ago.html

Weisburd, D., Bernasco, W., & Bruinsma, G. (Eds.). (2008). *Putting crime in its place: Units of analysis in geographic criminology.* Springer Science & Business Media.

Wheeldon, J., & Harris, D. (2015). Expanding visual criminology: Definitions, data and dissemination. *Current Issues in Criminal Justice, 27,* 141–162.

Wigdor, D., Shen, C., Forlines, C., & Balakrishnan, R. (2007). Perception of elementary graphical elements in tabletop and multi-surface environments. In *CHI '07: Proceedings of the SIGCHI conference on Human factors in computing systems.* New York, NY: ACM Publications. doi:10.1145/1240624.1240701

Wild, C. J. (2013). iNZight into Time Series and Multiple-Response Data. *Proceedings of the Joint IASE/IAOS International Conference of Statistics Education for Progress Organised by the International association of Statistics Education (IASE) and the International Association for Official Statistics (IAOS).* Macau, China: IASE/IAOS. Retrieved from http://iase-web.org/documents/papers/sat2013/IASE_IAOS_2013_Paper_2.5.3_Wild_ppt.pdf

Wild, C. J., & Pfannkuch, M. (1999). Statistical thinking in empirical enquiry. *International Statistical Review, 67*(3), 223–265. doi:10.1111/j.1751-5823.1999.tb00442.x

Wild, C. J., Pfannkuch, M., Regan, M., & Horton, N. J. (2011). Conceptions of Statistical Inference. *Journal of the Royal Statistical Society. Series A, (Statistics in Society), 174*(Part 2), 247–295. doi:10.1111/j.1467-985X.2010.00678.x

Windhagera, F., Zenka, L., & Federico, P. (2010). Visual Enterprise Network Analytics – Visualizing Organizational Change. *7th Conference on Applications of Social Network Analysis.*

Wirthmann, A., Karlberg, M., Kovachev, B., & Reis, F. (2015). Structuring risks and solutions in the use of big data sources for producing official statistics – Analysis based on a risk and quality framework. *Eurostat.* Retrieved from: https://ec.europa.eu/eurostat/cros/system/files/Big%20Data%20Risk%20Paper%20Version1.pdf

Wong, I. (2006). Using CensusAtSchool data to motivate students. *Australian Mathematics Teacher, 62*(1), 38–40.

Wong, P., & Thomas, J. (2004). Visual Analytics. *IEEE Computer Graphics and Applications, 24*(5), 20–21. doi:10.1109/MCG.2004.39 PMID:15628096

World Bank. (2014). *Myanmar-Systematic Country Diagnostic: Ending poverty and boosting shared prosperity in a time of transition.* Washington, DC: World Bank Group.

World Food Programme. (2012). *WFP in Myanmar: Looking forward 2013-2017*. Yangon: World Food Programme, Myanmar. Retrieved from http://www.wfp.org/content/wfp-myanmar-looking-forward-2013-2017

Wortley, R., & Mazerolle, L. (2008). *Environmental Criminology and Crime Analysis*. Willan Publishing.

Yakout, M., Ganjam, K., Chakrabarti, K., & Chaudhuri, S. (2012). InfoGather: Entity Augmentation and Attribute Discovery by Holistic Matching with Web Tables. *Proceedings of SIGMOD 2012*.

Zaiontz, C. (2015). *Real Statistics Resource Pack*. Retrieved from http://www.real-statistics.com

Zaslavsky, O. (2009). Mathematics educators' knowledge and development. In R. Even & D. L. Ball (Eds.), *The professional education and development of teachers* (pp. 105–111). New York: Springer. doi:10.1007/978-0-387-09601-8_12

Zeelenberg, K. (2016). *Challenges to Methodological Research in Official Statistics*. Presentation at the 2016 International Methodology Symposium, Gatineau. Retrieved from http://www.statcan.gc.ca/eng/conferences/symposium2016/program

Zikopoulos, P., Eaton, C., deRoos, D., Deutsch, T., & Lapis, G. (2011). *Understanding big data: Analytics for enterprise class hadoop and streaming data*. New York: McGraw-Hill Osborne Media.

About the Contributors

Theodosia Prodromou is a Cypriot-Australian mathematician, statistician and mathematics educator, who joined the University of New England in July 2009 to lecture in Mathematics Education. She taught primary and secondary Mathematics in different countries of Europe, and Australia. She has experience of teaching mathematics education to pre-service teachers and in-service teachers within primary and secondary and post-graduate programs. She is involved in European and International funded or unfunded projects. She is a chair of the Australian GeoGebra Institute.

* * *

Elaine Barclay is Associate Professor in Criminology at the University of New England, New South Wales, Australia. Her research over the past 20 years has focused on crime in rural communities. She coedited Crime in Rural Australia 2007 published by Federation Press.

Ayse Aysin Bilgin is an Associate Professor in the Department of Statistics at Macquarie University in Sydney. Her research interests include statistics education and applied statistics especially in health sciences. In 2009 she was awarded a Vice Chancellor's Citation at Macquarie University and an Australian Learning and Teaching Council Citation for 'Outstanding Contributions to Student Learning' for enhancing learning and teaching in statistics through different assessment tools, timely feedback and learning support that encourages independent learning. In recognition of her expertise, she was elected to be the Vice President of the International Association for Statistical Education between 2016 and 2017. She teaches undergraduate and postgraduate students in various topics such as Operations Research, Data Mining and recently she developed and started to teach the Capstone unit – Statistical Consulting – for the students majoring in Statistics.

Barteld Braaksma is Innovation Manager at Statistics Netherlands.

Joseph (Chien-Hung) Chien is the director at Australian Bureau of Statistics. He was awarded Sir Roland Wilson Foundation PhD Scholarship for 2016. His research analyses complex labour market dynamics to better understand the micro drivers of productivity. He combines semantic web and network analysis methods to study the connections between firms and employees and their impacts on productivity.

Belinda A. Chiera is a Senior Lecturer in Statistics at the School of Information Technology and Mathematical Sciences, University of South Australia. She has many years of experience in statistical methods, particularly in Big Data analysis centered on the analysis of high-dimensional communications networks, social network analysis and climate system modelling.

Ric Clarke is the director, Emerging Data and Methods at Australian Bureau of Statistics. He leads a multidisciplinary capability development team in the delivery of innovative prototype solutions for official statistics. This work includes the investigation of new methods and technologies for representing, integrating and analysing complex digital information from diverse sources - such as survey and administrative collections, transactional data, and sensor measurements. Areas of current focus include the Semantic Web and linked data, machine reasoning and learning for information discovery, content extraction from unstructured data, and the visualisation of multidimensional data.

Franck Cotton, after completing scientific and engineering studies in École Polytechnique (http://polytechnique.edu/) and ENSAE (http://ensae.fr/), joined INSEE's Business Statistics Department in 1986. He then occupied different position and is now advisor to the Director of Information Systems. His main fields of work include international cooperation, data science (open, linked and big data), statistical metadata, computer science and enterprise architecture. He is a member of several Eurostat groups (ITDG, SERV task force, DIGICOM...) and of the UNECE Modernization Committee on products and sources and CSPA implementation group. He represents INSEE in the Datalift (http://datalift.org/) and Teralab (https://www.teralab-datascience.fr/) projects. He also launched and co-chairs the Semantic Statistics (http://semstats.org/) workshops and is the editor of the XKOS specification.

Daniel Gillman is an information scientist with the Office of Survey Methods Research at the US Bureau of Labor Statistics. His research interests there include classification, metadata, standards, and terminology. He leads the team at BLS to build an agency wide taxonomy of terms in support of data dissemination and web site redesign. As part of that effort, he is building an implementation of the taxonomy in RDF. He is part of the collaborative effort to modernize an international metadata standard, the Data Documentation Initiative (DDI). DDI is based on the Generic Statistical Information Model which he also helped build. As part of the modernization of the Consumer Expenditure Surveys at BLS, he is instrumental in adopting the DDI for guiding metadata management for the surveys.

Thida Chaw Hlaing is a Research PhD Student at the University of New England, Australia. She got M.Sc in Agriculture Economics from Kyushu University, Japan in 2008. She has completed three postgraduate diploma degrees in the field of: Development Study (IDEAS, IDE-JETRO, Japan, 2003); Environmental Planning and Management (YTU, Myanmar, 2001); Japanese Language (YUFL, 2000). She has been working as a Planning Officer for the Department of Planning, Ministry of Agriculture, Livestock and Irrigation, Myanmar since 1996. She had experienced of working with International agencies under LIEN. Remarkably, she worked as a national project coordinator for EC-FAO Food Security Programme "Linking Information and Decision-Making to improve Food Security in the selected Greater Mekong Sub-Regional Countries, Cambodia, Lao PDR and Myanmar" from 2010-2012.

Malgorzata W. Korolkiewicz is the Program Director for Master of Data Science and lecturer at the School of Information Technology and Mathematical Sciences, University of South Australia. Her research interests and experience include quantitative finance, financial risk management and environmental modelling.

Timothy Kyng is a senior lecturer in the Department of Applied Finance and Actuarial Studies at Macquarie University in Sydney. His research interests include statistics education, statistical modeling, financial education and literacy, quantitative finance and actuarial science. He has both academic and professional qualifications, being a Fellow of the Institute of Actuaries of Australia and of the Financial Services Institute of Australia. He teaches postgraduate courses on financial modeling, investments and finance. He has substantial experience in both industry and academia. He has had a long involvement in professional actuarial finance education. His PhD thesis covered the valuation of executive share options using exotic option pricing theory. Tim's recent research has covered issues such as portability of long service leave, mathematical analysis of retirement village contracts, software used in academia and industry, employee share option valuation, financial education and literacy, and methods for valuing exotic options.

360

Federico Polidoro is Senior Researcher at Istat. He is head of the unit "integrated system on economic conditions and consumer prices".

Julian Prior is an Associate Professor in the School of Environmental and Rural Science at the University of New England (UNE). He lectures in natural resource policy, agricultural and natural resource extension, and environmental Impact assessment. His research and consultancy interests are in the fields of natural resource and agricultural policy, community-based natural resource management, community adaptation to climate change, and building effective farmer groups. For the 20 years prior to coming to UNE, he worked in natural resource management and agriculture in Australia and overseas, while employed by a range of government and non-government agencies and international development organizations. He has undertaken extensive international consultancies in Africa, Asia and the Pacific. He is an Australian member of the Landcare International Steering Committee.

Busayasachee Puang-Ngern is a PhD candidate in the Department of Statistics at Macquarie University in Sydney. She has a scholarship from Chulalongkorn University in Thailand to pursue her study in Master of Actuarial Practice, Master of Research in Statistics and also her current PhD in Statistics at Macquarie University since 2012. During her PhD studies, she works as a tutor for undergraduate and postgraduate students in the subject of Generalized Linear Models, Statistical Theory, Introductory Statistics, and Quantitative Business Decisions. Her research interests are in statistical modeling, data science, and insurance.

Jacques Raubenheimer is currently a research fellow in biostatistics with the Translational Australian Clinical Toxicology programme in the discipline of pharmacology at the Sydney Medical School, University of Sydney. He was previously a lecturer at the Department of Biostatistics, School of Medicine, Faculty of Health Sciences, University of the Free State. He is a Microsoft Certified Trainer and holds the Microsoft Office Specialist Expert certification for Microsoft Excel, as well as the Microsoft Office Specialist Master Instructor certification.

Antonino Virgillito is a Senior IT Engineer at Istat. An expert in Big Data, web technologies, business intelligence, he holds a PhD in Computer Engineering with a specialization on large-scale distributed systems. Before joining Istat he was a post-doc researcher at INRIA-IRISA and University of Roma "La Sapienza". Dr. Virgillito is author of more than 40 publications in international conferences and journals.

Jane Watson is Professor Emerita of Mathematics Education in the Faculty of Education at the University of Tasmania in Australia. Her major research and professional learning interests are in statistics education and she is currently focussing on data modelling to enhance STEM in the primary curriculum.

Kees Zeelenberg is Chief Methodologist at Statistics Netherlands.

Index

Stay Current on the Latest Emerging Research Developments

Become an IGI Global Reviewer for Authored Book Projects

Premier Reference Source
Solutions for High-Touch Communications in a High-Tech World

Premier Reference Source
Advanced Research on Biologically Inspired Cognitive Architectures

Premier Reference Source
Workforce Development Theory and Practice in the Mental Health Sector

Premier Reference Source
Resource Management and Efficiency in Cloud Computing Environments

The overall success of an authored book project is dependent on quality and timely reviews.

In this competitive age of scholarly publishing, constructive and timely feedback significantly decreases the turnaround time of manuscripts from submission to acceptance, allowing the publication and discovery of progressive research at a much more expeditious rate. Several IGI Global authored book projects are currently seeking highly qualified experts in the field to fill vacancies on their respective editorial review boards:

Applications may be sent to:
development@igi-global.com

Applicants must have a doctorate (or an equivalent degree) as well as publishing and reviewing experience. Reviewers are asked to write reviews in a timely, collegial, and constructive manner. All reviewers will begin their role on an ad-hoc basis for a period of one year, and upon successful completion of this term can be considered for full editorial review board status, with the potential for a subsequent promotion to Associate Editor.

If you have a colleague that may be interested in this opportunity, we encourage you to share this information with them.

Printed in the United States
By Bookmasters